BON VOYAGE!

BON VOYAGE!

The 𝕮𝖊𝖑𝖊𝖌𝖗𝖆𝖕𝖍
Book of River and
Sea Journeys

Edited by Michael Kerr

For Teri, who has survived an afternoon's
rowing on the Serpentine and much else besides.

First published 2010 by
Aurum Press Limited
7 Greenland Street
London NW1 0ND
www.aurumpress.co.uk

ISBN 978 1 84513 603 1

10 9 8 7 6 5 4 3 2 1
2015 2014 2013 2012 2011 2010

Typeset by Saxon Graphics Ltd, Derby
Printed and bound in Great Britain by Clays, St Ives plc

CONTENTS

INTRODUCTION

Balance is essential in any craft taking to river or sea. It's useful, too, in any vessel designed to contain writing about great journeys by water. This one weighs lone canoeists against military fleets, cargo ships against coracles, sailors intent on a record against writers in no hurry at all, cushioned cruises on the *QE2* against jagged raft rides down the Missouri, and still, I hope, keeps an even keel. While it was being provisioned in the good port Archives, however, it was threatened with capsize by the weighty presence of two men. One was Henry Morton Stanley, journalist, explorer and finder of David Livingstone. The other was John Ridgway, paratrooper, Atlantic rower and scourge of executives on bonding exercises.

Stanley is best known for one of the sharpest soundbites in history ('Doctor Livingstone, I presume.') It's one he may have contrived later at his desk rather than delivered at the time. More importantly, his scoop in tracking down Livingstone in November 1871 on the eastern shore of Lake Tanganyika has overshadowed his later and much greater achievement: solving the last great geographical mystery of Africa by mapping the Congo River.

The *Daily Telegraph* had a sizeable hand in making that expedition possible. Not only was the paper one of Stanley's two sponsors (matching the £6,000 put up by the *New York Herald*), but it also provided him, indirectly, with two of his three assistants. When Stanley set off from a sandy beach on Zanzibar on 17 November 1874, he was accompanied by five dogs, 352 bearers and three white men. The three (all of whom would perish along the way) were Frederick Barker, a clerk at the Langham Hotel where Stanley had stayed while in London, and two brothers, Frank and Edward Pocock, the crew of a yacht owned by the editor of the *Daily Telegraph* and moored on the River Medway near Maidstone.

During his expedition Stanley filed some ten dispatches, which the paper appears to have published in full, his accounts running from top to bottom of the broadsheet pages for column after column, unrelieved – except in one case by a map – of any illustration. If they are grey in the type, they are certainly not in the telling; they are full of 'the enthusiastic energy with which we rushed through the lands of the cannibals', and it was tempting to reproduce them wholesale here. But this is not a Stanley anthology. His story has been recounted many times — by himself, by biographers such as Tim Jeal and, most recently, by Tim Butcher (of whom more later) in his book *Blood River* – so I have used just two of his dispatches. One tells the tale, as the original headline puts it, of 'A land of ivory houses' and 'The thirty-two battles'. The other shows a softer side of a man who has often been characterised as one of the most brutal of imperialists: it is Stanley's letter to the father of the Pococks, detailing 'the sad, sad story' of Frank's death.

Ridgway may be a less resonant name than Stanley, but he crops up time after time in the *Telegraph* cuttings files, as participant, as commentator, and occasionally as both. Having rowed the North Atlantic with Chay Blyth in 1966, he made a failed attempt to sail solo non-stop around the world in 1968, before going round three times in company. He was paddling alongside his daughter, Rebecca, when she became the first woman (in 1992) to canoe round Cape Horn. In many of the manilla envelopes I sifted, I found reviews of his ten-or-so books; reviews by him of the books of John Fairfax (*Rowing Alone Across the Atlantic*) and Nicola Milnes Walker (who in 1971 became the first woman to sail direct and alone from Britain to America); and appreciations by him of figures such as Francis Chichester: 'I admired him most of all for showing that in a world of computers and planned obsolescence there was still room for the individual who feels truly alive.'

Ridgway is as puzzled by those who sit in front of computers for a living as he is repelled by the machines themselves. Nearly twenty years ago, when he was about to set off on one of the trips chronicled in our files, he was introduced round our office by the then editor of the 'Weekend' section, Will Ellsworth-Jones. Smacking one of his massive paws down on the edge of my desk, he leaned over my shoulder as I was editing a story, and told me: 'You poor little bugger, tied to your terminal.' The revenge of the clerk would have been sweet, but cheap, so Ridgway gets his due here. He is seen through the eyes of others: by Duff Hart-Davis, who joined him and Andy Briggs for the final leg of their record-breaking non-stop circumnavigation of the globe in 1984; and by Trevor Fishlock, who was in at the beginning and end of an adventure that took the whole Ridgway family across the

Atlantic and the Pacific, round Cape Horn, to the ice of Antarctica and back home.

Giving Stanley and Ridgway cabin room while barring them from the bridge has allowed me to do justice to the richness and variety of the *Telegraph* archives. There are stories here of men and women who battled their way round the Horn and of a columnist who paddled four miles on the Ure to the lower end of Wensleydale; of an intrepid pair who felt the full force of the Mississippi, in flood, in an 11ft inflatable, and of a press-junket hack who felt – well, nothing much at all, because he was transported over the Caribbean on a floating hotel 16 storeys high. There are glimpses of life (and death) on tall ships, narrowboats and submarines. There are portraits of seasoned masters and callow crewmen – and of a nanny, who saved her two charges when the liner *Lusitania* was sunk by German torpedoes in 1915. There are the testimonies of tough types who clearly knew what they were about, and there is the admission of Tim Moore, building and then trying to sail his own raft down the Klarälven in Sweden, that he hadn't a clue what he was up to.

In common with many *Telegraph* readers (who are twice as likely as the average Briton to count sailing as a hobby), some contributors to this anthology have served their time at the tiller. But much of the writing is by non-initiates; by writers who admit to feeling uneasy on a boat even when it is moored. Among them are Elizabeth Grice, who was sent to interview Ellen MacArthur in February 2001 after she had become the youngest and fastest woman to sail round the world single-handed. With a photographer, Grice was taken out in an inflatable to meet MacArthur on *Kingfisher* when she was three miles from Southampton. As they struggled on board with all their gear and in heavy lifejackets, Grice almost slipped back into the Solent and had to be grappled on to the deck. She spent two hours with the yachtswoman (who was 'quite shy') in the cramped, unventilated cabin and returned to her desk at Canary Wharf in London in such a rush to file her story for that night's paper that she only realised then that she was still wearing the yellow lifejacket. None of this haste is evident in the piece she wrote, which communicates powerfully both the claustrophobia of the place that for three months MacArthur had called home and the drive of the woman who inhabited it: 'At 16, I suddenly realised that all the books I had were about single-handed sailing. I didn't realise till then how obsessed I was by it. Then when I bought my little corribee, *Iduna*, I stripped her down inside and removed a bunk. So there was only one left. I did that without ever consciously thinking I would sail on my own.'

MacArthur told Grice that as a child she had borrowed and reborrowed from the school library books by Sir Francis Chichester, Robin Knox-Johnston and Chay Blyth. She didn't mention Joshua Slocum, the one they all followed, but she would be a rare soloist if his *Sailing Alone Around the World* (published in 1900) were not somewhere on her shelves. The man and the book have inspired countless sailors, writers, and writers cum sailors. Jonathan Raban, one of the doubly skilled, has written that Slocum has become 'the archetype of the American wanderer: creating himself on the page, he drew a classic hero, as resilient, as full of signification in his own rough-diamond way, as Huckleberry Finn.'

Fascination, rather than inspiration, is probably the word for the strange case of Donald Crowhurst. His attempt to win a round-the-world yacht race in 1968 ended in insanity and – probably – suicide. As Jasper Rees points out in Chapter 8, 'It is an extraordinary story that will withstand endless retelling, which is why a succession of writers and artists have found themselves drawn to it like hyenas to carrion.'

The same is not necessarily true of a lot of the maritime feats of speed, distance or survival that fill the cuttings envelopes in the Telegraph Media Group's warehouse. They made news, and then they died, brief as a flare. There was nothing, or no one, to make them last. The professional writer, whether joining in the great adventure or trying to sum it up, is generally more likely than the professional sailor to produce an account that endures beyond the news story of the triumphant homecoming or the instant paperback that follows. The writer, whether wholly at home on a boat or not, can sometimes reveal what the sailor, who is not only often single-handed but, by necessity, single-minded, either misses or doesn't think worthy of note. One is fretting about readability, the other is chasing a record. As Chay Blyth put it in October 1970, on the eve of his attempt at the first-ever non-stop circumnavigation of the globe from east to west, 'the object of the exercise is to get bleeding round, in the best possible time.'

Could there be a greater contrast between that declaration and the purpose – if that's the word – of Jenny Diski in taking a cargo ship across the Atlantic?

A long sea voyage was the only point of the trip. Why? An exercise in sensory deprivation, I suppose. To find out what happened when one day followed another, one mile followed another and each was exactly the same as the last. What was a person left with when there was no landscape except the curve of the horizon, and no anticipation in arriving somewhere you wish to be?

Not only did Diski not care how long the ship took; she didn't even care where it was going. Many of those who take holidays on cruise ships are similarly uninterested in ports of call; they sign up to empty their wallets in the shops and casinos and to broaden their waists in the restaurants. *Oasis of the Seas* – the world's biggest cruise ship as I write this but doubtless due to be supplanted shortly – was made for them.

Peter Hughes, who had a preview before the maiden voyage at the end of 2009, was not taken with it (definitely an 'it' rather than a 'she'):

> If it is a ship, it's a town ship. Three quarters of *Oasis* is in maritime denial. Until you reach the open decks – or your cabin, if you have one of the 1,481 with an outside balcony – you're barely aware of the sea...Life on these ocean waves is essentially urban living, more metro than matelot. You walk in off the street – well, off that whopping new terminal – straight on to a street, paved, lined with shops, bars, cafés and a pizzeria. There is even a car parked in the middle. It's a racy two-seater, a slinky replica of a 1936 Auburn.

The *Queen Mary*, launched the year the real Auburn rolled off the production line, would have been more to his taste. When she left her cradle on the Clyde to sail all of fourteen miles to the sea at Greenock, she made a splash in the journalistic sense, too. Our front page of 24 March records that people poured into Glasgow by train, car and even plane, and gathered along the banks of the river in caravans and tents. Admittedly, there weren't then the competing attractions of *Britain's Got Talent* and *Strictly Come Dancing*, but a turnout of a million-and-a-half spectators is still impressive. The *Queen Mary*, we declared – and this in news story rather than opinion piece – was 'the world's finest ship'.

Our readers over the years have expressed similar certainty over their favourite cruise lines. Figures published by the Passenger Shipping Association in May suggested that 1.65 million Britons will take a cruise in 2010, an increase of more than seven per cent compared with 2009 and more than double the figure for the year 2000. One in ten package holidays booked is now a cruise, compared with one in nearly thirty in 1997. Many of those bookings are made by regular *Telegraph* readers; thirteen per cent have been cruising and they are more than twice as likely to take a holiday afloat as the average British adult. One cruise line, indeed, owes its very survival to our readers. Swan Hellenic almost disappeared when its American parent company, Carnival Corporation, decided that it wasn't delivering enough profit. Readers took up the cry 'Save Our Swan', prompting Lord Sterling, former chairman of P&O Cruises, to rescue the line from extinction.

If the Church of England used to be the Tory Party at prayer, Swan Hellenic was and, in some respects, still is the *Daily Telegraph* at sea — though perhaps not as obviously as in 1999, when Graham Turner, on a cruise round the coast of India, summed up his fellow passengers like this:

> ... apart from a sprinkling of aristocrats and the occasional nouveau riche, they are all members of that endangered species, the traditional British bourgeoisie: bankers, barristers, admirals, brigadiers, retired tea-planters, Tory politicians and medics of every conceivable variety. They board the *Minerva* with an enormous sigh of relief, as if passing through the portals of their favourite club. And then they talk and talk...and talk, as if for the previous year they have been starved of intelligent and congenial conversation. There are no awkward silences. In fact, there are no silences of any kind, except in the library.

The *Minerva*, the *Queen Mary*, the *QE2*, the tiny *Hebridean Princess* (another floating club, whose membership is restricted to fifty at a time) — all of them have inspired affection among our readers and writers, but perhaps none has given rise to as much sentimentality as the *Canberra*, which throughout her life was seen not so much as a ship but as a floating extra county of Britain. Jan Moir, who sailed on the 'Great White Whale' in 1996, shortly before she was decommissioned, took a while to warm to her, feeling not so much 'a wave of affection, more a vague queasiness at the wild profusion of swirly patterned carpets'. But even she could not deny that illustrious history. Starting as a long-distance liner, the *Canberra* carried thousands of 'ten-pound Poms' on their assisted passage to a new life in Australia. As a single-class vessel from the 1970s, she made cruising affordable for many who had thought it was beyond their means. Then, famously, in 1982 she was requisitioned as a troop carrier and despatched with the Task Force to the South Atlantic.

Twenty-five years on from the Falklands War, the former ITN reporter Michael Nicholson, who had sailed on HMS *Hermes*, recalled for the *Daily Telegraph* how the Task Force had set off amid 'a crazy mixture of commotion and ceremony': 'Surely no one, on that April morning, really thought we were going to war. It could only be a matter of days before it was settled by diplomacy. It seemed such a nonsense...8,000 sea miles to save a thousand so-called Brits?'

Operation Dynamo, forty-two years earlier and much closer to home, saved 338,000 British, French and Belgian troops under German assault on the beaches of northern France. The *Daily Telegraph* of 4 June 1940 reports an Admiralty communiqué issued the evening before concerning 'the most extensive and difficult combined operation in naval history'. It is one of the earliest accounts in which the name of 'Dunkirk' was closely associated with a certain 'spirit'.

Spirit of a similar kind, combined with journalistic cunning, was demonstrated by the American journalist and writer Martha Gellhorn in stowing away on the first hospital ship to reach Normandy after D-Day. In coverage to mark the fiftieth anniversary of the landings, we republished her report:

> We sailed by daylight, alone in a presumably mine-cleared lane. Suddenly we were at the edge, then inside, the greatest naval traffic jam in history. Battleships, destroyers, transports (I know nothing of ships) were strewn haphazardly across the water, a seascape solidly filled with ships. It was so enormous, so awesome, that it felt more like an act of nature than anything man-made.

'Act of nature' is a suitable phrase for another of the journeys described in this anthology, one that involves neither man nor boats: it's the great migration, by hundreds of thousands of wildebeest and zebra, from Tanzania to Kenya across the Mara river. As they swithered and dithered, the Nile crocodiles awaiting them in the waters below, David Blair willed them on. Anthony Peregrine was less charitably disposed towards the fish of the Languedoc coast, but then he was as keen to eat as the crocs, having set out early with trawlermen from the resort of Le Grau-du-Roi. His assignment: to record the last journey of a turbot, from net to dinner plate.

Of the other oddities gathered here, one of my favourites is a report of 1958 of an attempted crossing of the Irish Sea from Wexford to Fishguard by six men in a curragh, or coracle:

> Originally it had been intended to use a raven for navigational purposes, the idea being to launch the bird when in doubt with the certainty that it would head straight for land. But the only raven available, 45 miles from here, turned out to be a cripple and most reluctant. In any case, the

owner demanded £5 for the loan. A crow offered as a substitute was deemed to be unsatisfactory for temperamental reasons and the curragh went off birdless.

The curragh set out at the initiative of the BBC, the plan being to provide film for an archaeological programme proving the remote common ancestry of the peoples on both sides of the sea. All six of the crew wore cowhide outfits 'simulating the dress of our Neolithic ancestors'. Such recreations and their participants feature here in various forms: there is an interview with that voyager on glorified hay bales, Thor Heyerdahl, who tells Helena de Bertodano that he nearly drowned in a millpond at five and for years afterwards was terrified of water; there is a rave review by the literary editor David Holloway of Tim Severin's *The Brendan Voyage* ('the reactions of a sensitive man with a feeling for words to the sort of adventure that is beyond most people's wildest dreams'); and there is an account by Richard Grant, participant as well as reporter, of an attempt, 150 years on, to replicate Livingstone's discovery of Victoria Falls. The figurehead for that expedition was Livingstone's nearest modern equivalent, Sir Ranulph Twisleton-Wykeham-Fiennes, 3rd Baronet, OBE. On the first evening, Grant reports:

> The ex-SAS man and veteran polar adventurer, who got those fingers frostbitten at the North Pole and sawed off the dead fingertips when he got back to his garden shed in Exmoor (going down to the village midway through the process for a fretsaw blade that snagged less on the bone), confessed that 'creepy-crawlies' unnerved him and he disliked them intensely.
>
> His wife, Louise, patted him reassuringly on the leg. 'I'm the absolute opposite,' she said. 'Snakes, spiders, I love them all. I want to pick them up and get a good look at them.'

There was less comedy and considerably more daring in Tim Butcher's expedition in 2004. A new *Telegraph* man in Africa, he set out to get under the skin of the continent by going back to where its modern troubles had begun – with the scramble for riches set off by Stanley's original journey of discovery through the Congo. In the most chaotic of African countries, he followed Stanley's 1,870-mile route from one side to the other.

Stanley and his companions had travelled heavily armed, and with the most modern medicines available to guard themselves against tropical disease. Butcher had a penknife and a packet of baby-wipes. He did not have the blessing, let alone the sponsorship, of the *Daily Telegraph*. The foreign editor, having told him in a formal letter that the trip was too dangerous for the paper to endorse, later sent him a handwritten note adding: 'For God's sake be careful.'

But he went anyway, faced down the Congo, and returned home to write *Blood River*, a book that has been both critically acclaimed and a bestseller. On serialising it, the *Telegraph Magazine* chose an extract that, while it conveyed the perilous and painful nature of his journey, dealt with a stretch he had covered by motorbike rather than boat. I am grateful to Tim Butcher for permission to use a different passage in this anthology, one in which he describes a trip on a UN-leased vessel named *Pusher Number Ten*: 'My diary tells me we sailed for seven days, but it felt as if I travelled years back in time. After leaving Kisangani, we did not stop at any other town until Mbandaka, 1,000 kilometres downstream, and in between I felt as though I saw an Africa unchanged from that which Stanley saw.'

In between Stanley's time and Butcher's, 130 years of journeys by river and sea have been chronicled by our writers. One of the quirkiest is reported by Mark Law in Chapter 9. A Frenchman, Baron Arnaud de Rosnay, set out to cross, by sailboard, the sixty miles of the Bering Strait between Alaska and Siberia. He would arrive in one of the Russians' most closely guarded military zones. And he hadn't told them he was coming...

A NOTE ON THE CONTRIBUTIONS

As I did in *Last Call for the Dining Car: The Telegraph Book of Great Railway Journeys*, I have drawn for this anthology on the archives of both the *Daily Telegraph* (which began publishing in 1855) and the *Sunday Telegraph* (1961).

Most articles appear at roughly the length they were originally, two notable exceptions being HM Stanley's first dispatch about his Congo expedition and David Blair's about the great migration over the Mara river, both of which are extracts from longer pieces. Here and there I have made cuts and tweaks – usually to avoid repetition of background detail in successive news reports or features about the same event – and amended original headlines and standfirsts to accord with the nautical theme of this book.

For readers unfamiliar with *Telegraph* newspapers and their ways, I should point out that 'Mandrake' is a diary column title that was first used in the *Sunday Telegraph* and is now shared by both papers. One diarist used to refer to his assistant as 'Boy Drake'.

Chapter 1
I NAME THIS SHIP...

---

8 MAY 2004

CRUISING BACK INTO FASHION

CONCORDE IS DEAD; LONG LIVE THE QUEEN MARY 2.
STANLEY STEWART, HAVING SAILED ON THE SHIP'S FIRST
TRANSATLANTIC VOYAGE, HOPES WE ARE FINALLY
LEARNING THAT SPEED IS NOT THE POINT

'I saw Clark Gable once,' the Merry Widow confided. 'On the first *Queen Mary*. He was playing shuffleboard with his wife. What a man. So virile, so American.'

The Merry Widow was an irrepressible figure of relentless good cheer borne on big toothsome smiles. She had designer sunglasses, dyed blonde hair, a Hermès scarf and an American beau on her arm, though not so much Clark Gable perhaps as Walter Matthau. From the breast pocket of Walter's check suit, two miniature flags protruded – the Stars and Stripes and the Union Jack, in their matching livery of red, white and blue. Theirs was a special relationship.

'We are not married, you know,' Walter announced gallantly over dinner one evening. 'We have our own separate lives, and don't feel the need to formalise things.' The Merry Widow, cast now as the Merry Mistress, smiled unhappily at him from the other end of the table. Walter owned oil wells in Texas. 'Though course I jes' love her to bits,' he went on.

Standing in the stern of the *Queen Mary 2* as she slipped her moorings in Southampton for her maiden voyage to New York, the Merry Widow was momentarily overcome. Her smile faltered and she dabbed at her mascara.

On the quayside a military band played 'Rule Britannia'. Streamers were launched over the decks where the passengers lined the rails sipping Champagne. A flotilla of small boats followed us out of the harbour as twilight descended on the low hills of Hampshire.

The *Queen Mary 2* is an unexpected resurrection of a great tradition. Thirty years ago, when the first *Queen Mary* was pensioned off to tawdry retirement as a tourist attraction in Long Beach, the received wisdom was that the age of the great ocean liners had come to an end. With the advent of jet aeroplanes, no one would want to spend a week getting to New York.

Although it is the phenomenal rise in the cruise ship market that has made her possible, the *QM2* is not a cruise ship. She is not restricted to dawdling in the Caribbean or the Mediterranean. She is a proper ocean liner with a deep draught, sleek hull lines, and powerful mid-ship engines. She is capable of crossing the North Atlantic in any weather, at speeds up to 30 knots, and a portion of her schedule will be devoted to doing just that. Against the odds, she is the first ship of her type to be launched in more than forty years.

She is also the largest ever launched – the longest (at 1,132ft), the broadest, the tallest and, at £550 million, the most expensive. She is almost twice the tonnage of the first *Queen Mary* and would make the Titanic look small. As a *Blue Peter* project, she is pretty impressive.

In 1973, a 13-year-old, Stephen Payne, wrote to *Blue Peter* to say he thought it had been wrong to describe the *QE2* in *The Blue Peter Annual* as the last of the great liners, adding, with innocent bravado, that he intended to build another one. Twenty-one years later, at the naming ceremony of the *Queen Mary 2*, the *Blue Peter* team came aboard to present its designer, the same Stephen Payne, with his Gold *Blue Peter* Badge.

The new ship trades on the glamour that used to be so much a part of transatlantic crossings. Cunard liners carried politicians, film stars, writers, royalty, jazz singers, femmes fatales, robber barons, high society and low life between New York and London in a manner that allowed them to meet over cocktails and deck quoits. In the unreality of the ocean liner, love affairs, friendships, life-long enmities, political alliances, business deals and unexpected children were all conceived. The ships were the bridge of the special relationship.

When Churchill travelled to America, fortified with Mother Sill's Sea Sick Remedy, they had a shelf installed by his bath so he could read, smoke, drink brandy and carry on correspondence while enjoying a soak. When the Duke and Duchess of Windsor sailed for New York they set a new record for the number of trunks — seventy-two. Marlene Dietrich managed to time her dinner entrances every evening to perfection, appearing at the top of the *Queen Mary*'s grand staircase only after everyone was seated.

When I first crossed the Atlantic, at the age of three, aboard the *Ascania*, I was a child prodigy in the competitive world of deck shuffleboard. Apparently they still speak of me in hushed tones in clubs for retired Filipino seamen. A year later the *Ascania* was scrapped and the opportunities for deck shuffleboard seemed to be gone for ever. But just when I thought it was safe to throw out the deck quoits, the *Queen Mary 2* hoved into view. I begged a ticket and set sail for New York.

Much has already been made of the ship's decor, which has been criticised as Vegas-at-Sea. The Vegas comparison is tabloid exaggeration, but the *QM2* does fall short of the design standards that made Cunard liners icons of style. Among the ten restaurants and fourteen bars there are some wonderful public spaces — the Queen's Room, the largest ballroom afloat, the Britannia Restaurant, the Illuminations Theatre and Planetarium, the splendid library — but decor tends to be bland. My cabin, in B1 class, was spacious, with a television providing a wide range of on-demand films, and lots of wardrobe space. Sadly, the design standards were more international hotel chain than classic ocean liner glamour.

Still, ocean liners are not a matter of curtain swatches. Only a stony heart would not miss a beat at the sight of this blue-hulled apparition. Taken as a whole, the *QM2* is a dream boat. Days aboard fell into a pleasant rhythm. After breakfast the more studious repaired to the lecture theatre where one could learn about dinosaurs, Utopia, Mozart's operas and Wagner. The best talks, by Simon Schama, were entitled 'Rough Crossings', a rehearsal for his next book on the nature of the transatlantic relationship. Afterwards, at lunch in the King's Court, a French family were discussing, over roast beef, how compromised little England was by her American connections, culturally as well as politically.

Meanwhile, in the casino, Walter was dropping $100 a spin on the roulette wheel. With a smile as wide as Texas he made losing seem rather jolly. He spotted me loitering and gave me a $100 chip. I would have preferred to have cashed it in and put it towards the mortgage but Walter would have been disappointed. I put it on two, and lost. Walter guffawed and slapped me on the back.

Upstairs in the gym an elegant gay couple from Chicago trimmed further ounces from their sleek figures, before repairing to the herbal steam baths of the Canyon Ranch spa, where irritatingly beautiful and fit young people were available to place warm stones along your spine. Five decks below, four John Bull figures, clutching pints of bitter, played darts in the Golden Lion pub. One deck up and the first corks of the day popped in the Champagne bar, while next door in the Mayfair shops a young man was buying his fiancée a silver bracelet. 'A little chain,' he cooed. 'A little chain to hold you.'

In the Royal Court Theatre, the Merry Widow was sighing over extracts of *Romeo and Juliet* played by students from RADA. Half an ocean liner forward, and another five decks up, I checked my email in the wood-lined library to find that Rupert Murdoch still hadn't coughed up the money he owed me. Through the bow windows the Atlantic, tufted with white caps, was beginning to swell. Spray shot over the starboard bows, and slight tremors ran through the ship, like a shiver down its spine.

At afternoon tea in the Winter Garden, where a real harpist played among unreal foliage, I tried to explain cucumber sandwiches to the New Yorker at the next table. 'I don't get it. Something's missing here, right.' He pulled the bread apart and furrowed his brow at the pale cucumber inside. Beyond the windows, couples bundled in coats braved strong winds on the decks. In the passageway outside the theatre I met the Merry Window hurrying aft. 'Scarf-tying class at four,' she called. 'Mustn't be late.'

The days glided effortlessly towards evening. Three of our six nights at sea were designated formal dress. A couple of the evenings included an invitation for drinks with the captain, known on the *QM2* as the Commodore. I hurried along to the Queen's Ballroom only to find that I was obliged to share him with at least 300 other guests. He looked to have everything you would have wanted in a captain, including a white beard.

At dinner the wine glasses began to shift. The seas had been mounting and the ship was now rolling and pitching dramatically. A tray of plates went on the far side of the restaurant. I was dining in the Todd English, the best of the *QM2*'s restaurants, and the only one for which you need to book. The food throughout the ship was first-rate, but Todd English is a chef to savour.

By the time I got back to my cabin, a journey made like a stage drunk, a full gale was blowing. Clutching the rails of my balcony I gazed out on black mountainous waves and wondered what it must have been like in such seas on the first Cunard ship, the *Britannia*, a paddle steamer that would have fitted into the *QM2*'s ballroom.

The Atlantic threw everything at us, except mercifully for icebergs. Not once, but twice the gales reached force ten. If the guests looked a trifle queasy, the crew were delighted. No one can predict a ship's handling in heavy seas with 100 per cent accuracy. The *QM2* came through with flying colours. On the final day, as if to reward her prowess, the seas abated, the sun shone and the decks blossomed into life.

We woke early for our arrival in New York. On the observation deck, muffled passengers were peering into the mists. Convoys of little boats had already attached themselves to us – pilot boats, tugs, coastguard boats and half a dozen NYPD police launches – as the great liner blindly followed a line of navigation buoys towards an invisible New York.

The Verrazano Narrows bridge, across the entrance to New York harbour, materialised like a ghost out of the mists. This bridge is what determined the height of the ship. As we passed beneath it there was less than 20 feet to spare. A fire tug sprayed arcs of coloured water – red, white and blue.

The growing convoy of boats, like Lilliputians round a blue-and-white Gulliver, escorted us past the Statue of Liberty. From port side on the top deck we gazed at her, eye level. On the starboard side the Merry Widow was waving a tiny Union Jack at the incomparable skyline of Manhattan. News helicopters buzzed round us, sending live feeds to the nation's breakfast programmes. Walter was shouting into his mobile – 'Hey, turn on the TV. We're coming into harbour.'

With three deep blasts of the ship's horn, we came to a halt on the west side of Manhattan. Tugs, dwarfed beneath the great hull, swung us into our berth. We stuck out past the end of the dock by more than 100 feet. Another military band, this one playing 'Yankee Doodle Dandy' and 'New York, New York', was marching on the quay where Mayor Bloomberg waited to greet the arriving passengers.

Quite by coincidence, two berths along lay Concorde like some exquisite bird with its wings clipped. She was lashed aboard a barge, presumably on her way to yet another aviation museum. Thirty years ago Concorde was the future and ocean liners the past. Who would have predicted that the demise of supersonic transatlantic travel would have coincided with the launch of a great liner such as the *QM2*? Perhaps it signals some new maturity – an understanding that, in travel, speed is not the point.

THE QUEEN MARY TO GO TO SEA TO-DAY

1,500,000 TO WATCH HER START HISTORIC VOYAGE

Clyde Weather Forecast – Sunny periods, with occasional showers; light easterly wind; mild.

Today, eighteen months after her launching, the *Queen Mary*, the great Cunard White Star liner, will leave her birthplace on the Clyde on her historic fourteen miles journey to the sea at Greenock. The Clydebank last night had the appearance of an army under canvas. Tens of thousands of people remained there all night, in tents, cars and caravans. All through the early hours of this morning thousands more were pouring into Glasgow by train, car and aeroplane.

It was disclosed yesterday that the *Queen Mary* will be rated at 80,773 tons of gross. Her maximum speed will probably be 33 knots. She will leave the fitting-out basin at Clydebank at 10.45 a.m., and is expected to anchor off the Tail o' the Bank at Greenock at 2.30 p.m. Tonight she will be floodlit.

Camp fires twinkle along Clyde

**From our special representative
Glasgow, Monday.**

The advance guard of the 1,500,000 spectators who will watch the *Queen Mary* go down the Clyde tomorrow were taking up positions on both banks of the river this afternoon, nearly twenty hours before the ship is due to pass. Tonight camp fires are twinkling at scores of places between Clydebank and Greenock. Thousands of sightseers, some of whom have motored from England, are camping out for the night, some in tents they have brought with them, others in their cars or in caravans. There are many family parties. One man and woman, near Erskine Ferry, had brought five children, including a six-months-old baby, to share their all-night vigil. Among those taking early positions are the ambulance workers. They will sleep under canvas.

Tonight special trains are being run from all over England and Scotland. Before dawn tomorrow the roads leading to the river will be blocked with people and cars. Glasgow has already been invaded by enormous crowds outnumbering even the great concourse which came to see the launching of the *Queen Mary*.

More than 1,000 policemen, some drafted from other counties, will be on traffic duty in Dumbartonshire and Renfrewshire. Hundreds of road signs bearing the laconic legend '*Queen Mary*' have been erected in Glasgow and country roads. A fleet of loudspeaker motor-vans will move among the crowds and assist the police in their efforts to prevent a traffic tangle. The Renfrew police have been deluged with trunk telephone calls from motorists asking information. Some have telephoned from as far afield as Devonshire and Cornwall. Many inquiries about aerodrome facilities have also been made by intending air travellers.

 Meanwhile all is in readiness for the *Queen Mary* to leave on her historic journey. Late this afternoon I went over part of the interior of the great ship. Hundreds of men and women were working at top speed on the final preparations. The organisation of the large number of workers was perfect and there was not the slightest confusion amid the bustle. The ship is astonishingly far advanced, even in trivial detail, and almost looked as though she could sail on her maiden voyage to America tomorrow. In the main saloon, tables and chairs were set out under dust covers. The decorative panelling shone gaily. Scores of women were polishing and dusting. Others were tacking down the luxurious carpets. Men were trying the lifts. Bedding was being carried aboard. Most of the public rooms and many of the cabins looked ready for use in all their shining newness. Everywhere wood and glass panelling looked crisp and clean. A truly remarkable job of 'freshening up' the ship has been accomplished over the weekend, since the thousands of visitors ended their invasion on Saturday.

On the bridge Commander Sir Edgar Britten, captain of the ship, was having a final conference with the pilots, Capt. Duncan Cameron and Capt. John Murchie. Outside the first-class saloon was one of the busiest men in all the ship – Mr A.E. Jones, the chief steward. Some of the 800 staff who will be under his control, including waiters, pantry staff, bar keepers and stewards, were bustling about arranging the disposal of equipment. New cutlery, china and supplies of food were being stowed away in their places. 'A big job, but I am enjoying it,' Mr Jones said with a smile.

Most of the food for the maiden voyage will be taken on at Southampton in May. The all-electric kitchens stood ready to cook the first meals. Chefs were carefully surveying their new domain. Two special sections of the catering department are devoted to children and invalid foods. The kitchen for invalid foods is near the two ship's hospitals, and also comes under Mr Jones's control.

Today a diver made a descent to examine the fitting-out basin near the *Queen Mary*. He reported that all was clear for the great ship to move out into the channel. This morning the cruiser *Southampton* was warped from her position in the fitting-out basin alongside the *Queen Mary* and taken to Rothesay Dock nearby. She will remain there until the giant liner has gone.

Throughout today conferences of officials have dealt with every possible contingency that may arise when the *Queen Mary* goes down river. Special weather forecasts sent to John Brown's yard at frequent intervals have been anxiously scanned. Present indications are that conditions will be fairly favourable.

A suggestion was made that the pilots might be assisted in their work by an aeroplane flying low overhead. From the air the shoals and mudbanks of the narrow river can be seen clearly as on a map. A system of light signals, it was suggested, might be used from the 'planes to assist the pilots in negotiating bends in the river. But the pilots have indicated their complete confidence in taking the *Queen Mary* downstream without aerial or other aid. The tender *Paladin* and a Clyde tug will lead the *Queen Mary* downstream, while two tugs will be at the stern. Three more tugs will be kept in close attendance, ready to give instant assistance if necessary.

THE QUEEN MARY TWICE AGROUND IN CLYDE

BY **HECTOR C. BYWATER**, *DAILY TELEGRAPH*
CORRESPONDENT ON BOARD R.M.S. QUEEN MARY

GOUROCK, TUESDAY EVENING

After an adventurous voyage from her cradle at Clydebank, the *Queen Mary*, the world's finest ship, is now safely anchored in deep water in the Firth of Clyde. None of those who made the passage in her will ever forget the thrilling moments of this trip. It began and ended in the happiest conditions, but for a few tense minutes the shadow of disaster seemed to hover near the ship. Fate played an untimely card by sending a strong gust of wind out of the south-east at the worst possible moment, but this scurvy trick was defeated by splendid seamanship.

When I boarded the liner at nine o'clock this morning preparations for the start were well under way. During the night the wind had driven so much water into the upper reaches of the Clyde that the pilots decided to advance the time of sailing by one hour. At 9.45, therefore, four tremendous blasts of the ship's sirens heralded our departure. From all over John Brown and Co.'s shipyard thousands of workmen, by special permission, dropped their tools and hurried to the dockhead to bid farewell to the ship they had laboured to create – 'The lady with the £5,000,000 look,' as they call her. Five minutes later the huge electric capstans on the foredeck began to turn, paying out great lengths of 9in. manila hawsers, which were made fast to bollards on the dock side. The tugs at our stern exerted their full powers, and, under the combined drag of warps and tugs, the Queen of the Seas moved slowly and steadily out of the dock.

There was neither fuss nor noise. Staccato orders from the first officer, stationed in the bows, supplemented by commands from the bridge, transmitted through loud-speakers, told the men on board and ashore exactly what to do. The delicate manoeuvre of drawing the mighty hull out of the cramped basin into the narrow river, straightening her out and pointing her head downstream was accomplished without the slightest hitch. Exactly twenty-five minutes after the first rope had been cast off, our bows were clear of the dock. At this moment two tugs astern exerted their utmost power, and cleanly and smoothly, the ship was sent on a course exactly parallel with the dredged channel leading to the sea.

At 10.25 the deck trembled slightly as the mighty turbines came into action. The *Queen Mary* had begun her first voyage. Salvoes of cheers came from the massed ranks of Clydebank workmen as we slipped by. I was told, and can well believe, that some of the older hands were overcome with emotion as they watched their beautiful ship leaving them. Indeed, as we passed a monstrous crane, which served as an improvised grandstand, one could sense the emotions of these craftsmen, who are, in their way, great artists.

At 10.30 the ship's stern was level with the dock and we were bowling downstream at what I reckon to be a good six knots. Our Red Ensign astern hovered gaily in the breeze, with the Blue Peter – the sailing flag – at the fore, and the John Brown and Co. house flag at the main masthead. Just as all were congratulating themselves on a perfect start the elements took a hand in the game. Standing at the after end of the boat deck I felt the great force of a sudden gust of wind that came sweeping down the river.

It struck squarely against the lofty hull, and, almost instantly, I saw that our stern was being swept across the channel. It was precisely at 10.35, when we were abreast of Dalmuir Light, that the inevitable happened. No human foresight, or effort, could have prevented what followed. In less than sixty seconds the wind had buffeted the ship out of her course and laid her diagonally athwart the river. The stern took the mud on the Renfrew bank, and almost simultaneously the bows scraped the foreshore on the Dumbarton side. So slight was the jar that scarcely anyone on board felt it. But the ship took a slight list to port, and there was no gainsaying the fact that we were aground and completely blocking the river Clyde. Below us, less than 20ft from the side of the ship, sightseers on the Renfrew bank gazed up at our towering decks and, unwitting of the gravity of the situation, attempted to exchange jokes.

We remained aground – or, rather, lightly embedded in the mud – for exactly twenty minutes, which seemed so many hours. But, in fact, things were by no means so bad as they seemed. It was still a full three hours to high tide, and our gallant tugs were already at work. At 11.18 I took a bearing and found that we were moving again; inch by inch it is true, but definitely moving.

All seemed to be going well when another fierce blast of wind impinged on our sky-scraper hull. I could see our bows drifting inexorably across the river, despite the frantic efforts of the tugs. Then came a sharp tinkle from the engine-room telegraph, and our engines were put full speed astern. Even at this thrilling moment I noticed the complete absence of vibration. We seemed to be clearing the Dalmuir bank with a few yards to spare when, at 11.45, the bows of the ship again struck the mud. This second involuntary stop lasted ten minutes, but once more our trusty tugs, helped by our own engines, tore us from the unwelcome embrace of the land. Again we were steaming down the channel, and though another awkward moment was believed to be awaiting us at Bowling, on the northern bank, where the fairway is very narrow, our fears were disproved. At 12.15 we were passing Erskine Ferry. From then onwards the time-table of the voyage was as follows:

12.25. — Donald Quay Light, Old Kilpatrick; ship turning north to follow deep channel.
12.30. — Approaching Bowling.
12.40. — Passed Bowling without mishap.
12.45. — Dunglass Castle, where the *Queen Mary*'s sirens blew a loud blast in honour of Henry Bell, who, 124 years ago, built the first steamer, the *Comet*. His memorial stands on the hillside.
1 p.m. — Abreast Dumbarton Rock.
1.40. — Passing Port Glasgow, its shipyards and cranes packed with spectators.
1.55. — Passing Greenock.
2.20. — Off the Tail of the Bank.
2.25. — Anchor let go.

Extraordinary scenes of enthusiasm greeted the passage of the ship down the fourteen miles of river. The cheering was almost continuous, and every vessel, great and small, gave us a welcome, either from diminutive steam whistles or full-throated sirens. These compliments were punctiliously returned by the *Queen Mary*, the power of whose own sirens baffles description.

Only an expert Clyde pilot could say whether this great ship, freighted with the hopes of a nation, was in real danger this morning when she took the mud off Dalmuir Light. Personally, in view of the fact that there was still three hours to high tide, I believe the misadventure was more spectacular than serious. Certainly none of the officials on board showed a trace of alarm. From beginning to end the vessel herself exhibited wonderful manoeuvring qualities, and although from Port Glasgow to the Tail of the Bank we were steaming at a fair speed, there was not even a tremor from the engines.

A FLOATING EXTRA COUNTY OF BRITAIN

THIS TIME NEXT YEAR, *CANBERRA* WILL SET SAIL ON HER FINAL CRUISE. WHAT IS IT ABOUT THIS SHIP THAT ENGENDERS SUCH AFFECTION? **JAN MOIR** TROD HER SWIRLY CARPETS

By night, he is Sir Philip Fortesque Cholmondley Raymond, the Brylcreemed star of the ship's olde-time music hall revue. By day he is Phil Raymond, cruise director on the *Canberra*, the maestro of merriment, the man in charge of entertainments. From his office on the promenade deck, where a jokey sign reading 'Without Compliments!' is propped against his computer, he chortles: 'Oh, any afternoon it's easy to find me. I'll be out there holding a baby or kissing an old lady.'

Raymond has an instant laugh and a deep suntan. The gold chains at his wrist and throat sparkle against his white uniform, which, in turn, emphasises a paunch that suggests an enjoyment of the good life. He has worked for P&O for fifteen years and adores his job. 'Where else would I get the chance to act, dance and sing every day and see the world? Although it is hard work, you know. It's not like *Hi-de-Hi!* on sea.'

Like most of the ship's company, Raymond is distressed at the recent news that the *Canberra*, after thirty-six years in service, will be decommissioned in September next year. 'She is a very special old girl — they could never afford to build something like her again.'

In her long career, she has sailed more than three million miles. First she was a long-distance liner on the Australian run, carrying thousands of emigrants, paying £10 each on fare-assisted passages, to new lives in the New World. Since the 1970s she has been a one-class cruiser, opening the oceans to those who had previously considered a cruise holiday beyond their means.

Famously, she was requisitioned as a troop carrier during the Falklands War and served with the Task Force for ninety-four days. Two destroyers, two frigates and a Cunard container ship were lost in the South Atlantic, but the Great White Whale, as she was known by the soldiers, came home intact.

It is sad for everyone, then, that this 44,807-ton slab of history is sailing into the sunset, but for the crew and ship's company it is a deep, personal wrench. One third engineer from Barnstaple wrote a letter to P&O's chairman, Lord Sterling, begging him to reconsider his decision. The chef de cuisine, David McLachlan, who began his career on the *Canberra* twenty-one years ago, is also unhappy. 'She was my first ship and I'm not looking forward to her going. Not many are. I think they should spend £100 million, take her out of commission for a year and do her up. Maybe I shouldn't say that, but that's how I feel.'

And Phil Raymond feels the same. 'Babies have been born and people have died on this ship. She's even been to war... so many memories.' The fate of the ship has yet to be decided. Senior staff at P&O are said to be considering offers. No one knows if she will be sold or broken up and the thought of her being turned into scrap is almost more than Raymond can bear. 'I will chain myself to the propeller if they take her away and turn her into razor blades,' he says.

Why, exactly, is she so special? 'You must have felt it when you came on board,' says Raymond. 'You must have felt the special atmosphere. Everybody does. Didn't you think to yourself, there is a real warmth about this ship?'

Actually, no. I had not been hit by a wave of affection, more of a vague queasiness at the wild profusion of swirly patterned carpets. Padding along the corridor to my D deck cabin didn't feel like striding through the midships of a great liner, but like climbing aboard the mezzanine level of a three-star Midlands hotel.

Nevertheless, there is much to marvel at, not least the departure, for cruising is the only modern form of transport still attended by a sense of ceremony. At Southampton Dock, P&O's home port for 150 years, well-wishers and families jostle for position in the 'waving' areas as the ship slips her moorings at 6 p.m., serenaded by a brassy fanfare from the Hampshire police band. She leaves a trail of paper streamers in her wake, tossed ashore by passengers and left curling in huge mounds of pastel spaghetti on the dockside.

An hour later, we pass Cowes to starboard and then set a south-westerly course through the Channel. On the bridge, nothing much seems to be happening; just a handful of blokes in smart uniforms silently scanning the horizon with binoculars.

The wings of the ship – an old-fashioned design feature – jut out over the superstructure more than 100 feet above the ocean. From here you can see right down the length of the ship, taste the salt on your lips, relish the freshening breeze. Given half a chance, I would have dragged my bunk and parked up in this wonderful place for the rest of the trip; falling asleep under the stars to the quiet thrumming of the engines.

Looking down over the rail at the faraway, inky sea, you realise that this would be the perfect place to commit suicide. 'Are you thinking about suicide?' asks Navigator Rob Powell. 'Don't worry, everybody does. And contrary to popular opinion, it's a very unpleasant way to die. From this height, it would be like smashing into concrete. And if that didn't kill you, the temperature of the water would give you a heart attack.' Has anyone ever done it? 'Yes,' he says, quietly. 'A member of the crew. A few years ago. But I'm certainly not going to tell you about that.'

Below decks, the 1,659 passengers and 899 crew are settling into the routine that will shape the fourteen days of this Riviera Romance cruise. In the two restaurants, the first-sitting diners have finished their fruit salads and the second sitters are tucking in to their soup.

Food is of paramount import to the cruisers, and chef McLachlan knows what his customers want: roast beef and two veg and plenty of it. 'British people tend to stick to what they know. I once tried to take Beef Wellington off the menu, and there was a near riot...We serve a lot of tripe and onions, yes, even when we're sailing through the Caribbean. A lot of them were brought up on it. They love tripe and they expect to see it on the menu.'

After dinner, at the Bon Voyage Dance in the Ocean Room, Phil Raymond's entertainments officers do their best to forge a party atmosphere. James Gorton, who has been with the company for a year, spends his evening asking wallflower women to dance. 'You can't possibly enjoy doing this,' I say, as we foxtrot across the sprung floor. 'Ho ho ho,' he says, as if he's just heard the most fabulous joke ever. 'Of course I enjoy it. And I get asked to dance quite a lot, actually.'

'Perhaps that's because you're so tall,' I reply, inanely. 'No – ho ho ho. Ha ha ha,' he guffaws, as if he is swinging Dorothy Parker across the boards.

He previously worked on US cruise ships – a terrible experience, he recalls. 'Say what you like about the English, but at least they're good at deck games. You've got to explain everything twice, three times to the Americans. Even something as simple as quoits.'

We assemble for a barn dance, dominated by elderly ladies with fierce grey perms who dance excellently. 'Isn't the Ocean Room lovely?' one remarks when we swap partners. If you must have nautical decor, then I suppose a ship is the place to have it, but the orange chairs decorated with anchors, the blue sofas with cockleshells, the woven compasses and the flotilla of clipper ships foaming across the curtains seems – to me, anyway – to be one seafaring motif too far. 'It's lovely,' I shout. 'Very cosy.'

Although it is proudly billed as a one-class ship, with public rooms open to all, the *Canberra*, of course, does have a tacit class system. 'You get what you pay for,' explains one veteran cruiser (twenty-six trips), as we stomp through a St Barnard's Waltz.

For this fourteen-day, seven-port Med cruise, the most expensive accommodation – for two adults travelling together – is an AA-grade suite at £4,580 per person. A German couple called Klaus and Katrina, who dine each night at the Captain's Table, are most certainly in the best berths on board. 'The worst thing is,' says Klaus, patting his wallet, 'that the ladies see this as an excuse to fill their wardrobes.' Katrina rolls her eyes heavenwards. 'Only three new long dresses and a few cocktail dresses,' she whispers. How many? 'Five.'

The cheapest berths – £1,057.50 per person – come via a deal called Friendly Fours, based on four adults travelling together and sharing a Z-grade cabin on F deck with separate toilet and washing facilities and no porthole; entertainments, meals and books are thrown in.

In the pubby Cricketers bar, the offstage Phil Raymond is warmly greeted by a crowd of Glaswegians ('heavy gamblers, great fun, they come every year,' he says) whose children are neatly kitted out in Rangers FC away strips.

In the Crow's Nest bar at the prow of the ship, men in lemon leisurewear and blazers buy glasses of Buck's Fizz (cocktail of the day, £1.50) for ladies in floaty scarves and strappy gold sandals. There is an excellent cocktail pianist, Diana Jarret-Harris, who signs off each midnight by saying: 'Remember, everybody, I love your faces.'

The morning dawns bright. After a breakfast of bacon, egg and black pudding – none of that foreign muck, matey – many go to press their noses against the plastic grilles of the five shops and gaze at the merchandise inside. When the stores open, there is a queue to buy postcards. Round the pools, sunbathers stake out their territory with towels and handbags, then stick their noses into magazines.

Whenever Captain David Lumb ventures off the bridge, he is besieged by passengers desperate to have their photograph taken with him. 'These days, the most important thing for a captain is to be sociable and charming,' he says, throwing an arm around a delighted old lady and smiling cheesily for the lens.

Up in his spacious quarters the captain reveals that he will be retiring in December, aged sixty, after forty-two years with P&O. 'So the *Canberra* will outlast me by nine months. It is all very sad, but these things happen,' he says. 'Some of the modern ships feel impersonal and cold, but this one has always felt like a friend. The *Oriana* is a hotel that floats, but the *Canberra* is a ship that happens to have a hotel on it. There is a big difference. Maybe not so easy to operate, but much more fun to drive.'

Captain Lumb has never been scared nor seasick, not even when the *Canberra* was caught south of Acapulco in winds of 70 knots with 60ft waves crashing around. 'We ended up heaving to, and she rode out the storm. A couple of windows were smashed, but apart from that we were OK.' He has only once had to lower a lifeboat and then it was to pick up some yachts-men who had capsized. Nine years on, the captain and the yachtsmen still exchange Christmas cards.

The captain would not like the ship to be turned into a dockside resort or a maritime museum, two suggested options. 'It would be kinder if she was scrapped. It is better that she goes with dignity.' Last year he visited the *Queen Mary*, berthed in Long Beach, California. She is an entertainments centre. 'She really is a bit of a mess,' he says. 'I would hate that to happen to the *Canberra*.' Then he excused himself to host the Captain's Cocktail Party.

This takes place in the Meridian Lounge, where sunburnt revellers in evening dress select glasses of gin or whisky from silver salvers and chat merrily. Bill Bridges, a builder from Manchester, is celebrating his fiftieth birthday. That morning – in the ship's salon – he had his greying hair dyed bright ginger to mark the occasion. 'I really wanted a blue rinse, but they refused to do it,' he says. 'My wife loves it, but the kids are a bit upset.' On a couch, one Scottish couple, with the loving animosity that only decades of marriage can bring, bicker happily: 'Sandy, open your dinner jacket,' she chides. 'Elspeth, shut your mouth,' he retorts.

The crew are on social duty and some, including the deputy purser, Johannes Ming, wear tiny medals on their left breast, testament to the fact that they sailed with the ship to the Falklands. 'This might sound strange,' he says, 'but I wouldn't have missed it for the world.' Officer Ming – a Swiss – pointed to the swirly carpet of the Meridian Lounge at his feet.

'I worked right here. This was the recuperating ward. My office was just there, in that little galley. We would feed the soldiers and look after them and talk to them, just like we do with the passengers. They were so young, you know. And some of them were very badly hurt.'

Towards the end of the war the Meridian – which is now resonating with festive piano music, the ho-ho-ho-ing of Raymond and his jolly officers and the chinking of glasses — became the holding area for 1,000 Argentinian prisoners of war. The Bonito Club upstairs — where I had been sunbathing earlier — was the operating theatre.

After all this, cynics need no more convincing. Who cares about the silly clipper-print curtains when you are travelling on such a remarkable ship? Think of kindly Officer Ming, a civilian sailor caught up in a war, padding around a converted cocktail lounge offering fatherly comforts to wounded young men a long way from home. Think of the hopes and dreams of the emigrants, sailing off into the unknown of Australia. And spare a thought for the people couched together in Z deck, gutsy enough to want to see a bit of the world, eating the same food and playing at the same roulette tables as those who have paid four times as much for the privilege.

The real joy of the *Canberra* is that she allows the British to be British — in all their eccentric, picky, happy-go-lucky glory — no matter where in the world she sails. There are those who might sniff at the thought of fry-ups in Sorrento or tea and scones in the Baltic Sea but, for me, the notion of a grandfather from Bolton tucking into a plate of tripe and onions as the *Canberra* steams into Honolulu Harbour is one of indomitable magnificence.

The party begins to wind down in the Meridian Lounge. People drift off to dinner, to play cards, to read a book in the quiet of their cabins. And outside in the darkness, the old girl, with all her memories welded into the thick, deep hull, ploughs on without complaint through the Atlantic.

A TOWN LIKE OASIS

THE BIGGEST CRUISE SHIP IN THE WORLD STARTS ITS MAIDEN VOYAGE TODAY. **PETER HUGHES** HAD A PREVIEW AND FOUND IT 'MORE METRO THAN MATELOT'

Back in the days when oldfangled ocean liners were evolving into shiny new cruise ships, sea dogs had a way of distinguishing between the two. A liner was a ship with a hotel built inside it; a cruise ship was a hotel with a ship built around it.

It's a distinction, along with almost every other maritime convention, that has been blown out of the water by the £800 million *Oasis of The Seas*. Never mind the hotel stuff, *Oasis* is hardly a ship.

For those just back from Planet Zog and who may have missed it, *Oasis*, which embarks on its maiden voyage today, is the biggest cruise ship ever built:

– So big that if stood on end it would be taller than either the highest skyscraper at Canary Wharf in London or the Chrysler Building in New York.

– So big that it can carry 6,296 passengers at a time.

– So big that it needs at least 312,000 passengers a year — that's more people than live in Coventry. It has to fill up every week because it only makes seven-night cruises.

– So big that British travel agents are worried they may not find enough aircraft seats between Britain and Florida to supply it. Four out of ten British holidaymakers booking a West Indies cruise with the ship's owners, Royal Caribbean, are choosing to go on *Oasis*.

– And so big that $75 million has been spent on tripling the size of the Port Everglades terminal at Fort Lauderdale from where it sails, and new docks have been built around the Caribbean to berth it.

It is not a thing of beauty. The first sight is of a colossal wall, sixteen storeys high, pixelated with balconies. It will keep Channel Five going with programmes about monster machines for years. But is it a ship? Not in any traditional poop and fo'c'sle sense, it isn't.

Royal Caribbean admits as much. The company refers to it as 'our float-ing nation'. That may be a little extravagant, but only a little: the ship's population of 8,461, which comprises all those passengers, plus 2,165 crew, is more than half that of the island of Anguilla.

If it is a ship, it's a town ship. Three quarters of *Oasis* is in maritime denial. Until you reach the open decks – or your cabin, if you have one of the 1,481 with an outside balcony – you're barely aware of the sea. As the song so nearly goes, 'Join Oasis to see the world, and whad'ya see? You see a city.' Life on these ocean waves is essentially urban living, more metro than matelot.

You walk in off the street – well, off that whopping new terminal – straight on to a street, paved, lined with shops, bars, cafés and a pizzeria. There is even a car parked in the middle. It's a racy two-seater, a slinky replica of a 1936 Auburn. On *Oasis* you may question what they have done, but you can't question the panache with which they have done it.

That street – Royal Promenade – is one of the ideas carried on from Royal Caribbean's two smaller classes of ship, *Voyager* and *Freedom*, both vast in their day. Of course, the *Oasis* Promenade is bigger: big enough for there to be a bar at its centre. It's called the Rising Tide because it ascends very slowly through three decks. It's like a pod from the London Eye; it has the same 32-person capacity. But the Rising Tide only goes up and down, not around and around.

It's proclaimed as the first on any ship, though I confess the point of it escaped me. As did 'the cosy charm of an old English pub', which was prom-ised in the Globe and Atlas. Besides being among the few places where smoking is permitted, it is lit like a power cut. So for 'cosy charm', read 'nicotine-fumed', and instead of English pub imagine New York dive.

Royal Promenade is one of seven 'neighbourhoods'. Note the urban terminology. Nothing nautical there: there might at least have been some-where called Buoyz n the Hood. Rising Tide doesn't really count because that sounds like a social trend, but the Schooner Bar does have pictures of ships, part of a $10 million, 7,000-item art collection.

No paradox, then, that for me the most convincing bit of *Oasis* was easily the most metropolitan. Central Park nestles in a cleft in the heart of the ship, open to the sky and bounded on either side by five-storey blocks of balconied apartments. The effect is of an exclusive little mews with outdoor cafés and sidewalk tables outside Vintages wine bar and Giovanni's trattoria.

Throughout it all runs the 'park', actually a garden containing

ninety-three different plant varieties, lilies, ferns, crotons, ginger and trees
that will grow to more than twenty-four feet. Hanging gardens, four floors
high, of ferns and flowering vines cascade down either side. Unless the ship
rolls, you would have no idea you were not in one of the more moneyed
quarters of Boston or New York.

The ship's steakhouse, Chops Grille, and the smartest restaurant, 150
Central Park, are here, too. There are twenty-four different eating places on
board — 'dining options' in cruise-speak — half of them levying a cover
charge above the cost of the cruise. In 150 Central Park it's $35 (about £21) a
head.

The reason *Oasis* is so spacious is that it is so wide. Its beam, 208ft, is almost
double the 'Panamax', the maximum width for a ship to get through the
Panama Canal. Oasis is registered at 225,282 tons, which is a measurement of
volume, not weight. That makes it more than 30 per cent bigger than the
previous supersized cruise ship, Royal Caribbean's *Freedom of the Seas*. But size
isn't everything. 'We don't build a big ship for the sake of it, just to be the
biggest in the world,' said Robin Shaw, Royal Caribbean's vice-president
and managing director for the UK and Ireland. 'The fact that the ship is big
gives us the opportunity to do so many more different things you couldn't
do on a smaller ship.'

In Royal Caribbean they call it 'working on the wow'. You would be
suffering from severe synapse deficiency not to be dazed by the scope and
scale of the *Oasis* wow. The Boardwalk, another of the neighbourhoods, is
themed as a Fifties Coney Island-style esplanade with ice-cream parlour and
a Johnny Rockets hamburger joint. In the centre is a working carousel, its
exquisitely carved and painted animals rising and dipping to a steam organ's
tinny chords.

At the end of the Boardwalk, right in the stern, is the AquaTheatre, an
amphitheatre where the stage is a pool. All told, there are twenty-one pools
on board including whirlpools, two of which stick out from the side of the
ship like an epaulette high above the ocean. The AquaTheatre pool is
almost 18ft deep. It's used for swimming and scuba diving lessons by day
and for a water show at night — part Peterhof Palace in Russia, with foun-
tains spurting 65ft in the air, and part Olympics, with synchronised diving
and gymnasts bouncing off a trampoline, it's an unusual performance. The
climax is a heart-stopping leap from a 55ft platform. Eat your heart out
Acapulco. The La Quebrada divers may jump from higher, but they're not
trying to land on a moving ship in what must look like a puddle.

It's when *Oasis* tries to be a conventional cruise ship that it is least successful. The brutish architecture of the ship's superstructure glowers over the open, top deck, which seems to be fenced by so many five-bar railings that it appears as corralled as a stockyard. And to provide enough loungers for thousands of sunbathers means jamming them together as tightly as piano keys.

Get back to the action quick and have a round of mini-golf, shoot some hoops on the basketball court, conquer a climbing wall, surf the high-pressure rapids of the Flowriders and dangle from the zip line 80ft above the Boardwalk. It's pretty tame, more dawdle than zip. Whatever became of deck quoits? Inevitably, the spa is the largest at sea, the fitness centre the biggest and the jogging track the longest.

And for children, *Oasis* is the most ginormous adventure playground on the planet long before they venture into their own neighbourhood, where there's a children's theatre and science lab. At night, as well as the jazz and the dancing, the karaoke and the guys doing stand-up in the comedy club, there is a full-blown Broadway musical in the Opal Theatre. Currently it is *Hairspray*, the story of Tracy Turnblad, who finds celebrity after her discovery on a television dance show. Very appropriate: Tracy would have been on *Oasis* like a shot.

As for me, I have some reservations. I am personally baffled that anyone should choose to go on holiday with 5,998 strangers; I am professionally puzzled that someone should do so while paying £4,269 a head for the most expensive suite — the gargantuan one on two floors with a whirlpool bath and a baby grand piano that plays by itself. Still, they can console themselves in the shop selling Breitling watches and, if they can get up a party of fourteen, they can have a private dinner at the Chef's Table for $75 each.

I have other questions. *Oasis* is being joined by a sister ship next year, so how is it that cruise ships are getting ever bigger when the trend everywhere else in the holiday business seems to be to downsize for greater individuality and more personal service? Economies of scale is Royal Caribbean's response.

And what is the effect on communities in places such as Jamaica and St Maarten, where a lot of cruises already call, when 5,000 or more passengers can now go ashore from a single vessel? Robin Shaw explained that they had been working with port authorities for six years. 'There is a significant economic benefit to these places and they welcome us,' he said.

But does a ship like *Oasis*, a destination in itself, need to go anywhere? Adam Goldstein, the company president, was emphatic about the importance of ports of call. 'Research continues to show that people are still very interested in where ships will take them,' he said. He unequivocally ruled out the notion of seven-night cruises to nowhere.

The big test, though, is whether *Oasis* works. Smallish rooms are fine for creating a feeling of intimacy, but they do fill up quickly. Every time I tried to get into either Johnny Rockets or the Seafood Shack fish restaurant, there was a waiting list of at least an hour, and we had only 4,000 guests aboard. Shows and restaurants can be booked online pre-cruise. I strongly recommend it.

When I arrived at the ship, it took four hours for my luggage to reach my cabin. With the petulance of a man who had been up almost twenty hours, had no change of clothes, needed a shower and in five minutes' time was expected for dinner, I called a man in Guest Relations. 'It is hard to find one piece of luggage among 15,000,' he said unhelpfully.

Did I detect a note of pride in the way he said 15,000? Undoubtedly, it is the biggest collection of suitcases ever to put to sea. I knew that ought to have made me feel better.

UNLADYLIKE

Sir – Must our finest liner, proud flagship of our merchant marine and successor of the two great *Queens*, always be referred to in newspapers and BBC bulletins by that hideous technological computerised post-codish term 'Q E 2'? Can this mode of appellation not be limited to Boeing jets, motorways and so forth?

J.C.B. Deakin
Lancing, Sussex

Chapter 2
THE BRITISH ISLES

---

20 FEBRUARY 1993

THE SPIRIT OF SAIL LIVES ON

BRIAN JACKMAN, IN THE STORMY WESTERN ISLES OF SCOTLAND, JOINS THE 100-YEAR-OLD LORNE LEADER, ONE OF ONLY THREE TRAWLERS OF ITS KIND NOW AFLOAT IN BRITISH WATERS

With a clap of thunder, as rat-tat-tat bursts of hail bounced off our oilskins, we slipped from our moorings on the Argyll coast and went rolling out into Seil Sound.

The winds were gusting at force six, kicking up white horses across the channel, but the *Lorne Leader* took them in her stride. A Brixham trawler from the age of sail, she had survived a century of storms since her oak hull was laid down at Galmpton, Devon, in 1892. Now, still under sail in this, her centenary year, she seemed to revel in the wild weather of Scotland's Western Isles.

We passed the green islands of Scarba and Luing to port and anchored for the night in Seil Sound. There, after supper, I lay in my bunk, lulled by the boat's gentle movement, listening to her timbers creaking and muttering in the darkness of voyages long past when she trawled for sole and turbot in the North Sea.

In her heyday there were hundreds of these graceful old workhorses of the sea. Now *Lorne Leader*, with her black hull, gaff-rigged sails and 20ft bowsprit, is one of only three still afloat in British waters, a beautiful survivor of an almost vanished breed.

Between 1910 and 1984 she worked in the Baltic, first as a fishing boat and later as a Swedish sail-training vessel. In 1985 she was bought by Don Hind, her present owner, a Glaswegian ex-merchant seaman, one-time sculptor and veteran sailing master.

With his wife, Gilly, he lovingly restored her for her new role in the chartering trade. 'She's been patched up, re-caulked and repaired so often that little of the original vessel is left,' says Don, 'but her spirit is still very much alive.'

Now, every year from April to October, the *Lorne Leader* plies among the Western Isles on six-day cruises. Her home waters extend from the Firth of Lorne as far north as Skye and south to Iona, Jura and Colonsay. On board are a crew of five and room for a dozen passengers.

Conditions are cramped but comfortable, with hot showers and flush toilets — a far cry from the 'bucket and chuck it' days of the old-time smacksmen. Meals, miraculously conjured up in the tiny galley by Dorothy McPhee, the ship's cook, are huge and wholesome, eaten at a communal table in the oak-beamed saloon.

Next morning the wind was still gusting at Force Six, the sky full of tearing clouds. The squally weather that had greeted my arrival at *Lorne Leader*'s home port of Craobh Haven was the fallout from a vicious depression, which had come howling in from the Atlantic and was now collapsing over the Scottish hills.

We left anchor and motored out into the Firth of Lorne. There, hauling on a bewildering cat's cradle of sheets and halyards, we hoisted sail and bore away towards the Sound of Mull. The air was rain-washed, luminous and clear. Looking up Loch Linnhe I could see the snow glittering on Ben Nevis, thirty miles away.

To port rose the hills of Mull, sombre summits obscured by cloud. Their Gaelic names set my scalp tingling: Creach Beinn (Plunder Mountain); Sgurr Dearg (the Hill of the Red Deer); and Dun da Ghaoithe (the Hill of the Two Winds). Now, as we entered the sound, they provided a dramatic background for Duart Castle, medieval stronghold of the chiefs of Clan MacLean. By the end of our first full day's sailing we were safely anchored again, this time in Tobermory Harbour, where we would spend the night.

From now on every day would be like this. Every morning we would up anchor and be under way by breakfast time. We'd sail when the wind was favourable, motor when it was not, and aim to be at our next anchorage in time for a late-afternoon shore excursion, walking or bird-watching in the hills.

The cruise combined sailing with bird-watching, and a resident ornithologist, Trevor Smart from Wolverhampton, was on hand to point out the puffins and black guillemots whirring away beneath our bowsprit. Sadly, we never saw the rare white-tailed sea eagles, which are now regularly breeding again in the Western Isles after an absence of half a century. But there were plenty of compensations: Arctic skuas, red-throated divers and, once, the thrill of a peregrine hurtling past the boat in pursuit of a panic-stricken oyster-catcher.

While we were under sail there would be sudden energetic bouts of rope-work as we tacked or gybed our way between the islands under the watchful eye of Nick Clamp, *Lorne Leader*'s young Bristol-born mate. He'd learned his seamanship aboard a square-rigger based in Malta, but much prefers the Hebrides.

'The possibilities here are endless,' he said. 'These are the finest cruising grounds in Europe. We may get big winds, but there is always somewhere to find a safe anchorage at the end of the day.'

Just how true this was we discovered the following morning. We had hoped to sail north from Tobermory, to the island of Rhum, and maybe climb by night to the top of Hallival to listen to the unearthly caterwauling cries of 10,000 pairs of Manx shearwaters that breed there in burrows beneath the turf. But first we had to round Ardnamurchan Point, the Scottish Land's End.

Ardnamurchan is the most westerly point on the British mainland and notorious for heavy seas when the wind is in the west. Green waves broke against our bows and came sloshing down the wooden decks as we hoisted sail and went plunging out into the teeth of the wind. 'Wear safety harnesses and clip on at all times' was the order of the day; but as we continued to wallow in the deepening troughs, our skipper, Tim Ebdy, prudently decided to go about.

As soon as he had brought her round she began to run with the sea instead of fighting against it. With the wind at our backs the sails filled in taut, sweet curves. 'She's really flying now, isn't she?' he said proudly. 'She must be making close on nine knots.'

Instead of going to Rhum we sheltered in Loch Spelve, on the east coast of Mull. A pair of golden eagles had built their nest on a cliff above the loch-side and, as we watched, the male came gliding past, close enough for us to see his hooked beak and fierce glittering eye.

Then we were away again, this time cruising south to Loch Tarbert on the west coast of Jura. In many ways this remote inlet was the high point of the voyage. Its windswept hills were as lonely as the Falkland Islands, its shores ringed with mysterious sea caves and raised beaches of smooth grey pebbles. Red deer watched us like Apache scouts from the surrounding crags; but apart from these, and the great northern divers in the loch's black waters, we had the place to ourselves.

The evening was golden, the loch a mirror. But during the night the wind got up and in the morning the hills were cobwebbed with hanging cloud. A low front was passing through, said Tim. In the Hebrides the weather is constantly changing: a storm one moment, sunshine the next. Sometimes it rained even as the sun was shining, throwing huge rainbows across the hills.

On the last leg of the voyage we sailed home past the notorious whirlpool of Corryvreckan, the 'Speckled Cauldron', which lies in the straits between Jura and Scarba. In a heavy sea, with the tide running strongly, its roar can be heard more than five miles away; but we passed by at slack water when the cauldron was quiet.

We returned to Craobh Haven as we had left, with half a gale blowing and the sky filled with mile-high clouds. But by now we had found our sea legs. We had begun to understand the bewildering nautical world of throat halyards, bobstays and flying jibs.

In six days we had sailed 150 miles and were proud of what we had achieved. Most of all, we felt the deepest affection for *Lorne Leader* and found it hard to say goodbye. Long after I had gone ashore for the last time I could still feel my body gently rocking to her easy rhythm.

THE WRITING'S ON THE RIVER

IN A SEARCH FOR THE SOURCE OF THE HUMBER, GRAHAM COSTER TRAVELS THROUGH 200 YEARS OF ENGLISH LITERATURE

Apart from a steady procession of ships sliding past the lighthouse, I had only the seabirds for company. There were thousands of them – waders such as dunlin, knot, oystercatchers – thronging the mudflats. The far shoreline was a powder-grey silhouette of refineries and chimneys. Behind me, in the words of the region's finest poet, Philip Larkin, 'bluish neutral distance / Ends the land suddenly beyond a beach / Of shapes and shingle': the North Sea. This was Spurn Point, the narrow spit of land that formed the end of the Humber Estuary. You could go no farther.

David Livingstone searched for seven years, and fruitlessly, for the source of the Nile. I rather hoped to wrap things up more quickly. Besides, it would be difficult to get utterly lost heading out of Hull. But I could understand the good doctor's quest. Where did a great river start? At one end, it was spanned by mighty bridges, flanked by the exuberant nineteenth-century architecture of a mercantile city. So how far to the dwindling mountain stream at the other?

If you were following the Thames, you could start at Canary Wharf nowadays and take a path all the way back through *Three Men in a Boat* country to a spring trickling out of the ground in a Gloucestershire field – but suppose you chose one of Britain's other major rivers? Larkin wrote of 'the widening river's slow presence' as the train trundled him to Hull: I wanted to find the Humber's distant source.

Allan Jones was leaning on the railings down at the Minerva Pier in Hull's old docks district. He was a landscape designer: that new redbrick estate just along the Humber's north bank – he had landscaped that, on the site of the old Victoria timber dock. It turned out he knew all about where the Humber came from.

'Well, it's an estuary, really, not a river,' he explained. It was fed by several rivers including the River Hull itself, which came down from Driffield and joined just beyond Victoria Dock. Farther back, it split into the Trent and the Ouse, and off the Ouse branched the Aire, and if you traced that to where it rose, you would find yourself up in the Yorkshire Dales near Malham — if you did not get sidetracked on to the Calder and end up in Heptonstall instead. I was getting an inkling of Livingstone's travails.

But the main tributary of the Humber, joining as the southern arm of the fork, was the Trent. 'Follow that,' nodded Jones. 'It's a very interesting river.'

Faxfleet sounded like a copy bureau — an incongruous name for a boarded-up farmhouse and a couple of hay-barns looking out over the river levee to where, twelve miles upstream from the Humber Bridge, the river bifurcated — but from here I could see Jones was right. Thousands upon thousands of birds agreed with him: the Ouse wound away to the north-west, but they swarmed above the Trent.

The length and meander of the River Trent were truly amazing in more than miles. I found myself calibrating the distance I had come in English writers. On Humberside, lines from Larkin had come into my head. Now the Trent headed down into Lincolnshire, and in Gainsborough, where the old millstone from Mercer's Mill had been incorporated into the paving of a new riverside garden, I found myself in the setting for George Eliot's *The Mill on the Floss*. Go south yet farther, all the way down through Nottinghamshire, and the Trent had taken you into D.H. Lawrence country.

Finally, after swinging west and then north up through the brewing town of Burton-on-Trent — down in the water meadows by the river there was still a small well from which Bass drew the spring water for its beer — I was in Stoke-on-Trent, and the 'Five Towns' of Arnold Bennett.

Such a vast meander through literary and industrial history also made me wonder how a river could wander so whimsically. The Thames flowed basically due east; the Severn more or less south-west. Weren't rivers ultimately trying to get to the sea? So how come the Trent and the Humber could start and finish on different sides of the country and manage to describe three sides of a square in between?

In Stoke library's local archives, I found someone to take me back to the start of the century and furnish an answer. In a paper on 'The Life History of the River Trent', presented to the North Staffs Field Club in 1908, A.L. McAldowie argued that it was originally three rivers. The upper Trent had flowed south into the Thames, the Nottinghamshire Trent had drained east into the Wash, and then a third river had cut across west to east to capture both, and link together a course that wandered all around the outline of the Pennines. 'There is a struggle for existence in inanimate nature as well,' pronounced McAldowie, 'and a survival of the fittest at the expense of the weaker.'

It had never occurred to me to see lazy, babbling rivers as pitiless canni-bals. But, when you thought about it, the gravitational rush of water was an implacable law. I had an image of a spruce, tweed-suited man with a tart Scottish humour holding the wood-panelled room rapt ninety years ago. I would have liked to have met A.L. McAldowie.

Not that there was much of the Trent left once you got to Stoke-on-Trent. The name was literally apt, for the river ran underground and the city centre sat on top of it. The only place where it emerged, said Gwynne Weston – when I dropped into the tourist information office – was beside the A500 roundabout. I seemed to have come a long way indeed from Larkin's poetic celebrations. But surely I was getting near to the source?

'Biddulph Moor,' said Gwynne Weston. She rummaged in her files and came up with a single, undated newspaper cutting picturing a weed-grown well. 'But it's difficult – that's as far as I can help you.'

The last leg took me up on to the Staffordshire moors north of the Potteries, and the finest scenery of the whole trip. At Knypersley, where the Trent had been dammed to create a sylvan reservoir, I followed the stream up through the woods. At last, you were up in the hills – approaching Biddulph Moor you had a fabulous view east of the main purple ridge of the Pennines. And, as the river became younger, shed all its grown-up baggage of mills and power stations and ships to become an innocent brook, so, appropriately, I was coming into one last literary domain.

Mow Cop was just a mile or so to the west: those magical, scary fantasies about *The Weirdstone of Brisingamen* and *The Moon of Gomrath* that were the best books you had ever read when you were eight or nine – hereabouts was Alan Garner country.

Elaine and Mel ran the Biddulph Moor grocer's. 'It never varies, never dries up,' said Elaine when I dropped in to ask about the source of the Trent. 'In the drought of '76, everybody used it to wash their cars – all queuing to get down.'

Biddulph Moor, a sprawling village on top of the hill, had its Spar shop and hoppa bus tootling around the modern bungalows like any other, but to find the place where a river emerged from the ground was also to discover how the distant past still trickled out into the present.

Why, I asked Elaine, was the field where the Trent rose known (so I had read in the Stoke archives) as 'Fortunes of War'? Elaine sent me to see Mary Chaddock, who had lived in the village all her life and whose grandfather had built its chapel. She said: 'My grandmother used to tell me it was called that because Cromwell shod his horses there.'

She then sent me to see Mr Booth around the corner, who was nearly ninety – his grandfather had been born at the Trent Head Farm – and he had once found a cannonball from the Civil War in nearby Gun Battery Lane.

'You drive down the lane over there,' Mel had said back in the shop, pointing west towards the fields, 'and it's like looking at a hundred years ago. It's like the top of the world up here.'

It turned out to be a surprisingly short walk to the source: down to the end of Trentley Drive, a basketball hoop on the end wall of the last house, over a stile, and there was the small well down in the dip. There seemed to be no spring or flow, just a still puddle: that was all.

But a descending line of holly trees blazoned the first yards of its course down the valley, 170 miles across the country, through two centuries of English literature, several more of English history, vast aeons of geological erosion and natural selection, and out to sea.

COUNTRY DIARY

JONNY BEARDSALL

It's a sharp, fantastically beautiful winter's morning. Kneeling in the frosted grass, I struggle to untie the frozen knot on the rope securing the old canoe to a fence post in Wensleydale. Almost forgotten, this fine craft has been hidden in the bottom of a hedge on the riverbank since the spring. It is green, about 17ft long and takes two people and a couple of lurchers if everyone sits still. It cost me £275 second-hand a decade ago and it never disappoints me.

I glance at my watch. It's just after 7 a.m., so the children will only just be stirring in their beds. If I do this sort of thing, I'm usually alone because it is impossible to find a willing front-seat paddler. Today, I've persuaded Marcus, a stray master of foxhounds from the Old Berks, to join me on this four-mile expedition to Kilgram Bridge.

'Is this really such a good idea?' he asks, as we slide the boat down the bank and he notices the thin sheet of pack ice that has formed during the night along the water's edge. 'What I mean is, do you think we'll end up wet?' I assure him not. It would be dangerous to fall in today.

Assuming I am not about to fall in, I'm wearing several layers under an old combat smock, a pair of trousers over my jeans and wellies, and have shoved on a big fur hat. 'Look, I'm not dressed for falling in...just paddle when I say paddle and we'll be OK,' I whisper. In a tartan lumber jacket, he looks similarly overdressed and would not float well.

There is not a cloud in the sky, nor a hint of breeze as we push off in silence, trying not to disturb the fifty or so greylag geese that are still sitting on the water beyond the bend. Of course, they spot us and are soon airborne. If you don't clump the sides of the canoe with your paddle, you can see much from the river; a less wary brace of mallards and a moorhen edge away, while a cormorant dives for a fish and a mink — well, we think it was a mink — disappears into a bankside hole.

Minute by minute, the sun is nudging its way over the fell above us, turning the surface of the water to brilliant gold and burning off the last palls of ethereal fog. I'm at the back steering, Wolfie and Jake are shivering in the middle and my friend is in the bow.

After a mile, we round a bend and face our only test…the Coverbridge Rapids. Well, in truth, no one else would describe them as rapids, but I've been turned over in them before, so they are not to be pooh-poohed. Marcus sees the boiling water under the arches of the bridge and stops paddling. 'What do we do here?' he asks, looking around anxiously. The dogs, too, look at me and begin to whimper. I growl at them – in 1916, Shackleton ate all his dogs before paddling hard for South Georgia.

It is simple. The current, if you keep digging, will carry you rather speedily to the left bank, where the only hazard is from overhanging willows that have a nasty habit of tipping you into the water. 'Aim for the middle arch of the bridge and head for the centre of the frothy bit,' I suggest. 'And, whatever happens, you must keep your paddle in the water.'

Terrific fun, this. It's not exactly a scene from *The River Wild*, but fearless Marcus, he who rode a Grand National winner, is starting to gibber as we fight to stay upright in the minor maelstrom. Waves are breaking over our bows and the dogs, I fear, may capsize us. They are whining, Marcus has frozen on his paddle, and I am trying my hardest to keep us out of the trees. It is, I swear, a close call but, phew, we all survive.

Canoes are considered a scourge in some parts because they upset the fish. I've never upset anyone here because the sight of a canoe where I paddle is almost unheard-of. Any anglers I wave to could not be more amused – I suppose it's the dogs and the fact that we don't look like canoeists.

BOY'S OWN TERRITORY

GAVIN BELL VENTURES INTO THE LAKELAND REALM OF ARTHUR RANSOME

You can sail from the North Pole to the Amazon in a day. Along the way you might see the Peak of Darien and the 'roof of the world' – the summit of mighty Kanchenjunga – and all you need is a 13ft dinghy with a brown sail and a bold crew who know where to find the secret harbour. Lots of pemmican and a spirit of adventure will also come in handy.

If there is a world in miniature it is the lakeland of Arthur Ransome, the author who created a magical realm of navigators and pirates in the lakes and fells of Cumbria. This year marks the seventy-fifth anniversary of *Swallows and Amazons*, the first in a series of a dozen books relating the escapades of a bunch of children who sail to the ends of the earth in their imagination, and in reality to the ends of Windermere and Coniston Water.

Their fame has spread as far as their expeditions – The Arthur Ransome Society (TARS) boasts more than 2,000 members, with groups in North America, Australia and Japan exchanging news and views on the exploits of Captain John and his crew through such august publications as *The Outlaw* and *Ship's Log*.

The Museum of Lakeland Life in Kendal is a focus of anniversary celebrations with an exhibition of manuscripts, sketches and personal items from its Ransome collection. Among them are pages of the typewritten first draft of *Swallows and Amazons*.

The story begins with a boy called Roger running up a steep field to 'Holly Howe' farm in wide zigzags, imagining he is a tea-clipper tacking against the wind. The farm is actually Bank Ground, on the eastern shore of Coniston Water, where Ransome spent summer holidays and met the children of a friend who inspired his stories.

The lakes are busier than they were when Ransome was writing in the 1920s, but the farmer's field and the view from it are unchanged. A greensward slopes down to tranquil water where swallows dart among old slate boathouses for the fun of it. A wooden jetty is screened by a chestnut tree that is said to produce formidable conkers, and in early morning you can hear the beat of swans' wings over the water.

Across the lake, the 2,635ft Old Man of Coniston presides over the fells like a mythical rock of ages, or as it is known to *Swallows* aficionados, Kanchenjunga. If ever there was a natural playground to fire child-like imagination, this is it. In the room where Ransome sat contemplating the view, you can almost see Roger and his shipmates setting sail on an adventure beyond the Peak of Darien.

Ransome was an adventurer himself. The son of a college professor, he went to Russia in 1913 to study folklore and ended as a war correspondent for the *Daily News*, and then special correspondent of the *Manchester Guardian* covering the Russian Revolution. He played chess with Lenin, married Trotsky's personal secretary, Evgenia Petrovna Shelepina, and set up home with her in Estonia and Latvia.

On their return to England, he bought a cottage near Windermere and began writing children's stories – unwittingly sparking rivalry in the lakes. The problem is that he never clearly identified locations in the books. Instead he mixed places and changed their names, provoking claims by champions of Windermere and Coniston, and providing endless hours of conjecture for The Arthur Ransome Society.

He once confided in a letter to a young fan: '. . .the lake is Windermere, but in the book I stole a few bits from Coniston and mixed them in for the sake of disguise, because we didn't want everybody to know our best places...' He did, however, provide an important clue – the secret harbour on 'Wild Cat Island' was really at the south end of Peel Island on Coniston Water, where he camped as a boy.

The best way to explore this far-flung outpost of the *Swallows'* realm is to hire a boat, and pootle along wooded shores beloved by Ruskin and Beatrix Potter. Now and again wisps of smoke rise from a steamer chugging down the lake, but all else is peace, and the most energetic sign of life is a seagull landing on a buoy.

The secret harbour lives up to its name. A cove hidden by rocks, it leads to a path that rises to a clearing where Ransome and later the young adventurers of his books camped among ferns and ancient oaks. It has the air of a fairie dell, a place to enchant adults and children alike.

For a tour of Ransome's Coniston, step aboard a 1920s launch named after him that visits sites associated with the books and a film based on them. A commentary by the skipper, Gordon Hall, becomes like a pub quiz, in which almost everybody seems to know the answers. Pointing out the

'River Amazon' (a shallow creek) and 'Octopus Lagoon' (a reedy pond), he affirms: 'Do not be put off by shams or substitutes they show you on Windermere. This is the real thing.'

On Windermere, they also have real things – notably Ransome's sailing boat and a dinghy renamed *Amazon* that both featured in his stories, and the splendid Victorian steam yacht *Esperance*, better known to *Swallows* fans as Captain Flint's houseboat.

All of them are on display in the Windermere Steamboats & Museum at Bowness-on-Windermere, and pilgrims on the Ransome trail will find the dining table in *Esperance* set for a tea party, complete with green parrot in a cage, as it was when Captain John and his crew visited. Michael Cates, the museum director, is happy to report that his boats have been swamped by friendly boarders: 'I've been overwhelmed by the interest. The magic is still there.'

Intrepid explorers might consider hiking up Kanchenjunga, aka The Old Man of Coniston, where the crew of the *Swallow* left a note attesting that they reached the summit on 11 August 1931, along with a halfpenny in a small brass tin. The tin has long since disappeared, but ramblers will be rewarded by the same magnificent views from Antarctica to the Amazon, and even the Isle of Man.

A less strenuous excursion is to the hamlet of Rusland, in the Furness Fells between Coniston and Windermere. There Ransome and his wife lie in a corner of an old churchyard beneath a pine tree, amid countryside that is the quintessential bucolic playground of his books.

In the slate-built church there is a fine collection of needlepoint prayer cushions, and among them one is adorned with crossed pennants and a familiar legend – Swallows and Amazons For Ever.

SKELETONS IN THE WASTELAND

UGLY ESSEX? NOT AT ALL, SAYS **CHRISTOPHER SOMERVILLE**, AFTER TOURING RURAL HAUNTS ALONG THE THAMES

'The Thames estuary? Down below Tilbury?' expostulated a Home Counties acquaintance. 'But that's all white stilettos and Capris, isn't it? All…oil refineries and container depots. Wouldn't bother if I were you.'

It's understandable for anyone who has not explored the margins of the Thames downriver from London to dismiss its haunting landscape. The southern or Kentish shore might be allowed to have some charm from Herne Bay onwards. As for the northern Essex coastline – from Tilbury Docks and Canvey Island to Southend and Foulness – forget it.

Certainly there are huge oil-refinery complexes, power stations and their marching lines of pylons, and wharfs where giant vessels ride. But tucked away along the shore I found, during a few autumn days' exploration by land and water, elements of another, quieter and more rural world.

Tilbury Docks announced themselves as a forest of skeleton jibs bristling from a dead flat horizon. Silhouetted against this cranescape, a solitary Romany-faced rider clopped up the dock road on a magnificent, high-stepping palomino. Travellers still graze their horses on the green marshes that line the Thames estuary.

Developers and industrialists are not the only ones to have cast covetous eyes on London's river. In July 1667 the Dutch made a cheeky raid up the Thames, destroying much of the ancient church of St Catherine at East Tilbury. That prompted King Charles II to have a pentagonal, moat-girt fort built at West Tilbury, just a cannon-shot from where the modern docks now sprawl.

It was not the Dutch but the French who posed a threat to English sovereignty two centuries later. Three miles along the shore I found Coalhouse Fort, a grim, grey, bastion-bulging strongpoint built in the 1860s under the supervision of General Gordon of Khartoum.

Just above the fort stood St Catherine's Church, towerless since the

Dutch raid, its 800-year-old walls a jumble of traceried windows, tiny round-headed doors, and an antiquarian's maze of arches blocked with stone and flint. General Gordon's men started building a new church tower to commemorate their hero, but gave up after raising only one storey.

From East Tilbury a network of narrow country lanes between high hedges brought me among the chimneys, silos and flaming towers at Coryton and Shellhaven oil refineries. So characteristic of the Thames estuary landscape, this plunge from the rural human scale into the enormities of the refineries: great silvered cylinders and smoking chimneys the height of skyscrapers; miles of pipework, gantries, ladders; gaunt flare towers topped with intense orange flames.

Standing on the shore here I looked across Holehaven Creek to Canvey Island, where big ships pull in to the Thames-side jetties to discharge their cargoes. In Tudor times Canvey was a patchwork of marshy islets, used for sheep-grazing and visited by milkers with tiny three-legged stools strapped to their buttocks. The wild Canvey ewes were famous for their cheese.

In 1620 an ingenious Dutchman, Joos Croppenburgh, built sea walls to form one island – accessible only by ferry until this century. Dickens chose Canvey for the concealment of the convict Magwitch in *Great Expectations*. Since the Second World War the eastern half of the island has filled up tight with housing, but on the west are swathes of undeveloped grazing marshes, while Benfleet Creek and Hadleigh Ray run along the landward side of Canvey through an archipelago of saltmarsh islets.

'I've got the very man for you,' my Canvey Islander friend Chris Fenwick had said, when I told him I was coming to do some estuarine exploring. 'My Uncle Jack. A proper Essex skipper, born and bred on Canvey, who knows the estuary like the back of his hand. He's just back from Antigua. If he's not too busy, he'll find us some moody spots.'

Smallgains Creek on Canvey's eastern point felt moody enough at 5 a.m., its mudbanks and channels dully gleaming in the dawn light. Jack Fenwick's yacht, *Breakaway*, slipped out into the estuary, Uncle Jack at the helm. This is a man who has seen and done it all in every corner of the seven seas, but who still prefers his native creeks, muds and marshes. 'I can walk out of my house before breakfast,' he said, 'hop over the sea wall and be among the wild birds. Where else in the world could I do that?'

On the cabin table Chris spread out his uncle's charts of the estuary. 'I thought we'd go across to the Medway and potter about among these creeks,' said Jack. 'I used to go poaching there when I was a boy. They've always been lonely old places.' His fingers traced the names, dark and ominous, littered across the mouth of the Medway – Deadmans Island, Slaughterhouse Point, Blackstakes, Bedlams Bottom, Horrid Hill.

With a scrap of jib up we batted across the Thames. Right in the throat of the Medway, between the Isle of Grain and the Isle of Sheppey, the Martello tower built to deter Napoleon stood dwarfed by the twentieth-century furniture of the Kentish shore – power stations, pylons, sand and gravel works, Grain's container port lined with long-necked, four-legged cranes, fussing black tugs bullying monstrous cargo ships.

Thames and Medway hereabouts are still working rivers. But tucked away round the corners and down the creeks lie odd villages, forgotten jetties and hundreds of those low-lying marsh islands that the tides are gradually repossessing.

It was brewing up into a stormy day. Anvil-headed clouds drove squally showers across the estuary. We let the anchor go in the choppy waters of Sharfleet Creek and settled down to laze and chat in the shelter of the black mud shelf of Burntwick Island. The ribs of wooden ships stuck up out of the mud. 'Hulks,' said Jack. 'There used to be a lot of convict ships moored here. A lot of stiffs in that island, too.'

'Plague of London burials,' amplified Chris. 'This area was London's dumping ground over the centuries.'

The sun broke through, turning the creek water from turbid brown to brilliant jade green, lighting the dark mud with gold shadows. After lunch we slept, all three, poleaxed by salt air and the gentle rocking of the boat. Towards evening the wind abated and we went puttering up to moor at Queenborough's jetty, on the western flank of Sheppey.

Next day dawned fair and flat. 'We'll run up to Rochester,' said the skipper. We sailed between two squat stone forts, built on the marsh islands of Darnet and Hoo to repel the Napoleonic invaders who never came. Inland, the graceful spire of Hoo St Werburgh was silvered by sunlight. By the shore at Hoo Marina, the old Nore lightship lay redundant in her rusty scarlet paint.

Back across the Thames estuary later in the day, Jack moored *Breakaway* in the mouth of Smallgains Creek to wait for the ingoing tide. Terns pounced screaming on shoals of fish, cormorants stood on sandbanks holding ragged black wings out to dry and a seal slipped soundlessly into the creek. 'Unknown area, really, all the river east of London,' said Chris Fenwick. 'People think it's all industry and wasteland. But that's their loss, isn't it?'

SAILING INTO SERENITY

SAM LLEWELLYN, IN THE INNER HEBRIDES, FINDS RAIN, ROUGH WATER – AND PERFECT PEACE

We were eight miles of tortuous single track from the not-very-big main road, standing on a slipway facing a dark sea loch. There were gulls over-head. Behind us was the short line of houses that makes up the town of Tayvallich. Garlinda looked about her. 'Bit quiet here,' she said. The sound of her boat rumbling off its trailer and into Loch Sween was deafening, by Tayvallich standards.

There we were, five people and five boats on the slipway. The boats were 21ft Drascombe longboats, open yawls of great seaworthiness. The people were Garlinda, Hextall, Bertie, Dave and me. The sun was shining and it was very quiet.

We pushed the boats into the water and sailed south, past the caravan park that surrounds the ruined Castle Sween. At the mouth of the loch, we slammed through a fierce robble of tide into the harbour of Eilean Mor, the largest of the McCormaig Isles.

On the summit of the island is a building that was once a Celtic chapel, then a bootleg distillery, now a ruin. From this eminence you can get your bearings. Across five miles of sea to the west is Jura; to the east is the Mull of Kintyre. And hull-down on the southern horizon is the island of Gigha. We decided to go there.

It started as a bright, sunny canter over a sparkling sea under a sweet curve of sail. As I placed a strand of chilli sauce on a delicate confection of Mother's Pride and Cumberland sausage, sooty tendrils of cloud were reaching out from the Mull of Kintyre. Under the cloud, the sea turned slate. Casting lunch aside, I hopped to the uphill side of the boat. The wind hit the sail like a boot. Behind and in front, the little tan wisps of canvas of the other boats clattered as they shortened sail.

There are twelve sea miles of open water between Eilean Mor and West Tarbert Bay on Gigha. We burrowed on through the black waves, pumping to stay afloat. Gannets dived on mackerel shoals. The wind went up to force six. A huge motor yacht surged past. Slowly, distant Gigha changed from three disconnected lumps into a landmass, and finally to green hills faced with grey rock.

West Tarbert Bay is a bleak hook of granite lashed with icy williwaws. After the open sea, it was as comfortable as an armchair by the fire. We landed on a white beach, and walked through a landscape with flowers from all seasons: primroses were flowering with bluebells and foxgloves, and the wiry grass was studded with early purple and military orchids.

Next morning we sailed past a great northern diver patrolling the mouth of Craro Bay, a seal-crowded complex of rocks and turquoise water at the south end of the island. Behind the beach, a woman in a shower-cap turning hay gave us directions to Achamore Gardens. We passed a church-yard with nineteenth-century granite columns and a twentieth-century plastic mourning windmill.

Candelabra primulas burned scarlet in the shadows. Rhubarb-leafed gunnera, half-grown, stood head-high. Tender plants thrive in Achamore's Gulf Stream climate. Embothrium flame-trees burn like bonfires among oak and sycamore. Self-sown echiums thrust their 10ft blue spikes into the mild salt breeze.

We left that afternoon for Islay, seven miles west. The weather was high and blue, the forecast dire. The sails flapped. The boat's wake was the faint-est curl of turbulence under the stern. We saw a black ridge of back, rolling out of the sea for a moment, ending in a small, hooked fin, then vanishing. Then it came again, closer. A minke whale.

Islay's anchorages include Lagavulin, which sits next to Laphroaig; round the coast are Bowmore, Bruichladdich and Port Ellen. We rejected them all in favour of the Ardmore Islands. Here we anchored in shallow water among the reefs, ate lobsters bought from a Gigha fisherman and played mandolins while the rain rattled on the tents.

Next morning, the quarrels of a colony of breeding sooty terns thirty yards away drowned out our conversation. We left in a splatter of leaping sea trout, watched by a couple of dozen seals and a yawning otter. Here in the islands, the wild world is so much in control that it is almost impossible to disturb it.

There is not much chance of disturbing Jura, either. We pulled into Craighouse harbour (Bertie first, as usual) in a rising northerly breeze. The island has 200 inhabitants, twelve of them employed in the distillery behind the hotel. Deer wander through the village's gardens. In the bar of the Isle of Jura Hotel there is desultory talk about the Overland Route, a proposal to institute a new, fast ferry service from the mainland via Jura's only road to the much more populous Islay. Some would see the ferry as a commercial opportunity. The inhabitants of Jura see it as a source of rush and pother, and are opposed to it.

Moored to the end of Craighouse quay was a charming blunt-nosed steamship with a red funnel. This is the puffer *Vic 32*, last survivor of the race of steamboats that in the first half of the century carried all the heavy freight of the Highlands and Islands. Nick Walker, its captain, is a seaman-like figure with beige corduroy trousers, a hacking jacket and a promising crop of tomatoes in his wheelhouse.

The puffer's hold has been converted into a capacious saloon and comfortable accommodation for twelve. For people who do not want the expense of yacht charter or the unpredictability of open boat journeys, the puffer is the best way to visit the islands.

The gale blew itself out as we sat tasting distillery produce in the hotel. By lunchtime we were in the threshold of the Sound of Islay, moored to a tiny, lonely quay, sitting on close-cropped turf with sea pinks, watching a skua beating up a gull.

Then we spotted a wood – and on Gigha woods mean gardens. This one concealed Ardfin, an acre or two of sub-tropical paradise inside 20ft-high walls. Here, perfectly sheltered from the wild weather, there is a rill, much Geranium palmatum and a pseudopanax. There is an ideal tea tent with excellent cakes, and a Dutch gardener called Peter.

In such warmth and shelter, it was hard to imagine bad weather. As the tide washed us up the Sound of Islay, it got easier. The western corner of the sky was weighted down with a fat black lump of cloud. The weather forecast said gales. North of the Sound, the swell came rolling in unbaffled from the open ocean, and the mountains were vanishing in the rain.

By teatime the cloud was universal, the shore was a smudge and the five white boats hurdling the long black hills of water looked ridiculously small. The entrance to Loch Tarbert was invisible in the rain. David handed out his usual meticulous cups of tea (lapsang souchong: take pot to kettle, brew for 4.8 minutes while rolling 40 degrees; pour). Rain lashing into our mugs, we followed our bearing through the reefs that boiled and growled left and right. And suddenly, surprisingly, we were in.

West Loch Tarbert is the most remote loch in the Inner Hebrides. There are caves all around its shores, in which primitive altars have been found. Bodies used to be stored here en route for the burial grounds of holy Colonsay and Iona. It was very, very quiet. Another line of bearing across a grey mile of loch, straight at a cliff. The cliff parted, revealing a channel 20 yards wide, then a maze of channels. Finding inner West Loch Tarbert is more like potholing than sailing. But finally there we were. There are no roads, no waves. It is a land of shadows.

So we dropped the anchors and lit the stoves. Far away, the gale screamed in the mountain passes. On the dark loch in the middle of the great dark island, the lamplit tents rocked gently. Soon it would be dawn.

Chapter 3
EUROPE

14 AUGUST 1999

RETURN TO THE EDGE OF THE WORLD

IN 1930, THE LAST INHABITANTS OF ST KILDA –
BRITAIN'S STRANGEST AND REMOTEST ISLAND – WERE
FORCED TO LEAVE THEIR HOMES. LAST WEEK, TWO
OF THEIR DESCENDANTS RETURNED, TO COMMUNE
WITH GHOSTS AND DEFEND THEIR LOST HERITAGE.
NIGEL RICHARDSON SAILED WITH THEM

They met for the first time on the bridge deck. Norman Chalmers, carrying an accordion in a much-stickered case, had just stepped jauntily aboard from the Glasgow dockside.

'Hello,' said Donna Brown, née Ferguson. 'I'm your long-lost cousin.'

'Oh aye, right,' replied Norman. 'You're the Ferguson person?'

And so, with this moment of touching understatement, began our voyage through the seas of consanguinity – and the stacks and eddies of the North Atlantic – to the strange and wonderful Land of the Puffin Eaters.

For Norman and Donna this journey was to be a form of homecoming. Our destination: the remote specks of granite and grass known as St Kilda, where for 3,000 or more years their grandparents and countless generations before them eked an existence in almost complete isolation from civilisation, before abandoning the island forever in 1930.

Humans should never have been there at all, by rights. The archipelago of St Kilda is a savagely unforgiving environment, 110 miles from the nearest point on mainland Scotland, 45 miles west of the outermost of the

Outer Hebrides; fit only for creatures highly adapted to the murderous moods of the open ocean: watercannon winds, three-month-long mists, and seas that can splinter boats to sawdust.

The first recorded mention of St Kilda comes in a fourteenth-century manuscript called *Scotichronicon*, which describes it as 'on the margine of the world, beyond which there is found no land in these bounds' – the Ultima Thule of Greek mythology made manifest. Ever since, the St Kildans have been a source of wonder and fascination to so-called civilised man – damned yet uncorrupted, both heroic and degenerate. Theirs is the story of the Noble Savage, and it touches heights of sublime, often hilarious madness.

Our course was now set for the vortex of that mad world, and what better conveyance than a ship of fools, of holy fools, some would say, the *Rainbow Warrior*? The *Warrior* is flagship of the environmental campaigning organisation Greenpeace, which contends that St Kilda is now under threat from oil pollution.

It is a concern shared by the National Trust for Scotland, which owns the island group. Now the humans have gone, St Kilda is one of the great avian gathering places: it has the largest gannet population in the world and the largest colonies of both fulmar and puffin in Britain, as well as being one of the most important breeding stations in north-west Europe.

Largely for this reason it was designated a World Heritage Site in 1986 – Britain's only such site. In 1997 the government licensed adjacent areas of the Atlantic for oil drilling. So far the nearest 'tranche' being developed is 75 miles away, though tranches as close as 25 miles are up for grabs. For Greenpeace, and the polyglot crew of the *Rainbow Warrior*, St Kilda may be remote, but it is in the front line.

The *Warrior* slipped down the Clyde on a humid, thundery evening, on its 'SOS St Kilda' mission to publicise this potential threat to the island's fragile eco-system. Out on deck Donna, a 43-year-old freelance researcher, and Norman, a professional musician (in both a folk band called Jock Tamson's Bairns and an avant-garde outfit called The Cauld Blast Orchestra), shook out the branches of their family trees: 'I think her father was my grand-father's brother...'

'I remember his wife ran a wee campsite behind the house...'

As both live in Edinburgh it seems slightly strange they have not met before, but it is certainly no surprise that they are related – in the entire recorded history of St Kilda, there were only five surnames: Ferguson, Gillies, Mackinnon, MacQueen and MacDonald. The precise connection between these modern St Kildan cousins is that Norman's grandmother's cousin, Mary MacQueen, married Donna's grandfather's brother, Neil Ferguson, in 1929.

The wedding was the last to take place on the island – though both had moved away by that time, they returned to get hitched in the tiny church there. The following year the last of the St Kildans – a demoralised rump of thirty-six souls – were finally driven from their wind-blasted Arcadia and into the modern world.

The evacuation of the island, by HMS *Harebell* on 29 August 1930, was a cause célèbre. Rubberneckers lined the docks at Oban to witness the beaming down of these oddballs into the twentieth century – 'You'd be thinking you were going to a football match,' according to one of the evacuees, Neil Gillies. When the ship came within earshot of the crowds, Gillies called out: 'What are you looking at? There's nae hairs on us.'

Oh, but there were. They were a bizarre lot, these ancestors of Norman's and Donna's, with their penchant for eating anything of a flying, feathered variety they could inveigle into their gins and snares. They may have put in long hours in the church but, to put it mildly, they were not Politically Correct when it came to puffins, gannets and fulmars. In 1840 they were even responsible for killing the last great auk in the British Isles – apparently they thought it was a witch.

Over centuries, islanders slaughtered many, many thousands of birds: ate their flesh and eggs, sold their oil, even wore their skins on their feet. Puffin for breakfast, dunked in porridge; fulmar for lunch, with a spud or two. Couldn't read or write, spoke a strange form of Gaelic considered little better than animal grunts by their Anglo-Saxon betters, and as for their feet…According to some accounts, St Kildans had been genetically modified by all the barefoot bird-snaring they went in for up on the crags and cliffs.

They had prehensile toes, some said six on each foot; they had thick wrists and super-strong thumbs. 'Sometimes,' Norman told me, 'I say the reason I have big ears is that St Kildans used to fly down from the cliffs.'

Ironically for a feudal throwback – St Kilda was owned by the MacLeods of Dunvegan, to whom rent had to be paid annually – the island ran itself on communitarian lines. They shared possessions and workloads and had no use for money. Crime, was unknown.

As far as mainlanders were concerned, such anomalies were precisely what made the St Kildans the Most Backward People in Britain, our very own South Sea exotics. Edwardian postcards of islanders in their shawls or beards, with their severe centre-partings, beetle brows and slightly mad stares, were airily labelled 'Natives of St Kilda'. Cruise companies such as Martin Orme & Co., the forerunner of Caledonian MacBrayne, made a killing in the summer months by promising passengers 'glimpses…of the primitive ways of life that are vanishing.'

Well, contact with us twentieth-century sophisticates did eventually see to it that the St Kildan way of life vanished. Islanders realised that life did not have to be a matter of grim susbsistence. They wanted mangles and antimacassars, they wished to twirl a parasol now and again, and they may even have discovered bacon and eggs. And so, with the departure of HMS *Harebell* from St Kilda's harbour, ended an experiment in human sociology that had lasted for countless years beneath the belljar of the North Atlantic sky.

The unique nature of that experiment became increasingly apparent as our *Rainbow Warrior* ploughed more and more of the Malin Shipping Forecast Area beneath her bows. The weather was mild and balmy – freakily so, considering our northern latitude – and as we contemplated the placid circle of sea in which we moved, Donna likened the experience to being in a bubble, moving through a mesmerising continuum of time and space.

It's the space you notice – what Norman called St Kilda's 'palpable sense of remoteness'. We sailed for thirty-six hours from Glasgow, seeing not a single ship, before spying shapes to port on a warm and misty morning. Raptly attentive, Donna now confessed to having butterflies.

Slowly, the islands of St Kilda, with their fang-like satellites of stack and rock, grew in size and detail beyond the ship's rail. Norman had visited St Kilda before. 'It's a symbolic place as well as real,' he said as minke whales and dolphins surfaced around us. 'The idea of a community that lived in harmony. *Tir nan Og*, in the Gaelic. The land of the eternal young, the place over the horizon.' It was Donna's first visit, and her breath was near taken away.

Later she would murmur to me that, 'These truly have been among the best days of my life.' For now, silence was more eloquent. And silence is what we had for our approach to the main island of Hirta, save for the soughing of the *Warrior* through the waves, the unearthly requiem of countless thousands of gannets, and a series of plangent airs played by Norman on the tin whistle he had brought along with his squeeze-box.

Ninety-eight years ago, HMS *Bellona* passed this way before us. Like us she would have edged into the broad mouth of Village Bay and faced the fan-shaped settlement of stone houses and enclosures sloping gently up towards swelling hills. Though the right-hand end of the bay is now disfigured by grey army buildings – serving the missile tracking station in the centre of Hirta - the view is essentially unchanged, Unlike us, though, the *Bellona* was on vital state business back in 1901.

A brass band accompanied the *Bellona*'s captain ashore. While bemused villagers looked on, the captain read a solemn declaration announcing the death of Queen Victoria and the accession of Edward VII. The band then started to play 'God Save the King', whereupon the villagers fled in fright to those swelling hills.

It is not until you have seen the settlement of St Kilda that you can truly appreciate the absurdity of this story. The houses and walls, and the strange, igloo-shaped storage houses with turf roofs called cleits which dot the land-scape, are a defiantly scribbled statement of human endurance that has no point of similarity with life in mainland Britain.

So dispersed are the man-made configurations of stone, so widespread the scattered boulders, that it is impossible to tell where the one ends and the other begins. The whole of Village Bay and the surrounding hills look like the ruins of a once mighty civilisation, a Hebridean Thebes. But St Kilda was never mighty. Even in its pomp, towards the end of the seventeenth century, there were scarcely 200 inhabitants.

We anchored in the bay and took an inflatable to the concrete jetty. The prosaic geometry of the Army settlement there was briefly dismaying. But as we crossed a meadow to the street of houses – this begins some 50 yards to the north-west – the mood changed.

Sad yet peaceful, the ruined human habitations of St Kilda are like a graveyard; here, an extinct way of life rests in peace. On the day of the evac-uation, the village postmaster, Neil Ferguson, had thought the same thing. 'It was weird passing the empty houses,' he recalled. 'It was just like looking at an open grave.'

The single-storey houses are as humble as stone crosses, bespeaking the apologetic simplicity of the St Kildans. There are sixteen houses, strung out along the gently curving 'street' – a path of turf and stone – for some 200 yards. Six of them have been repaired and re-roofed by volunteers on NTS work parties. The rest remain as shells, without roofs or doors, carpeted by dandelions and thistles.

I wondered to Norman what it must be like to pin down your past so precisely to a set of stones and a still-blackened hearth. 'I feel lucky to have such a defined place that I come from,' he said, 'a strong rock in my sense of being. I don't have ontological anxiety about where I fit.'

These houses where Norman and Donna fit have a door, two windows, and a fireplace and chimney at each end – the bare requisites of a child's drawing. In the hearths are slates bearing the name of the last inhabitant: 'No.8 1930 – empty. Formerly Callum MacDonald – "Old Blind Callum"; 'No.11 1930 – Christine MacQueen.'

Donna finds the house belonging to her family – it is one of the re-roofed houses and the NTS is using it as a store. Here, where hard hats, paint and wellington boots ('assorted sizes') are stacked, her great grandparents ate their puffin brekkies. Another restored house serves as a little museum. Beside a picture of two moustachioed villagers, Donna pauses: 'This chap looks tremendously like my grandfather.'

Norman: 'That's Donald's brother.'

Donna: 'So that's my grandfather's brother.'

Norman: 'Aye, and that's my grandmother's brother...'

'It is like putting together the pieces of a jigsaw,' she says. 'I feel complete having seen it.'

It was an infinitesimally small world. Though St Kildans did occasionally escape their Atlantic fastness – principally in the 1850s, when forty-two emigrated to Australia – only one ever returned: Ewen 'California' Gillies. He returned three times, in fact, after increasingly prosperous spells in Australia, New Zealand and the Gold Rush state, until the islanders asked California to leave for good: they couldn't stand him banging on about what he'd seen and done.

Their universe was this agglomeration of tiny, mountainous outcrops whose biggest island, Hirta, is no more than about two miles by one-and-a-half at its longest and widest points. They were not, though, short of perspectives; Hirta has three peaks above 1,000 feet high. The biggest, Conachair, slopes on its seaward side to the tallest sea cliffs in Britain, where gannets and fulmars bank and hover in unimaginable and endless permutations looking (Norman's description) like specks of dandruff far below.

Standing on Conachair's summit – pneumatic moss underfoot and blown by balmy breezes – we gazed on seas that stretch unbroken to Newfoundland; seas capable of unimaginable malevolence that on this scorching summer's day were benign as the Serpentine. It was nigh impossible to imagine just how grim life here could be.

But we were in for a salutary reminder that humans are only ever here on sufferance, that this is one of those rare and fragile places that remain red in tooth and claw. As we continued down the slope of Conachair, near the wreckage of a Beaufighter that crashed in 1943, we were strafed by great skuas, big angry birds known here as bonxies. They came in fast, at head height, requiring us to fling ourselves to the ground.

The human experiment that was St Kilda is over. The birds and the wind and sea own it now. Though Norman and Donna feel a sense of connectedness, St Kilda is not home to them. 'When they cleared off the people they cleared off the culture,' Norman said. Now the fight is on to preserve the wilderness that St Kilda has become.

Perhaps the concern expressed by Greenpeace and the NTS over possible oil pollution is alarmist. But history suggests that the human propensity for destroying that which is good and vulnerable needs guarding against. To illustrate the point, Norman returned to the village street and read from a letter written in 1931. This letter was sent by an islander called Alex Ferguson to his brother Neil.

For some time after the evacuation, it was the islanders' habit to return to St Kilda in the summer months. Alex had arrived in mid-June of 1931, less than twelve months after the evacuation, to discover that the village had been ransacked the week before by a Belgian trawler crew: 'Every article of value stolen, doors and windows smashed...All the back windows in the Manse are smashed and every article of value removed.

'Your house is left uninhabitable. If you left any money above the fireplace it too has gone.'

Alex Ferguson did not allow himself to brood too long on this outrage, however. 'I snared twelve puffins on Friday night,' he added proudly. And no doubt in those heady clifftop moments, when he once more dangled his bendy rod above those hapless beaky birds, all seemed right again on the margine of the world.

AN ENGLISHMAN AT SEA IN GERMANY

PETER HUGHES FINDS HIMSELF ONE OF ONLY TWO
BRITONS ON A GLORIOUSLY TEUTONIC SHIP

A confession: I approached the MS *Deutschland* with curiosity and trepidation. I had long been curious to see how a ship so unequivocally German could appeal to a British clientele. My trepidation was how to deliver 1,500 words without once resorting to cheap jokes about *Das Boot*, or slipping in a mention of 'Don't mention the war', or wondering who bags the sunbeds for the day.

On this last concern, the ship pre-empted me. In the very first edition of the daily programme there was this request: 'We ask you not to reserve deck chairs with books, towels etc.' So it's true...

My cruise took me from Venice to Rome. We called at Cephalonia, Messina and Salerno – hard not to think of the war with an itinerary like that – but for me the most distinctive part of the journey was the MS *Deutschland* herself. At a time when cruise ships are becoming ever more homogenised, and the whole notion of cruising is being prescribed by suits in Miami, it was a joy to find a ship so idiosyncratic. 'The past is a foreign country: they do things differently there,' wrote L P Hartley. The same goes for the MS *Deutschland* – nostalgia is all part of the act.

First, some facts. Built in 1998, she is not a big ship. At 22,400 tons and carrying a maximum of 520 passengers, she is less than a third of the size of the *QE2*, and a minnow compared with today's monster vessels. Nor does she traipse around the same old circuit of ports, but spends her year ambling about in the sunshine, first in Europe and then in the Middle East, before wintering in South Africa and the Indian Ocean.

Old cruise hands used to make the distinction between a ship with a hotel inside and a hotel with a ship built round it, and the MS *Deutschland* belongs emphatically in the latter category. Take a simple example: corridors. On big modern ships they are tunnels tapering to some featureless infinity. Not here. The corridors are lined with fluted columns, the carpet pattern is broken at roughly two-cabin intervals and the cabin doors are faced with a faux fruitwood veneer. Throughout the ship there seems more wood panelling than in the whole of London's clubland.

The 'Golden Twenties' are evoked in the ship's nomenclature. The Adlon Library echoes the name of Berlin's most famous hotel; Salon Lili Marleen's name is from the old love song. There is the Kanzlerzimmer (Chancellor's Room) and the Kaisersaal (Emperor's Ballroom), where the huge chandelier, painted ceiling and little table lamps under pleated shades are a funny mixture of stately home and show lounge. It's a formula that must work because there are now plans to build a sister ship. It will be bigger – for between 600 and 700 passengers – and designed more for the British and American markets, which I hope won't mean losing the MS *Deutschland*'s high style and triumphant European feel.

Or its remarkable detail – the engraved glass, bevelled mirrors, cornices and marquetry, the marble pillars, gilded capitols, ivory painted panels, ruched blinds and deep pelmets, the timber and brass. The Kino cinema is art deco; the outdoor tables of the Lido Café, with their white cast-iron chairs and globe street lamps could have come straight off Berlin's Unter den Linden boulevard. The art on board has the touch of real collectors' items – not pictures bought by the square metre.

There was an odd disparity between the ship and its passengers. The ship was much less formal than I had expected, whereas the passengers were more so. Not that things weren't efficient. As the passengers' guidebook puts it in describing the laundry: 'These services work fast and reliable.'

Embarkation, though, was so relaxed it seemed almost casual, whereas the passengers all appeared to be impeccably dressed for an activity smarter than the one in which they were engaged. The women were permanently in heels; one man sat in the sun in a tweed jacket and jeans. The dress code never stoops to 'smart casual'. When it wasn't black tie, which it was for two nights out of five, it was 'semi formal' ('jacket and tie for gentlemen, casual elegance for ladies').

Elegance is one of the defining words for the MS *Deutschland*. The à la carte restaurant is 'elegant', as is high tea, which is served 'in a traditionally English manner' to the accompaniment of light classical music. It has its own dress code: 'We kindly ask you...not to enter the Lido Terrace during the Elegant Tea Time with shorts.' It was not a huge risk because few shorts were ever worn.

I went to the Elegant Tea Time and it was, well, elegant, in a *Room with a View* kind of way. The Lido Terrace is painted ivory, with more engraved mirrors and ruched curtains, these ones gold. It is done out as a grand conservatory — an orangery, perhaps, or winter garden — with loom chairs and big windows on three sides. A spruce pianist in a light-grey jacket and pink shirt, with an ivory smile, played an ivory piano in an ivory room straight out of Merchant Ivory. He tickled the ivories through Liszt and Lloyd Webber and a witty variation on that irritating little Microsoft tinkle you get when you turn on a PC. He even got a laugh out of the 'Moonlight Sonata'. At one point a tiny man in an ivory shirt with guava stripes materialised and burst into 'La Donna è Mobile'. He was a pocket tenor. One serious concern was my inability to speak German. As far as the ship was concerned there was no problem. It conscientiously catered for its minority of English-speaking passengers (five on this cruise). Waiters, room stewardesses, reception staff, all slipped unhesitatingly into English. There were English news-sheets, menus, daily programmes and announcements. And in each port at least one shore excursion had an English-speaking guide.

The passengers were less accommodating. Inez, a spirited young blonde, asked why I had not equipped myself with at least a smattering of German before coming on board. Her husband, Peter, gave a considerate laugh. 'You see what I have to put up with,' he said, skilfully deflecting the attack to the inadequacies of men generally rather than of Englishmen or, more specifically, this Englishman.

'I am not proud of not speaking German,' I blustered. 'But you have to admit you can travel very much farther speaking English. In fact I would learn Spanish before German.' 'Or Chinese,' mumbled Peter. 'I wanted to tease you,' said Inez with the satisfaction of one who was not only fluent in my language but could use it to my embarrassment. In a lift the next day another woman inquired amicably why I was on a German ship without being able to speak German. 'Because you all speak English,' I replied lamely. 'We don't,' said a man behind me.

Music is a big part of life on board, and the standard of musicianship is high. While the Ambros Seelos Gala band — nine piece, no less, and renowned in Germany — was playing dance music in the Kaisersaal, the Deutschland Trio was performing in the Salon Lili Marleen and David Warwick was on the keyboard in the Alter Fritz Bar. David was the only other Briton on board — the other English-speakers came from Singapore and America. Born in England, he has lived in Germany for some years, but not so long to affect his repertoire: 'I try not to go too German,' he said. 'Not too many waltzes.' You can see the temptation. At the crew show there was a lot of schunkeln — linking arms and swaying to lilting traditional songs.

This is a ship with none of the usual occupational therapy of cruising, no napkin folding, line dancing, macramé or bingo. No comedian, either. But there was a soprano who sang 'Somewhere over the Rainbow' while an acrobat, suspended by straps from the ceiling, performed the splits above her.

The MS *Deutschland* is showing her age in a couple of respects, though not in her fabric, which is immaculate. There are still two sittings for dinner in the main dining room with tables allocated for the duration of the cruise; there is no public internet and only the owner's and executive suites have private balconies. Cabin doors and room safes are unlocked with real keys.

An MS *Deutschland* cruise is splendidly, refreshingly and uncompromisingly different. For British passengers it's like adding another country to the itinerary. And, as with any extended foreign travel, it does help to speak at least a few words of the language. It's not necessary, but it will put Inez in her place.

GO WITH THE FLOE

JOANNA KAVENNA WARMS TO THE VASTNESS AND SILENCE OF THE ICE KINGDOM OF GREENLAND

Under a pale sun, I was standing on deck and shivering beneath six layers. The only sound was the lapping of the waves and the grinding of the ship against the ice. The ice was lying in overlapping circles on the surface of the sea. The whales had come earlier, a fleet of black-tailed monsters rolling in front of the ship.

The ship was cruising along the western coast of Greenland. We had begun at Kangerlusuuaq, a former US air base in the south, and were moving slowly north, along the ragged coast, through dazzling fjords and archipelagos of icebergs. The destination was Ilulissat in the mid-west, a town by the Quaanaaq ice fjord. The view from the ship was always extraordinary — stark red cliffs and the icecap glinting in the distance. The land is too northerly and wind-blasted for trees. The bergs were fascinating — some were tall and elegant, some squat and ragged, some bright blue, others brilliant white — and made slapping sounds as they bounced on the waves.

I could sit on deck for hours staring at the view, with only the disconsolate figure of my partner to distract me. He liked the salmon suppers and the ice, but the land's remorseless emptiness concerned him at first. On the third day, he anxiously suggested that we seemed to be circling around the same lump of rock. He wondered if anyone else had noticed. Then he took to fidgeting wildly in the daily lectures on Arctic geology.

In some ways the cruise was like an anti-holiday, stripped of fabulous monuments, intriguing ruins, cities and towns. Herman Melville described the Greenland ice fields with a gothic flourish as 'the profoundest of solitudes to a human observer'. It's not the sort of phrase you would splash on a tourist poster. Still, there's something compelling about the vastness and silence of the land. Greenland is home to some of the most northerly settlements in the world, with ice covering 708,072 square miles, or 85 per cent of the island's total area. The ice is nearly two miles thick in places. The land is billions of years old. The entire coast seems to be one long, gigantic rust-red cliff face. The icecap lolls across most of the country, ice so heavy it has forced the land down, creating a vast trough in the middle.

From the ship I could see great rifts of ice, formed into black and white stripes, receding for thousands of miles into the interior. There are no roads between the settlements; travel is possible only by boat or plane. Amid all this are scattered, tenuous villages, perched on rocky promontories. We would travel for hours without sighting anything; the villages were invisible until we were practically at the shore.

There are only about 60,000 Greenlanders, and they live along the coasts, the only ice-free part of the country. 'Greenlander' is the term used for the mingled population of Danes and Inuit that emerged during the twentieth century. There's a long history of intermarriage, but as you go further north the Danes seem to fade out, and the settlements are more Inuit.

From a distance, the settlements seemed scenic enough: the small wooden houses painted in bright colours, the boats lined up on the shore, white Arctic hares bounding on the hillsides. Then we would find the harbour was far from quaint, scattered with rubbish, with the houses hemmed in with more junk, broken boats, piles of seal flesh, a dead dog or two. Sometimes we found the Inuit skinning seals and spreading the skins out on wooden frames to dry.

Thanks to generous Danish social services, the people have been liberated from dependence on the harsh environment, but they have also lost something of their raison d'être: there is not much to do in a polar village to replace the traditional activities of hunting with harpoons, making clothes from furs and skins and building moss houses.

There is a sense of aimlessness to many of the villages, and alcoholism is rife. The Inuit stand in the harbours trying to sell narwhal tusks: extraordinary metre-long ivory horns, spiralled like drill bits, that were traded down from the north in the Middle Ages, fetching their own weight in gold and presented to kings and queens as unicorn horns.

The only crowded tourist town was the final stop, Ilulissat, which stands on the edge of a fjord filled with bergs of every shape and size. The ice is the overflow from a glacier that seeped into a fjord and was crushed into piles as high as St Paul's Cathedral.

The glacier is like an ice machine, or ice kitchen, as it's often called. From Ilulissat these vast bergs drift towards the south, winding their way towards Newfoundland, gradually melting. Local legend has it that the iceberg that sank the *Titanic* drifted out of the Ilulissat ice kitchen before making its way to a historic collision.

The only view as we turned south was the glistening ice cap and the red mountains of the coast. As we were chilled out of the ice kitchen, I found myself thinking of the Greenlanders battening down the hatches for the winter, when the icebergs would all stand still, trapped in the frozen fjord.

TO NORMANDY, ON THE HOSPITAL SHIP

FIFTY YEARS ON FROM D-DAY, WE REPUBLISH AN ACCOUNT BY THE AMERICAN JOURNALIST **MARTHA GELLHORN** OF THE JOB DONE BY THE MEDICAL TEAMS

It was the first hospital ship to reach Normandy. Two that sailed earlier hit mines and sank. Before the war it had been a comfortable passenger boat ferrying comfortable travellers between Harwich and Holland. Now, brilliantly white, identified by huge red crosses, it stood out with strange innocence among the surrounding grey and camouflaged warships.

A military policeman stopped me and asked me my business. I said I was just going to interview the nurses, the women's angle for *Collier's*, the American magazine I was working for. Nobody gave a hoot about the women's angle, it served like a perfect forged passport. As soon as I got aboard, I found a toilet and locked myself in.

I had no authorisation, travel orders they were called, to witness the Invasion. I came out of hiding to find us anchored beyond the harbour in darkness, the night of D plus 1. No one questioned my right to be there. It was a civilian ship, the British master and crew were merchant service, the American medical staff had arrived that day from the States.

The lower decks were gutted to make three vast wards, filled with 426 wood bunks, and a large operating theatre. There were four doctors, six nurses, fourteen medical orderlies and perhaps six stretcher bearers. I never managed to count them. It seemed an impossibly small group to care for 426 wounded men. It was, and these men and women, without any experience of war, did the impossible job calmly and superbly. We sailed by daylight, alone in a presumably mine-cleared lane. Suddenly we were at the edge, then inside, the greatest naval traffic jam in history. Battleships, destroyers, transports (I know nothing of ships) were strewn haphazardly across the water, a seascape solidly filled with ships. It was so enormous, so awesome, that it felt more like an act of nature than anything man-made.

Naval guns were firing over the beach to unseen land beyond the high bluff that edged the beach. On shore, bulldozers scooped up and detonated mines. Tanks, looking toy-size at this distance, moved slowly up four dirt roads that scarred the bluff. Before us now was a weird forest of tall iron rods, like pieces of railroad track, with shreds of barbed wire trailing from them. Inshore a mass of landing craft jumbled together or raced between ships and shore. Far below, bodies floated face down, swollen greyish sacks, drowned infantrymen. Afterwards they seemed the saddest casualties; their landing craft lowered its ramp too soon, overladen soldiers stepped off into deep water, those who could not flounder to land died here.

We anchored outside the iron posts at the position called Omaha Red, in the American sector. Immediately a small landing craft bobbed alongside. From our deck crewmen winched down a big wooden box like a lidless coffin. Somehow the men in the tiny moving craft lifted a stretcher into the box, which was then winched up the high side of the ship. The first wounded soldier to arrive was an unconscious German.

We had six water ambulances that could be lowered and raised to the boat deck; each held six litter cases and as many walking wounded as could crowd aboard. With landing craft also serving as water ambulances and the winched lidless coffin, the wards filled quickly.

A very young man, with a colourless drawn face and open unblinking eyes, lay on a table in the middle of the ward. Whoever picked him up sent his story, by word of mouth, with him. He had been blown out of the turret of his tank and lay watching and hearing his comrades burn to death inside it. He was unwounded and could not move or speak. Shell shock. The only one. Medicine has progressed since 1914-18. A nurse shot him full of pentathol; he was put on a bunk, covered with blankets and left to sleep. Twenty-four hours later, he was all right, at least in his body.

A soldier with a smashed shoulder and a soldier with a smashed knee were worried about a French boy, lying on a bunk between them. He was our only innocent bystander. The boy, about sixteen, wore peasant blue clothes and had a piece of shrapnel in his back. The soldiers thought it was hard on him, a civilian with people he could not talk to and going to a strange country. 'Can you help that kid, Miss?' The French boy was tight-lipped about his wound. He was fearful for his family still in the battle zone. He said the Germans burned his house before they left. He was afraid he would never get home and see them again. I soothed him with invented certainties and the French kid smiled and both soldiers said: 'Thank you, Miss.'

'That Ranger over there, Miss, he's in a bad way, can you do something?' Quickly find a nurse. 'Miss, this man here needs water.' A soldier with two bloodied bandaged legs, talking for a man next to him whose head was shrouded in bandages. Nobody complained, except for one deeply unpopular German, and no American soldier asked a service for himself. They watched out for each other; it was very moving to see this gentleness of hurt men. They were all stoical with a degree of pain that no one unwounded can imagine.

The walking wounded on B deck told each other where they'd been hit, their units, intense shop talk, and asked the inevitable American question, 'Where're you from?', looking for another from the same state who would know the same things. One called out: 'Miss, is there anything to eat? Guys here haven't eaten since England.' But no one had thought of food.

Two little pink-cheeked cabin boys in red monkey jacket uniforms appeared from nowhere. Presumably in peacetime they served in some officers' mess, and were here now as a wild comic oversight. They knew where to find food. We made thick sandwiches of bread and corned beef, all there was, and filled teapots with instant coffee, heaping in sugar. Teapots were easy to carry and perfect for pouring into mouths of men who could not sit up or use their hands.

At dusk it was decided that the water ambulances could not weave through the iron posts in the dark with the tide going out. Two young stretcher bearers would arrange onshore to collect wounded men for pick-up at first light. We waded the last strip of water on to a beach of big sliding pebbles. White tapes marked a mine-cleared track that curved inland from the edge of the beach to a green tent marked with a red cross. Troops and tanks and ammunition trucks were all moving between these white tapes.

In the tent a tired quiet young man said he would send the wounded to an LCT (tank-landing craft), now marooned on the shore. It grew dark quickly. The fine white ship blazed with light, according to the rules of the Geneva Convention. Furious shouts rang out from shore, from landing craft, and the light was doused.

The stretcher bearers laid the wounded down in two rows with their heads against the metal walls in the hold of this strange tank carrier. How many were there? Forty? We could not see them and they were unnaturally silent, so I feared they were too badly wounded to speak or unconscious; we would have a cargo of dead and half-dead men in the morning. Now our ack-ack opened up at both ends of this stretch of beach. The noise was appalling, and though the sky bursts are very pretty, twinkling in the dark, they also rain down shell fragments. Tracers added to the unappreciated beauty of the scene. I had the impression that the German planes were spraying the beach with machine-gun fire. Two turned into fiery falling comets and blazed in giant bonfires to the right and left of us, lighting up the shore. In this red flaring, the beach looked like a deserted junk yard, with the boxy black shapes of tanks, trucks, munition dumps.

We went under the canvas roof of the hold to keep our wounded company, feeling miserable that we had collected these poor men in one place to get them wounded again or killed. The Oerlikons on our LST (tank-landing ship) had opened up and the noise inside that metal hold was like having your ears drilled with a spike. It was a short and violently noisy raid. Someone shouted from shore that we had brought down four German planes. In the silence afterwards I heard two of the wounded talking in low voices. I walked over to them and realised they were speaking German; we had a hold full of wounded German soldiers.

The water ambulances collected us in pre-dawn light. Back in the wards, dim bulbs hung on wires. Everything looked worse. The men, in the remnants of their uniforms, the cloth cut away from their wounds, looked older than one night could age them, and thinner. The nurses were blanched by fatigue. All night the doctors had operated, the nurses and orderlies had worked, without rest. This was the quiet of exhaustion. A nurse put the palms of her hands against the small of her back, arched to ease strain, smiled and said: 'They're good boys, aren't they? They're real good boys.'

More and more wounded men were brought to the ship. The decks were slippery with blood, and littered with heaps of bloody bandages. One soldier died on that ship but he was already far along the road to death when he reached us. When at last the men in the wards felt the ship moving and breathed fresh sea air and heard the new silence around us, the atmosphere lightened into hope.

In the early evening, I stood at the bow, watching the shore of England approach, realising I knew nothing about any of these Americans and Britons: no names, no backgrounds, no accounts of the fighting. I only knew the extraordinary quality of them all.

A bone-tired nurse came out for a breather. She said: 'We'll do better next time.'

STREET FULL OF WATER

MICHAEL KERR TRAVELS UP AND DOWN
VENICE'S MAIN ARTERY

To the Grand Canal, with seven guidebooks, a dozen rolls of film and a small bag of cynicism. This is the high street of the most written-about, most photogenic city in the world; but it is also a high street in which, to paraphrase Mary McCarthy, the syllables Tintoretto are heard slightly less often than *il conto* (the bill). And so it was, scarcely three hours after arriving, and having made only the mildest of protests, that I allowed myself to be bundled into a gondola by my wife. Our helmsman took us down minor waterways, past the house of Marco Polo, the statue to Daniele Manin, scourge of Venice's Austrian invaders, and a mark chiselled on a wall, a good three feet above our heads, signifying the level of the last *acqua alta*, or high water. His commentary was friendly but perfunctory. Surely, I thought, our entry into the Canal Grande itself, the Canalazzo, inspiration of countless writers, artists and musicians, would draw from him some poetry. We swung into it. His eyes brightened. His mouth opened. And the words came: 'Is nice, huh? All thee nice palaces are on thee Grand Canal, huh?'

Well, what could he add? Even Henry James had to admit that in Venice 'originality of attitude is utterly impossible'. Besides, our gondolier was right. The Grand Canal is lined by 200 palaces. Though many now serve as museums, glass showrooms and municipal offices, they still bear the names of popes and aristocrats. The canal remains, as James (now Jan) Morris put it, 'the register of the nobility'.

It is also a tradesman's entrance. Venice has not been an island since the 1840s, but the trains, buses, cars and lorries that cross on two bridges from the mainland are not yet permitted to drive all the way into town. They stop at the north end of the Grand Canal, and passengers and freight switch to small boats and long barges. Along the two-and-a-half miles of this waterway, which runs all the way to St Mark's, comes everything that cannot be wheeled on a trolley or carried on shoulders, from sides of beef to toilet bowls, from the television sets that Venetians crowd round in the evenings to the high fashion and low tables that they order from Milan. By means of this thoroughfare, tourists reach the sights, workers arrive at their shops, hotels and desks, and Venice is fed, watered, lit, fuelled, furnished and even cleansed. Grand Canal it is, but not too grand to admit the dustcart.

The city's refuse arrangements, of course, are given little thought by most of those travelling the canal. Their eyes are on the churches and the *palazzi*, their minds wrestling with the distinctions the writers of their guide-books profess to discern between buildings Gothic, Byzantine and Renaissance. Fingers jab at the page and out the windows of the *vaporetto*. There is the quay from which Byron, torch in hand, dived in to swim home from a party; there is the warehouse that Titian and Giorgione, having dropped their brushes at the sight of the flames, helped to save from a fire; and there is the palace of Nicolo Balbi, who was so keen to see it finished that he slept outside in a boat for months, caught a cold, and died before he could move in.

Its palaces are many, but the Grand Canal's bridges are few. Only three cross it: the Scalzi, the Accademia and, in the middle, the Rialto. At the height of Venetian power, merchants from throughout the world came to the Rialto district for coffee, cloth, spices and gold. The first state bank in history, the Banco Giro, was established here. The flesh trade thrived, too: by the start of the seventeenth century, according to a traveller from Somerset, Thomas Coryat, there were 2,000 courtesans in the city, 'whereof many are esteemed so loose that they are said to open their quiver to every arrow'. If they repented later, they probably queued for the confessional in the little church of San Giacomo di Rialto. Here an inscription reads: 'Around This Temple Let The Merchant's Law Be Just, His Weight True, and His Covenants Faithful.' Some have slipped a little from those high standards: at a canal-side restaurant we drank one bottle of wine but were charged for two – an error corrected with little grace. I congratulated myself for 24 hours on this evidence of sharp practice. Then we ate at a more modest place, which promised a 10 per cent discount to readers of a certain guidebook. I had only to leave the book on the table to ensure the deduction was made.

'We send all over the world,' a stall-holder by the Rialto boasts. But the merchandise is not what it was: gaudy glassware, carnival masks, and sweat-shirts bearing the logo of the 'Hard Rock Cafe, Venice' (there's no such place). Prices can be steep. Still, if a tourist cannot leave Venice without a lapel badge of that little genie-baiter 'Aladino', why should he not be charged 96,000 lire (£37)?

Prices are more moderate at the Rialto markets. Long before first light steals across the canal the little boats are putting in here, piled with cabbages, onions, kiwi fruit and pears; with milk, bread, cheese and yogurts; with buckets of daffodils, roses, marigolds and gladioli. As fish are heaved ashore the gulls wait for a slip and a plop; the fat cats stretch lazily, confident of later feasts.

Beyond, the dirty cream *vaporetti* labour up and down, their passengers at this hour toting briefcases rather than backpacks, burying noses in newspapers rather than guidebooks. For these people the Grand Canal is the road to work. But only to them is its street furniture unremarkable. In place of junction markers there are the *dame* — pilings lashed together like giant primary-school pencils. In place of parking meters there are the *paline* — mooring poles in the colours of aristocratic families. In place of bus-stops there are pontoons that roll under the feet.

Then there are the vehicles. There is the gondola, of which enough has been said, and its pensioned-off two-man version, the *traghetto*, which plies from bank to bank. There is the *vaporetto*, which puts in with a sound like a spin-dryer coming to rest but still fails to kill the romance of Venice at night. Then there are the barges of burden and the police boats and the ambulance boats and the fire-brigade boats, the last manned by five men in anoraks who seem to do little but round up small craft as if they were stray dogs. And there are the water taxis, whose boy-racer drivers twitch at the city-centre speed limits. It was one of those who took us from our hotel to the airport, and even as we blanched at his tariff we admired his James Bond urgency.

The Grand Canal, of course, should generally be taken at a slower pace — if not quite as slow as that of the Venetian post office, which has its HQ here. For dawdling, the most famous spots are the cafés Florian and Quadri, on the Piazza San Marco, and Harry's Bar. I spent a quarter of an hour amid the gilt and mirrors of Florian's, seated opposite two moustachioed American queens in their forties. 'Just think,' drawled one, 'that's the greatest square in the world out there.' My thimble of espresso wasn't quite up to that standard, but at 5,300 lire (£2.14) it was an early-season bargain.

I called in, too, at Harry's Bar. This is one of those establishments whose staff are highly conscious of its celebrity; so conscious, indeed, that when a customer walks in they assume he is trying to frame a picture in his mind's eye rather than buy a drink. So they left me alone for a minute or two to set the exposure. When the vodka martini did come, however, it was as good as its reputation. This was the sort of stuff that rotted Hemingway's brain.

It did strange things to mine, too. Shortly afterwards, I found myself at the other end of the canal. Opposite the bus station and the car park, the only ugly pitch in the city, stood a woman trying to sell baseball caps and posters. Was it for a bet or a dare or a punishment? Surely Shylock himself could not have made a profit here? I stopped this train of thought just in time. It wouldn't do to feel too sorry for a merchant of Venice.

A WHOLE RAFT OF PROBLEMS

TIM MOORE TAKES TO THE RIVER IN SWEDEN, AFTER A BOTCHED BIT OF DIY

When I stepped out of our hotel shower to find Lilja flicking through channel after channel of lurid filth, I felt more than ready for the wilderness. What world was this where a father could not leave his 10-year-old daughter alone with the remote control at breakfast time? (Answer: a Swedish one.) Lilja's enthusiasm, though, was already beginning to wane. We had an hour before our bus came, and she spent it in Karlstadt's H&M, cramming in memories of commercial civilisation to sustain her through the looming mall-less void.

Middle children are by tradition rejected and ignored, but my daughter's initial glee at getting the nod ahead of her big brother had been eroded with every new detail of what she'd let herself in for. The following morning we'd be building a raft out of logs, and for four days thence we'd sail this down the Klarälven, in tribute to the million tree-trunks a year that until 1991 made the aquatic journey from forest to paper mill. The one consolation for her was the third member of our party, now waiting for us at the bus stop: my wife's Icelandic-born, Stockholm-resident teenage nephew.

An already lofty 17-year-old when I'd seen him last, in six short months Hugi − *Starsky & Hutch* fans may be disappointed to hear it's pronounced Hoo-yih − had soared into an imposing colossus, by temperament and physique the definitive gentle giant. It's difficult to think now of how else he could have been more perfectly equipped for what lay ahead. Gills, perhaps.

The bus took us to a remote riverside campsite that would double as our trip's finish line. Here we were kitted out by a sombre quartermaster, and lined up with four other groups for a raft-building tutorial. I'd confidently anticipated that our craft would be assembled using the technique that had served me so well throughout my DIY career: mess everything up, enlist someone competent to sort it all out, then shamelessly pose for a triumphant photo alongside the finished result. This happy vision took more vivid shape as our instructor, Frederik, chuntered on about clove hitches with the throwaway air of a man long accustomed to audience inattention. Besides, even I could manage the odd knot – a rare legacy, along with dumb insolence and the third verse of 'Swing Low, Sweet Chariot', of my time with the 34th Hammersmith.

The revelation that our supplied tents – ancient and malodorous frame-and-guy-rope affairs – lacked instructions and a full set of pegs offered a first suggestion that we might find ourselves short of practical initiative. The second came when Lilja noticed that the Dutchmen pitching camp beside us with wordless proficiency had changed into uniform: matching T-shirts emblazoned with sponsors' logos and the legend 'Klarälven 2006'. It wasn't until the morning after, though, as we tramped out of a coach and into a wet field thirty miles upstream, that the full extent of my misjudgement made itself apparent.

'There,' barked a suddenly forthright Frederik, directing each group towards a jumbled mountain of sawn-off telegraph poles as he tossed boxes of rope out of a lorry. 'Your raft will be three logs deep, and six by three metres, in total 2,000 kilograms of logs. Make sure those knots are okey-dokey, unless you like to see your logs go on holiday without you.' It was the last time anyone used the 'h' word.

Following the example of other groups Hugi and I stripped down to our pants, and as the rain intensified set about the task that would account for the next nine hours: the effortful selection, extraction and relocation of two tons of muddy logs from pile to river and the innefectual lashing together of these therein. In lighter moments the experience recalled *Jeux Sans Frontières*; at others it was all a bit *Bridge on the River Kwai*. There was nothing Lilja could do but watch us fall over and drop logs on each other's feet, which we did rather a lot.

'You think that was the bad part?' beamed Frederik as in frail half-triumph we tied the last knot, securing a tarpaulin cover to our raft's little aft-ward shelter. Ever keen to recalibrate our morale-ometers, he promptly regaled us with tales of relationships destroyed by the maritime rigours we were about to embark on. A highlight was the dishevelled newlywed who had stomped into the office, snatched up her car keys and bellowed, 'Thank you for letting me see what a prick he is!', before speeding off alone. Frederik's parting words were a reminder that if we'd had enough, we just had to phone and he'd come and pick us up. Another taunting beam. 'But that will cost you 2,000 kronor!'

All the other groups bar a Dutch couple and their young son had long since set sail when we poled ourselves out into the Klarälven's broad, rain-swollen current. In a moment we were rotating downstream, gently serene between riverside ranks of towering evergreens; the contrast with the splashy disorder of the construction process was bewildering. Here it was, the *Huckleberry Finn* voyage I'd foreseen this trip to be: plenty of idle drifting and straw-chewing, seasoned with practical japery and outsmarting the odd brigand.

The fantasy was swiftly holed below the waterline. We spotted the semi-submerged rock from half a mile away, but forewarned is not forearmed when you're trying to impose your navigational will on two tons of wood with a punt pole and three canoe paddles. Impact was a dismal, creaking thud, and though the steady current soon spun us clear, the implication that such incidents would be a regular feature drained Lilja's modest reserves of optimism. 'Daddy,' she inquired in a cracked whimper, 'how much is 2,000 kronor?'

Another lesson soon grimly learnt was that far more than a simple wish to do so was required to make land for the night. Hugi nobly climbed into the canoe that we towed behind us to facilitate the landing process, but only after ninety minutes was he able to lash a rope round a tree and haul us in. By then it was past dusk, and he'd fallen in twice. Supper was cold hot dogs and fish balls straight from the tin; the tents were semi-erected in blackness, rain and silence.

The insistent pattering that awoke us accurately foretold of a lot more dimpled water in the day ahead. Crammed together under our tarp shelter, just downstream we passed the group of boozy young Englishmen who the day before had beaten us out of the blocks by four hours, their raft now stuck in one of the 'log traps' that had been a prominent feature in Frederik's exhaustive rundown of hazards. That shouldn't have cheered us up, but my how it did.

Retribution came as we prepared our first hot meal, packet soup boiled up on a spirit stove. Our lethargic progress proved dependably deceptive – I knelt to set the stove to simmer, and when I looked up, we had somehow drifted right across the quarter-mile-wide river and were soon being thwacked by overhanging foliage. One hefty bough brushed aside my shrieky flails to bequeath our shelter an extravagant asymmetry which halved its internal space. Another of those and the whole thing would have been dashed clean off the deck, taking with it all our possessions; only Hugi's burgeoning mastery of the big stick saved us.

We hunkered down in what was left of our shelter, drenched and exhausted as shipwreck survivors. The Klarälven broadened and mean-dered; once we saw a grebe, another time a hill. There was some excitement when I spotted a beaver, but it proved to be a submerged log, which we hit. Long periods of bored discomfort interspersed with moments of blind panic and terror – I had taken my 10-year-old daughter to war.

Making land in the traditional wits'-end, random manner brought us to the bottom of a farmer's garden. Though Sweden's right-to-roam law is tilted very much in the freelance camper's favour, Hugi felt it prudent to ask permission. But there was no sign of life, aside from great clouds of rain-proof mosquitoes and a slavering half-breed wolf in a cage festooned with rusty scythes. At Hugi's insistence we left an explanatory note, which even as he wrote it I could hear being read out at a coroner's inquest.

The bulb in our only torch blew just as we'd got mine and Lilja's tent up; bundling inside to flee the buzzing bloodsuckers, she reacted so flamboy-antly to an imagined spider's web brushing her face that we had to put it up all over again in the dark. Our stove proved no match for the elements, and we were sipping mugs of tepid Dolmio when the Dutch family pitched up out of the sodden gloaming. It felt like being rescued. When the cheery and hyper-competent father revealed his career as an insect-repellent salesman, and handed us a tube of military-grade product, I wondered if he was real.

There didn't seem many more ways we could fail to have fun, but the next day ticked every remaining box. We ran aground on rocks twice, and on sand thrice, the latter requiring Hugi and me to strip, jump in, and heave two tons of timber against the current. One of my shoes shed a sole; Hugi's mobile went missing, presumed drowned. In our desperation to buy torches and cooked food at the only settlement of note along the route, Hugi capsized the canoe and nearly lost both it and his will to live. When I got the lifebelt to him on the fifth throw, the look in his eyes had devolved from fear to the resigned forgiveness of a saintly martyr.

'The river's going the wrong way!' yelped Lilja soon after we'd hauled him aboard, and for once her doomsaying was justified. A huge whirlpool was lazily drawing us towards its repulsive maw, a rotating mound of filthy foam and flotsam, and only after a brutal hour of galley-slave paddling did we inch ourselves clear. Throughout it rained as if God had forgotten how to make it stop. If the day before had been *Three Berks in a Boat*, then this was the *Raft of the Medusa*.

The heavens were finally drained dry as we pitched camp in a tussocky field, and with our wrinkled toes warmed by the sunset and a blazing heap of barbecue coals I saw it was at least possible to imagine shaking Frederik's hand, rather than pinning it behind his back as Hugi belted him unconscious. This rapprochement intensified as the last of the alcohol trickled soothingly down my throat, and a squadron of geese honked overhead beneath a billion stars. A moon-dappled river and clear sky wasn't enough for Lilja, though. 'Listen, Daddy,' she whispered as we lay in our mouldering tent. 'It's a lovely car, on a lovely road.'

Fifteen hours later we thunked up on to the campsite river bank under blue skies, trailing a wake of scummy detritus acquired during the morning's alarums. The shelter was no longer worthy of the name, and the crucial binding that held the two halves of our raft together flapped loose in the clear water, with the front section sharply tilted nose down: somehow, we had made wood sink.

We stumbled out on to the bank, and stood there blankly picking at bite scabs with rope-burned fingers, terra firma swaying under our river legs. For the umpteenth time I begged Hugi's forgiveness for dragooning him into this endeavour; now that it was over he claimed with apparent sincerity to have relished the challenge. I might have at least pretended to agree had Frederik not then appeared, reminding us we weren't going anywhere until the raft had been dismantled, all lent equipment correctly packed away, and every piece of rubbish cleansed and placed in the correct recycling bin.

'I can't tell you how much I want to go home,' mumbled Lilja as she sluiced out the beer cans, although she had, and often. Months later, after a Hallowe'en sleepover, she told me of her ability to blot out unwelcome things by simply pretending they weren't happening. I couldn't help asking if this was a technique she'd tried on the raft. 'All the time,' she hissed, gloweringly aware that I'd just broken an agreement never to speak of our Swedish misadventure again. 'And it never, ever worked.'

FROM SEA TO SUPPER TABLE

ANTHONY PEREGRINE TRACKS THE FINAL JOURNEY OF A TURBOT

The turbot we had been following all day ended up at table 10, on the plate of Mr Escoffier — which was a stroke of luck. Granted, this was Marcel Escoffier, the magnate, and no descendant of the more celebrated Augusto — but with a name like that and eighty-six fish-eating years under his belt, his opinion demanded respect.

'Succulent,' he said of the flat-fish. 'Evidently fresh.'

Spot on. Just a few hours earlier the turbot — several turbot, in fact, had been hauled from the deep and dumped, twitching, on the trawler deck. Its nearest and dearest had barely time to grieve before it was in the kitchen of Le Gafetou restaurant, flanked with potatoes and ready for the onward journey to table 10. From sea to stomach in less time than it took early-season holidaymakers to get their first sunburn.

This is, of course, no less than you expect in a little Mediterranean fishing port. The image — the experience — demands fresh fish consumed as moon and lights twinkle on the harbour and briny while your beloved beams in something backless. Le Grau-du-Roi doesn't disappoint (though you must bring your own beloved).

As well as being unpronounceable — the name emerges as a Pawnee incantation from Anglophone mouths — Le Grau-du-Roi is the most appealing fishing village resort on the French Languedoc coast. That's because it is a fishing village first and resort second, thus fulfilling the Mediterranean holiday ideal of authenticity. Beachwear daftness has invaded its narrow streets — with Italian ices, pineapple-shaped jewellery and shell figures — but the harbour at its working heart remains the preserve of the trawlers, men in overalls and mangles of mechanical tackle.

The place exudes the romance of reality…and is therefore the perfect spot to discover how fish progresses from natural habitat to the dinner-plates of the Mediterranean dream — or, to put it another way, to study a day in the death of a turbot. And guides come no better than the Bense family who, owning both a trawler and a restaurant, cover the entire process. They know more about Mediterranean fish than the fish know themselves.

They also have news of Eric Cantona. 'Lived here when he played with Nimes Olympique,' says 47-year-old Charles Bense as he takes the 18-metre *Verseau* down the channel, past dormant shops and cafes, to the sea. Ernest Hemingway, too, knew Le Grau — visited in the 1920s and appreciated the dace, apparently. This is more pertinent cultural background than is usual at 3 a.m. — and so carries us through the hour to the fishing grounds, six miles off the Camargue coast, where turbot and sole are thought to be lurking.

The sun is nowhere near up as Bense's crew of two feed out the 80-metre net, fix the metal wideners to keep its mouth open and withdraw to wait through the four-hour, four-knot trawl. It is time to drink coffee and talk fishing talk...of Spanish fish piracy, of our luck that today the sea is calm as a convent, and French fishing's luck that beef is currently considered toxic. Mad-cow madness is price support from heaven for Mediterranean fishermen.

Before it struck, French fishing had seen earnings cut by 25 per cent in real terms in five years. Large-scale producers with high fixed costs — mainly on the Atlantic coast — had been hit hard, knocked out and/or bought up by the dreaded Spanish. If a French industry survives in recognisable shape, it is because so much of it, like the *Verseau*, is in the hands of small-scale, family enterprises that are prepared to grit their teeth when the going gets rough. Up to a point, anyway.

These are the one-boat outfits that give Mediterranean fishing ports their bobbing, backs-to-the-world atmosphere, assuring supplies to shoals of quayside outlets; every other shop and restaurant in Le Grau-du-Roi boasts fresher fish than the one next door.

But it doesn't do to get too romantic. The local market is nowhere near enough. Le Grau has thirty-three fishing boats, and there's only so much that village and visitors can soak up. Ninety per cent of the catch goes to Paris or Lyon, and so, just like fish from Grimsby, is at the mercy of international fishing currents.

The Mediterraneans naturally reckon their fish is of better quality but, as Charles Bense points out, how many people, Mr Escoffier aside, can truly distinguish an excellent turbot from a merely adequate one?

There may not yet be EU fishing quotas in the Med — as there are off the Atlantic coast — but they are under discussion. Meanwhile EU officialdom wants cuts of 40 per cent in the French fleet – and there's no question of licences for newcomers wanting to join Bense in Le Grau. Thank heavens, indeed, then for mad cows and sane fish – but, says Bense, the effect is artificial, temporary and sad. When it dissipates, things will again look choppy for the bobbing boats of the Mediterranean. As dawn breaks, it doesn't seem possible that much could be wrong with the world – but we aboard the *Verseau* are not the first ones to be fooled by the dawn.

It's now 8.15 and macro-economic gloom is forgotten as the net is winched in – a lyrical, even biblical, moment…though less so when it happens three times every day of your working life. 'It's not unknown for men to get caught up in the cables and winched round,' says Bense.

Suddenly, the sunbaked deck space is writhing with seafood of all species, a United Nations of fish which, like real UN members, don't like close proximity with others they rarely meet. Sombrero-sized octopuses strike out, flowing across the boards like weary old men who, having lost all their bones, remain determined to escape. One wonders who ever first looked at such a thing and said: 'Mmmm, I feel hungry.' Eels wriggle, tiny crabs edge away – and, yes, here and there in the heap, the target turbot flap convulsively, as if undergoing electro-shock therapy. 'They can go on like that for a couple of hours,' says Bense.

Certainly, they're still at it as the crew, Jean-Louis Malabave and Jean-Claude Marquet, sort out, crate and ice the gasping scrum. Whiting and hake fly this way, squid, sole, red mullet and sea-snails the other. More disagreeable items – venomous scorpion-fish and a well-armed crustacean called la galère – are handled with care, as is the angler-fish, with its built-in fishing rod dangling before its mouth.

Sardines, by contrast, are unwanted – 'Can't give them away,' says Bense – and go back over the side with the few other tiddlers that not even the French will eat. Seagulls are less fussy. Appearing from nowhere – moments before, the sky was clear – dozens wheel and pounce and the source of Cantona's most celebrated pensée is instantly obvious.

Two further trawls bring up more turbot, but the overall haul will struggle to make the Fr7,000 (£950) Charles Bense needs daily to stay in business. 'Weather's too clear,' he says. 'Fish aren't stupid. They can see and hear the net.'

After fourteen hours, we head for home – dodging windsurfers on the approach – and for the computerised fish auction that kicks into life as soon as any of Le Grau's thirty-three boats lands. The *Verseau*'s catch is sold in minutes to an amphitheatre of buyers who appear to be doing anything

— chatting, joking, sleeping, smoking — except buying fish. They are, though, wide enough awake to stop the price — descending fast on the 'scoreboard' from a notional maximum — when it suits them. They wait rather longer than Charles Bense would like, so his earnings are merely low-average.

'Only 10 per cent stays locally,' he says. 'The rest will be in Paris or Lyon in the morning.' Along with cut-price stuff from Eastern Europe, he grimaces.

Earlier, Bense's elder brother, Joe, had his pick of the haul for the family restaurant on the seafront — and so our turbot is spared the auction. By early evening, it is at Le Gafetou on the kitchen work surface, being cleaned, prepared and sprinkled with white wine by Joe's wife, Ann-Marie. 'You can always tell a fresh flat-fish, because it's never entirely flat. It curls up slightly,' she says. Now the focus of professional attention, it looks individual, special and worth Fr85 (£11.50) – as it certainly didn't flopping with the mob on the trawler deck.

Beyond the restaurant's huge windows, the sun has faded over the vast sea, giving way to night-shift shimmering. Couples with light laughs and lighter clothes are grinning in expectation of fresh fish and more besides. The turbot, with its pre-steamed potatoes, is in the oven for ten minutes as kitchen staff nearby prepare bourridesa with angler-fish, and bouillabaisse with more or less everything, including scorpion-fish, which remain evil-looking even in a stew.

At table 10, Mr Escoffier is waiting with his wife and looking out over the Mediterranean 25 yards away, near which he has lived all his life. 'It still retains a magic,' he says. By now, at least, the turbot is part of the magic – a strange destiny, perhaps, for a fish. Across the village, Charles Bense has a couple of hours before he's off again in search of others.

SAILING AWAY ON A SEA OF VODKA

AS A TRAINEE ON A RUSSIAN TALL SHIP, **MALCOLM MACALISTER HALL** PAYS FOR A THRILLING VOYAGE WITH A SORE HEAD

The real danger came at us from an unexpected quarter. It wasn't so much the 900 miles of deep, hostile water between Aberdeen and the Norwegian town of Trondheim, close to the Arctic Circle; nor the heaving decks of the mighty Russian ship; nor the 100ft drop from the crow's nests; nor even the cabbage soup.

Here, aboard one of the world's biggest sailing ships, the principal threat to life and limb was the vodka in our cabin, downed with a Russian toast – 'Nasdarovya! Nasdarovya!' – that began to haunt me in my fitful sleep.

My small but gruelling role in this year's Cutty Sark Tall Ships' Race started as it finished – with a sore head. Press-ganged by an old friend, Iain, into signing on with the colossal Russian square-rigger *Mir* for the first leg of the race, I arrived in Aberdeen to find eighty-three ships from sixteen nations packed into the harbour. Iain, home after several years in Canada, took me on a tour of his old haunts.

These were pubs. People I had never met and can now no longer remember pressed drinks into my hand. Amid a riot of parades, parties, bands and screeching seagulls, the stern-faced granite city was making whoopee, as nearly a million visitors marvelled at the soaring masts and tipped £13 million into the town's tills.

Two blurry days later – or it might have been three - the lumbering armada eased out of the harbour in a barrage of foghorn blasts. As schooners, barques, brigantines and full-rigged ships massed around the start-line offshore, the scene resembled a huge nineteenth-century sea battle. Only the cannon-fire and exploding powder kegs were absent.

Gripping the yardarms 150ft above the *Mir*'s decks, the teenage Russian cadets unfurled the dizzying 30,000 square feet of canvas – twenty-six grimy sails, billowing out and snapping tight in the southerly wind. Some looked as big as tennis courts; 360ft of steel, assembled in the Lenin Shipyard in

Gdansk ten years before, surged forward. The start gun boomed. The cadets raised a wild cheer.

From here, it would be a week to Trondheim, north towards the edge of the Arctic. A bracing chance to recuperate, it seemed, after our fierce schedule in Aberdeen. Below decks, on the noticeboard, were the ship's rules. Rule 1: no alcohol allowed. But I hadn't reckoned on our shipmates in cabin 147, with its choking fug of socks.

Six of the bunks were occupied by the ship's band, members of St Petersburg's Andreyev Balalaika Orchestra. With ten of us shoehorned into this hutch, the cabin was a chaos of musical instruments, stage costumes, lifejackets, wet towels – and vodka. 'I thought there was no drinking on board,' I said to Pavel, 32, who despite his sausage fingers played a tiny balalaika with lightning skill.

'Ha!' he grinned, waving a bottle of Moskovskaya and tipping a quarter of a pint into a glass for me, 'in this cabin, it's Russian rules. That means no rules! Nasdarovya!' And so began a full nightly programme of toasts, wrestling matches among the bunks, and other festivities. The only problem was that there was a race going on, and Iain and I were supposed to be helping.

The *Mir*'s complement included forty-one regular crew, seventy-six cadets on four months' sail training from the Admiral Makarov merchant navy academy in St Petersburg, and us – forty-eight paying 'trainees', mostly German and British, ages seventeen to around seventy. And this was no cruise.

The catering was rough – wet cutlery dumped in heaps on plastic tables, soggy pasta, cabbage, meatballs – and the WCs were rougher. 'Work on deck is obligatory,' noted the introductory bumf. We were assigned to the watches – Iain and I to the midday-4 p.m. and midnight-4 a.m. turns.

For the first few days and nights the mighty ship raced northwards before a steady southerly wind. As the 50ft steel bowsprit cut through the dark we did spells as lookout, bundled against the cold. And as Andrei, our bosun, barked orders in Russian we jogged this way and that in the footsteps of the cadets to haul sheets and braces, huge rough ropes that ascended skywards to the sails and yardarms in an infernal cat's cradle of rigging.

Feisty pensioners and Edinburgh schoolgirls hauled ropes with the rest. Among our crew were an Aberdeen oil executive and his wife, a retired stonemason who had worked on York Minster, and a woman who had left a corporate career to run her father's farm in Scotland. There were students, a Tesco customer service manager, and Alan, a refrigeration engineer from Fleetwood. He typified the breed.

'I'll have a bash at anything, me,' he said as the *Mir* sped across the wave-tops on a sunny afternoon. He recalled other holiday highlights: on the Cambodian border during a military offensive, and a booze-up with Tamil Tiger fundraisers in India. 'You've got to get out and meet people, haven't you?', he added. 'They're not going to come to Fleetwood, after all, are they?'

We gazed over the rail. For days the horizon had been empty. Reputed to be the fastest square-rigged ship in the world, the *Mir*, under its highly regarded captain, Viktor Antonov, had had a string of wins, including last year's Cutty Sark race and the transatlantic Columbus race in 1992. We had left the other square-riggers miles behind.

At night we practised the knots the cadets had taught us in halting English, and Thomas, a medical student from Trondheim, briefed us on what to expect of his home town: how the houses there sometimes blew up when illicit moonshine stills exploded in back bedrooms, and that a famous delicacy was lutefisk, cod soaked in caustic soda until it turned to jelly. 'That's a particularly horrible-sounding speciality,' he said. 'I've never tried it.'

With the ship racing along at up to 13 knots, it seemed we would be there days ahead of schedule. In one 24-hour spell we had covered 260 miles. Then we hit the doldrums. The *Mir* slowed, then stopped, rising and falling on a queasy swell. The great sails hung limp. Fulmars flew round the ship.

Disabled and lost in a grey windless haze, the ship invited morbid comparison with its Russian namesake, the space station at that moment spinning helplessly far above us with a crashed computer. This was a back-breaking interlude as Andrei, brow furrowed and chain-smoking in frustration, had us hauling constantly on braces and sheets, spinning the huge steel yardarms and trimming sails to try to catch imaginary puffs of wind. The computer screen on the bridge showed our speed: 00.00 knots. For nearly two days we wallowed here, other ships catching us, their towering stacks of sail spied now and then on the horizon.

On Sunday, however, a strong wind sprang up from the north-east. Twenty-four hours' hard tacking would bring us to the finish line. As we dozed in our bunks, the intercom would bark us awake at any hour: 'Sailing alarm! Sailing alarm! All hands on deck to tack ship.'

This was a huge operation – a blizzard of commands, bleary-eyed cadets sprinting this way and that, forty people hauling on the mainsheet, the decks ankle-deep in rope. The skies were bright now on our midnight watches as we edged farther into the northern summer, the horizon a permanent glow of pink. Snowy peaks stood out on the distant Norwegian coast – and the band gave a concert. They played haunting, beautiful gipsy romances.

They had played Carnegie Hall, and toured Japan and Europe with the 75-strong Andreyev Balalaika Orchestra, formed in 1888 and once the Imperial Russian Court Orchestra. Now, said Pavel, they played six days a week at a radio station in St Petersburg for $100 a month. He lived with his elderly mother and Juliet, a little dog that the band's guitarist had found dying on a snowy street in winter. Much of his money went on rent. 'It's very hard to live in Russia now. So I work as a carpenter, too, fixing doors and things for people...'

The ship itself was in similar straits. The cadets were on the equivalent of $1 a day. 'We have no money – only impressions and memories from this trip,' said Alexei, a trainee radio operator from Belarus. 'We got 35 Deutschmarks [about £13] at Aberdeen, just enough for a phonecard to call our parents, and some beer. But it was my dream to come on this ship. It's a memory for life.' In their threadbare trousers and old uniform jackets, the cadets had to make do with the most rudimentary equipment. One day, when the deck needed sanding, a piece of glass was smashed and the jagged shards issued as scrapers.

Just keeping the ship running was the work of miracles. The Makarov Academy was all but broke. 'Last year the only money we got was from the passengers, and we covered all our expenses through our own work – repairs and everything. We have to count every penny,' said one officer. 'The cadets usually get $4 a day – but the academy has no money and refused to contribute anything. At the first German port we could only pay them 25 Deutschmarks, and they didn't know what to do with it – buy a beer, or phone home.'

On the Monday, just after 6.30 a.m., we crossed the finish line first among the big Class A ships. No flags, boats or Champagne at the end of this first leg – just open ocean, nothing in sight, the position plotted by satellite. Next day, after 956 nautical miles, we sailed up the fjord to the leafy town of Trondheim, famous for its exploding houses and lutefisk.

I was disappointed to find all the houses neatly in one piece and lutefisk out of season. Never mind. It was time to celebrate, as usual. 'My house in St Petersburg is your house. Nasdarovya!' said Yuri, who played the mandolin-like domra, squeezing the breath out of me in a farewell bear hug. He and the band gave us such a titanic vodka send-off that I felt a bit funny for both of the next two days.

LITTLE WONDER

IF YOU WANT TO BE A CUSTOMER RATHER THAN A NUMBER ON YOUR CRUISE, IT PAYS TO THINK SMALL, AS **STANLEY STEWART** DID EN ROUTE TO NORWAY

Through the Western Isles of Scotland there sails a wee ship that breaks every rule of modern cruising. She carries fewer than fifty passengers, she does not have a blackjack table, and she never goes anywhere near the Caribbean. She seems to belong to another age, when travel was a more leisurely and a more elegant affair.

The *Hebridean Princess* has the restrained atmosphere of a well-appointed members' club. She is all polished brass, varnished teak and white linen tablecloths. She has a wood-panelled dining-room, a conservatory for after-noon tea, a library with deep leather armchairs, and an inglenook fireplace. The smallest luxury cruise ship in the world, she has standards of service that went out with the Charleston. To those who have sailed her, she is heaven on the high seas.

Last summer saw the launch of a sister ship, the *Hebridean Spirit*, which boldly goes where the *Princess* rarely ventures – to foreign seas. The idea is an ambitious one – to take the unique atmosphere of the *Princess* and try to replicate it in a new ship that will cruise a range of itineraries from Scandinavia to Sri Lanka.

In Edinburgh I joined a loyal, if slightly sceptical, band of former *Princess* passengers for the inaugural cruise through the fjords of southern Norway. At first glance the passengers had the look of disapproving in-laws. The specialness of the *Princess* was an article of faith for these people. The new ship had a lot to prove.

The *Hebridean Spirit* was moored in Leith Docks, next to the Royal Yacht *Britannia*, and the two ships seemed to share the same nautical gene pool in their smart livery of navy blue and white with red trim. Appropriately, Princess Anne had dropped round earlier to christen the ship. At five o'clock we were piped aboard by the ship's piper and we gathered along the rail as we slipped our mooring and turned out towards the North Sea.

'Do you know the *Princess*?' asked an elderly lady from Aberdeen. For a moment I thought she meant Princess Anne. But to the passengers aboard the *Hebridean Spirit*, there was only one *Princess*.

When I confessed I had never been on the *Hebridean Princess*, it was a moment before my companion could recover herself. Finally she said: 'The bonniest wee ship you could imagine. Not so much a ship as a second home. We all love her.'

When news got round about the man who had never sailed the *Princess*, passengers queued up to tell me about her. Among these ardent evangelists, I began to feel like a heathen.

The purser, a rather faded music-hall turn, made a Frankie Howerd face of disapproval. People wondered what I had been doing with my life. Foolishly I tried to drop into dinner conversations that I had followed the White Nile to its source in the Mountains of the Moon, traced the length of the Silk Road and ridden a horse 1,000 miles across Outer Mongolia. But my fellow passengers were unimpressed. If I had not watched the sun set over St Kilda from the rail of the *Princess*, I had not really been anywhere.

Among the places I had not been were the Norwegian fjords. Norway's coast is such a spectacular confusion it is as if the country had been dropped from a very great height. Its mountains have split asunder, allowing the sea far inland, while its shores have shattered into thousands of tiny islands. It has been a classic cruising destination since the 1870s, when Thomas Cook first brought tourists here to marvel at the mess left by one of God's clumsier assistants.

Over morning coffee I watched the brooding heights of Lysefjord fill the windows of the Skye Lounge. Cruising is travel for the sedentary, the ultimate armchair journey. You take to the armchair while the ship does the travelling. Surrounded by books and maps and slices of poppy-seed cake, I could see that I could get used to this novel and appealing arrangement.

Inaugural cruises are famous for their mishaps, from the *Titanic*'s iceberg to the *QE2*'s toilets. Built in Italy as a luxury cruise ship in 1991, the *Hebridean Spirit* had been brought back from Malaysia at the end of last year, stripped down, and completely refitted and refurbished. In the circumstances the crew and officers managed to look admirably relaxed after what had clearly been a hectic few months. Only days before the cruise, some hitch in the water system had flooded the cabins and a carpet fitter had had to be summoned in Great Haste from Great Yarmouth.

At the head of this Herculean task force was Michael Fenton, the

managing director of Hebridean Cruise Lines, one of those who are determined to reverse the trend in cruise ships to larger and larger vessels.

The newest ships, reminiscent of vast housing estates, carry as many as
3,000 people. Each of these behemoths is launched in a blaze of publicity in
which airport runways, high-rise buildings and the populations of provin-
cial towns are marshalled in a fevered attempt to describe their scale. The
irony is that cruise operators have managed to convince the cruising public
that the bigger the ships the better the cruise. This is an Orwellian fiction.

The Hebridean Cruise Line takes a different tack — that in cruises, as in
much else, small is beautiful. With a maximum of 98 passengers, the
Hebridean Spirit has a more intimate atmosphere. The staff know everyone by
name, and by the end of the voyage so will you. What's more, no one will
try to persuade you to sing 'My Way' to a karaoke machine.

But small also dictates the nature of the itinerary. The ship's size, only
300 feet long, allows access to harbours and anchorages that larger vessels
cannot reach. On the Norwegian fjords this meant visits to the monastery
of Utstein, to the old manor house of Rosenblat, to the little fishing port of
Skudeneshavn, with its traditional white houses, and to Espevar, where the
Hebridean Spirit docked for the day in a harbour so tiny that I thought we
were going to have to run our mooring ropes through the windows of the
harbour cottages and tie off to the bedposts.

As in many of the harbours we visited, no cruise ship had ever docked at
Espevar before, and the whole village turned out for the fun. I walked across
the island to the windward shore where I swam in a bay that I had all to
myself. Had I arrived with 2,000 fellow passengers, my bay would have
looked like Benidorm and the village of Espevar would have sunk beneath
the weight.

The *Spirit*'s passengers needed no convincing that small is best. But what I
wanted to know was how the *Hebridean Spirit* compared with the *Princess*. Did
she manage to live up to the formidable reputation of her sister vessel?

Almost. It was clear that the *Hebridean Spirit* could never entirely match
the old-world charm of the *Princess*. But the feeling among the passengers
was that the new ship was a fine addition to an illustrious tradition. The
cabins won universal praise for their comfort and style. The lounges were
beautifully appointed, the food was outstanding, the waiters and stewards
were attentive, and the itinerary was excellent, bringing us to hidden gems
along the Norwegian coast under the guidance of the wonderful Bard
Kolltveit, former director of the Norwegian Maritime Museum in Oslo.

But above all was the atmosphere. The *Hebridean Spirit* was like a country-house party. There was a smattering of lovable eccentrics, a convoy of lively widows whose husbands had sloped off to the Great Cruise Ship in the sky, a sprinkling of tanned Americans, a retired colonel, a pianist strong on Noël Coward and the swing tunes of the 1930s, a flustered but enthusiastic host, and not nearly enough fanciable girls. I soon knew everyone else aboard, and I was buoyed along by the pleasure of good company and good conversation.

A feature of every Hebridean cruise is a gala black-tie dinner. With the ship moored in the silent waters of Osterfjord, in the long Norwegian twilight, the evening ended with a few wee drams and a lot of boisterous Scottish reels on the mizzen deck. The elderly lady from Aberdeen marked my card for 'Strip the Willow'.

Between energetic figures of eight, I asked her how she had enjoyed the cruise. 'Terrific,' she cried, whirling me off my feet. 'Makes me feel sixty again.'

Chapter 4
AFRICA

MR STANLEY'S MISSION

THE RIVER LIVINGSTONE
A LAND OF IVORY HOUSES
THE THIRTY-TWO BATTLES
TO THE EDITORS OF 'THE DAILY TELEGRAPH'
AND 'NEW YORK HERALD'
LOANDA, WEST COAST OF AFRICA, SEPT, 5, 1877

On Jan. 4, 1877, we came to the first of what proved a series of cataracts, or, to use a more correct term, falls, below the confluence of the Lumami and the Lualaba, or the Lowa, as the river was now called. Our troubles began now in earnest. We were hunted like game. Night and day every nerve had to be strained to defend ourselves. Four times on Jan. 4 we broke through the lines of canoes brought out against us, and finally we were halted by the Baswa Falls, in S. lat. 0deg. 32min. 36sec. The savages seemed to think that we had no resource left but to surrender and be eaten at their leisure. Again and again were we compelled to repulse the furious charges that they made to drive us over the Falls. The people of the Falls Islands also came up to assist the cannibals of Mwana Ntaba. After constructing a fence of brush around on the forest side, [we placed] the best sharpshooters in position for defence. For the ensuing twenty-four days we had fearful work, constructing camps by night along the one marked out during the day, cutting roads from above to below each fall, dragging our heavy canoes through the woods, while the most active of the young men – the boat's crew – repulsed the savages, and foraged for food. On Jan. 27 we had passed in this desperate way forty-two geographical miles by six falls, and to effect it had dragged our canoes a distance of thirteen miles by land, through roads which we had cut through the forest. Our provision in the meantime we had to procure as we best could. When we had cleared the last fall, 0deg. 14min. 52sec. N lat., we halted two days for rest, which we all very much needed. In the passage of these falls we lost five men only.

After passing this series of rapids, we entered upon different scenes. The river was gradually widening from the usual 1,500 or 2,000 yards' breadth, to two and three miles. It then began to receive grander affluents, and soon assumed a lacustrine breadth, from four to ten miles. Islands also were so numerous that only once a day were we able to obtain a glimpse of the opposite bank. We had reached the great basin lying between the maritime and lake regions. The first day we entered this region we were attacked three times by three separate tribes; the second day we maintained a running fight almost the entire twelve hours, which culminated in a grand naval action at the confluence of the Aruwimi – the Welle (?) – with the Lualaba. As we crossed over from the current of the Lualaba to that of the Aruwimi, and had snatched a glance at the breadth of the magnificent affluent, we were quite taken aback by the grand preparations for our reception. Fifty-four canoes came rushing down on us with such fury that I saw I must act at once if I wished to save the expedition. Four of our canoes, in a desperate fright, became panic-stricken, and began to pull fast down stream; but they were soon brought back. We dropped our stone anchors, formed a close line, and calmly waited events.

Down the natives came, fast and furious, but in magnificent style. Everything about them was superb. Their canoes were enormous things, one especially, a monster, of eighty paddlers, forty on a side, with paddles 8ft. long, spear-headed, and really pointed with iron blades for close quarters, I presume. The top of each paddle shaft was adorned with an ivory ball. The chiefs pranced up and down a planking that ran from stem to stern. On a platform near the bow were ten choice young fellows swaying their long spears at the ready. In the stern of this great war canoe stood eight steersmen, guiding her towards us. There were about twenty – three-fourths of her size – also fine looking; but none made quite such an imposing show. At a rough guess there must have been from 1,500 to 2,000 savages within these fifty-four canoes. I cannot think that these belonged to one power. I imagine it was a preconcerted arrangement with neighbouring tribes, got specially up for our entertainment. We had, however, no time even to breathe a short prayer or to think of indulging in a sentimental farewell to the murderous cannibalistic world in which we found ourselves. The enemy, in full confidence of victory, was on us, and the big monster as it shot past us launched a spear – the first. We waited no longer; they had clearly come to fight. The cruel faces, the loudly triumphant drums, the deafening horns, the launched spear, the swaying bodies, all proved it; and every gun in our little fleet angrily gave response to our foes. We were in a second almost surrounded, and clouds of spears hurtled and hissed for a short time – say, ten minutes. They then gave way, and we lifted anchors and charged them, following them with fatal result.

We were carried away with our indignant feelings. We followed them to the shore, chased them on land into ten or twelve of their villages, and, after securing some of the abundance of food we found there, I sounded the recall. To the victors belong the spoil – at least so thought my people – and the amount of ivory they discovered lying useless about astonished me. There was an ivory 'temple' – a structure of solid tusks surrounding an idol; ivory logs, which, by the marks of hatchets visible on them, must have been used to chop wood upon; ivory war-horns, some of them three feet long; ivory mallets, ivory wedges to split wood, ivory pestles to grind their cassava, and before the chief's house was a veranda, or burzah, the posts of which were long tusks of ivory. We picked up 138 pieces of ivory which, according to rough calculation, would realise, or ought to realise, about $18,000. These, I told the men, they must consider as their prize-money. In this fight we only lost one man.

Our expedition was, however, becoming thinned in these repeated attacks made on us by such piratical cannibals. We had lost sixteen men already. There were no means to return to Nyangwe, for we had resolutely put six cataracts between us and the possibility of returning; besides, we were about 350 miles, according to the course of the river, or 296 geographical miles, north of Nyangwe. Why should we not ascend the Welle, and try by that road? But I felt almost convinced I was on the Congo. I was in N. lat. 0deg. 46min. Looked I where I might on my chart, I saw I was in the midst of a horrible, hateful blankness – a meaningless void. Yet to fight three or four times each day, our ammunition would not last. Nature even could not sustain such a strain as we experienced. The increasing breadth of the river below this last great affluent pointed a way of escape. I could abandon the mainland, and lose myself among the islands. I thus should pass by many affluents, but it could not be helped. The main thing, after all, was the great river itself, the receiver of all affluents.

The boat led the way to the islands. The first attempt was unsuccessful, for the channels, after taking us by half-a-dozen islets, exposed us again to the savages, and we, of course, were again compelled to fight. After two or three attempts we learned to distinguish the mainland from the islands, and we glided down for five days without trouble, further than anxiety for food. Driven at last by pressing hunger to risk an encounter with the savages, we came to a village in N. lat., 1deg. 40min., and E. long., 23deg, where the behaviour of the natives was different. These canoes advanced to meet us, and addressed some words which we did not understand. The canoes retreated, but, having told my little fleet to drop anchor, I allowed the boat to drift down, and anchored opposite the village, at only twenty yards from the shore. We made signs that we wanted food, showed copper bracelets, cowries, red and white necklaces, cloths, and brass wire – in short, resorted to our usual way of opening friendly communications when permitted by natives disposed to be friendly. The negotiations were long – very long; but we were patient. What made us hopeful was their pacific demeanour, so opposite to those above, and at last, after five hours, we succeeded.

That day, after twenty-six fights on the Great River, was hailed as the beginning of happy days. We certainly were now the happiest fellows in existence. When the old chief came to the bank to negotiate with the white stranger, we lifted our anchor and steered for him. My coxswain and self sprang ashore. Our canoes were anchored 400 yards off. The kindly visage of the old chief was so different from the hateful faces we had lately seen, that I almost crushed his hand, making him hop, out of pure love. My coxswain – a braver soul was never found within a black skin, but more of him by-and-by – he too hugged everybody all round, and hugging matches took place. The boat boys grew enthusiastic, and they also followed the example of Uledi the Coxswain. In the meantime the old chief drew me apart, and pointed to the face of Frank, which gleamed white amid the dark skins of the soldiers in mid-river. 'Ah! he is my young brother,' I said. 'Then he must make friends with my son,' said the chief; and Frank was accordingly hailed and told to come ashore, and the solemn ceremony of brother-hood ensued – the white man's and black man's blood were made to flow in one current, and a covenant of eternal peace and fraternity was concluded.

'What river is this, Chief?' I asked.

'*The* River,' he replied.

'Has it no name?' I asked.

'Yes; the Great River.'

'I understand; but you have a name and I have a name; your village has a name. Have you no particular name for your river?' (We spoke in bad Kikusu.)

'It is called Ikutu Ya Kongo.'

The River of Congo!

There was, then, no doubt, though we were still about 850 miles from the Atlantic Ocean, and over 900 miles below Nyangwe Manyema.

We spent three days at this village in marketing, an era of peace long to be remembered by us. We saw also four muskets here, and we augured from this fact that the perils of our desperate voyage were over. It was a false augury, however. One day's run brought us to Urangi, a populous country, where there was one town about two miles long, and our friends introduced us to these people. The first introduction over, about 100 large and small canoes appeared, and began trading. One thing after another disappeared. A man lost his mat and clothes; my cook lost a copper plate or dish; a gun was snatched at, but recovered without trouble. I arranged with the king that all trade must be done in the canoes. Every body was then contented. Next day we began to prosecute our voyage, two native canoes leading the way to introduce us to the tribes below. The 100 canoes that were employed in doing trade and visiting, the day before, now contained neither women nor children, but men with muskets and spears. We, however, did not regard it as anything extraordinary, until our guides at a signal paddled fast away, and we were at once assaulted.

'Form close line!' I shouted; and 'Paddle slowly down river close to the island.'

My boat's crew rested on their oars, allowed all the canoes to pass by, and we followed after them. Two out of each canoe, and two out of the boat, with myself, maintained a running fight for two hours until another tribe joined in the chase. The pirates of Urangi returned, but Mpakiwana took the fight up and maintained it, until we came to another tribe, and this tribe carried on the chase, charging furiously sometimes, then being repulsed but endeavouring with admirable pertinacity to effect the capture of one of our canoes. Frequently were we all compelled to drop paddles and oars, and defend ourselves desperately. At three p.m. the last of our enemies abandoned their designs, and we steered for the islands again.

On the 14th of February we lost the [TEXT ILLEGIBLE] channels, and we were taken — too late to return — along a current which bore us towards the right bank to the powerful tribe of Mangara, or Mangala, of which we had heard so much, sometimes as very bad people, at other times as great traders. The fact that they pursued trade caused us to imagine that we should be permitted to pass by quietly. We were woefully deceived. Despite the war drums and horns summoning the tribe to war, as it was near noon, and a bright sun shone, and there was sufficient stretch of river to take a good observation, I would not lose such a splendid opportunity to fix the position of this important locality. I ascertained it to be N. lat. 1deg. 16min. 50sec; by account 21deg. E. long. I closed my sextant, and put it away carefully, and then prepared to receive the natives – if they came for war, with war; if they came for peace, with gifts.

We cast loose from Obs Island, and started down stream. Sixty-three canoes of light, even elegant make, very soon approached. Some of the natives were gorgeous in brass decorations, and they wore head-dresses of the skins of white goats, while skins of the same colour hung down their shoulders like short mantles; the principal men having robes of crimson blanket cloth. We ceased rowing. When they were about 300 yards off I held a crimson cloth up to view in one hand, and a coil of brass wire in another, and by signs offered it to them. My answer was from three muskets, a shower of ironstone slugs, and four of my boat's crew and one in my canoes sank wounded. A fierce shout of exultation announced to the hundreds on the banks their first success. We formed our usual close line, and allowed the canoes and boat to float down, every rifle and revolver being required here. The battle consisted of bullets against slugs. We were touched frequently, boat and canoes pitted, but not perforated through. Dead shooting told in the end. Breechloaders, double-barrelled elephant rifles, and Sniders prevailed against Brown Besses, though for two hours our fate was dubious. The battle lasted from twelve o'clock to near sunset. We had floated down ten miles during that time; but we had captured two canoes, swift as they were. We had moreover dropped anchor for an hour, protecting a storming party, which took a village and burnt it. At sunset our people sang the song of triumph; the battle was over. We continued floating down in the darkness until about eight o'clock, and then camped on an island. This was the thirty-first fight, and the last but one.

We clung to the island channels for four days longer, unseen by any of the natives, for the river was here very wide – between five and ten miles. At a place called Ikengo, a great trading people, we found friends. We made blood brotherhood with many kings, and collected a vast deal of information. This tribe was one of the cleverest and most friendly of any we had seen. We halted three days with them. We met no armed force also to oppose us in the river below Ikengo, though a few canoes indulged in the customary little distractions of savage life by firing slugs at strangers; but, as no one was hurt, we permitted them to have their pleasures without regarding them. In the words of a dry humorist – one of my soldiers – 'We ate more iron than grain.' Six miles below the confluence of the river – called the Kwango by Europeans – and the main 'Livingstone,' we had our thirty-second fight. We proposed to halt in the woods and cook breakfast. We were collecting fuel to make a fire, when a quick succession of shots from the bush startled us and wounded six of our people. We had not the slightest idea that any tribe lived in that vicinity, for it seemed all forest. We sprang to our arms, and a regular bush warfare began, and ended in a drawn battle, the two sides mutually separating with a little more respect for each other. The advantage we gained was that of being permitted to stay in our camp unattacked.

I have stated this was our thirty-second fight, and last. So far as inter-change of bullets between natives and ourselves went, this is true. But we have been many a time on the verge of fighting since. However, diplomacy, vast patience, tact, and stern justice saved us from many a severe conflict. Soon after quitting Nyangwe, I had issued orders – knowing the propensi-ties of many of my people to take advantage of our strength – that whoever molested a native or appropriated anything without just return, would be delivered up to native law, the punishment of which would be certain death or eternal servitude. These orders were not always regarded. I had purchased several of my people who were guilty of theft from native power by extraordinary sacrifices of money, until we were almost bankrupts from this cause. The time came when it was necessary to place everybody on half-rations from our poverty. Yet the knowledge that we should be unable to make further sacrifice to save thieves did not restrain some from commit-ting depredations on native property. These were surrendered to native law. When five men had been thus dealt with my people began to awake to the fact that I was really in earnest, and I heard no more complaints from the natives.

A terrible crime in the eyes of many natives below the confluence of the Kwango and the Congo was my taking notes. Six or seven tribes confeder-ated together one day to destroy us, because I was 'bad, very bad'. I had been seen making medicine on paper – writing. Such a thing had never been heard of by the oldest inhabitant; it, therefore, must be witchcraft, and witchcraft must be punished with death. The white chief must instantly deliver his note-book (his medicine) to be burnt, or there would be war on the instant. Now my notebook was too valuable, it had cost too many lives and sacrifices, to be consumed at the caprice of savages. What was to be done? I had a small volume of Shakespeare, Chandos edition. It had been read and re-read a dozen times, it had crossed Africa, it had been my solace many a tedious hour, but it must be sacrificed.

It was delivered, exposed to the view of the savage warriors. 'Is it this you want?' 'Yes.' 'Is this the medicine that you are afraid of?' 'Yes; burn it, burn it. It is bad, very bad; burn it.'

'Oh, my Shakespeare,' I said, 'farewell!' and poor Shakespeare was burnt. What a change took place in the faces of those angry, sullen natives! For a time it was like another jubilee. The country was saved; their women and little ones would not be visited by calamity. 'Ah! the white chief was so good, the embodiment of goodness, the best of all men.'

MR STANLEY'S MISSION

THE DEATH OF FRANK POCOCK

Subjoined is the letter addressed to the father of Edward and Francis Pocock by Mr. Stanley Loanda, Sept. 2, 1877

My dear Mr Pocock — By means of my despatches to the *Daily Telegraph*, you have, no doubt, an idea as to the reason that induces me to write to you. The subject is very serious and sad. I would to God that Frank had to tell you about my death rather than I should be compelled to write about Frank's. The feeling is still fresh in my mind how I hankered after that long, long sleep from which there is no waking; for we were passing through a most troublous period, and hunger and sickness had destroyed all that enthusiastic energy with which we had rushed through the lands of the cannibals. I had lost many men in our incessant wars with the natives; sickness and despair had worried many others to their graves. Still our work seemed to have no end, and we could not see one ray of hope ahead. Our sick list grew heavier and heavier, until we had but sixty-three persons fit for work. I had about fifteen men down from ulcers and ten from dysentery and debility. So long, however, as I had Frank, and my boat's crew, I felt myself able to endure and fight it out — savages or cataracts, it mattered not much which. If there were hostile tribes we felt ourselves able to cut through them; if there were forests across which roads must be made, we would make them; if we had to pull our canoes over mountains, we would do so. It was only a question of time. And all this while Frank cheered me on, and said, with me, 'We must and we will do it.' There were two series of cataracts and rapids. The upper one consisted of six separate falls; the lower of seventy-four, with great and small rapids, fifty-seven of which only were important. Of these latter obstructions we had already passed thirty-five, and there were only three more really dangerous. It was in attempting the thirty-seventh fall — Masassa — that Frank lost his life.

The truth is that Frank died through his own rashness and his immense contempt for the water. He had been placed on the sick-list, because for ten or twelve days previously he was incapacitated from duty through ulcers on both feet of a most painful kind, and a man in that position ought not to have assumed the responsibility of commanding 'active-duty' men to proceed to execute a dangerous work, and to take him with them, when he could actually do nothing to assist them or superintend them. Frank was scarcely able to stand, least of all to climb the rocks to take a good view of the dangers ahead, so that he might judge of his situation. What does Frank do? He crawls on his knees to the canoe – the rescue canoe – manned with the most daring fellows in the Expedition, headed by the most desperate and courageous young man I ever knew, and, despite all remonstrances of the crew and chief, he orders them to cast off.

Still Frank might have been safe if, when the last chance was given him, he would have permitted himself to reflect upon his own condition – his own distressing, pitiful condition. The chief acted prudently enough in what he did, though he would have done better and more to my satisfaction had he carried out exactly what I had taught him when over forty-one falls and rapids I was leader. This chief steered his canoe into a cove just above the fall, and started to reconnoitre, to take a good look at the fall, and he came back and told Frank that it was impossible to shoot it – that, in fact, it was a very bad place. Frank would not believe him, but sent the youngsters to survey the spot and report upon it. They returned with the same story, that the fall was very bad. I have no doubt that had Frank been able to view the scene himself he would have agreed with them, but, seated in his canoe, unable to move, he thought, as he came down river to the cove where they were consulting, that he had seen in mid-river a place clear of falling water and waves, and he of course argued with the crew upon the strength of that. It seems that he remembered what I had told him a few days before – that, whenever he was going to risk the lives of others in a dangerous undertaking, it was not fair to give the final word without exposing to his companions all the dangers of it, asking them to give their judgment upon it, and if that was against the undertaking that they should not be compelled to go on. Frank hinted to the crew at this time that he knew exactly who had told him of this, and therefore, lest he should be charged by me with having risked the lives of others, he would say nothing.

'But,' he asked, 'tell me what am I to do. I have eaten nothing today; and here am I lame, unable to move. Will you leave me here to die of hunger?'

'Oh, no,' said the chief. 'I will send at once for your food, and for men to carry you; and in a couple of hours they will be here.'

'Oh, very well,' said Frank; 'do as you please,' and he assumed the look of one badly and disagreeably used. Then he told them that they were always afraid of the least little wave, and other querulous things, which only a sick man would have said. Poor Frank was only pushing himself nearer and nearer to death.

The chief then said, 'Little Master, we are not afraid of the river. I think I have proved I am not, and, if I say the word, these boys of mine will follow me to the bottom. Master has told us not to play with the river — not to do anything foolish — and if Master was here, he would tell us that the fall was dangerous. But if anything should happen, if you will take the blame, I say I and my people are ready, and if we die we die, if we are saved we are saved.'

'Oh, never fear; I will take the blame. Nothing will happen. Did I not see the river as we came down? Cast off, then, and let us go.'

Five minutes afterwards they were over the falls, in the depths of a fearful whirlpool, and out of the eleven men that went down but eight came out alive. Presently Frank was seen with his face up, and the chief sprang after him, but before he could reach him they were both drawn into another whirlpool immediately, sucked down, whirled and tossed about, and only the chief came out, faint and exhausted.

Twenty miles below Frank's body was seen floating down river, a wonder and a terror to the tribes, who could not imagine where the white man had come from; and then his remains were seen no more.

I have told you as much as I know, and a good deal of what I have heard, but as I have proposed to the commander of the *Sea-gull* and the English and American Consuls that they should question officially about all causes relating to Frank's death, you may hear more.

Meantime, dear Mr Pocock, believe me when I tell you that I feel his loss as keenly as though he were my brother. Sorrow is difficult to measure, and is expressed by different people in different ways. My tears are over, the indescribable grief I felt when I was assured that I should see my amiable, faithful Frank no more has lost its intensity; but even now, whenever my mind recurs to those days of danger, despair, and death, I feel my heart sinking when memory recalls the day I lost Frank. My pity and sympathy are also roused each time I think of you. I had flattered myself of the pride I should feel when I should be able to tell you that there was not a finer, braver, better, young man in the world than your son, Frank. Now, what is it I can show you, what can I tell you, but the sad, sad story of your son's death?

Whenever you think what a pity it is, believe me I can echo even your very thought. Whenever you sigh for his fate, believe that there is one who sighs with you. Whenever you grieve, believe that I sympathise truly in your grief.

HENRY M. STANLEY

P.S. — I shall take charge of the papers, letters, and journals of Edward and Frank until I can send them to you safely. Their more interesting papers, which I am sure you will be glad to see, I shall send by mail.

HIPPO!

CANOEING THE SELINDA SPILLWAY IN BOTSWANA –
A FEAT POSSIBLE ONLY EVERY THIRTY YEARS OR SO
– IS ARGUABLY THE MOST EXCLUSIVE ADVENTURE IN
THE WORLD. IT'S ALSO POTENTIALLY LETHAL, AS
NIGEL RICHARDSON DISCOVERED

Hilton – Hilts to his friends – thought it was a boulder. Then the boulder moved as he canoed across the top of it. A couple of tons of hippopotamus rose behind him, its gargantuan jaws yawning to reveal a pink mouth equipped with huge, razor-sharp teeth before snapping shut like the mechanism of a refuse truck.

In that split-second Ryan, in the canoe behind, was convinced his drinking buddy was a goner. But the jaws had missed the man and hit the canoe. Screaming "Hippo!", Hilts spilt into the water as the hippo dived. Ten feet to one side, I watched aghast as the seconds ticked by and Hilts struggled to get back in his boat before the hippo found him. Suddenly it felt absurdly hubristic to be here at all, on this latter-day River Styx, amid such remote and dangerous wilderness. Was Hilts to be a sacrificial offering?

We were attempting to complete a pioneering canoe trail across the north-eastern corner of Botswana, one of the wildest tracts of southern Africa, where vast herds of elephant and buffalo roam, and hippos lurk like unexploded depth charges in river drop-offs. If we succeeded, it would be a feat not accomplished before in living memory.

The Kalahari Desert covers almost the entirety of Botswana, but in the far north the Okavango River flows down from Angola, its channels and lagoons spreading into the ragged and fluent shape of a scarecrow's hand: the wildlife-rich Okavango Delta. Every thirty years or so (the last time was in the early Eighties) the waters that feed the delta – and the Kwando River to the east – rise to such an extent that they flood a normally dry channel of grassland immediately to the north called the Selinda Spillway.

The spillway, which reaches a width of 100 yards in some places but even at high water is seldom deeper than a man's height, snakes south-west to north-east for nearly sixty miles through the 300,000-acre Selinda private game reserve, a former trophy-hunting concession now given over to upmarket, eco-friendly tourism in a handful of safari camps.

The rising waters are a mysterious hydrological event in which faultlines in the earth's crust also play their part. And this summer – Botswana's winter – the waters have been flowing further and deeper than anyone can remember. As you read this, the spillway continues to fill up at both its western and eastern ends, the two channels separated by a daily diminishing section of dry land.

By canoeing this miraculous and temporary river we hoped to confer on ourselves a kind of immortality – not quite what Achilles' mother had in mind when she dipped him in the Styx, but a modest immortality nevertheless. As Hilts had said, 'We'll be among just a handful of people in the world who can say they have canoed the Selinda Spillway.'

Apart from the sheer hell of it, the purpose of the trip was to see how feasible it would be for tourists to do the same later in the season. It's a 'thumbsuck' – anyone's guess – how long the waters will last, but it should be possible to canoe at least part of the way well into October.

Given the rarity of the spillway phenomenon, not to mention the intrepid nature of the undertaking, this can justifiably be called the most exclusive adventure in the world, and it had attracted an appropriately exclusive bunch of white southern African adventurers (plus this white-kneed journo). Hardened bush hands who have dropped a charging elephant at twenty paces, then gone back to sharpening their bowie knives on their chin stubble, were rendered dewy-eyed by the prospect of canoeing the spillway.

They included Grant, our khaki-clad trail leader, and man-mountain Ryan, a former big-game hunter who now runs a wildlife camp in Tanzania. Around the fire at Motswiri bush camp on our first night, we nursed goblets of Famous Grouse as Grant delivered his briefing to a soundtrack of amphibian burps and blips from the encircling waters.

'The spillway is quite confusing, I won't kid you,' he said. 'No one really knows the way. Generally you just go with the flow.' After advice on the necessity of wearing sunblock, keeping hydrated and watching out for V-shapes on the water's surface (indicating submerged obstacles), he broached the hippopotamus issue: 'If the worst comes to the worst, and you do get dumped out of your canoe by a hippo, swim for the bank. The thing to keep in mind always is that they're more scared than you. They're cacking themselves.'

We appreciated the thought, but the fact is that hippos are responsible for more human deaths than any other African animal (apart, of course, from man himself). When the comical fatty with his pink undersides and bemused Oliver Hardy stare encounters hairless bipeds at close quarters, he tends to turn homicidal.

Who slept entirely free of doubts that night? Certainly not Hilts. The last thing he had said to his wife when he left his home in Durban, South Africa, early that morning was that he had a thing about hippos.

At 8.30 the next morning our four two-berth fibreglass Canadian canoes, with bedrolls and baggage loaded between the seats to provide ballast, nosed off through tea-coloured water in which land grasses waved like Ophelia's tresses. Ahead of us went the camp hands and cook with tents, equipment and food, to set up lunch and evening camp in suitably shady spots on the riverbank.

The spillway was very shallow at first. No chance here of lurking hippo. The water coiled lazily back on itself, while the flooded vehicle road ran through the coils like the perpendicular lines through a dollar symbol. At one point we paddled past a sign that said 'Restricted road. Authorised entry only.'

Grant has driven the vehicle road countless times. He knows this territory like the back of his hand. But seeing it from the water was different, like rereading a familiar novel in a foreign language. For the animals, too, it was an unknown quantity. 'They're still learning that they've got water,' he said. This probably accounted for so few sightings of big game on the first day – just a lone bull hippo, 100 yards away on the far bank, nursing a wound on his back and manifestly no threat to us.

We relaxed, lulled by the splash and rhythm of the paddles and the tickle of paddle-drip on our bare legs. Dead trees with branches the shape of forked lightning lined the banks, a flock of pygmy geese flapped across our bows. Pied kingfisher hovered and dived. 'Red-billed wood hoopoe,' said Grant, cocking an ear. 'The Zulu call it "cackling woman."'

In the afternoon we canoed over the intact skeleton of an elephant resting on the spillway bottom, and circled back over it, mesmerised by the sight of the huge skull, both noble and sad. As the evening light turned the surface of the spillway pearlescent shades of blue and lilac, Grant and Ryan caught bream, which we cooked over the camp fire that night. And no fears troubled our sleep.

It was after lunch on the second day that fear raised its head and flashed its jaws. We had snoozed on the river bank and were now paddling gently through apparently shallow waters. But below us, in a sandy hollow, slept a one-eared hippo (the other ear he had almost certainly lost to a lion).

When Hilton's canoe brushed the top of him, he rose from the water in a reflex of anger and fear and bit hard. Later, studying the teeth marks on the back of the canoe, we realised that he had missed Hilton's back by no more than the span of a hand.

But the danger was not over. The hippo had managed to tilt Hilts into the water. As he scrambled to get back in the canoe, he disclosed later, a thought had flashed through his mind: what would it be like to spend the rest of your life without legs? After what seemed like minutes, but was probably no more than five seconds, Hilton managed to haul himself back into his waterlogged canoe.

He paddled furiously to the bank, where we joined him to assess the damage and relive the moment. When he saw just how deep and wide were the teeth marks in the back of the canoe – and how close they were to where he had been sitting – the colour drained from his face and his jaw went slack.

'I saw him come right out the water,' said Ryan, holding his hands wide apart to mime those colossal jaws opening and snapping shut. 'In my mind he'd got you, Hilton.' Twenty yards away, in the middle of the spillway, old one-ear continued to watch us balefully. Hilts fumbled to light a cigarette – his lighter had got wet – then, in a state of shock, did a strange thing: he handed out his business card to everyone. By a grim irony, the hippo had chosen to nearly kill the sales, marketing and public relations manager of one of southern Africa's most famous and highly respected safari and conservation companies. My first thought was: does publicity get any worse than this?

Unwittingly Grant had an immediate retort, in the form of his own rhetorical question. 'I tell you what,' he said, 'this is an adventure, eh? Why do people love Africa? Because it's safe?'

And he was right. Statistically what had just happened is extremely rare – hippo will almost always move out of the way if they hear or see you coming – but the African bush is not bound by the legislation of the Health and Safety Executive. Having stepped straight from my highly regulated, risk-averse Western culture, I was feeling uniquely alive to be sharing a habitat with huge, intriguing animals that could as easily kill me as scratch themselves. Or, as Ryan said laconically, chewing a blade of grass, 'Africa is not for sissies.'

It was time to get back on the bike. But the mood of the group had changed. In place of the banter, and the eager spotting of animals and birds, we canoed through pools of reflective silence broken only by the splashing of paddles – and the warning drum of those paddles on the sides of our canoes whenever we saw darker, deeper water. 'Everyone is contemplating the hippo,' said Grant quietly.

Over the camp fire and the scotch that evening the incident was gone over as obsessively as if we each had handsets with which to replay and freeze it at different moments. Filthy jokes followed, then thrillingly grue-some near-death stories of the bush: of a man who had half his face eaten by hyenas and another who now wears a corset after being disembowelled – by a hippo. We were exorcising our fear.

On the third day we walked nearly nine miles strap across the dry middle section of the Spillway to reach the eastern channel (by now the waters may well have joined and the walk will not be necessary). On this eastern side floodplains spread from the spillway's banks. Sedge grew high at the water's edge, blocking our view, making us nervous. 'Ambush alley,' said Grant, indicating the gaps in the sedge. 'There are a load of hippo here. A lot.'

Before reaching the end of the trail – the luxurious Selinda Camp, a five-star treat after the grunginess of three nights of fly-camping on the river bank – we saw a breeding herd of elephant at the water's edge, and in golden afternoon light a bull crossed the spillway right in front of us. We also stopped to inspect the carcase of a buffalo, killed by a lion within the previ-ous 48 hours. The putrefying skeleton, still red with blood and fringed with membrane, buzzed with flies. 'He's nice, eh?' murmured Ryan affection-ately. 'A beautiful old boy.'

But it was another hippo that bade us bon voyage on our historic paddle. On one of the spillway's final bends, as we were dreaming of hot showers and cold beers, he rose, snorted and displayed his fearsome dental weap-onry. 'A big bull,' said Grant. 'He's cranky for sure. Howzit, boy?'

'Dammit,' said Hilts, 'my heart can't take much more of this.'

A BEAST OF A MASS MOVEMENT

IT'S ONE OF THE GREAT DRAMAS OF THE NATURAL WORLD: THE MIGRATION OF WILDEBEEST AND ZEBRA FROM TANZANIA TO KENYA ACROSS THE MARA RIVER. **DAVID BLAIR** WATCHED IT UNFOLD

You could sense the agony of their indecision. A herd of wildebeest stood frozen in their tracks a few hundred yards from the raging torrent of the Mara river. They stared at the swollen brown waters, broken by rapids hurling white spray across a surging current. Two Nile crocodiles lurked on glistening black rocks beside the river. The flared nostrils and bulging eyes of three hippos emerged from the middle of the waterway. Thick bush and long grass lined the riverbank, offering ideal cover for a lion ambush. I saw all these hazards from my vantage point a little down the river. The wildebeest had been weighing them up for several hours.

The plains beyond the river must have been cruelly tantalising. Green, rain-ripened grass stretched to the foot of the Olooolo Siria escarpment. Vast, distant formations of black clouds heralded still more rains on the other side. I knew the wildebeest could smell the heavy rainclouds because I smelt them, too. I watched, transfixed, as they grappled with their decision. To cross or not to cross? It was only my second day in the Maasai Mara, Africa's most famous wildlife reserve, in south-western Kenya, and already I was hooked.

This herd of about 100 wildebeest was the vanguard of the great migration, the largest movement of land mammals on earth. Huge herds entered the Maasai Mara a few weeks ago in search of fresh grazing, crossing into Kenya from the Serengeti.

The herd began moving in single file towards the river. They walked with painful slowness, pausing after every few steps to raise their heads and stare at the torrent once again. It took the best part of an hour for the wildebeest to cross 100 yards of open ground and reach the edge of the river.

The herd halted for a long, final stare and another bout of agonised indecision. Then a lone wildebeest moved ahead of the others, tripping down the bank and plunging headlong into the Mara. Slipping on wet rocks, it lurched into the deepest waters and swam furiously, only its head and horns visible above the spray. Another wildebeest followed, and another. Then the whole herd was surging forwards and splashing into the river, slipping on treacherous, shining black rocks or thrashing wildly in the rapids. The current pushed them far downstream. I watched a calf floundering behind its mother as waves buffeted its tiny head.

By now, the leading animal had reached the rocks on the far side and was scrambling for the bank. After a few seconds of frenzied movement, during which the helpless wildebeest would have been easy meat for any predator, it clambered to safety and galloped on to the green plain beyond. Others managed to follow, but as they emerged unscathed, I watched a crisis erupt behind them. One wildebeest lost its nerve just before entering the water. In panic, it turned and galloped away. Its terror was contagious and a split-second later dozens of animals were turning away from the river.

Every wildebeest that took the plunge into the Mara had survived, including the struggling calf. No lions emerged from the bush and the crocodiles remained motionless. But about thirty animals had turned back at the last moment. Some were calves, separated in the confusion from mothers that had managed to cross. With more than half the herd safely on the far bank and darkness falling, these wildebeest faced a night in lion country, deprived of the safety of numbers.

EGYPT MINUS THE MULTITUDE

THERE WERE 400 SHIPS PLYING THE NILE BETWEEN
LUXOR AND ASWAN, BUT ONLY SIX CRUISING LAKE
NASSER. **PETER HUGHES** ENJOYED THE DIFFERENCE

For 4,000 years, ever since a pharaoh first raised a sail, or his slaves an oar, Nile cruises have plied between Luxor and Aswan. The modern voyage typically takes three days and at times can be almost hectic. There is a schedule to keep and the river gets crowded. In high season, with everyone wanting to do the sightseeing at the coolest times of day, you can be piled into sites already heaving with visitors from other boats. In some places the cruise ships berth ten abreast, so passengers on the last vessel to arrive have to traipse across nine other ships to reach the shore. Nevertheless, a Nile cruise remains one of the classic journeys that everyone should make at least once.

There are ways to calm the pace. You can choose a longer, more relaxed itinerary or travel on one of the smaller and slower sailing cruisers called dahabeeyahs. In whatever style you do it, your trip will almost certainly include a day trip by air from Aswan to Abu Simbel. However, there is a real alternative. Go to Abu Simbel by all means: it's one of the fabled spectacles of the planet. But do it the way the ancients did. Go by boat.

Cruise ships can't pass the dams at Aswan, so you have to change vessels before spending another three days' cruising south on the waters of Lake Nasser. It could hardly be more different. If you want a measure of just how different, consider this: on the Luxor-Aswan section of the river there are some 400 cruise ships, though they seldom all operate at the same time. On Lake Nasser, there are six.

Lake Nasser was created by the Aswan high dam, which was completed in 1970. Named after Egypt's second president, Gamal Abdel Nasser, it's one of the largest man-made lakes in the world. Nearly a third of its 340-mile length is in Sudan.

Whatever its economic benefits — electricity, increased agricultural land — it also brought devastation to the riverside in what was the old kingdom of Nubia. More than 50,000 people, whose homes were to be inundated, had to be resettled. With surprising vehemence one of my guides in Cairo declared, 'What Nasser did to the Nubians was a crime.'

Not just people were moved. Some of the oldest monuments of human civilisation were uprooted, dismantled and reconstructed above the lake. The temples of Abu Simbel are the most famous but there were more than twenty others. Garnered from the river banks by international teams of engineers and archaeologists, they were taken to safety in an extraordinary rescue operation instigated by Unesco. One temple, Amada, was put on rails and dragged uphill, intact, for more than a mile, 900 tons of it. All nine sites visited on this cruise would be under water had they not been transplanted, by anything up to 35 miles. Now they have been grouped along the lake shore in three small clusters, making them easier to see and manage.

With the exception of Abu Simbel, the temples are small, but their chamber walls are adorned with some of the most graphic tableaux in Egypt, vibrantly coloured paintings and reliefs. Together they make a high-definition documentary of dynasties already ancient to the ancient Greeks. We had our own guides and we had the temples to ourselves, landing at each by launch, and escorted by two white-uniformed policemen toting automatic rifles. A gesture, one suspects, if not a job, for the boys.

Our ship was the *Kasr Ibrim*. Built in 1997 in the style of a Twenties steamship, expressly to work on Lake Nasser, it was not dissimilar to the old post boat that plied between Aswan and Wadi Halfa, in the Sudan, at the turn of the last century. Its picture is in the Nubian Museum at Aswan, which was donated eleven years ago by the Egyptian government as atonement for the indignities done to the Nubian people and the near eradication of their culture.

The post boat was little more than a steel hull with a large, colonial-style pavilion on top. *Kasr Ibrim* is like that, but its pavilion has four storeys. The interior, efficiently air-conditioned, is art deco in style. The lounge would pass for a set in an episode of *Poirot*. Besides the parquet floor, timber panelling and hefty, period armchairs, the room is planted with wood-clad columns. Their capitals are like stylised lotus flowers, the 'blooms' illuminated behind alabaster lights. The decor is a front — the ship has more modern facilities than the retro style would suggest. All but seven of the sixty-five cabins have balconies; ten of them are suites. There's a sauna and Turkish bath on the bottom deck and a pool and Jacuzzi on top. Every cabin has a fridge and a bath, whirlpool baths in the suites. I would reduce *Kasr Ibrim*'s official five stars to four, if only because every meal but one was a buffet. As for the food, travellers of the early twentieth century would be familiar with the menus of meat-and-much-veg, fish from the Red Sea, all served in copious quantities.

We sailed at 7 a.m. Our departure was imperceptible. Before I realised, we had left our berth in front of an echoing terminal building at Aswan and its small, disconsolate population of security men. Now we headed south, upstream, into the Nubian Desert, on grey-green water dimpled by the breeze.

To the west ran a low, flat bank of buff-coloured sand; to the east a range of small hills, jagged like the rim of a broken dish, and dark in the morning shadow. About a mile separated them. It was a scene empty of life – no birds or boats on the water, no sign of habitation on the land. Correction: at five past nine I saw a single fisherman in a small, white boat way off to starboard. There was another, four hours later, although where this one was headed, or had come from, was a mystery.

The land was a void of blackened rock in which every hollow and crevice was filled with unblemished drifts of beige sand. Only sailing in polar regions have I seen such empty places, although there the colours are different, and, of course, the temperature. By midday, in late May, the sun was caustically hot, even in the shade of the parasols on the top deck. That first morning we crossed the Tropic of Cancer.

The lake widened and then tapered. The hills seemed to swap banks. At first they were on one side, then the other. For a time they became distinctly pyramidal, nature's little parody of man's efforts downstream. Later they rose on both banks, growing almost to the stature of mountains. They pressed in on the channel to form what must have once been an impressive gorge but today are no more than narrows.

We passed the occasional navigational marker and two other cruise ships making for Aswan. At 5 p.m. we stopped, nosing into shore on a rocky island where mooring posts awaited our lines. This is Ramses country. Or it was 3,250 years ago when Ramses the Great, the most famous of all the pharaohs, ruled Egypt. He was Ozymandias, Shelley's king of kings, whose 'sneer of cold command' chilled his desert domains. 'Look on my works, ye mighty, and despair!' goes the poem: if you substitute the word 'cower' for 'despair', you understand the purpose of the monuments he built on these banks of the upper Nile, a land strategically important and rich in gold.

At the rock temple of Beit al-Wali, relocated just upstream of the High Dam, the wall paintings show the pharaoh smiting Hittites and taking slaves. He is also seen accepting gifts of giraffes, gold and ivory from grateful Nubians.

Ramses raised temples as politicians put up campaign posters. Many were decorated with statues of himself. They were instruments of propaganda, designed to impress, if not intimidate, the locals. They also sated Ramses's vanity. At the El Seboua temple he is depicted as a god, a heresy he would never have got away with at Luxor where Amon-Re was chief among the deities. Millennia later, the Romans, who seldom missed an imperial trick, had images of the emperor Augustus, kitted out as an Egyptian king, added to the temple of Dakka as an embellishment.

In the temple of Derr, which has some of the best wall paintings of all, Ramses appears as both king and god. But the apotheosis of his self-promotion is at Abu Simbel. We arrived in time to have lunch on deck, while the boat drifted offshore in front of the colossi of Ramses's ultimate temple. Now and then the captain would turn the ship so passengers on each side could share the view.

Abu Simbel has a polish and swagger that the smaller, unsung temples along the lake do not. That is partly down to Ramses and his unerring sense of the spectacular — the four 70-feet-high statues of himself alone land him top of the extravagant league of personality cults. But it is also because we are back on tourism's beaten track.

For me Abu Simbel represented both the continuation and the conclusion of the distinctiveness of the Lake Nasser cruise. The continuation came in the afternoon when I had the rare experience of sharing the entire Abu Simbel site with just five other visitors. The conclusion came that night at the *son et lumière* and its sonorous, bloated commentary. Simultaneously translated into half a dozen languages, and bereft of sense in every one of them, it relieved itself of such lines as: 'Memory, like the night, is but a promise' and 'The plenitude of the pharaoh is the splendour of his reign'. Ramses, of course, would have loved it.

Chapter 5
ASIA & AUSTRALASIA

---

6 MARCH 1999

FUN? THIS WILL TEACH YOU

IN EASTERN INDIA WITH SWAN HELLENIC,
GRAHAM TURNER LEARNS THAT KNOWLEDGE COMES
FIRST – AND SHOPPING IS AN UNSPEAKABLE SIN

'Liturgically,' said the Bishop of Oxford, 'this is a difficult time to be going on a cruise.' It was Ash Wednesday, the beginning of Lent, and we were eating breakfast on the deck of the *Minerva* in the sultry heat of Calcutta. But there is no theological hurdle that an Anglican prelate cannot negotiate. The bishop smiled expansively. 'We shall just have to make a special dispensation,' he said.

He clearly felt that his flock was all around him. 'Whenever anyone asks me where the Church of England is today,' he murmured complacently, 'I always tell them: "On a Swan Hellenic cruise".'

More than any ship I have sailed on, the *Minerva* is a people-like-us affair. Its devotees – and at least 80 per cent of the passengers are repeat customers – share a range of attitudes. They believe, for example, that television has fallen into the seedy clutches of the yob element and that there is simply nothing worth watching these days. They would never be seen dead on any ship carrying a sizeable number of American passengers because it would be, as one put it, 'a cultural desert'. And they regard those who waste their time ashore shopping rather than soaking up the local culture as intellectually enfeebled. As far as they are concerned, shopping – like sex – is meant to be an entirely private activity.

Their extraordinary like-mindedness springs from the fact that, apart from a sprinkling of aristocrats and the occasional nouveau riche, they are all members of that endangered species, the traditional British bourgeoisie: bankers, barristers, admirals, brigadiers, retired tea-planters, Tory politicians and medics of every conceivable variety.

They board the *Minerva* with an enormous sigh of relief, as if passing through the portals of their favourite club. And then they talk and talk... and talk, as if for the previous year they have been starved of intelligent and congenial conversation. They talk over breakfast at 5.30 before setting out on four-hour coach journeys. They discuss the doctrine of karma in the swimming pool. They even mull over the latest lecture while working out in the ship's modest gym. There are no awkward silences. In fact, there are no silences of any kind, except in the library. I have never before seen such instant and unfailing cordiality among the British. If you are looking for an extended family, the *Minerva* is not a bad substitute.

The cruise was to take us around the coast of India. After a glimpse of Calcutta, a city still ringing with imperial echoes, we inched our way down the reaches of the Hugli river on the first leg of our journey. And, having listened to a perfectly seemly lecture about the mysteries of Hinduism, we caught a startling glimpse of its earthy reality at Bhubaneshwar, which bills itself as the Temple City. There had been veiled references in the lecture to what sounded to me like phallic symbols. To make sure I had not misunderstood, I asked our guide what the main point of it was. 'Hindus believe,' he replied, 'that if ladies find a man who is, let us say, well-endowed, they will lead a happy life. So a lot of unmarried ladies come here every Monday to pray that they will find such a thing.'

We were to see many temples – Hindu temples, Jain temples, Buddhist temples, temples to Shiva, temples to Vishnu, elegant temples, temples of mesmerising vulgarity. At each we dutifully took off our shoes before entering. But when we were asked to do the same at the Catholic church in Cochin, where Vasco da Gama was buried before being ferried back to Portugal, a former Tory MP would have none of it. 'The only doctrinal point on which the C of E is united,' he declared, 'is that we wear shoes in church.'

As the days went by, we discovered that this was no pleasure cruise, at least in the hedonistic sense. Our fellow-passengers were eager to learn everything about India – its religion, history, architecture, art. They were ready to suffer anything – interminable bone-shaking journeys in non-air-conditioned coaches (one of which boasted an ants' nest) on appalling roads, with 'natural' lavatory facilities, in relentless heat – in pursuit of that knowledge. Getting up at five in the morning, said one woman, was no problem. At school, she had had to run a mile before breakfast every day.

The intervals between our forays into the interior were packed with lectures, four a day when we were at sea. 'Good heavens!' said one woman, as she tore herself away from a self-improving novel. 'It's time for another lecture! We live by the clock, don't we? I'm sure it's good for our aesthetic soul.' One session was mouthwateringly billed as 'Stories of Empire'. 'Actually,' said the lecturer apologetically, 'it should have read "Stones of Empire".' It was another talk about imperial architecture. Not a single member of the audience moved. Nobody even groaned.

Non-intellectual diversions are severely rationed. 'We don't do entertainment,' said the cruise director. 'No origami, no embroidery and no folding of napkins in the lounge.' When, in Madras, a handful of ladies begged to be allowed a little time ashore to buy saris, a militant non-shopper inquired: 'Just who are these women?' In Kandy, we visited the gilded glories of the Temple of the Tooth, which houses a relic said to be one of the Buddha's molars, and learnt everything we had ever wanted to know about Sri Lanka and elephants.

Back in India, there was no escape from the kindly eye of the elephant. Our Tory MP swore that he had seen a pink one – and before lunch. On the way from Cochin to visit the Syrian churches of Kottayam, we came upon yet another pachyderm at the heart of a procession collecting offerings for a temple. This was not one of your low-key campaigns. The procession was led by five drummers, a bell-ringer and a wild-haired holy man wielding a sword, which he deployed vigorously when anyone tried to take his photograph. 'He's an ascetic who speaks in the name of God,' explained the guide. 'At drop of a hat, he will go into a trance and tell you what you need to give to please the god.' Heaven alone knows what he does if your offering does not come up to scratch.

In Goa, we encountered another holy man. At a splendid temple in the hills, he was interceding with Vishnu on behalf of a group of pilgrims from Bombay who were apparently having family difficulties. For half an hour or so he bombarded the idol with prayers, with much beating of breast and wagging of finger. Finally, he collapsed into the arms of his acolytes. 'Warm work,' I said to him sympathetically. He was not amused.

'It's all supernatural,' explained one of the group. 'He doesn't feel anything. The god just comes into his body and then he can guide us as to what we should do in the future.' So what wisdom had he brought back from his trance? 'That we should lead a more peaceful and contented life,' the pilgrim replied. They had spent sixteen hours in a coach for that.

We disembarked at Bombay after what had been a fascinating, if arduous, odyssey. The *Minerva* is undoubtedly the busiest cruise ship afloat. Its schedules are not for the faint-hearted. The cabins are perfectly adequate for those who regard luxury as effete, the food is good and the company delightful.

In one way, though, the most extraordinary thing about the entire trip was that not once on all the long coach journeys did anyone ask for a comfort stop, although the vast majority were well over pensionable age. This was the spirit that built the Empire. Nonetheless, it was a considerable relief to sink into my airline seat for the flight back to London.

THE BEAUTIFUL AND THE DAMMED

IN CHINA'S THREE GORGES AREA, **MICHAEL KERR** SEES SIGHTS THAT ARE ABOUT TO BE SUBMERGED

Six-fifteen in the morning on the Yangtse. The navigation markers were still lit – pyramids of light looking like tiny metal sailing boats in the muddy water. A junk puttered past yards from the stern of the *Viking Century Star*, but in the mist its helmsman was no more than a shrouded huddle and the brief flare of a cigarette.

Grey-walled flats and houses lined both banks. Below them lush terraces of rice paddies fell to the water. But there was not a light on in a village, not a soul stirring in a field. It seemed odd that while a tourist on a cruise vessel was up and about the peasants of China were still in their beds. Then realisation dawned. These homes had been cleared – of every stick of furniture and every person who had used it. In five years' time, the buildings and the fields below them would be under water.

Spookier still, our ship was gliding over settlements that had already been consumed, their people among the two million who, by 2009, will have been forced from their homes and seen them flooded. Theirs are the villages of the dammed.

China is building another Great Wall, this time across its principal river. With the steel and concrete of the Three Gorges Dam, the Yangtse is to be tamed and put to work. Last year the dam's giant sluices were closed and within a fortnight the river had risen to 440ft above sea level. By 2009, the trick will be repeated, the waters reaching 580ft.

The Chinese government says the project will not only make the river more navigable but protect its middle and lower reaches from the sort of floods that, in the past century alone, have claimed a million lives. The dam's turbines will provide as much electricity as 10 nuclear power plants, increasing national output by 10 per cent.

Or will it? Critics say that the dam, which is being built on an earthquake fault and will hold back a lake 400 miles long, is a disaster waiting to happen. Even if it doesn't break, silt and sewage – pumped untreated into the river from many cities – could build up behind it, leaving 10,000-ton ships stuck in a bog.

Whatever the truth, the Three Gorges area, famed for its tree-clad chasms, celebrated in Chinese prose and poetry, will be changed for ever. Hence the posters and the brochures urging us to 'Go now and see it while you can'.

British tour operators have long been offering cruises on the Yangtse, but on Chinese ships. I joined the inaugural trip of the *Viking Century Star*, which is a joint venture even in name. A Chinese state enterprise, New Century, built the ship and provides the nautical staff; but the hotel side of the business is managed by Viking River Cruises, a company based in Basle that has been operating in Europe since 1997 and which offers cruises in cities from Paris to St Petersburg.

Chongqing, where we boarded the *Century Star*, is a two-hour flight from Beijing. It's nearly 1,000 miles from Shanghai and the ocean, but will effectively be turned into a seaport when the Three Gorges dam project is finished. It's a grey and smoggy city, erupting with buildings of a startling ugliness. A French tour company rep was heard to mutter that her clients would love the Three Gorges, but mustn't see Chongqing in daylight.

For the launch cruise, the greyness was dispelled by dragon dancers and a brass band; and if the port was lacking in the quaintness of Viking's European destinations, the ship was not short of comforts. Viking claims the *Century Star* is the best-appointed cruise vessel on the Yangtse. It is certainly a few notches above the rustbuckets we saw during our four days. Better victualled, too: it has a Western-style kitchen that served up not only Chinese food (surprisingly bland on our trip) but also anything from a steak to a (delicious) spinach-and-ricotta-cheese parcel.

Viking bought the vessel when it was almost built, and it falls short of the standards of the European fleet. An air conditioner roars in the dining room. A slight vibration can be felt from time to time through the floors. But neither of these will ruin anyone's holiday.

Cabins are spacious and comfortable, with mod cons including a phone, a television and even a socket that takes a three-pin British plug. If you want a hairdryer, however, you have to ask for one at reception. As Viking's chairman, Torstein Hagen, put it, 'Our customers are not so fussed about the hair, anyway; they are more concerned about what is going on inside the head.'

In Europe, history and heritage are what draw Viking's customers – but on the Yangtse both of them are being submerged. One survivor so far has been the Shibaozhai Temple, an extraordinary twelve-storey wooden building that hugs the side of a 720ft cliff. As we filed off the ship to see it, we passed a graphic showing how an island and a mini dam would protect the temple come the next rise in the waters. It had all the believability of a *Thunderbirds* set.

In a pond in a courtyard at the temple's summit, there lay a grey-black creature about two-and-a-half feet long, in the shape of a flattened spoon with a broad handle. Tiddlers flashed silver around it. Coins had been dropped in the pond, so I dropped another to see whether the giant would move. It didn't, so I took it for a fake.

Then one of the guides told me it was a salamander, caught by a fisherman in the Yangtse in 1987. It would move only when driven by hunger to snatch at one of the tiddlers, he said; hence the local saying, 'As lazy as the salamander in the temple'.

Laziness wasn't a failing in evidence on the ship the following morning. A dozen of us, having been told we would be entering Qutang Gorge, the shortest and narrowest of the Three Gorges, at seven, were up well before then to see it, the river banks closing in, the cliffs rising sheer from the water, clothed in green. But the light was flat, monochromatic; not for nothing does Viking bill this cruise the 'Misty Mountains of the Yangtse'.

The light was better and the water clearer in the Lesser Three Gorges area, on a tributary of the Yangtse, the Daning. Having docked at Wushan and boarded a smaller vessel, we spent the best part of a day here, setting off at 10 a.m. on a five-hour round trip that included a picnic lunch on shore.

Our guide had promised that the Daning would be narrower, its walls higher, the scenery more dramatic. We would see the boat-shaped coffins that the Ba people had installed in ancient times on natural shelves on the sheer cliff face. And so it all came to pass. But he had made another promise, and after half an hour he had still not delivered.

'When do we see the monkeys?' asked a travel agent from Florida. 'You said there'd be lots of them. So where are they?'

The guide, as scrawny as the American was stout, told him there would soon be a subject worthy of his lens. There were more than 10,000 rhesus monkeys living along the Lesser Three Gorges. 'We have no birth control for the monkeys,' he said with a smile. 'No family planning for them.' Public joking about government policy was not something I had expected in China. Nor was voluntary candour.

As we entered the Lesser Three Gorges, the guide had told us that a bridge built as recently as 1987 would have to be rebuilt because the rising

Yangtse would stop only 10 yards below it. 'This bridge,' he said, 'is a very big, very expensive mistake.'

No one is likely to say that publicly about the dam, where we arrived the following day. We had been warned that we would not sleep through our entry into the locks that precede it. I was woken around five by a loud clang and the sensation of being at the bottom of a well with a giant laughing maniacally at me from the top. The giant, possibly, was someone bellowing orders through a loudspeaker.

Through the cabin window I could see nothing but a grimy concrete wall with a set of metal rungs climbing it. I opened the window, got a lungful of diesel fumes, and immediately shut it. The *Century Star* spent the best part of four hours going through the locks, with five other ships, all belching fumes. The smoggy waters of the Yangtse.

Our penultimate stop was an exhibition about the building of the dam, complete with scale models, photographs of heroic workers and an exhibit about the Chinese Sturgeon Institute. (The dam will prevent the sturgeon returning upstream to spawn, so the institute is netting the fish and, once they have spawned, returning their fry to the Yangtse.) Then it was on to the dam itself, to gaze on concrete, ponder on the volume of water it was holding back and worry about what might happen if it burst.

There's a peculiar poignancy in being a tourist in the Three Gorges area, for you are seeing a sight that will not be preserved for future generations but that will be denied them. The exhibition had been all about what would be gained: the floods that would be avoided, the waters that would be made navigable, the towns that would be supplied with power. There was no mention of what would be lost.

A HYMN TO THE WATER GODDESS

GRIDLOCKED TRAFFIC HAS PROMPTED THE PEOPLE OF
BANGKOK TO GO BACK TO THE RIVER AND CANALS.
STANLEY STEWART JOINED THEM

According to the captain, the water goddess was an unpredictable old bat.
He had spent his life mollifying her. Every morning he lit incense and threw
her offerings. Every year at the Loi Krathong festival he honoured her with
a beautiful miniature boat, loaded with candles and coins. Nothing
mattered, he said. You could never trust her.

The captain had long fingers with rings like miniature shrines. He wore
an amulet against misfortune, and tattooed serpents on his arms. He was a
Bangkok sailor. It was not blood that flowed in his veins, he declared
proudly, but the muddy waters of the Chao Phraya.

In the old days Bangkok was the Venice of the East and sailors were its
cabbies. 'The highways are not streets or roads,' reported Sir John Bowring
in the mid-nineteenth century, 'but the river and the canals. Boats are the
universal means of conveyance.' Right up to the Second World War all visitors arrived in the city by boat. I wanted to follow in their wake and discover
what remained of Bangkok's watery past.

Upriver in the ancient capital of Ayutthaya, I boarded the *Mekhala*, an old
rice barge converted into a cruise boat. It had polished teak decks, rattan
chairs and cushioned sofas, and cabins with nautical prints on lacquered
walls. The captain sat amidships at a small wheel. He had a proprietorial air
not only about the *Mekhala*, but about the entire river. He had spent his life
on the Chao Phraya. Welcome, he said as we slipped our berth. We might
have been stepping across the threshold of his home.

The Chao Phraya is to Thailand what the Thames is to England: the
nation's politicians are rarely diverted from its banks. It is a working river,
full of freighters and tramp steamers and barges. Huge rafts of teak logs
drifted downriver with the loggers camped, like ill-fated holiday-makers, in
the middle of these floating islands.

Beneath cargoes of gravel and sand, the barges lay so low in the water they appeared to be sinking. The crew waded the decks ankle-deep in river, nervously lashing and unlashing ropes. The tugs that pulled them were the character actors of the Chao Phraya: cavalier craft painted in jaunty colours. Like the barges, they were home to the boatmen and their wives. The awnings were bedecked with laundry, the cabin walls with cooking pots and family portraits, and the windowsills with geraniums.

Our captain, who until recently had been one of the tug-boat fraternity, made disparaging remarks about the seamanship and private lives of the other pilots as he smiled and waved at them. The river was a happily incestuous world, riven by rogue currents and gossip.

We moored for the night at the Temple of the Short Chicken. Monks flapped about the grounds in orange robes while tribes of pariah dogs howled. By the water's edge a Buddha, wearing an Isadora Duncan scarf, smiled demurely at passing sailors.

In the temple I had a go at the shaking sticks. This is a rather useful wheeze by which the faithful can discover their fate. Kneeling before the Buddha you shake a little vase of numbered sticks until one drops out. The number of the stick corresponds to a prophecy. I shook 74. It didn't sound lucky. An elderly monk handed me my fate on a pink slip of paper. The steward on the boat translated: 'You shall be ill and find sad stories. You have made sin in former lives.'

He poured me a stiff drink. I felt as if I had been taken over by aliens. Who were these former lives? They could be anybody: serial killers, child pornographers, estate agents. God knows what they got up to.

Dinner consoled me. It was a splendid affair, taken at a table in the bow, by candlelight. The delicacy of the dishes was in direct proportion to the unpronounceability of the names. The starter was goon moo sab followed by tom yam goong. The main course was gaeng khow wan gai and nuea num mon hai.

I retired to the bar. The steward had his own problems. He could not decide whether he should be a monk or a kick-boxer. A life of spiritual enlightenment had its appeal, but as a career move there was much to be said for kicking people in the head for large sums of money. Shaken by the depravity of my own past lives, I advised celibacy and submission. The captain, however, felt professional violence was the thing. I went to bed late and dreamt I was Attila the Hun.

In the morning I found the captain sticking lighted incense into the garlands of jasmine that hung from the bow and throwing bits of breakfast into the river. The incense was for the spirit of the boat; breakfast for the spirit of the river. 'Anything to keep the old girl happy,' the captain muttered.

We pushed out on to a grey, still surface. Along the bank were the kind of houses in which Rat and Mole would have delighted. They stood on stilts above the water's edge, the current tugging at their feet; boats were moored at their doorsteps and verandas hung over the water to make every meal a picnic. Gardens of morning glory floated on the river and buoyed nets caught breakfast while the family slept. In the early light people were at their morning ablutions. They waded down their front steps into the wide warm bath of the Chao Phraya, the men in tattoos and shorts, the women in sarongs.

By midday we were sailing into Bangkok amid thickening crowds of barges, ferries, river taxis and sampans. Bridges spanned the river and the city's glittering temples began to rise from the banks. Beyond the gilded roofs of the Grand Palace and the wonderful profile of Wat Arun, Temple of Dawn, lay the Oriental Hotel, its old 'author's wing' almost hidden among the trees.

The Oriental has long been a fixture of expatriate society and a favourite of visiting celebrities from Noël Coward to Marlon Brando. Joseph Conrad cadged drinks in the bar, the King of Siam was impressed by the plumbing and Somerset Maugham was almost thrown out when he threatened to die in one of the rooms. The Oriental has been called the Old Lady of the Chao Phraya, the Hostess of Bangkok. More recently, she has been rightly described as the best hotel in the world. She has the ambience of a club.

Bangkok has not always shown its appreciation for the river that created it. With the modernisation that came in the 1950s, the city turned its back on the water. Many of the canals were filled in, and the city spread along new and faceless avenues. This affront to the water goddess did not go unpunished. Bangkok is sinking at the rate of five inches a year, considerably quicker than Venice. In the rainy season when the river swells, the streets often revert to their watery past.

The city boasts some of the greatest traffic jams this side of the M25. An average Bangkok motorist spends forty-four days per year in traffic and much thought has been devoted to in-car comfort. Cellular phones, televisions and food-warmers are commonplace. Petrol stations do a roaring trade in the Comfort 100, a portable potty that allows motorists to relieve themselves in situ.

The river and the canals are now the only escape. Many of the canals on the Thonburi side of the river survived the purge and are now the city's most delightful thoroughfares. As for the river, hotels and offices are hurrying to relocate along its banks. River transport is now the best way of getting about the city.

Turn down any of the alleys towards the river and you leave a world of traffic for one of people. At the end of lanes of coconut sellers, warehouses, riverside cafes and floating jetties, the river buses and taxis arrive and depart in a dramatic wash of water. Piers are called tha, and the Chao Phraya River Express runs the length of Bangkok from Tha Phibun to Tha Ratchasingkhon.

At Tha Tien I disembarked to have my fortune told. Wat Po is the greatest of Thai temples, a confusion of gilded chedis (towers), marble pediments, soaring roofs of green and orange tiles, serpents curling above the gables, mirrored pillars. Somerset Maugham was overcome: 'It makes you laugh with delight to think that anything so fantastic could exist on this sombre earth.'

I found a fortune-teller inside the main gate. He peered myopically at my palms, his face so close to my love lines he appeared to be smelling them. My future was sweetly scented long life, great riches, many wives, few problems and a successful family holiday some time in 1998. One couldn't have asked for more. He didn't once mention my past lives. I gave him a generous tip.

Across the river in Thonburi I took to the long-tail boats that serve as taxis through its maze of canals, or klongs. Here one finds old Bangkok, a leisurely water-borne world. Schoolchildren were waiting with their satchels on the front steps for the river bus, while women in big hats went shopping in sampans, paddling between open-fronted shops and riverside stalls. Old ladies rowed between the houses, calling through the open shutters, selling charcoal, vegetables, cut flowers and newspapers. The postman, sorting letters, passed in a little motor launch.

We cruised far out along the Klong Bangkok Noi into the Klong Kut. We were leaving the city behind and the canal was narrowing between coconut groves. People were taking swims from their doorsteps. We came upon a floating market, a village affair, where the sampans of buyers and sellers nudged between a row of canalside shops.

Life in these watery lanes seemed to have taken on the peaceful rhythms of the river lapping the porches. It was just the place to escape one's past lives.

THE GERMAN WHO CANOED TO AUSTRALIA

BY **NICK SQUIRES** IN SYDNEY

A German adventurer who spent seven years canoeing from Europe to Australia during the 1930s, only to be interned as an enemy alien on the eve of the Second World War, is finally being feted for his extraordinary and ill-fated journey.

Oskar Speck, an amateur canoeist and unemployed electrician from Ulm, set out to paddle from Germany to Cyprus in May 1932, hoping to find work at a copper mine. Seven years and four months later, on 20 September 1939, he landed on a remote island in the Torres Strait, just off the coast of northern Queensland. Using two canoes, the first of which was adorned with a swastika, he had travelled more than 30,000 miles.

During his epic voyage Mr Speck was robbed, shot at, hailed as a god and accused of being a Nazi spy, although the extent of his Nazi sympathies is unclear. Belatedly, Sydney's National Maritime Museum is devoting an exhibition to his strange and dangerous search for work.

Mr Speck lost his job as an electrical contractor in Hamburg in 1931. He was desperate to leave Germany, then in the grip of economic depression. 'The times were catastrophic,' he later recalled. 'All I wanted was to get out for a while.'

Travelling on a tight budget, with limited supplies of tinned meat, choc-olate, cheese and condensed milk, he paddled down the Danube and Varda rivers to Bulgaria and Yugoslavia. After reaching the Mediterranean at Thessalonika in Greece, he hoisted a small sail and island-hopped through the Aegean. The kayak then hugged the coast of Turkey all the way to Cyprus. By this time, according to the exhibition organisers, the prospect of life in a copper mine was less attractive than a journey into the unknown.

Postponing his job hunt, Mr Speck paddled on to Syria and made his way to the Euphrates river, where he was shot at after refusing hospitality from local tribesmen. Undaunted, he continued to the Persian Gulf, where he had to order a replacement kayak.

In his white pith helmet and khaki shorts, Mr Speck then skirted the west coast of India, around Ceylon, and went up the east coast to reach Burma in 1936. He financed his trip by giving lectures along the way, including one to a troop of Boy Scouts in Madras.

Pursued by curious journalists from local newspapers, he proceeded down the west coast of Siam toward Malaya and through the Dutch East Indies. On arriving in Timor, he was beaten up by suspicious locals and suffered a perforated eardrum. Yet such mishaps failed to dampen his enthusiasm for further discovery. Black-and-white cine film, taken by Mr Speck during this phase of the journey, shows that he had become a passionate anthropologist. Timorese villagers are filmed performing a dance with swords; Balinese children use a bow and arrow to spear fish in shallows; and New Guinean tribesman are shown killing and eating a large turtle.

In 1939, as Hitler prepared to invade Poland, Mr Speck, who was suffering from bouts of malaria, arrived in Dutch New Guinea. On New Britain, off the east coast of New Guinea, he was hailed by locals as a god.

This was to be his last adventure. Three weeks after war was declared in Europe, he landed on Australian territory. After so much trauma and excitement, his final destination turned out to be an internment camp for enemy aliens in Victoria.

Although at one point Mr Speck demanded to be placed alongside 'fellow National Socialists', the Speck exhibition curator, Penny Cuthbert, said there was no other evidence that he was a committed Nazi. 'It's debatable,' she said. 'His friends have always said he had no sympathy for them.'

On his release, Mr Speck set up a successful opal-dealing business in Sydney. He died in 1995, aged 88, apparently with no regrets. 'Everywhere I went I was surrounded by crowds of people,' he said in a rare interview. 'No one had ever seen this type of boat before. But I had no idea in 1932 that I would end up in Australia.'

BUSY DOING NOTHING IN THE BACKWATERS

JAMES BEDDING WATCHES THE WORLD GO BY FROM A RICE BOAT IN KERALA, SOUTHERN INDIA

Parachuting out of my dream, I opened my eyes to watch the horizon rocking gently through the mosquito net. A blur of swallows swooped low over the water hyacinths, feet from my floating bedroom window. A hundred feet up, a dozen egrets flapped their wings rhythmically, pulsing across the sky towards the rice paddies.

'Breakfast is ready, sir,' shouted a voice, coughing. I clambered out from under my mosquito net on to the coconut matting floor, got dressed and climbed out through the door of my cabin. Sitting on a table in the lounge were my fried eggs with toast and a flask of milky Indian tea.

I sat on one of the rattan chairs under the coconut-frond woven canopy that served as a roof and listened to the lake waking up. I could just make out two songs, coming from radios on different shores of the lake perhaps a mile away, their sinuous, nasal melodies intertwining. From somewhere else I could hear the thwack of washing being slapped against a stone. From closer by came the plosh of a boatman poling across the lake.

Exploring the canals, lakes and waterways of Kerala – the 'backwaters' – on a converted rice boat, miles from any roads, is seriously soothing. Making sure I relaxed was a team of three. Sivadas and Sahadevan took turns to operate the engine or steer, or punted together, one at each end of the boat. And then there was Syph, pronounced Sayeph – the coughing captain/cook/host/guide/navigator – a cheerful 29-year-old moustachioed Keralite with a disarmingly offbeat view of the world and a charming way with the English language. (The night before he had reassured me: 'No mosquitoes here, sir, here salt water. Only some mosquitoes live on the houseboat, sir. Permanent residents, sir. Like foreign people blood, sir.')

Most of the time I simply sat in supreme idleness, sipping tea and watching Kerala go past. Children fished in canals with bows and arrows; men stood chest-deep in the water, retrieving bags of mussels and piling them into canoes; women in dazzling saris walked along the canals under the mottled shadows of the palms, a flickering rainbow of colours shimmering along the bank above their reflection.

These backwaters, which stretch for about 50 miles along the coastal strip from Quilon in the south to Cochin in the north, form a network of about 1,200 miles of waterways punctuated with large and small lakes. Tiny islands are formed on the low-lying land and many areas are inaccessible by road. Passing through smaller canals, we would often jostle with locals zipping around in open canoes. At the beginning or end of the day we would pass launches packed with people being taken to or from work by their employers. On larger canals we encountered double-decker launches, which Syph said were local water-buses, connecting bigger villages.

Our boat was about 70ft long. It had previously been used for carrying rice or other cargo. Now, with a floor and roof put in, and divided up with a bathroom, double bedroom and large lounging area with windows – actually large flaps in the canopy, propped open with poles – it carried visitors on cruises.

Twice a day we would drop anchor, and Syph would go astern to his little pump-up stove to start one of his fabulous creations, throwing in fistfuls of spices. I would know when the turmeric went into the pan because the crew would erupt into a coughing and sneezing fit that had the boat shuddering. His meals were mouth-watering: fresh fish fried in a mixture of masala spices, accompanied by vegetables cooked with coconut, ginger, mustard seeds and curry leaves, which somehow all arrived at my table hot.

Between meals we motored and punted steadily northwards from our starting point near Quilon, reaching Alleppey about forty-eight hours later. Navigating was hit-and-miss; there was no map, so I had to talk through the alternative routes with Syph, some of which required extra money for petrol.

Like lanes, roads and motorways on land, the different waterways each had their own flavour. At times we would pass over a lake, the water indistinguishable from the sky, an identical pale grey, but for the dots of floating clumps of water hyacinth. I would watch the sea eagles hunting, the scavenging brahminy kites and countless snakebirds – like cormorants with long, thin necks. On one lake I saw a flock of about forty, swimming away from us like a forest of dancing snakes.

On the smaller canals we would pass through villages with coir factories, where women were spinning fibres from coconut husks into a twine that would be used to make coconut matting. They earned perhaps £1 a day, Syph said; the men little more for fishing.

Occasionally, on the narrow, shallow canals where we had to travel more slowly, Syph would turn off the engine and Sahadevan and Sivadas would punt us along on 15ft poles, heaving the boat gently through the shallow waters. At those times the boat fell blissfully quiet. The indolence was intoxicating.

Now and again we stopped off for a visit on land (the approach to the snake temple of Mannarassala was lined with thousands of small stone statues of cobras). That Sunday morning there must have been a couple of thousand worshippers milling around the single-storey stone buildings, making offerings, reaching out to holy men for turmeric paste — said to protect against poison — and pressing in their hundreds against an iron grille to see the 93-year-old high priestess making offerings in a darkened courtyard.

On the way we passed a long canoe with at least two dozen paddlers inside; Syph said it was a village racing boat heading for the temple to worship. We later saw one of these upturned on land — an unimaginably thin and elegant boat, 131ft long, according to a sign, carrying a crew of 120, although it was less than 5ft wide.

Opposite stood a church — like many round here, topped with a triumphant Jesus, arms outstretched. Inside, in front of a garishly painted wooden altar that reached up to the ceiling, we chatted to the sacristan, who had had the job for 63 years. He said the wooden-roofed, heavily rebuilt church was about 1,500 years old and that more than a thousand families worshipped there.

Most relaxing of all, perhaps, were the evenings. We would moor on a lake, I would take a dip, then read by the light of a hurricane lamp while Syph, spluttering over the turmeric, would prepare spicy wonders in his tiny galley. After dinner, we would chat over a beer. He told me how he had fallen in love with his wife at school when he was 16 and she 14; and how, as she is a Brahmin and he of a lower caste, they had been forced to keep their love secret; and how, when her parents found out two years later, they immediately took her out of school and started arranging a marriage for her with a boy from the same caste. Syph returned from his annual leave in the army to elope with her; and, with the help of his father — an atheist, communist journalist who had no truck with the caste system — they married in secret. Her family told the police he had kidnapped her but, thanks to his sympathetic army commander, the couple were left alone. Now she looks after their two small children, while Syph messes about on boats.

Soon it was time to turn in. In the distance I could make out chanting. Syph said it was the month of the Vedas, with the Hindu temples blaring out holy scriptures through loudspeakers, clashing with the calls to prayer coming from the mosques. Only the churches were silent. 'They pray inside,' said Syph. 'Only Muslims and Hindus have direct contact to God, sir. By speaker.'

We turned off the hurricane lamps and I went to bed under my mosquito net, while the crew prepared to sleep aft in the open air. I watched the fishermen's lights twinkling at the far side of the lake, accompanied by thousands of croaking frogs. I listened to the spicy mingling of the Hindu Vedas coming over the lake, rising and falling with the breeze, mixing on their journey to God, as I drifted on my floating bed off to the land of dreams.

HOT GOSSIP AND HOTTER CURRIES

CATHERINE STOTT HAS A SPICY TIME IN SOUTHERN ASIA

'Now that is what I call a dreamboat,' said Al, the Washington attorney, as he pointed to where *Seabourn Spirit* bobbed at anchor in Singapore's cruise terminal. This sleek craft has all the appearance of a very fancy private yacht; indeed, it is aimed at people like Al who can afford their own yacht but would rather not have the bother. And – as with owning a yacht – if you have to ask how much it costs, you can't afford it.

Since her launch in 1989, *Seabourn Spirit* has joined the elite band of boutique cruisers that has redefined civilised cruising. She and her sister ship, *Seabourn Pride*, have a shallow draught that enables them to put in at islands barely charted, to nose into exclusive yacht marinas and to insinuate themselves up rivers and into secret harbours where larger craft dare not venture.

The exquisite finish of the ship strikes you the minute you step on board: blond wood, creamy marble, good paintings, and nautical brass judiciously used. 'I am your personal attendant, Lotta,' said the Swede who escorted us to our suite (no such thing as a humble cabin on this ship).

When I saw it, I was glad it wasn't my first cruise because that would have spoilt me for any other ship. The suite was wonderfully well appointed, from the six-feet-wide bed to the five-feet-wide picture window, the desk with its personally printed writing paper, the TV and video cabinet, the drinks cabinet stocked with the 'free' tipples we had been invited to specify on the booking form.

Already there was a bottle of champagne chilling, and two crystal flutes. Rare orchids reposed in a crystal vase. Tropical fruit in a crystal bowl gave off an exotic scent. Beyond the walk-in dressing room, with its personal safe, was a marble bathroom with proper bath-tub and twin hand-basins, fluffy robes and a great cache of prettily-packaged bath unguents. And since all gratuities were included, no embarrassment about how much to tip.

The two-week winter cruise from Singapore and back was to take us to Penang, Kuala Lumpur, two days in Bangkok, Kuching and Pulau Tioman.

The first day was spent at sea, cruising towards Penang — a good time to acquaint ourselves with the ship and our fellow passengers.

Next door to me (why can't we have next-door neighbours like this in England?) was a most elegant New York female of a certain age who had once been a colonel in the US Army and had on one occasion parachuted out of an aeroplane in a ball-gown. Later she became a war correspondent. She was six feet tall, blonde and had a stunning wardrobe and a tongue as sharp as the crease in her silk pants.

Then we had the Berlin tycoon-ess with her eight matching Louis Vuitton suitcases each filled with slinky 'cruise-wear' — and her matching, macho toy-boy; a loquacious Dublin hotelier who hired a motorbike, fell off and broke his arm; and a sparky Californian divorcee who had had copious affairs with movie stars and who served up such 'hot dish' (American for good gossip) that we all stayed up, enthralled, well past our usual bed-times.

This cruise line has a policy of looking after single travellers — 'we see to it,' they say, 'that singles are always included in the social mainstream (unless they prefer to be left alone). Our officers and staff personally invite and escort single guests to parties, dinners, dances and other events.' A lone Texan lady so enjoyed the company of one of the staff that she has put him on her personal pay-roll as an escort, for a year.

Our first port of call was Penang, whose Batu Ferringi beach ranks as one of the world's finest. I much enjoyed the visit to the kampong, a village on stilts, at the edge of the jungle, where we had Malaysian breakfast. Lewis, a New York magazine editor, stared, pale and aghast, at his noodles. 'Oh great. Green food. Just what I need for my hangover.' As we toured the neat homes, certain American ladies expressed surprise at the lack of loos. 'Don't worry,' the guide told them. 'They have the whole jungle out there.'

Malaysia may have the world's fastest-growing economy, but it also has the slowest roads. As we were stuck on an embryonic motorway en route to Kuala Lumpur in fierce heat, our guide inflicted torture on us by singing old Cliff Richard songs. Then he told us that if you eat monkey your dog will bite you, and that the Malay mothers put Guinness on nappy rash. The Irish hotel-keeper told him that was a terrible waste.

In the 10 years since I was last there KL has transformed itself from a tumble-down colonial remnant into an impressive sky-scraper city where a genuine attempt has been made to preserve the worthwhile; the fairy-tale railway station of Moorish influence remains, as does the Tudor-style 1890 Royal Selangor Club, once at the heart of colonial life. Its economic power made even market shopping expensive for the British.

Two days at sea, cruising off the coast of Indonesia, took us northwards to the Thai island of Ko Samui, which is destined to become the next Phuket, their somewhat over-worked current dream island. Here, tourism is being developed quite sensitively so far and the tallest structure I saw was the biggest imaginable golden Buddha.

Lunch was on the beach of the Imperial Hotel under a spreading sea grape tree: langoustine roasted with a hint of lemon grass, crab baked with ginger, satay of lobster and mango of the palest yellow. After lunch you could have a massage (not of the 'Bangkok' variety) on the sand for £2.

The food on board *Seabourn Spirit* was of an elaborate kind, cooked by an Austrian chef. It was rather too rich for those of us who are now more used to food that speaks for itself rather than through its sauce, although the desserts were wickedly wonderful. However, a friend who has recently returned from a *Seabourn* voyage says that a lighter touch is now in force.

At the Verandah Cafe you could eat breakfast or lunch, inside or outside, from a splendidly health-oriented buffet.

On each cruise there is a guest chef: ours was Singapore's TV cook, Violet Don, who cooked us a sensationally spicy dinner which caused a Dutchwoman to sneeze so violently that her diamond earrings shot into the curry. Violet also gave morning cookery lessons which were much appreciated by me and a trio of gay caterers from Oregon.

And then Bangkok for two days, with a fascinating entry up the Chao Phraya river, where you could really see how close the jungle comes to the city and how crowded the banks are with temples and gold-tipped curving roofs. The traffic in Bangkok is now so horrendous that seeing the city by water is much more rewarding.

To get to the Oriental Hotel for dinner we split into threes and hailed tuk-tuks, those spluttery, motorised, hooded tri-shaws. Our driver looked for all the world like a guerrilla and had about as much charm.

Now, the Oriental is the most famous hotel in Bangkok, but our guy hadn't heard of it. He ploughed into murderous traffic, asking the way a dozen times, crossing and re-crossing the river as darkness fell, and our eyes streamed with the choking pollution. But it was worth it. We finally crossed the river by the Oriental's private teak ferry boat, to the fairy-lit outdoor restaurant, and dined on the terrace from a series of fragrant dishes.

The two-day crossing of the South China Sea was sometimes turbulent. The Norwegian captain insisted that seasickness is all in the mind and told us that 'the waves make it better for the sleep'. Many of the passengers were relieved, though, to reach the calm of the Sarawak River. Since reading

Redmond O'Hanlon's brilliant book, *Into the Heart of Borneo*, I had wanted to come here. It is now known as 'the Land of the Hornbill' ('Land of the Headhunter' was ditched since it was not thought to be doing much for tourism).

Little remains from the time of the White Rajahs apart from a few noble residences, but although Kuching is now a thriving city, all along the muddy river bank are the Iban villages on stilts, each with its longhouse, and you feel from the intense and humid heat that the jungle is very, very close.

The prime tourist attraction is the Sarawak Museum, designed a century ago to simulate a town house in Normandy, for some mad reason. Inside there is a wonderful recreation of a longhouse, complete with skulls hanging from the ceiling, showing exactly how life is lived along the river-bank; and a gruesome display of blow-pipes and other vicious weapons and, of course, the celebrated '*palang*' – a piece of bone introduced horizontally into the male member. 'Oh, I had that done ages ago,' said Lewis, our New York wit.

As we approached Singapore nobody wanted to get off the ship. 'I could live in this suite quite happily for the rest of my life,' an American woman said. 'Surrounded by staff, just calling room service. I think that is probably my vision of heaven.'

Chapter 6
ANTARCTICA

---

10 FEBRUARY 2007

TO THE LAST PLACE ON EARTH
ON A RUSSIAN ICE-BREAKER, **PETER HUGHES**
JOURNEYS TO THE FAR SOUTH

Tomorrow we would reach the huts. For eighteen days we had sailed south, 4,870 miles into the whiteness of Antarctica. Our voyage began in South America but we passengers had travelled from all over the world. Some had come for the wilderness, many for the wildlife. I was among those on a pilgrimage and tomorrow we would arrive at the shrines.

They are two of the Antarctic's historic huts, sturdy sheds, prefabricated in London of timber and dreams and assembled nearly a century ago in the most isolated spot on earth. From them Ernest Shackleton and Captain Scott set out with sledges for the South Pole. There was no saying we would get to them. Yesterday we had been all set to land at McMurdo, the big American scientific station, close to another of Scott's huts. But there was too much ice in the sound and it was too windy to fly in by helicopter.

In the Antarctic you have to recalibrate your senses. Everything is scaled up. Nature is at its most uncompromising, history at its most remorseless. It is the coldest place on the planet and the most remote. It is a realm of extremes, and that would include our disappointment if we were unable to make it.

This was a rare journey. The Antarctic has been seen by fewer travellers than any other continent. No one set foot on it until 1821 and it was less than 100 years ago that Roald Amundsen reached its pole. In so many senses it is the last place on earth: the last to be seen, the last of the continents left for most people to see. On this voyage we saw more of it than all but a handful of scientists and explorers can ever hope to.

We travelled from Argentina to New Zealand, to make a semi-circumnavigation of the west coast. Our ship, a Russian icebreaker, is the only passenger vessel in the Antarctic capable of making the voyage. In fourteen years it had done so on just five other occasions. We journeyed from the mountains of the Antarctic Peninsula to the white wastes of the Ross Sea, from snow peaks reflected in glazed black water to an infinite pale plain of ruffled ice scattered with spectral icebergs. They rose, suffused in a milky light, like the ramparts of ruined castles or the broken spires of dilapidated cathedrals. Some were as big as towns, surreal citadels of some frozen legend. We saw fifty-three species of birds, five types of seal, four kinds of whale and we voyaged back north via the albatrosses and yellow-eyed penguins on two of New Zealand's sub-Antarctic islands.

It took a month. We carried Zodiac inflatable boats and two helicopters to take us ashore and an expedition team to guide us. It was led by a swashbuckling Canadian, with rings in his ear and a beard like a Plantagenet knight's, called Shane Evoy. We had a team of lecturers to educate us, headed by Bob Headland, holder of the Polar Medal, wearer of a grey polar beard and possessor of the voice and graces of a BBC Home Service announcer. He is also an eminent historian at the Scott Polar Research Institute in Cambridge. We were eighty-nine passengers, mostly retired, from sixteen nations; the majority were American, Australian and British.

We sailed from Ushuaia on Tierra del Fuego. Ushuaia is the southernmost city in the world. The signs and postcards say so. Either that, or Fin del Mundo, 'the End of the World', which is not nigh, but here, at the very tip of Argentina. The city rises like a tidemark on a mountainside steep enough for some of the pavements to have steps. It is built in bright colours – yellow, blue and red – typical of settlements in the polar regions, and has their frost-pitted roads too. In winter it is a ski resort, in summer, a transit camp: everyone seems to be waiting to go somewhere else. For many it will be the Antarctic: polar travel is one of the town's prime industries. Ninety per cent of all Antarctic travellers leave from Ushuaia. They sail east along the Beagle Channel, a wide seaway lined by sharp-pointed mountains palomino with snow. These are the final vertebrae in the tail of the Andes.

It was in the buttercup sunlight of evening that the *Kapitan Khlebnikov* let go its mooring lines and headed down the Beagle Channel. The next town we should see would be in New Zealand in twenty-eight days. It is not a beautiful ship. The sleekest thing about it is the lifeboats. *Kapitan Khlebnikov* — *KK* to its passengers — is a 12,000-ton icebreaker, all power and no grace. A five-storey cube of an apartment block, painted ochre, looks to have been planted on top of a tug. Built in 1981 to keep the seaways clear around the coast of Siberia, *KK* was effectively a unit of the Soviet coastguard. The hammer and sickle is still emblazoned on the bow. It was designed to operate in temperatures down to minus 50C, has a bow of 45mm cast steel, and can smash ice up to 3m thick. Home port for the ship and most of the crew is Vladivostok. In 1992 *KK* underwent a change of life. It was chartered by the American company Quark to make expedition voyages to the Antarctic and Arctic.

The travel industry talks about 'soft adventure', the sort of holiday where you spend all day in the dust of safari but come home to a designer bathroom. If that is soft, the adventure of an icebreaker is distinctly firm. The cabins were made for the original huge crew of 150 Russian seamen, so they are not that spacious and the furniture is metal, albeit finished in an oak vinyl. If you share — and the single supplements are eye-wateringly expensive — one person will be on a sofa-bed. But the rooms are quiet, have their own showers, and windows that open to admit the polar air and the sound of crunching ice. More importantly, *KK* is the only passenger-carrying icebreaker of its class in the Antarctic: it will take you to places that no other cruise ship can.

If the day is to be active, the wake-up call comes over the PA at 6.30 a.m.; 7.30 if you are at sea. There is none of the malarkey of dressing for dinner, unless you choose a different sweater. The food, prepared by Austrian chefs, including — disastrously for waistlines — a pastry chef, was good, better than most of what you will ever eat in a dinner jacket. But while an icebreaker's element is ice, it first has to reach it.

Between Tierra del Fuego and the Antarctic lie nearly 600 miles of the most infamous water in the oceans. The Drake Passage can be placid — Drake Lake — or tempestuous — Drake Shake. If it puts its mind to it, it can come up with some of the most mountainous seas the Southern Ocean can amass. We would cross the Antarctic Convergence, where the relatively warm waters of the north meet the icy waters of the south, and the 60th parallel (60 degrees south latitude): Antarctica is defined by international treaty as the land to its south.

On the first morning it was 5C outside and we were making 14.5 knots. On day two those figures had come down to minus 1C and 7 knots. We had a 50mph headwind, it was foggy and the sea, grey as undercoat, came at us in sullen mounds. They squirmed their way beneath the ship and then arched their backs to tip us off. With no stabilisers, a smooth hull and all that superstructure, the *KK* is not the ship for such seas. We rolled and we jolted; we pitched and we yawed. The horizon careered up and down the windows like manic rollerblinds; passengers leant at zany angles as the decks rose, and then hurtled to the next handhold as they dipped.

On the wall of the passengers' lounge there is a pendulum measuring the ship's roll. I saw it swing to 30 degrees; old hands claim to have been to 48. It was a record the captain was not about to challenge; he changed course to find smoother water.

If outside the sea was riled, inside life was in the doldrums. We donned our name tags, told one another where we came from and attempted to memorise the other eighty-eight passengers' names. We attended introductory talks in the lecture hall on birds, seals and history, and wandered up to the bridge, which was only ever out of bounds when the weather was really bad.

We went on deck where, on the first day, I found myself face to face with a wandering albatross. It was keeping perfect station alongside the ship. Stocky body, brutal beak, hardly flexing its slender, sailplane wings, it was little more than its own 3.5m wingspan away and eyed me disinterestedly.

The ship turned into the lee of the South Shetland Islands and the Russian navigator got out his chart marked Arctowski Peninsula, the hook of land that points to South America. The peninsula, and its archipelago, is the most accessible and most visited part of the continent. After sixty hours at sea, we took to the Zodiacs to make our first landing.

That meant dressing – 'rugging up' or 'layering' as they have it in these latitudes. It's not the ambient temperature, which this day was comfortably above freezing, but the wind chill that gets you: in an instant it can turn a fresh winter morning into cold of such searing pain that you feel the skin will crack from your cheeks. On every landing Quark takes tents and food ashore in case the weather turns savage and prevents an immediate return to the ship.

One's fluid intake has to be judged carefully in these circumstances. Apart from the palaver of uncovering, it is protocol to return to the ship for any call of nature not made by a seal or a penguin. It is also protocol to paddle your boots in disinfectant before and after leaving the ship to reduce the risk of contaminating the continent with non-native species. It was my first practical indication of the vulnerability of this great white place.

We went ashore at Neko Harbour. The *KK* had anchored in a wintry lagoon, seemingly enclosed by rough cliffs of ice and daubs of dusky rock. In the distance was a range of immaculate white mountains gouged by shadow. The sea was black as liquorice and scattered with small blossoms of fluffy ice that looked like polystyrene. We landed at a narrow grit beach, safely away from a glacier slashed with blue fissures to our left. From time to time it rumbled with a kind of geological flatulence as the ice shifted. They call it 'Antarctic thunder'.

There were many emotions on landing. We were on the mainland of the continent, not an island, itself a trophy of sorts. There was consciousness of the sheer immensity of the Antarctic. One and a half times the size of the US, bigger than Europe or Australia, it is overwhelming. Almost everywhere else in the world distance has some comprehensible dimension: there is always another town to arrest the imagination. You never have to think of the whole country at once, let alone a continent. Here there is nothing: no fences, frontiers or limit. There is the pole in the middle and the continent's furthest edge, but few have the capacity to think what it means to reach either. And no colour is more boundless than white.

Here were our first penguins. It was a Gulliver moment, stepping ashore among all these busy little people tottering about the place, oblivious to the arrival of nearly 100 giants in bright yellow parkas. Within seconds of our climbing from the beach on to the snow, two shambled by within a metre, the edges of their beaks scarlet as if they had overdone the lipstick. You are supposed to keep a 5m distance from wildlife, but no one had told these gentoo penguins. It was my first encounter with a wild creature that had not treated me as a threat.

The colony was nesting, laying its eggs in little craters constructed with stones that other sneaky penguins kept trying to pinch. From above, on a hillside trail marked by expedition staff with red pennants, the rookery's nesting areas looked like scorch marks on a damask cloth; snow-free ground, required for egg laying, is at a premium. Close to, they were noisy with the birds' guttural cawing, and smelly. Imagine a fishy duck pen. The only other feature of the shore was a small orange hut, built by the Argentinians in 1949. Officially it is a refuge; more likely it was a subtle way of planting a flag on the peninsula. In the next cove, beside a cliff populated by blue-eyed shags, is an abandoned Argentinian research station.

Some twenty nations man more than sixty research stations in Antarctica. Their population is about 2,400 in summer, less than half that in winter. Antarctica has no government as such and no one owns it, although seven countries have made territorial claims, Britain among them. Others, including the USA and Russia, reserve the right to do so. But the issue of ownership is suspended – frozen, if you like – under the terms of the 1959 Antarctic Treaty. The treaty contains the principles by which the continent is run and its wilderness protected. Its commitment to preserving Antarctica's uniqueness was a rare instance of international idealism. Forty-five countries, representing 80 per cent of the world's population, are signatories and there has never been a significant challenge. The test may come in 2041 when the agreement banning mining expires.

Tourism should exercise it before that. It is an issue that will decide how the continent is to be treated. Should it be open to unlimited numbers of visitors? Should they have the run of the place, have hotels or be allowed to arrive by air? At the moment about 17,000 tourists come ashore a year – but the numbers are growing and 95 per cent is concentrated on the peninsula – the majority in just fourteen places.

The trouble is the treaty never anticipated tourism and has no machinery to deal with it. As Lars Wikander, the chairman of Quark, puts it, 'The treaty says the Antarctic is for science and peace. But what is peace? Some would say that tourism is peaceful because it promotes international understanding, but the scientists don't like that.'

Since 1991 the industry has regulated itself through the International Association of Antarctic Tour Operators (IAATO). Besides insisting on high standards of safety and behaviour, IAATO restricts access to the most sensitive sites and controls the numbers who go ashore. The failing of the arrangement is that no one is compelled to join the association and be bound by its rules. Wikander doesn't believe the situation can continue indefinitely. 'The treaty and IAATO are working on the immediate future to reduce the impact because of the increase in ships and visitors,' he told me. 'In the long term some say the only answer is to limit the numbers of both.'

In the meantime the treaty members' attitude can best be described as head-in-the-snow. Scientists may tut proprietorially about anyone else venturing on to 'their' continent, but that ignores tourism's growing demand to experience wilderness and evades the necessity for such demand to be managed. No one, for instance, is addressing the issue of land-based tourism when three South American countries are already using abandoned scientific bases as holiday lodges.

We pushed on south, down the peninsula and the archipelago off Graham Land, through the narrow Lemaire Channel, so scenic it has been dubbed the Kodak Gap, and into waters where other cruise ships seldom venture. The night before we reached the Antarctic Circle it snowed.

Now we were off Adelaide Island, at the end of the archipelago, in a meringue of pack ice. The *KK* shuddered as it cut its way through. Photographers with howitzer lenses kept vigil for the sight of seals or penguins, better still a whale. Glaciers, glowing blue, and crammed into valleys in massive accretions of gnarled ice, crumpled and split. On dark rock, snow delineated the finest cracks to give whole cliff faces a lacy veining. It was a negative landscape, where white was substance, dark ethereal. Except it wasn't just white. It was blue, purple, cobalt, green and a dozen shades of grey. David McEown, the *KK*'s 'artist in residence', always took ten tubes of different coloured paints when he went out to tackle a snowscape.

We saw orcas (killer whales) and minkes. A school of penguins porpoised beside the ship; rare Ross seals lounged on the ice, one with its pup, which was even rarer: the ship circled for a second look. We saw countless, wriggling crabeater seals and emperor penguins. One obligingly trudged around having its photograph taken.

The ocean curdled into a mottled skin of ice and greasy, near-freezing water. Beneath this stiff sheet a low swell undulated, bending it like a metal shutter. The Zodiacs rose and plunged, making boarding tricky for the next landing. It was one of our more esoteric afternoons. Peter I Island is an extinct volcano, less than 12 miles long and invariably wrapped in cloud. From a distance it looks like leftover Christmas pudding. 'That's the most I have ever seen of it,' said one passenger on his seventh trip to the Antarctic, peering at a brown cliff disappearing into the murk.

It was discovered in 1821 by the Russian explorer Fabian Bellingshausen and subsequently claimed by Norway. Heaven knows why. Uninhabitable and unapproachable, it is one of the remotest spots on earth. Therein lies its appeal to a group like ours. Bob Headland estimated that fewer than 800 people had ever landed, and most of them were from the *KK*, which was paying its sixth call. 'I guess if you collect islands, it's pretty important,' mused Brigitte, a Canadian passenger.

My Zodiac was the last to go. The incoming tide was building an ice barrier between ship and shore, but using the rubber boat as a squidgy icebreaker we pushed our way through a rough paving of broken glacier. By the time we reached the island the tide had taken all but two metres of the black stone beach and was still rising. There was time to wade ashore, listen to the geology lecturer, Prof. Norm Laska, deliver a three-minute dissertation on volcanoes, take a picture of what might have been a chinstrap penguin and scramble back to the boat. I am now one of fewer than 900 people ever to have set foot on Peter I Island.

The island was meant as a therapeutic comma to break the long voyage to the Ross Sea. A second punctuation stop was planned three days later at Siple Island but we never made it. We hit pack ice a metre and a half thick. Normally the *KK* would have dealt with it easily, but the surface was covered with 50cm of cloying snow. It acted as a brake. Overnight we travelled just 70 miles. The captain weaved, trying to find 'leads', channels, between huge plateaus of ice. Cracks zigzagged from the ship like bolts of cartoon lightning; slabs the size of playgrounds tilted and slid aside. A helicopter was sent out to scout for a way through. No go. By noon the *KK* was backtracking along the channel it had cleared.

On the fifteenth day we should have been approaching the Ross Ice Shelf. That morning, with 460 miles to go, we were still grinding through the pack. A PA announcement informed us that we were now the most remote ship in the world. But then the way cleared. Next morning we were in a treacly sea littered with only scraps of ice: the ice shelf was within 115 miles and at lunchtime we reached it, escorted briefly by some twenty killer whales.

'Shelf' is too domestic a word for something that so beggars comprehension. 'Land' would be more accurate because it has an area larger than France. To the explorers of the heroic age it was simply the Barrier, a great ice plate reaching 400 miles into the Ross Sea. From the water the edge appears as an endless white cliff, extending for 560 miles. It took two days to sail its length. The ice is constantly advancing, calving enormous icebergs. The biggest ever recorded broke from the shelf in 2000. It was the size of Jamaica. When James Clark Ross saw the shelf for the first time in 1841 he deduced that the entire plateau must be floating because it rode with the tide. As with an iceberg, however much you can see there is seven times more under water. In places it is more than half a mile thick.

After dinner we landed by helicopter. It was daylight at 11 p.m. There were diversions, such as peering into the turquoise depths of a crevasse and toasting our arrival with bubbly, but nothing could quell the insignificance of our own speck-like existence in this vast and empty place. It is a landscape that reduces people to pixels.

On the day we were unable to get to McMurdo, we flew instead to the so-called Dry Valleys, discovered by Scott on his first expedition in 1903. The ice retreated from them a few million years ago and everything else seems to have retreated with it. These are the carcasses of massive mountainsides skinned by katabatic winds, sudden avalanches of dense, cold air that come roaring off the polar plateau at hellish velocity. Anything not heavy enough to be embedded in the permafrost — grit, snow, ice, even colour — is blasted away, leaving the valleys stripped of everything but a dull primer of dusty brown. So desolate is the area that NASA has used it to simulate the surface of Mars.

The Antarctic at the best of times is so cold that most of it seems largely immune to the effects of global warming. Paradoxically, climate change is actually causing more snow to fall on the ice cap. Here there is little comparison with the Arctic, where the ice is steadily melting. On the Antarctic Peninsula the situation is very different. As the most northerly and warmest part of the continent, it is more sensitive to temperature change. Here a number of large ice shelves have disintegrated and glaciers are receding faster than predicted. The population of Adélie penguins, which thrive in sea ice, is declining, whereas the numbers of gentoo and chinstrap penguins, which prefer open water, are rising. It also seems as if stocks of krill, the shrimp-like creatures on which so much Antarctic wild-life feeds, may be reducing.

The wind dropped, the sun shone and the *KK* pressed its bow into the rim of the sea ice surrounding Ross Island. Penguins squirted out of the water and waddled up to inspect the ship. That day we reached the huts.

Both Shackleton's and Scott's huts were erected at the foot of the simmering volcano, Mount Erebus, 900 miles from the South Pole. They stand in a landscape which has the markings of an orca, jet-black lava patched with snow. There are five miles and three years between them. Shackleton's hut at Cape Royds, the earlier of the two, is where his fifteen-man expedition spent the winter months of 1908, in temperatures down to minus 42C. The following spring bitter weather and dwindling supplies forced Shackleton to turn back 96 miles from the pole. His hut nestles in the lee of a bank of lava, its timbers bleached like well-scrubbed pine. It could be a beach house. Propped up outside, in the manner of an incongru-ously chichi garden ornament, is a wooden wheel from an Arrol-Johnston motorcar the expedition took with them.

Under the supervision of a representative of the New Zealand Antarctic Heritage Trust, we brushed our boots to protect the floor and entered eight at a time. Ducking under the copper tanks of an acetylene lighting genera-tor we came into a surprisingly uncluttered room. The hut is being restored by the trust and some 400 objects have been temporarily removed. At the moment, therefore, it has more of the replicated feel of a museum than previous visitors remembered. But the bunks made of packing cases are still there; there is a sledge stored in the rafters, and Shackleton's private quarters are just inside the door. His signature survives on one box and so do many of the more domestic touches. A big iron cooker — Mrs Sams Range — stands like an altar at the end of the room; thick woollen socks hang on a line and, arranged on precarious shelving, are scarlet cans of tripe and onions, Irish stew, minced collops, Irish brawn and boiled mutton.

Scott's hut at Cape Evans is more sombre. It was almost completely buried in snow so, while much bigger than Shackleton's, it was darker. The history is darker too. Scott's polar party struck out from here on 1 November 1911. Five of them — Scott himself, Edward Wilson, Lawrence Oates, 'Birdie' Bowers and Edgar Evans — never came back. They died in March 1912 on their return from the pole, having made the desolate discovery that Amundsen had got there before them. It was eight months before a relief party from the hut discovered Scott's body and learnt of his noble failure.

There are shadows of the tragedy in every corner. The thought of it is ingrained in the floorboards where the explorers walked, chipped in the dishes from which they ate and reposed in the beds to which they took their plans, ambitions, anxieties and who knows what imaginings. I cannot remember feeling so privy to any history, let alone one steeped in such drama, as in this simple wooden building. There are no ropes, no glass cases, nothing but your own understanding between what you see and what happened. But it could be lost. The hut at Cape Evans is in urgent need of restoration.

Others have written that they could imagine an expedition returning at any moment. Not me; the place feels too abandoned for that. But I could believe that no one else had opened the door since Scott's men left. It has the faint smell of habitation, a mixture of leather and soot, and is crammed with the mundane things that people touched and used, still in the places where they left them. Oates's bunk is hung with pony harness and a dog collar; there are nine enamel teacups hanging from hooks; a kettle on the stove, candles with blackened wicks and drools of wax and, above a bed, a white toothbrush balanced on the rim of a mug.

Scott called it a 'truly seductive home', and there were certainly enough brand names around to remind them of what they had left in England — Fry's cocoa, Colman's mustard, Huntley & Palmer. There are some oddities too: rat traps and the wires from a telephone installed to connect with Scott's earlier hut on McMurdo Sound. There is scientific glassware in the laboratory and the red lantern in the dark room where Herbert Ponting processed not just his photographic plates but moving pictures as well. Slabs of stinky seal blubber are stacked at the entrance to the stable annexe where the ponies would have been restless in their stalls.

Unlike Shackleton, who had everyone mucking in together, Capt. Scott, ever the Royal Navy man, divided his hut into a wardroom for officers and mess deck for other ranks. It was at the head of the long wardroom table that he was famously photographed at his forty-third birthday dinner. The table is there. So is his bed, in a corner of the hut he shared with Wilson and 'Teddy' Evans. His fur sleeping bag is laid out ready for his return.

There was one more hut to visit. It is on Cape Adare, at the western end of the Ross Sea. The hut is tiny. Only four visitors are allowed in at a time, although originally it housed ten explorers. They were members of a British expedition led by a Norwegian called Carsten Borchgrevink, and in 1899 became the first people to spend a winter in the Antarctic. Their shack is the first human dwelling on the continent, man's first foothold on the far end of the earth. From a shelter no bigger than a potting shed has sprung activity that will decide the fate of a continent.

The Antarctic is mankind's last ticket to utopia; the last chance to keep part of the world much as it was made. It belongs to no one, is in thrall to no system or faith; it has no indigenous population, currency, language, borders or trade; no army or police or permanent settlement. No conventional government. Its inhabitants are the creatures that have adapted to live there. They accept us as equals, not intruders. The fact that the place is white, and sterilisingly cold, only adds to its aura of purity.

As the *KK* sailed on that glistening blue-black, ice-flecked sea, through the archipelago of snow and rock, past the high white ranges of the coast, it occurred to me that this is how it would be if the Himalayas were flooded to within 1,000m of their summits and we, like Noah, were floating among the highest peaks on earth. Carry that metaphor further and those peaks would be all that was left. Everything beneath them would be inundated, gone. And that, of course, is Antarctica — all that is left of our chance to begin again.

SLOW AND SOLITARY

CHRIS MOSS, ON A LEISURELY TRIP SOUTH,
IS QUITE HAPPY WITH HIS OWN COMPANY —
UNTIL HE MEETS THE PENGUINS

You can't rush to Antarctica. But you can get there in a day's sailing from the Argentine port of Ushuaia, see the ice and shoot back — or rather keel and rock and topple back as the Drake Passage does its worst. Then you can say: been there, done that, what next? But, after a long spell of not getting around to going (despite spending 10 years working in Argentina, just up the road from Antarctica in Buenos Aires), I decided to give the south of the south three weeks of my life. So, in mid-February I boarded the Russian ice-strengthened expedition ship *Akademik Sergey Vavilov* for a nineteen-day cruise with my stepfather, Joe, and eighty other passengers. When we pushed away from Ushuaia into the Beagle Channel, I wondered what I was letting myself in for: I don't like groups, or even parties, and a conventional cruise round, say, the Caribbean or Greece is my idea of hell. But the slow boat turned out to be a joy, providing me with two wonderful preambles: one mental, the other geographical.

The former came in the shape of time to think, read, reflect, look through the window at the choppy Southern Ocean, and be disconnected from the world. There is no mobile phone connection out at sea in the austral latitudes; and the on-board internet was too expensive to consider as a means of communication. I was also far away from news — the credit crunch in particular, which had become bothersome by late winter — and quotidian woes.

Armed with books on travel to Antarctica by Jenny Diski and Sara Wheeler, an anthology of Heroic Age narratives, a Bradt guide to the birds of the Antarctic Circle by Tony Soper, and some bottles of whisky, I lay back, thinking of nothing in particular. Surely the most appropriate thought when heading to the cleanest, whitest, blankest spot on the planet.

Joe went enthusiastically to every lecture. I skipped most of them, preferring not to have too much preparation for the wildlife and wonders of the ice. He also went to every meal. As an ex-rigger he wasn't bothered too much by the huge swell; I, on the other hand, had mild seasickness for part of the time and felt too queasy to eat. 'Great meatballs for lunch,' Joe would say after another trip to the dining deck. I focused on the horizon through my porthole or sought solace in Darwin's *Beagle* journal: he suffered terribly from seasickness and he was at sea for nearly five years.

After a long crossing from Ushuaia heading due east via the Falklands, I was able to experience the other preamble: South Georgia, inside the Antarctic Circle but as green as it is white, and as interesting for its human history as for its inhuman isolation. Following the screening of a documentary about Shackleton, which I did attend, and lunch, we sailed gently into the Bay of Isles. The sea was still high and heaving, but the Zodiac pilots decided it was safe to go in to Salisbury Plain, a beach that about 40,000 king penguins call home.

It was a penguinopolis at rush hour. When not fishing and flapping in the surf, the tall, sleek, orange-flashed birds were busy shuffling, flirting, clapping, slapping each other, trumpeting (their shrill, slightly comic, calling), having sex, feeding chicks, sitting on eggs and generally behaving like city folk. But kings are hypersocial and too interactive to be ordinary commuters, and when I stopped and allowed them to approach – I sat down to be at their eye level and avoid intimidating them – their manner, which is half swagger and half coy, reminded me of nothing so much as teenagers at a youth club. They would even club together to push one of their number forward so he would be closest to me, as if saying: 'Go on, check him out, don't be a chicken.' One or two got close enough to have a bite at my boot.

Of course, such encounters are an anthropomorphic delight. We imagine all sorts of emotions the birds probably don't have at all. Some were bullies, some were shy, one couple seemed to be bent on quarrelling all the time. There were many threesomes, as couples took along gooseberries for competition or just for fun. Reading their mating rituals was tricky, as they seemed to involve a combination of weird posturing, a little bit of slapping, and not much tickle at all.

Later, our on-board lecturer on seals and penguins, Kirsten, did impressions of what he called the king penguin's 'advertisement walk', with the male doing a hip-swinging saunter and glancing behind him to check that his date was keeping up. If she suddenly got lazy and wandered off elsewhere, he would pretend he had not been interested anyway and go and join another girl or lose himself in a gang. I would love to have pitched a tent among the penguins, but the South Atlantic Islands are all about minimum impact, so we went back to the ship for dinner and drinks.

South Georgia was a great introduction to Antarctic wildlife and the pleasures of king penguins, which you don't see on the Antarctic continent. Then there were the horrors of whaling stations and the dreams and dramas of exploration (I started reading *South* after seeing Shackleton's grave at Grytviken), and the energising delights of katabatic winds, chilly Zodiac rides and, by degrees, ice. We saw hanging glaciers, ice fields and, then, like a mirage in the distance, our first big icebergs.

But there are no shortcuts between the bottom of lonely South Georgia – its last cape is named Disappointment – and Antarctica. Three days on board had given me as much of an introduction as I would ever need to the power and might of the sea; now I had two more, heading in a southwesterly direction, when it would get colder (definitely) and rougher (probably).

Whether grey or blue skies lay overhead, the heft of the waves was always huge, sometimes rhythmic and pleasant, at others offering a waltzer of a voyage. In the dark, the sensation of wild winds spinning the vessel was heightened, but the ship pushed on like a metallic serpent, riding a sine wave of swell and keeping a steady 10 to 12 knots across the open sea.

I carried on reading *South*, comparing the trials and tribulations of Shackleton and his crew on their epic open-boat voyage from Elephant Island to South Georgia with my own minor discomfort. I got used to the swell and, when not reading or meditating on nothing, I joined Joe in the bar, made trips to the sauna and strolled around the decks. I discovered that deep drafts of ozone were more curative than any seasickness pill. My fellow passengers were aged between thirty and eighty, and mainly from Oceania. We had some laughs, a few beers and quite a bit of dawn communing – the morning light is amazing down south – but I still enjoyed my cabin and the solitary sessions.

When you sail south you don't exactly find the Antarctic continent. Rather, it gathers round you in the shape of icebergs, islands, coves and bays. Gradually, the coastlines draw closer and slowly begin to lose first the greens and ochres of mosses and lichens, then the black of volcanic basalt, and one morning you wake up and everything has turned brilliant white.

I first caught sight of what looked like sheer cliffs of ice – classic Antarctica – on a stretch of the voyage that took us from the flooded volcano of Deception Island in the South Shetlands to Charlotte Bay on Graham Land. I should probably have been observing the humpback whales that were breaching alongside the *Vavilov*, or gawping at the albatrosses and petrels, or studying the maps to make sense of the chaos of peninsulas, islets, bays and capes that make up the Antarctic Peninsula. But whiteness is enigmatic, and because a cruise is so far from being an overland expedition, you feel an urge to get off the boat and walk on the big slab of ice. Later that afternoon I went to another lecture, about ice, in all its varieties: frazil, grease, brash, shuga, pancake, white, drift, rafting and fast. That's from soft to hard, in case you need to know.

After a few false starts, we eventually got a chance to walk on the continent at Neko Harbour. A miniature conquest of sorts, it was also an opportunity to sit and ponder away from the group. The bay was calm and the sky a pinkish grey and slightly eerie, and there were sweeping views of distant mountains — a sun we couldn't see was illuminating their peaks — and of blue glaciers all along the coast. By early March, Antarctica is readying for winter, and this gloomy but atmospheric point on the map seemed entirely fitting for the end of the season and the end of our voyage south.

The return leg had its own wonders. The Gerlache Strait is not as famous as the Le Maire Strait but it is one of the Antarctic Peninsula's unmissable mini-voyages. A calm, narrow channel, lined by low peaks wrapped in ultrawhite glaciers, it is strewn with huge tabular icebergs and smaller bits of iceberg. During a slow morning cruise, we saw a couple of humpback whales rolling and blowing along one side, and then a Weddell seal and lots of fur seals basking on floating ice islands (the latter, unlike the Weddell seal, do not belong here — but thanks to global warning are, as one guide put it, taking over the world). The light, though, was the thing: it was end-of-the-world luminous, a bit Martian even, and the ice glowed aquamarine and emerald against a dreamy grey sky. In the afternoon it all became coffee-table photogenic: blue skies, white ice, calm waters, a lone cormorant on a steeple of ice, and twee chinstrap penguins hiking up snowy slopes.

A young leopard seal still studying to be a top-drawer predator chased us — once he had realised we were going anyway. A few bays away a group of kayakers saw an older leopard seal tear the head off a penguin.

But perhaps the ice was even more remarkable than the wildlife. I loved leaning over the bow just gazing at the shape and colours and — when in the Zodiac — peering down through the translucent water to try to make out the bases of the icebergs. I never did — Antarctic ice goes deeper and higher than you have ever dreamed. At times, I forgot where we were, and I even forgot the wildlife and my fellow passengers, and everything. If my cabin was a secret hideaway while at sea, then Antarctica, at least the few channels and bays I was able to explore, was the ultimate refuge from the everyday.

I can – sort of – understand why most people want a shortish hop to the Antarctic Peninsula. It ticks a box, yields amazing photographs, involves the shortest possible exposure to the perils of the Drake Passage – and, yes, it's cheaper. But if you have the time and the money, and don't mind some long stretches on big seas, prepare yourself for the slow trip and enjoy the prologues; the chances are you won't be going back again, so why rush?

Chapter 7
THE AMERICAS

---

12 APRIL 2008

BACKWARDS TO FLORIDA WITH SEVEN LUCKY TEETH

HAVING TAKEN A NARROWBOAT TO CARCASSONNE, **TERRY DARLINGTON**, HIS WIFE, MONICA, AND THEIR WHIPPET, JIM, SET OUT TO EXPLORE THE US INTRACOASTAL WATERWAY. HERE THEY ARE BECALMED IN NORTH CAROLINA

The population of Oriental was leaning on the rail to the marina and looking at the *Phyllis May* from five feet away. Not the whole 1,000 – a dozen at a time, in shifts. Cars would drive up and people would get out and do a quarter of an hour, and then get back in their cars and go and buy a disposable camera and come back. Monica was hiding in the boat. If she looked out they asked her – Did you sail her across the Atlantic? Did she go in a container? And then, She is the damn cutest boat I ever did see and What does she draw? And What is her horsepower? And Where are you headed?

The Tiki Bar was nearby, under a little roof, South Pacific-style. Traffic in Oriental is limited to 15 miles an hour, explained Bob, and the dogs roam free. The mayor is a dog. Bob was a boater, like nearly everyone else in Oriental – a nice man with a beard.

A dog like a teddy bear passed and a dachshund bustled by. A black retriever arrived and Jim went for the throat and nearly pulled me off my stool. They were waiting for us when we sailed in from the Neuse River, I said to Bob, and the dogs were waiting too. They were lining the quay. The local reporter was on board before the boat had stopped. Then the lady who does the town website, who looked like Sigourney Weaver, asked me, When you get off your narrowboat does the world look very broad?

We slept most of the next day, the gongoozlers nattering alongside. Some brought their lunch. A narrowboat is almost soundproof if you shut the windows tight and I was fathoms into sleep when someone hammered on the roof. I stumbled to the door and it was a pretty lady of a certain age — Will you come to dinner with us tonight?

Of course, I said.

Never seen her before in my life, I said to Monica.

When Bob came to fetch us, the shrimp boats had lit their anchor lights, which shone on their masts and rigging and poles, all folded up like the wings of a dragonfly. We rushed into the car with coats over our heads, through a blizzard of flashes.

Bob and Betty's house was a mile away. It was white-painted cedar, raised, in a large plot, with many windows. It was richly furnished, traditional-style but colourful, and the carpets were deep. Outside the sitting room a lawn and flowers, and 20 yards away the river, turning to ink. You couldn't see the other side. I sucked on a bottle of Newcastle Brown that tasted of barbecue smoke and maple syrup.

Bob had been in telecoms and Betty was an artist. They had asked Dick and Judy. To me Dick looked like Lyndon Johnson, and Judy like a beautiful spy. I wasn't far out — Dick had been a Washington lobbyist, and Judy in the CIA. I was a prostitute, said Dick — that's all lobbyists are — prostitutes. How long have you been married?

Forty-five years, I said.

My God — most of us are on our third wife and Monica looks so young!

She gets plenty of sex, I explained.

One day you'll find out where she gets it, said Bob, stealing my punchline.

Property here is much cheaper than up north, said Dick, and people who like boating come here to retire — we all know each other. The average age here is sixty-five. There is a small shrimping fleet with some Hispanic workers and the black guys live at the other end of town. We are forty-five minutes from New Bern, and three hours from Greenville. Tomorrow is ladies' night at the Tiki and the next night there are free peanuts on the bar. Then there is gentlemen's night and the next night is the marquee and a band. Saturday is the picking of the roast pig at Don's place and in the evening the rock group from Virginia Beach. On Sunday the croquet and then dinner at my place on Monday. We will come and get you for these occasions, and tomorrow we will see you at breakfast.

At seven o'clock next morning voices came across the road into the cabin. Some American gentlemen have a note in their voice that recalls the grinding of steel. Here it is considered a sign of masculinity, but to an effete European it sounds like someone grinding steel and For the love of God turn it down.

I got up and crossed the road to the café. Sitting on the stoop was Gabby Hayes, the bearded guy in braces from the old western films. Bob and Dick were inside at a table, with Clint Eastwood and Ernest Hemingway and Dwight Eisenhower. Sigourney Weaver was on a stool in the corner reading a book, and over there were Larry David and Johnny Cash. They were all looking at each other, like cormorants, from the corners of their eyes. Look, said Bob and Dick, we are having a great time!

One of the few useful things they taught me at Oxford was not to talk at breakfast, but I chatted as best I could with my new friends and bought two cups of coffee and a Danish to go and as soon as I could go politely, I went.

That evening Jim and I set out into the sunlight and walked under the big trees between the wooden houses, painted and pretty, in their open plots. There were lots of squirrels and they were tame, which is not to the advantage of a squirrel if a whippet is in town. Jim's screams echoed down the leafy avenues and more than once I was tempted to let him slip, but was not sure what a suburban American would say about havoc on his lawn and a shredded squirrel. For all I know they feed them and give them names and put them in the airing cupboard in winter.

We came to the new marina by the big bridge over Smith Creek and there outside a restaurant was an African-American gentleman playing upon the organ. Jim lay down on the cedar decking and I ordered a bottle of Samuel Adams and listened to 'Ferry 'Cross the Mersey' Ray Charles-style. You hear many more British songs in the US than you do in England. It is just like being at home, except you don't hear the songs at home, if I make myself clear.

A withered gentleman left his table. Is that a greyhound? he asked.

No, I said, a whippet.

The dog is being bothered by the music, said the withered gentleman. He went up to the African-American gentleman. Can you turn it down? You are bothering the dog.

The musician smiled and turned down the volume. I have a resolution that when on the waterways I shall think the best and not take offence. But I wish I had walked away from the withered gentleman.

My dog died, he said. She was a sheltie. She had cancer then she got it again. Cost me ten grand in chemotherapy and radiation in one year. She still died but when they took her away I could look her in the face. We are too far from the hospitals here – it is three hours to Greenville. My wife's got Parkinson's disease and so we will have to move. No one stays here very long.

When Jim and I got back into the boat it was empty but a large man with white hair fell into the front deck. I helped him up. Came to see your boat, he gasped. Jesus, what a boat – love it! I'm going to die soon. I've got cancer – it doesn't get much worse than that, does it? Come back to the Tiki Bar and drink with me.

You know Monica, I said later, there is something sinister about Oriental. Everyone has a terrible disease. There are no children. It is three hours to a big hospital – in three hours we can get from Stone to Glasgow. People move here because it is beautiful and because of the boating and because of the property prices but they are bored stiff and getting more and more ill and they are cut off from the world and their families and to ease the pain they drink all the time and smoke all the time and go to each other's parties. They are so sweet and so generous but they seem so needy I am afraid they will eat us up.

On Sunday we went to the Episcopalian church. The service was led by the ladies who look after things when the minister has put on the whole armour of God and gone to serve with the marines. During it we were asked, as usual, to greet each other. Peace, said a fairly withered man in a sports jacket.

Peace, I replied.

Peace and the love of God, said the fairly withered man, which passeth all understanding. He embraced me – What sort of engine does she have?

On the way out of the church he approached me again. It has been a privilege to have you at our service, he said, to share our Sunday on this God-given morning. What's she like in a beam sea?

They are so generous and kind, said Monica at lunch, laying her teeth by her plate.

Along this coast millions of years ago there were sharks that could have snatched the *Phyllis May* and broken her back and picked her clean of people and dogs. In the Tiki Bar Monica had made a friend called Bev who had a fossilised shark's tooth seven inches long. Bev had given Monica five teeth polished to jet – one to protect us each month to Florida.

Why do I hate Oriental so much? Why am I so cold? It seems unfair when everyone is so good to us. I lay waiting for five o'clock and tried to work it out. Heaven knows I will take a glass but I hate the relentless drinking -- being summoned to the bar at five o'clock every day – and their relentless smoking. I hate the contrast between the hostel for the Mexican girls who processed the shrimps and the wooden palaces by the water. I hate the way the streets where the African-American people live are left off the street map. I hate the lack of children, the way everyone seems to be playing a role, and people hanging around waiting for the next trip to the bar or the hospital. Rich, desperate, sick people, running away from their families and the world – My God, they are a bunch of bloody expats!

I do hope the good and generous citizens of Oriental will forgive me -- four o'clock in the morning is not when the mind is most clear or the heart most full of love, and of course I was scared. The captains had departed and to get back to the Atlantic coast we had to cross Carteret Country and to get to Carteret Country we had to cross the Neuse River and the Neuse River was four miles wide.

The makers of charts pour out alphabet soup and photograph it, and the charts are impenetrable even on a table at home. On the top of the boat before dawn, forget it. Daymarks are poles stuck in a river or an estuary. They have green or red squares or triangles on them. You go to the left of one and to the right of the other, or to the right of one and to the left of the other. Few boaters ever work out why, and none of them managed to explain it to me.

As you steer the *Phyllis May* you can see the beetle boat crawling along the four-inch GPS screen, but I was still scared. This was the first crossing in America on our own, and we were leaving at dawn regardless of a poor forecast, hoping to get over the river before the wind came up. We had been here ten days and, overwhelmed by hospitality, had lost too much time.

A banging on the boat – Hello, hello!

On the quay a white beard two feet long. The beard came out of the darkness into the boat and behind the beard a tall thin man with a stocking cap. He had two fruit-preserving jars under his arm full of something golden. I am Tennessee Ronnie, he said, and this is to help you through the winter. And here is a bag of apples.

How wonderful, Tennessee, I said, how generous. Is it honey?

In a way, said Tennessee Ronnie. It's Tennessee Brown – the best there is.

I just don't know what to say, Tennessee – you are from Tennessee?

Tennessee Ronnie's face saddened. No, he said, I was born in Arkansas, but only 20 miles from Tennessee. They are waiting for you at breakfast.

It was still dark but the breakfast crowd was in — Ike, Sigourney, the lot — Bob and Dick, of course.

Owya doon, they cried. They did not know the dark thoughts I had harboured in the night. Bloody awful, I said, I'm terrified. Haven't slept since midnight. The Neuse is four miles wide and I've never tried to navigate by daymarks before and it's going to be windy.

No trouble, said Johnny Cash, you leave the green ones on the left — follow the magenta track on your GPS screen — I walk the line.

You're telling him wrong, you old fool, said Ernest Hemingway. You leave the green ones on the right; it's an estuary. Terry, why is your dog so thin?

I picked up my coffee and muffins and went back across the road to the boat. My stomach didn't feel good and my brain was running without oil, making a grinding noise. Jim was shivering and whining. Monica was setting up the back-up GPS and looked pale.

I heaved out of the hatch and stood on the back of the boat. The breakfast crowd had come across the road and stood two feet from me and watched me put on my life jacket. You try putting on one of those life jackets with straps when you are disabled with fear and there are twelve people watching you, making remarks. I put it on sideways, then upside down, then the right way and reached over and shook hands with everyone and dropped into reverse and set out backwards for Florida.

Out of the slip, slowly into the harbour basin, avoiding the shrimp boats and yachts. I might be frightened of going to sea, but I can handle a narrowboat in flat water. I turned in my own length to scattered applause and looked back to wave goodbye. On the balcony of the café a row of people was holding cards a foot square.

I could see in the dawn light the numbers 9, 8, 9, 7, 9, 8, 9, 8.

I wonder which bastard gave me a seven. I bet it was that Sigourney Weaver.

Extracted from *Narrow Dog to Indian River* by Terry Darlington (Bantam Press), the sequel to *Narrow Dog to Carcassonne*.

4 JUNE 2005

THE LADY WHO LOVED THE RIVER

STEPHEN LACEY FOLLOWS THE TRAIL OF MARGARET MEE, WHOSE PAINTINGS HELPED ALERT THE WORLD TO THE VALUE OF AMAZONIA'S FLORA

At Manaus, 930 miles before it meets the sea, the Amazon is joined by another great river. Free of sediment, and stained by the tannins of rainforest leaves, it flows down from Brazil's remote north-western frontiers a clear Coca-Cola black.

'My beloved Rio Negro,' Margaret Mee called it. Over thirty years, beginning in 1956 at the age of forty-seven, this quiet, self-effacing Englishwoman set off, usually alone and for months at a time, on a series of expeditions by simple houseboat and canoe to paint the orchids, bromeliads and other fabulously intricate forest flowers along its banks, lakes and myriad tributaries, and those of the Amazon. The paintings — many owned by Kew Gardens— are among the most celebrated botanical studies of the twentieth century.

Little could deter Margaret Mee from getting out her sketchbook or setting up her easel. She would sit out in the intense heat and humidity and paint under flapping tarpaulin in wind and rain. She endured blood-sucking flies and biting ants; she was once nipped by a scorpion, and her parrot by a vampire bat. She caught malaria and hepatitis, was threatened by drunken gold prospectors (she always carried a revolver), and was forever having boat troubles — crashing, capsizing, losing belongings, and, once, falling overboard in pitch darkness. All this she describes with stoicism and great good humour in her diaries, whose republication in lavishly illustrated form last autumn was the final prompt I needed to go and see the wildlife riches of the Amazon for myself.

Although I am a passionate tropical traveller, I had so far shied away from a trip here to the motherlode, home to a fifth of the world's plant and bird species. I had been daunted by the horror stories of deforestation. This is a theme running through Mee's diaries, too. Sometimes she admits to bursting into tears on seeing areas she had once known and painted reduced to wasteland. Would I find that her paintings of Jacobin hummingbirds diving over scented white Gustavia flowers, and of tangled old trees loaded with epiphytes, were now just a poignant record of what we have lost? Did Margaret's Mee's Amazon still exist? I dreaded the answer, but steeled myself to find out.

Well, Manaus was a shock. A city of one-and-a-half million people, clogged with road and river traffic, it has a skyline bristling with everything from clanking industrial complexes and glinting apartment blocks to precariously stacked favelas, or shanty towns. Fascinating as it was, there was no sense of being in the heart of the world's greatest forest.

But after less than an hour's motoring upriver on the *Amazon Clipper*, the eight-cabin river boat that was to be my home for the first four days and nights, the complexion of the Rio Negro changed completely. Houses petered out and the trees closed in. Here and there, the forest line was broken by a white sandy beach. The light was dimming, but when we passed close to the bank I could see the great shield-shaped leaves of philoden-drons, plants Mee both painted and photographed, sprouting from the forks of tree branches. A dolphin breached, and a pair of green parrots flew with rapid wing beats over the canopy. I was starting to get excited.

The next day we were among the Anavilhanas, a chain of some 400 forested islands strung down the middle of the river, in intermittent rain, for the rainy season had just started. I had not realised how great an impact this rain has on the lowland forest, but you could tell by the tidemark way up the tree trunks. In some years, the water level can rise by more than 40ft, and it remains high for many months. The Rio Negro, already several miles wide, expands hugely, and you can navigate much of its flooded forest habitat, known as igapo, by canoe. Clearly, the tree-top orchids and brome-liads would then have become a lot more accessible to Mee – and the poor crew member who was sent up the trunks to bring flowers down for her to paint.

Mee's delight at her first encounter with Amazon plants and animals is palpable in her diaries. She could not sleep 'for listening to the magic sounds of the sleeping forest'. It was indeed a world away from her native Buckinghamshire, and the succession of art schools in and around London and Liverpool where she had studied and taught. With her husband, Greville, she had first come to Brazil in 1952 to visit her sister in São Paulo, immediately fallen in love with it and decided to stay. Inspired by the flowers around her, she began to specialise in botanical painting, and, financed by the sale of her work, to travel to remoter areas, where her blonde hair was guaranteed to astonish, and sometimes alarm, the Indians ('On seeing me, most of them fled or hid behind rocks').

Of course, the *Amazon Clipper* was luxury compared with Mee's transport, with air-conditioned cabins, private bathrooms and delicious foods, from palm hearts and strange fishes to pineapple meringue pie. I quickly developed a taste for caipirinha, the deadly Brazilian mixture of lime, ice, sugar and cane spirit.

Our party's daily routine was to leave the main waterways in the early morning and explore by canoe. In one beautiful backwater (igarape), we spied, in quick succession, blue and yellow macaws, a crimson-crested woodpecker and a pair of red-billed toucans. In another, at the water's edge, we met a flock of leaf-eating hoatzins, bizarre prehistoric-looking birds with claws on their wing joints, which were so taken aback by our sudden arrival that they almost fell off their branches, plunging back into the undergrowth in a cacophony of squawks and ungainly flaps. Like me, Mee was a dedicated bird-spotter, and was forever rescuing birds from cages and saving others from being shot.

With my binoculars, I could also pick out a number of epiphytes among the trees, the highlight being one of the gorgeous orchids from Margaret Mee's paintings, *Cattleya violacea*, which was sporting several stems of intense purple flowers, flared with yellow. Later in the day, on several occasions, we made a foray into the forest on foot, and I had the chance to rummage, touch and smell. Often, the ground banked up quickly and we were soon above the flood line. Avoiding a spiny Astrocaryum palm, I almost stepped backwards into a huge bromeliad, a species of Aechmea, low down a tree trunk, with a massive, cylindrical white flowerhead protruding from its giant rosette of barbed fleshy leaves. Aechmeas were among Mee's favourite dramatic subjects, and I could see why.

I was thoroughly enjoying myself. Heat and humidity apart, the Rio Negro's forests were also proving remarkably pleasant to walk in. There are no leeches and hardly any mosquitoes. I refused to believe this at first, but it is true. The black water is too acidic for them. The only time I was bitten during the trip (seven times in five minutes) was when I ventured on to the white waters of the Amazon itself.

Mee used to take a cleansing dip in the river every day, but for this first part of my trip I was a little hesitant. I had read about electric eels and stingrays, and those needle fish, candiru, that lodge themselves in your urinary tract. Night-time canoe trips with the *Amazon Clipper*'s captain, Mr Gomes, flashing his torch over the shoreline, were showing me how big the population of cayman was in these waters. And by day, I was seeing how quickly piranha appeared when a piece of meat was dangled on a hook.

At Novo Airão – a small, new town halfway along the Anavilhanas chain, surrounded by forest but abuzz with bars, internet cafés and satellite telephone kiosks – we watched spellbound as Marilda Medeiros, the owner of a floating restaurant, and her daughter Mariza dangled their feet off the dock and splashed pieces of fish on the water. From the depths emerged a long pink mouth and then a bright pink face, the first of several juvenile pink river dolphins to call in for breakfast.

Two days later, I took the plunge – a blissful swim off a white sand bar at dawn, after an uncomfortable first night on my new river boat, *Dona Tania*. Cramped, hot, and with only one communal bathroom, it was at least a more authentic taste of Amazon river life, and closer to what Mee would have experienced. The guide, Anand Pooran, had me and my fellow passengers eating out of his hand in no time, as he demonstrated how to get a drink of water from a forest vine, found us a red tarantula and showed us the nest of a hermit hummingbird, bound to the underside of a palm frond by cobwebs.

In her diaries, Mee is spying and recording some fascinating new bit of plant and animal life in almost every paragraph. The reality is even more overwhelming. Canoeing down the igarape, it sometimes felt as if I was in some naïve painting of the Garden of Eden, there were so many marvels arrayed in such quick succession. Bromeliads would be flaunting scarlet bracts, parakeets chattering in the waterside thickets, dolphins ambushing shoals of sardines, sunbitterns giving us flashes of their dazzling yellow-brown wing feathers on the river bank, and lemon and black caciques attending their pendulous nests, hung out of the reach of snakes on semi-submerged trees.

The presence of a troop of squirrel monkeys, and a three-toed sloth, so close to the jungle hotel, the Ariau Amazon Towers, however, was a bit suspicious. I hadn't seen such animals anywhere else. But we enjoyed watching the sloth wearily munching the broad, fingered leaves of a Cecropia tree, a distinctive plant notable for its symbiotic relationship with Azteca ants, which are offered food and accommodation in its hollow stems in exchange for help against insect attack.

The climax of this second leg of my trip was to be a night in the forest, sleeping in a hammock, which I was looking forward to. We disembarked near the Arara River and collected a local guide, Marcio, who farmed the piece of land we were passing through. (Slash-and-burn agriculture is permitted along the Rio Negro, but from what I saw it was patchy and small-scale, and the damage didn't extend deep into the forest. Trees can also be cut for private use, but are not, I was told, for sale.)

Our walk under the trees took us past more wonders – red passion flowers, strangler figs and ladder vines, termite and giant wasp nests and the robust little home of tent-making bats, woven out of leaves. Frequently, there was a flash of blue, orange or yellow from a butterfly, and an abrupt cry – 'I can see you' – from an annoying grey bird called the screaming piha. Eventually, we arrived at a small stream, and from the materials around them, Anand and Marcio rustled up a very commendable hotel and restaurant, even carving spoons out of the stems of palms, weaving plates and tablecloth out of the palm and heliconia leaves and catching a few shrimps to supplement our roast chicken.

All went well until after dinner, when we were feeling our way from the light of the roaring fire to the blackness of our hammocks. There was a great commotion under Anand's hammock, six feet from mine, and moments later, he confessed we had had a visitor, a coral snake, which Marcio had clobbered with his machete. It was a handsome creature, striped in scarlet and black, but apparently one of Brazil's most poisonous and too risky to have in camp. After that, peace reigned. I awoke several times during the night, but was always lulled off again by the sounds of the frogs and insects, and the rainlike patter of perpetually falling leaves.

The Hotel Tropical, the best in Manaus, is just the sort of place you want to arrive at after a spell in the bush. Luxury bathroom, crisp white sheets, a cold beer beside the wave pool. Here I met Gilberto Castro, a knowledgeable naturalist and successful businessman from Rio de Janeiro, who had accompanied Margaret Mee in May 1988, giving her the use of his boat and small house on the Cuieras River at the southern end of the Anavilhanas Islands.

On that trip Mee had a specific purpose: to paint the fabled moonflower, *Selenicereus wittii*, a species of epiphytic cactus that blooms in the dark for just a couple of weeks in May, each flower lasting no longer than a single night. Never before painted in the wild, it had eluded her on previous trips, but this time a likely plant was identified and a vigil mounted.

'Margaret was rather frail by then,' Gilberto told me. 'I remember lifting her on to the roof of my boat. She painted for hours in the sun, and then continued through the night, as the rest of us dropped dead with sleep.' By torchlight, she captured the whole life-cycle of the scented white flowers, from opening bud to withered petals. It was to be her last project, for later that year she was killed – not in the rainforest but in a car accident in England.

Long before her death, Mee's importance in the realms of botanical art and field research had been recognised with the award of an MBE and Brazil's Order of the Southern Cross. Foundations in both countries established in her name have since financed hundreds of young field biologists and illustrators, and have helped alert ever more of the public to the flora of the Amazon and the need to conserve it.

I asked Gilberto about the state of the rainforest today. Close to the towns and to the main waterways, there have been major changes, he said, but unlike other parts of the Amazon and in spite of recurrent threats from road-building, the Rio Negro region has remained, encouragingly, remarkably intact. The botanists I have since spoken to at Kew confirm this. I am sure you have to penetrate a lot farther now to see, as Margaret Mee saw, a family of tapirs bathing or a jaguar lolling in the sun, but certainly I felt I had tasted the world depicted in her paintings. It was intoxicating stuff.

8 MARCH 1997

RIVER OF FEW RETURNS

ON A TRIBUTARY OF THE AMAZON, **MALCOLM
MACALISTER HALL** JOINS THE *DON ALBERTO,*
A BOAT WITH A PIRATICAL-LOOKING CREW

We had been bitten to hell the previous night by tiny black insects in the Hotel Wilson's peeling accommodation, and I needed a midday drink. Across the dirt street was a little bar with a couple of wooden tables on the boardwalk.

Two men were lolling here, pouring beer into each other's glasses and spilling plenty of it. 'I'm Julio,' said one, unsteadily. 'And I'm Leo,' said the other. 'We've been drunk for two days.'

'Salud,' I nodded. 'What are you celebrating?'

'Absolutely nothing!' they replied triumphantly. 'Have a beer...' This seemed the perfect excuse for a party in Puerto Maldonado, a ramshackle Peruvian jungle town on the edge of the Amazon basin, set on the banks of the river fearsomely named Madre de Dios – Mother of God. Nothing much seemed to have happened here since the brief nineteenth-century rubber boom. Overlooking a vast lazy brown curve in the river, its corrugated iron roofs grilled sleepily in the heat. The shops were full of chainsaws and antibiotics. The trees stretched away on every side to the horizon.

We were looking for a boat down the Madre de Dios, across the border, and on to Riberalta in north-eastern Bolivia – nearly 300 miles. But down at the muddy riverbank by the sawmill there were only canoes. 'There might be a boat on Friday. Maybe,' said some loafers there.

It was like this for six days. Of all the uncertain ways to get around in South America – white-knuckle airlines, junkyard buses, deathtrap roads – river travel is the least predictable. We passed the time idling with people such as Julio and Leo. Like everyone here, they had a touch of gold fever. The flecks and little nuggets lay, hidden but in fortunes, on the bed of the Mother of God river.

'One guy made so much in six weeks that he just left his dredger moored in the river and took a plane out,' said Leo wistfully, as the afternoon drifted by. 'If you make money, you have to disappear before they kill you for it. Más cerveza!'

The next morning a man was waiting outside the Hotel Wilson, sure of a tip. 'There's a boat in, from Bolivia,' he said excitedly, cutting through my hangover in a flash. And there, with two big barges lashed to it, wallowing under the weight of four massive bulldozers it had brought upriver, was the *Don Alberto*, a wood-built, no-frills, jungle river workhorse. With their bare feet and gold teeth, the five-man crew looked like a bunch of pirates.

'Let's say $12 each to Riberalta, including food. It'll be about five days. We leave maybe tomorrow, maybe Saturday,' said Alejandro, the captain. We stocked up: mosquito nets, antibiotics and rum. By way of insurance, my girlfriend put a ring on her wedding finger.

'Meester, hay un cambio – there's been a change,' said Alejandro as we were slinging up our hammocks in the hold. They were words I would come to dread. He needed a signature from the customs post. It was closed. We now couldn't leave until Sunday. I could hardly believe it when, at last, in a terrific explosion of clattering and smoke, they fired up the engine and the *Don Alberto* turned out into the current.

The Madre de Dios curved ahead of us, smooth but swift, a brilliant tangle of green rising above its banks. The Brazil-nut trees towered over the others. Their giant companions had been logged long ago. Multicoloured parrots flew fast overhead; canoes slid by. Above it all spread the huge Amazon sky.

Below, in his oily shirt and trousers, Alejandro tended to his ancient engine with the skill of a surgeon. Much of it was held together with bits of wire and string. 'It's all worn out,' he shouted, 'but the owner won't pay for a new one.' Its unguarded flywheel and belts spun in a menacing blur of rubber and steel. The cook's five-year-old daughter, Esmerelda, played happily beside it, dragging a plastic Coca-Cola bottle on the end of a piece of thread. Apart from an oily one-eyed doll with no clothes, this seemed to be her only toy.

Meri, her mother and our cook, concocted greasy soup from brown river water and chicken gizzards in a choking shed on the back of the boat, her Hell's Kitchen of filthy pots equipped with a brazier made from a cut-down oil drum. Up above, two more doomed chickens squawked in a hen house on the roof. At the wheel, the crew flashed their gold teeth and worked the bolt of the ancient rifle that they kept ready in case any unfortunate wildlife should stray across our path. On the evening of the first day we rounded a curve, and there on the riverbank was a hand-painted sign. 'BOLIVIA', it read.

The *Don Alberto* spun crazily and ran on to a sandbank before we could tie up. The border control here, lost in the jungle, must be one of the lowliest postings in the Bolivian immigration service. The official studied my passport. Any problems now, and a week of hanging around would have been in vain. He looked up, unsmiling. 'So, you're from England,' he began, and paused. I had a sick feeling in my stomach. 'Tell me about the mad cows, please.'

A fast, dramatic sunset, then the *Don Alberto* nosed into the riverbank, and was tied to a tree. After a night of bad-tempered scratching in hammocks, the misty dawn revealed a derelict, engine-less gold dredger moored nearby. A tattered scarecrow figure emerged from it and begged a tow to Riberalta. He had more gold in his teeth than the rest of the crew put together, and raffish – if ravaged – good looks. He reminded me, ludicrously, of the actor Peter Bowles. It might be the big skies, or the gold in the rivers, but the Amazon is a country of dreamers. He was going to get this hulk fixed, he said, and make his fortune.

Even with the two barges and Peter Bowles's floating scrapyard in tow, the *Don Alberto* made good speed with the current, shooting through rapids, the crew whooping and wrestling with the wheel. Clouds of white butterflies settled over the boat. The thatched huts of Brazil-nut collectors sped by on the banks. And everywhere, the endless trees.

It was monotonous, hypnotic, fascinating. We lay in our hammocks, read, watched the jungle, and tried to teach the alphabet to Esmerelda. Suddenly, there were shouts from the wheelhouse. 'There, in the water! Look!' Up ahead a small deer was swimming across the river. Two of the crew raced for the old aluminium dinghy, wrenching furiously at the motor. 'Swim! Swim!' I silently urged this little creature as, for several minutes, it desperately tried to escape. But it was no match for two men circling it with a 25hp outboard, a rope and a machete. It was lassoed and dragged alongside; one of the crew sawed at its throat, and heaved it aboard. It made an awful, dying effort to stand up, its gaping neck spurting blood. Ten minutes later it was a sordid mess of meat in a plastic bowl outside Meri's kitchen. After this, I didn't breathe a word when I saw a small alligator, then a turtle, and then a big green iguana stalking along the bank.

We tied up in the dark, at a strange place of fires, shouts, women and arguments. Dawn revealed it to be a logging camp, with huge tree-trunks in the river, boats, barges. This ramshackle settlement was grandly named America. Alejandro went ashore for an ominously long time.

He returned, and took a deep breath. 'Meester, hay un cambio.' The boat tied alongside us had a broken gearbox. Its crew needed to go miles upriver, almost to the Bolivian border, to log trees. They wanted a tow. 'The owner is a friend of my boss – what can I do?' That was the bad news. There was no good news. No roads here, nothing.

We said goodbye to Peter Bowles, lashed the crippled boat and its barge alongside, and set off back the way we had come. Against the current, we were barely making walking-speed. A ragtag band of about thirty, our new shipmates lived in heaving confusion and squalor. Loaded with an old tractor, a canoe, guns, babies, women, dirty washing, pet monkeys and a dog, their boat and barge could have starred in a waterborne remake of *The Grapes of Wrath*. They returned from hunting trips with dead monkeys, turtles and beautiful big parrots, their red and yellow feathers bloodied, which made my girlfriend weep. 'Why is she crying? Those parrots are lovely with Brazil-nut sauce,' Alejandro said.

I was angry with myself for being angry about the parrots. Bolivia is one of the poorest countries in South America. This was survival hunting. 'We'll get less than $100 a month for dragging out trees that are worth $600 each,' said one of the men. 'We're exploited, but what can we do?'

The *Don Alberto* crept back upriver for an agonising two-and-a-half days. The rapids we had shot through in thirty seconds took a whole morning to negotiate. At last we cast off our passengers in a muddy chaos on the river-bank, turned and sped downstream.

Back at America, our two barges now sat low in the water, loaded with tons of timber, sacks of Brazil nuts, half-a-dozen passengers and a crate of fighting cocks. They, too, were unwitting players in the great daily struggle for survival.

'I've been upriver collecting Brazil nuts, but you can barely live on that,' said their owner, Juan. 'I'm taking these birds down to Riberalta to see if I can win some money. Your wife's brave to come on a boat like this.'

The *Don Alberto* ploughed on through the forest. We already knew that we wouldn't reach Riberalta on it. 'Meester,' Alejandro had said as we left America. They were going to stop for a couple of days, short of Riberalta, to load more Brazil nuts. But there was a road there, and a bus.

We rounded a bend to see a dredger spinning slowly in the middle of the river. Someone, madly, was trying to row the contraption with a pair of home-made oars. And there, grinning his wild gold grin, was Peter Bowles.

'He's crazy,' said Alejandro, as the crew threw him a rope. 'He thinks he's going to get rich with that thing. Sure, people make money from gold, but it all goes on drink and women – in a flash. The truth is he'll always be poor. Like us, I suppose.'

IN THE FOOTSTEPS OF HUCK FINN

BLUESMEN, BEAVER, DEER, THE PAW PRINTS OF A BEAR...
MAX DAVIDSON HAS AS MUCH FUN AS MARK TWAIN'S
HERO ON THE 'MONSTROUS BIG MISSISSIPPI'

Dawn on the Mississippi and the only sound, apart from the drone of mosquitoes, is the strumming of a guitar in the next tent. John Ruskey, Jesus look-alike, sole proprietor of the Quapaw Canoe Company, mixer of the best margarita between Memphis and New Orleans, is singing the blues.

'...angry women...gee, they make a mess out of you. . .' I have to strain to hear the words, an odd mixture of melancholy, sentiment and defiance. '...got to get me another woman...you can get you another man...' This is not the United States of the cereal commercials: happy families sitting around a breakfast table. It is a bleaker, lonelier world. Relationships between the sexes are as transitory as the Mississippi itself, that great watery highway through the heart of the nation.

At a quarter to six, as the first streaks of red are starting to appear in the sky to the east, John unzips his tent and pads down to the river. 'Felt so lonesome in the city,' he croons, as he washes his face in the murky water. 'Jus' had to get away.' In the wood behind the tents, the drone of mosquitoes is supplemented by birdsong and the croak of bullfrogs. Away in the distance, a boat sounds its foghorn, a single mournful note that lingers for what seems an eternity. By half-past six, we are drinking strong black coffee, scented with chicory, around a camp fire.

John's brother Chris, a doctor from Colorado Springs, crawls out of his tent to join us, followed by his sons, Nicky, eight, and Gavin, six. 'Morning, Uncle John,' says Nicky, wiping sleep from his eyes. 'Morning, Max,' croaks Gavin. Then a long, contemplative silence as four Ruskeys and a Davidson, on an all-male, back-to-nature canoeing trip, savour one of the last great wildernesses in America.

We are camped on a sandbank on an island in the middle of the river -- the perfect vantage-point to enjoy what Mark Twain called 'the great Mississippi, the majestic, magnificent Mississippi, rolling its mile-wide tide along'. The river is only about half-a-mile wide where we are, just west of Clarksdale, but the impression of vastness is overwhelming all the same. The trees on the far bank, silhouetted against the rising sun, are just tiny black stumps, a frame for the blue-grey expanse of water, gliding southwards like a giant conveyor-belt.

'Impressed, Max?' asks John.

'Definitely.'

I am here, in part, on a literary pilgrimage, hoping to reconnect with the world of *Huckleberry Finn*, one of my all-time favourite novels. The book is not as popular in the States as it was: the all-pervasive N-word, though quite natural in the mouth of a nineteenth-century white boy in the American South, does not play well with the PC lobby. On top of which, Huck Finn smokes a pipe. Big no-no in the twenty-first-century US. But its portrait of one of the world's great rivers exerts a timeless charm.

Twain, born Samuel Langhorne Clemens in Hannibal, Missouri in 1835, was brought up near a steamship landing. As a young man, he worked as a river-boat pilot, committing every bend, sand-bar and swirling eddy to memory.

The Mississippi Delta, the area in which we are camping, inspired some of his most evocative writing. Here is Huck, drifting downriver on a raft with Jim, a runaway slave: 'The days just slid along so quiet and smooth and lovely...It was a monstrous big river down there...Not a sound anywheres, perfectly still, just like the whole world was asleep...And we would watch the lonesomeness of the river, and kind of lazy along, and by-and-by lazy off to sleep.'

Somnolence is the keynote of the delta and, to some extent, the blues music it inspired. Farther north, the Mississippi pulses with life: bustling towns such as St Louis, Missouri and Memphis, Tennessee. Further south is New Orleans, still reeling from Hurricane Katrina. But here in the delta it is another matter. The Mississippi used to flood so often, and the flood-plain extend so far, that until proper levees were constructed in the 1920s it was madness to build anywhere near the river. Hence the wilderness. Hence the loneliness. Hence the blues.

'There isn't a bridge across the Mississippi between Memphis and Greenville,' says John, with a note of pride. 'That's nearly 100 miles. Around here, there isn't a building of any description on the river for 40 miles. New Yorkers come and are captivated. They've never seen anything like it.' I look across the river, where he is pointing, and see what he means. The sun is high in the sky, bathing the willows in a rich glow. The river is so still it is hard to tell which way it is flowing. Pieces of driftwood dot the virgin sand-banks. Above our heads, a flock of birds flies north in perfect triangular formation.

'Geese?' I ask.

'Pelicans.'

John set up the Quapaw Canoe Company in 1998, having come to Mississippi as an outsider — he was born in Colorado — and fallen under the spell of the river. 'It has gotten into my soul,' he says, with affecting simplicity. Improbably, given the beauty of the surroundings, his company is the only one of its kind, offering canoe-based camping holidays on the river. 'A lot of local people are afraid of the Mississippi,' he explains. 'Some of them can't even swim. There is a whole mythology of shipwrecks and accidents and drowned bodies floating downstream.'

As we sit admiring the river, perched on low-slung deckchairs labelled 'power loungers' (only in America), we are not totally alone. If there is little by way of leisure craft on the Mississippi, the river remains a major commercial artery. All day, while we are fooling around on our canoe, paddling this way and that, exploring the creeks and the tributaries, having Huck Finn-style adventures, huge tugboats ply the river, ferrying grain, oil, chemicals, scrap metal, cotton, industrial machinery — anything that moves.

The boats are pushing barges that are 250ft long by 30ft wide, and the biggest of them are pushing upwards of forty barges at a time. They make an extraordinary sight, inching past the sandbanks, and thanks to John's short-wave radio, we are able to catch snatches of the conversations, indelibly Southern in timbre, between the captains of the boats.

'Where yo' goin', dude?'

'Natchez. How abou' yo'self?'

'St Lou. Then back to Vick. Up an' down, up an' down.'

'Hear what happened t' Abe?'

'What happened t' Abe?'

'Got sucked into the bank five mile back. Bent port rudder. Darn fool. Had to be tugged out. Yo' don' want to get too close to those booeys.'

'What are booeys?' I whisper to John. 'Booeys is booeys. B-u-o-y.' 'Oh, you mean buoys. As in "boys". The "u" is silent in England.'

'What's the point of it, then?'

And there is no arguing with that. As always in America, that old dictum about two countries divided by a common language keeps coming back. Having mislaid my luggage at Newark airport, I am reduced to swimming in my pale blue M& S boxer shorts.

'Your skivvies,' says John.

'What's that? Oh, ah, yes. Skivvies.'

John, naturally, swims in the buff. He is becoming more like Iron John by the minute. After lunch – beer and turkey sandwiches on the power loungers – he takes us on a route march through the forest, carrying Gavin on his shoulders.

'All you need to watch out for is the poison ivy,' says John. 'I'll tell you if I see any.'

'Yep, mind the ivy,' says Gavin cheerfully. 'My daddy got some on his willy. He couldn't go wee-wee for...'

I march grimly on, cursing Twain and all his works.

But what beauties lie around us, in this magical, untamed wilderness. We see exotically coloured butterflies, a pair of beavers playing on the bank, the pale rump of a deer disappearing into the distance, even the fresh pawprints of a bear. 'Don't see many of them around here,' says John, impressed.

It is with real regret that I finally leave Ol' Man River 24 hours later, having paddled 30 miles downstream with John and family. Wesley Jefferson, a.k.a. the Mississippi Junebug, is waiting for us with the trailer. He is called the Junebug – a noisy local insect – because he is a part-time blues singer, with a booming baritone that you can hear in Memphis. I get to see him in action that same night, at Ground Zero, a trendy blues bar in Clarksdale, just opposite Madidi, a popular French restaurant co-owned by the actor Morgan Freeman. Junebug is right. Wesley does not just have a big voice, but an expressive one, by turns angry and mournful – pure blues.

Jennifer and Roger Stolle, my companions for the evening, are out-of-staters who have come to live in the delta because they have developed a passion for the region. She teaches English at an all-black secondary school in a run-down part of Clarksdale. He is blues-mad and runs a shop called Cat Head, where you can buy rare blues recordings, as well as folk art from the area.

After Ground Zero, too touristy for his purist tastes, we move on to Red's Lounge, a sleepy, dimly lit joint, where a solitary figure, hunched over his guitar, his eyes half shut, sings of love and loss and days gone by. There are only half a dozen people listening, drinks in hand; in the background, a young couple are playing pool. But this, for Roger, is the authentic world of the blues – a distinctive musical form, rooted in the delta and in its lonely, isolated communities.

The ghosts of the blues greats – Muddy Waters, Big Jack Johnson, the Jelly Roll Kings – are sounding in my ears as I finally get to bed, in a quirky little hotel called the Shack-Up Inn, another Clarksdale institution. Guests sleep in rickety wooden shacks and there is an in-house TV channel, on which crackly old LPs are played. 'You Know What My Body Needs' by Smokey Wilson; 'Strollin' with Bones' by T-Bone Walker and his Band. An entire – and splendidly evocative – sub-culture. As I drive out of Clarksdale next morning, Sunday, I pass church after church, every one packed. Some of them sport those jokey slogans so beloved of American pastors. 'Exposure to the son may prevent burning.' But on the car radio, like a memento of my trip, those Mississippi blues are still throbbing their magic, the words ringing across the cotton fields.

'God knows how I miss you/ All the hell that I've been through...Life throws you the curves/ But you know the swerves...'

Not great verse, perhaps, but redolent of a way of life that is distinctive and fiercely independent. The ghost of Huckleberry Finn lives on.

RUNNING THE RIVER WILD

THE MISSOURI, SAID TWAIN, 'HAS MORE GRIEF TO
THE MILE THAN ANY OTHER WATERWAY IN AMERICA'.
ROB STUART WENT DOWN IT – AND THE MISSISSIPPI –
IN AN 11FT RUBBER BOAT

Tornado alert sirens wailed over Kansas City. They were being tested in case the day's forecast of storms and tornadoes proved correct. With dark clouds gathering in the south, the two of us decided finally to heed the advice about being off the river in bad weather and pulled into the bank at Jackass Bend, some 25 miles downstream.

The garden of a large unoccupied riverside cabin seemed to offer both a good pitch for our tent and shelter from the increasing wind. As we settled down for the night, after our staple diet of pork and beans and bacon, the storm broke with cataclysmic power. Sheet lightning lit the sky a feverish yellow. Thunder drummed painfully in our heads.

But we were in less mortal danger from the storm than from the owner of the cabin. We didn't hear him drive up; the first we knew was when two headlights, on full beam, fixed on our tent. We stepped out into the rain, and there was Buck pointing a pistol straight at us.

In outback America one person's misjudgment can be another person's reason to pull the trigger. And Buck had ample reason to be suspicious, not least because we were trespassers. We attempted to explain, but it was only when Tony made the quirky remark, 'Isn't that car of yours a '66 Chevrolet Malibu?', that the bemused Buck lowered his gun.

'You were lucky last night,' he told us the next morning. 'It was only your accents that saved you.' He had assumed we were hitmen hired by his girlfriend's husband, who, he explained, was currently languishing in the local penitentiary. On our departure, as a gesture of goodwill, Buck handed us a bottle of wine and a tin of luncheon meat.

This was the rural frontier America that I had come to see, the America of the early pioneers and settlers, the trappers and traders – Daniel Boone, Auguste Chouteau, and of course Lewis and Clark, who in 1803 began their epic westward voyage up the Missouri and finally to the Pacific Coast.

Our journey – six weeks in the planning – was a two-and-a-half month trip down the Missouri and Mississippi rivers, 2,600 miles from Pierre, South Dakota, to New Orleans; our craft, an 11½ft Avon inflatable with a 4hp outboard engine. A fisherman unloading his catch of wall-eye at the wharf on Lake Sharpe, our starting point, stared in astonishment at our boat. 'You going down to New Orleans in that thing? Gee, you must have balls of steel!'

Our timing was unfortunate. The Missouri was abnormally in flood. Apart from keeping a wary eye on the constantly changing water condi-tions – boils, whirlpools, the treacherous wing-dykes and incessant strong current – we had to dodge uprooted trees, logs and flotsam. Ensuring that our two six-gallon gas tanks were topped up, that our maps were kept dry and that the boat was properly inflated were constant concerns. This was the river of which Mark Twain wrote: 'The Missouri has more grief to the mile than any other waterway in America.'

Perhaps we were protected by Indian spirits. Barely a hundred miles into our voyage, at Lower Brule, we met Joe Grassrope, a Sioux Indian. Joe, who had recently got out of prison, was eager for us to meet his father, a direct descendant of the last chief of the Kul-wi-cha-sha-oyate tribe. Swaddled in dirty sheets in his cramped bedroom, Joe's father seemed to me to be dying. A photograph of him in his younger days hung above his bed, his face a handsome, patrician profile. His son gave us a feather from the bald-headed eagle, a keepsake symbolising swiftness and courage. We lost Joe's gift some-where on the journey, but we never forgot the spirit in which it was given.

Such meetings, and there were many, demonstrated to us the other side of America's frontier spirit – an unstinting hospitality. Behind the plain-speaking manner ('No shirt, no shoes, no service' was the ubiquitous sign), there was always unquestioning generosity and encouragement.

In Nebraska, for instance, after three days of continual heavy rain we moored, cold and miserable, at Lazy River Acres, a small community of cabins with a cafe-cum-store. There was no question of our camping. We were offered a luxurious cabin, the 'children's house' as Willard and Lucille Koucher, our hosts, referred to it. (They had eighteen children and seventy-two grandchildren, and Willard had built the cabin for their visits.) At Bluemoons, the cafe, Joe and Carol Pecheville cooked us Bohemian stews and catfish dinners, and their friends entertained us lavishly.

South of Jefferson City, we witnessed for the first time the extent of the flooding. Camped on a small island, itself the product of the high water, we saw how the river had breached the levee on the south bank and swept unimpeded two miles inland. In the midst of the floodwater stood a solitary whitewashed farmhouse, deep in sandbags. Here in the Bible Belt, the flooding seemed to have a more religious significance.

We did a little praying ourselves that night. Tow-boats ply these waterways, powerful enough to push a fleet of thirty barges. At full throttle they throw up a tumultuous wake that rocks the river for three miles behind them. Here was one now, ploughing upstream at a tremendous lick; our island camp would be submerged and washed away in seconds. With our tiny torches we signalled frantically for it to slow down. Just in time, the tow's searchlight picked us up, and the engines cut their revs.

After 1,400 miles and four weeks of the Missouri, we reached the Mississippi at St Louis. We raised a glass – two large early-morning Wild Turkey whiskeys. But the celebrations were short-lived. Beside the spectacular riverbank arch that is the city's signature, we were confronted by three US Coastguards.

They asked to board our boat. I pointed to the inflatable. 'So where's the big boat?' demanded one. 'That's it,' I said, preparing to photograph the event. He shook his head disbelievingly. 'Goddammit,' I heard him mutter.

We were placed in 'hospitable custody' and taken to see Captain Cooper at the Federal Building. 'All pleasure craft have been banned from the river indefinitely due to the flooding,' he explained. I pleaded and argued with him, but to no avail.

We were not prepared to see our epic journey come to such an abrupt and anticlimactic end. Daringly, the following day, we tried to escape downriver. We were quickly pulled up and escorted back to Cooper's office. Secretly impressed, I think, with our determination to press on, the Captain offered a compromise, an escort to the next big town: 'What would you say to a tow-boat to Cairo?'

I feigned disappointment but my heart leapt at the prospect. A few hours later, comfortably ensconced in the guest room of the tow-boat *W.J. Barta*, our inflatable tied on the aft deck, we set sail with twenty-two barges of grain and coal.

We reflected on our astonishing luck. Two weeks into the journey we had had our luggage stolen at Nebraska City. When the news went out on local radio, offers of help poured in. We ended up with more clothes than we had lost. There had been one or two hair-raising scrapes on the river, but we had survived unscathed. So far.

'Do you find that the river mesmerises you?' I asked Kenny, the pilot, next morning over a huge breakfast. It wasn't a silly question. Tony and I had on several occasions almost toppled into the river half-asleep. 'Hypnotic, isn't it?' Kenny agreed. 'On a straight stretch, I set the steering, make a coffee and walk about a bit to clear my head.'

We had no such luxury, but back in the inflatable we imposed a strict regime of half-an-hour on, half-an-hour dozing in the bow. By whose grace we survived the tow-boat traffic south of Cairo I do not know.

Around Rosedale we had our first taste of the Deep South: our own profuse sweat. The heat became intolerable and the humidity reduced us to a complete torpor. The mosquitoes, on the other hand, thrived. 'The heat saps your energy, debilitates you, then you're meat for the insects,' said Ray, who had invited us to stay at his hunting lodge in the Ozarks.

Welcome as his hospitality was, the evening with two of his friends – one of whom claimed to be a member of the Ku Klux Klan – degenerated into aggressive, liquor-fuelled racism. 'We're the law down here. Do you understand?' said Dan. Since he was packing a Magnum, I didn't feel inclined to argue further. Outside were the din of the bullfrogs and the crickets and the clattering mayhem of dying mayflies round the porch light. This was the Deep South of the movies, *Mississippi Burning* in real life.

After that encounter, the river seemed a safer proposition. Or so we thought. South of Baton Rouge ('Nice name, but it could be Trafford Park, Manchester,' observed Tony) a terrifying storm hit us. The noise was incredible and the density of the rain blinded us.

With the increased tow-boat traffic and the swamping wakes, our situation became desperate. Somehow we found shelter in an overgrown bayou, under the canopy of a half-sunken fishing boat. The fetid air was seething with mosquitoes, and we sat sullenly, ankle-deep in water, keeping a baleful eye out for moccasin snakes and sucking on Life Saver mints. 'If we're going to go, let's go on the open river,' we agreed, and headed back into the storm.

Tony tirelessly bailed out the boat as I steered half-blind through the torrential rain. Then, as suddenly as the storm blew up, it cleared. In the distance we could see the skyline of New Orleans. We hugged each other. There was no room in the boat, nor in us, for flamboyant celebration.

As we sailed the last miles through the congested industrial landscape of the Mississippi, its banks festooned with gantries and refineries, with moored sea-going freighters, pilot boats, docks and belching chimneys, I tried to remember all the people and places we had encountered on our ten-week voyage. The small, often remote settlements – Chamberlain, Waverly, Glasgow, Chamois on the Missouri; Caruthersville, Helena,

Greenville and Vicksburg on the Mississippi — and the big hearts of the people who live there.

And I remembered Gloria, in Glasgow, Missouri. She fed us and arranged accommodation at Larry's Motel after a particularly gruelling day on the Missouri. We asked how we could repay her. 'When you boys meet someone down the river who needs your help, be sure to give it to them. Then you'll have paid us back.' A proud and simple ethic of mutual help. That, not the pistol-packing swagger and tough talk, is the real spirit of the American frontier.

A TASTE OF SOUTHERN COMFORT

POKER AND MOSQUITOES HAVE GIVEN WAY TO
AEROBICS AND BINGO, BUT PADDLE STEAMERS ARE
STILL A FINE WAY TO SEE THE MISSISSIPPI,
SAYS **MAURICE WEAVER**

Faced with the alluring prospect of a steamboat cruise on the Mississippi, I concluded that my first priorities must be to learn poker – so that I could cut a dash at the tables – and stock up with insect spray so that the mosquitoes wouldn't cut a dash on me. The film *Maverick* had made a lasting impression and I thought I knew what life on the SS *American Queen* was going to be like. I could not have been more wrong.

When Americans resurrect the romance of their past, they have an admirable talent for deleting the more scabrous aspects of authenticity. Aboard the floating gin palace that was my home for ten heavy-eyelidded summer days, gambling, guns and mozzies are strictly off-limits. What you do get is iced water, chilled air and a bye-byes chocolate on your pillow every night. This is as fine and dandy a reproduction of a nineteenth-century showboat as twentieth-century technology can create – the newest, biggest, costliest and most unashamedly ostentatious sternwheeler plying Ol' Man River.

I joined her at St Louis, in the shadow of the soaring arch that is 'The Gateway to the West'. The *American Queen* is the flagship of the only remaining fleet of passenger boats plying the Mississippi, Ohio, Missouri and Arkansas Rivers and her owners, the Delta Queen Steamship Co., have spent more than $40 million to bolster a folk dream. Her sister ships, the *Delta Queen* and *Mississippi Queen*, have been churning the milk-chocolate waters since 1917 and 1976 respectively, offering holiday-makers the unique experience of long-haul cruising without actually putting to sea. They provide a holiday for those who like to take their nostalgia with a spoonful of sugar. This being America, that sector seemed to include a large number of well-heeled widows.

A pink-iced floating wedding cake, the vessel towers six decks high with twin smokestacks flared like exploded cigars. On the outside she is a fretwork extravaganza, with a pilot's gazebo, a steam organ fluting brassy minstrel tunes and, neatly hidden, an outdoor pool. On the inside she is as fancy as a New Orleans bordello: en suite cabins, chintzy public saloons, chandelier-hung dining-room, bars galore and an on-board music hall with more plush and gilt than the Leeds City Varieties.

Our journey took us down-river through the heart of the Mid-West where the Good Book rules – which is why poker, the staple pastime of bored nineteenth-century steam-boaters, has gone. Round here gambling will get you in jug pronto these days. The *American Queen* tips its hat at tradition by providing a Gentleman's Card Room (and, for that matter, a Ladies' Parlour) with baize tables under fringed Victorian shades. But the odd game I saw in progress was as polite as a WI whist drive. There are plenty of other ways to pass the time, and most of my fellow travellers threw themselves into such pursuits as bingo, old-time dancing, quizzes and keep-fit with that unself-conscious enthusiasm that makes Americans so different from Europeans.

Every dawn I lay limply in bed listening to the thump of trainer-clad septuagenarian feet pounding the decks in pursuit of eternal youth. A sign said seven circuits equalled one mile. Every evening I would gaze in awe as the same people scoffed till they dropped. There were some gargantuan appetites on board and figures to match. To satisfy them, continental breakfast was available from 6.30 a.m. on the foredeck (I was told, although I never actually saw it), and from then till the early hours the calories queued and jostled for attention. Breakfast proper was traditional and superb. Lunch and dinner, presented with panache in the airy, high-ceilinged dining-room, featured high-quality fare in generous amounts, although somewhat short on imagination. Americans are eager but not adventurous eaters. As for the groaning late-night supper tables, cream-laden afternoon teas, never-ending bar snacks and the round-the-clock hot-dog stall, they are scenes I prefer to forget. A lawyer from Los Angeles told me cheerily he was there 'to pig out'. Hmmm!

These cruises are quite dressy affairs. You can get away with shirt and shorts by day, but at dinner collars and ties are de rigueur for men, and women are expected to put on a bit of a show, which they do with enthusiasm and a penchant for sequins. Most passengers were comfortably-off Middle American retirees – spry, friendly people with the parchment skin and shallow political horizons that result from vegetating too long in the Californian and Floridian sun. After-dinner conversations were rather limited.

One intriguing party of matronly ladies belonged to a group from Atlanta calling itself The Merry Widows. They took it in turns to schmooze and trip the light fantastic with a couple of slick fifty-something fellows, one with a ponytail, the other a lounge-lizard moustache. I assumed them to be gigolos on the make but learned later that they were professional escorts hired for the cruise. They certainly seemed to earn their keep.

Steam-boatin' is a curiously soporific experience in which time and space cease to have meaning; stifling days drift into steamy nights and the flat, featureless panoramas of the Mississippi Basin slip past. The Rhine it is not. The river is wide and smooth, and the only hint of being afloat is an occasional muted thumpety-thump as the flat hull breasts the wake of a passing cargo barge.

Branching into the narrower Ohio, heading for Cincinnatti, our final destination, we had a closer view of what sparse river-bank life there is. A 'riverlorian' gives daily lectures on the boat's progress, the history, the locks and other sights. There is even a mock-up of a chart room where passengers can check progress and play at being navigator. The mosquitoes had obviously died of hypothermia in the boat's fiercely air-conditioned interior. I reckon the river banks, once thick with them, have also been dusted down. I wasn't so much as nipped, not even when catching the sultry evening breeze on deck.

The skipper, high on his flying bridge, was a suitably colourful stand-in for *Showboat*'s Cap'n Andy. Capt. Lawrence Keeton, with his starched whites, bright-blue eyes and slow-burn Tennessee drawl, was seventy-seven years old and had been navigating the river since boyhood. Most days there was a port of call, Capt. Keeton sounding his siren as we rounded a river bend, then nosing his vessel in to the sloping bank as the locals came out to watch and cheer. They seemed happy to see 'their' river coming back to life. As for the towns themselves – well, Mark Twain would surely recognise some of these hot, one-horse streets and the God-fearing folk who inhabit them. They love to show visitors the sights: the oldest house in town; a villa where a Civil War general once stayed; the town museum. Many communities have greeters – ladies of a certain age with cherry-pie cheeks who gather on the quay to say 'Welcome'.

We found St Genevieve, Missouri, immersed in its annual fair, with craft stalls lining its streets. It was folksy, wholesome and unpretentious – a glimpse of an America far removed from *Miami Vice*. On the Ohio we stopped at Paducah, Kentucky, where I told a greeter called Mary-Ellen that the place I really wanted to visit was the neighbouring town of

Metropolis, 'home of Superman'. She ran me there in her Chevvy, and introduced me to the superhero's statue in the town square and the Superman Museum. Such is the hospitality of Middle America.

I must, in the interests of accurate reporting, note the fact that during our cruise the *American Queen*'s 50-ton paddle-wheel developed a crack and gave up the ghost. Capt. Keeton hinted at behind-the-scenes ructions with the Louisiana shipyard. Time was when we would have been stranded, up the creek without a paddle. But we just kept on cruising because what had really kept us moving, it turned out, was not steam power and a churning egg-whisk but two diesel-electric propellers. As I was saying, authenticity goes only so far.

BIG FISH IN THE BIG APPLE

MICHAEL KERR TAKES A BOAT TRIP IN NEW YORK
HARBOUR – WITH ROD AND REEL

Jon had served his time on the rivers of Montana, and it showed. Watching
him cast, watching the sweet flight of line, leader and fly, I was reminded of
Norman Maclean's *A River Runs Through It*, that hymn to the angler as artist.
But there was no mistaking our stretch of water for the Big Blackfoot.

Behind us was the slender span of the Verrazano Narrows Bridge. To our
right was Brooklyn; to our left Staten Island and, beyond it, Jersey City.
Directly ahead, crowded on the water's edge like commuters on a platform,
were the towers of Manhattan. We were angling in New York Harbour.

As soon as I had heard it was possible, I knew I had to try it. Thanks to a
ban on commercial harvesting and tighter controls on dumping, there had
been a huge increase here in twenty years in the populations of two hungry
predators: the bluefish and the striped bass. Both could be caught from a
boat. They could be taken nobly, on the fly, or crudely, by the likes of me,
with spinner or bait. And if the sport proved disappointing, the sightseeing
would not.

Joe Shastay was my guide to the game fish. A cheery fireman from Jersey
City, he works twenty-four hours on, seventy-two off, which leaves plenty
of time for his second occupation of charter-boat captain. Most of his
customers are New Yorkers, escaping with him for an evening's fishing
after a long day on Wall Street.

Mine was a daytime trip. I joined Joe and Jon Fisher, proprietor of a shop
called Urban Angler, at 10.15 at a marina on East 23rd Street at the East
River. Above us, the Empire State shouldered its way to heaven. Rich men's
toys – El Rancho, Real Escape, Phat Boy – rocked gently at anchor, rigged
with only slightly fewer security devices than are found in a New York
apartment. 'Do Not Board Without Permission,' said the notices. 'Alarm
Will Sound.'

Joe's boat, Mako, although more modest in length at 19 feet, lacked
nothing in power. We took off at a fair lick down the river. 'There's a 90 per

cent chance these fish are running. That's why I'm pushing it,' said Joe. 'We've got about a nine-mile run and it's against the tide.' That, at least, is what he seems to have said. Notes taken against the tide are as hard to read as they are to write.

As the boat hurtled along, I stopped worrying about seasickness and tried to stop a silly grin spreading across my face. Two days earlier I had crossed the harbour by ferry, a great hulking craft on which I had seen nothing – it was misty – and felt nothing. Now I was not so much on the water but in it, wind-beaten and bouncing with every bump.

I was on a cushioned seat with my back to the wheel. Jon was sprawled on the bottom of the boat sorting his tackle. Joe turned his head momentarily to the side and gestured to me. 'Over there...' he began.

But he didn't finish. The boat took off, and Jon with it, then came down with a mighty thump. There was a scream, an oath, an apology – and the sightseeing was curtailed. (Joe had been trying to draw my attention to the Domino factory on the quay, where a giant pair of claws was lifting the sugar that would later sweeten New York's coffee.)

If the logs don't catch you here, the wakes will. Our buffeting came, I think, somewhere near the Queensboro Bridge. Our passage thereafter, although no less exhilarating, was smoother: under the Williamsburg Bridge, the Manhattan Bridge, the Brooklyn Bridge, past South Street Seaport and the unmistakable towers of the World Trade Centre. Then, under the watchful eye of the Coastguard and the welcoming arm of Liberty, we swept into the Upper Bay. As we anchored north-east of the Verrazano Narrows Bridge, Jon was still nursing his tail bone but strong enough to crack a joke. 'Since when,' he asked, 'has fishing been a contact sport?'

As he and Joe began to discuss tactics – 'I've got this super-fast sinking line. How about a little bunker pattern?' – I took in the view. The sky, which had been grey when we left, was clearing, the sun sparkling on the water. I felt sorry for all those suits in their Manhattan offices, all those slaves scurrying between the canyons. We, said a madly macho little voice in my head, are the only livin' boys in New York.

'You wanna fish?' asked Joe. I did. I started with a spinning rod, following Joe's advice to cast and then let the line run deep – the fish were feeding near the bottom – while I counted to twenty before reeling in. 'Count slow – a thousand and one, a thousand and two...Some people say Mississippi, but thousands work fine for me.'

But not for me. Perhaps the fish had heard my beginner's question and

Joe's answer and knew that what was whizzing through the water ahead of them was 'a one-ounce jig with a rubber tail'. Still, it was only just after eleven o'clock. I had more than three hours in which to get lucky.

Joe had other ideas. He has been 'skunked' only once in 450 trips; he was determined to see me land a fish, and sooner rather than later. Taking a short boat rod, he baited the hook with a four-inch chunk of oozing fish guts, let the line drop to the bottom over the stern and then handed me the rod. I kept it there a moment, then jiggled to check I hadn't had a bite. 'You don't need to do that,' said Joe. 'Don't worry — when these fish bite you won't mistake it for anything else.'

On cue, the rod arched sharply. Having not fished for years, and having become a little squeamish about the whole business, I had wondered what I would think when this moment came. I didn't think at all. I whipped up the rod, bracing the butt against my hip and reeled as fast as I could, trying all the while to keep my balance in the rocking boat. If I lost the fish, I would be disappointed; but if I dropped the rod or fell in, I would be disgraced.

I didn't play the fish; I wrenched it in. The landing was a blur: a flash of blue-green, a white belly, Jon (or was it Joe?) bending with the net. Then the bluefish, a couple of feet long, was thrashing inside the boat.

There was a dribble of blood on the second knuckle of my right hand. 'Hey,' said Jon, 'is that yours or the fish's?' Mine. In my excitement, I had scraped my finger on the edge of the reel.

I watched as Jon gingerly unhooked the fish. Bluefish will eat whatever is put in front of them, including fish of their own species and fingers trying to free them. The triangular teeth snapped but missed. God, clearly, had decided that Jon had suffered enough today.

As the fish went back, I asked Joe whether, if I had kept it, it would have been safe to eat. Yes, he said, but the official advice was to eat no more than one a week. This was not because the harbour was dirty but because these are coastal fish and coastal waters generally are in a bad way.

Within ten minutes I had landed another bluefish, 28 inches long (we measured it) and weighing perhaps five or six pounds. I remained proud of this even when Joe told me that the boat's biggest bluefish weighed 16½lb and was caught, with a little help, by an eleven-year-old girl. I was proud, too, of my two-foot bass (boat record: 43 inches). It was a beautiful fish, its stripes little diamonds of gold stitched together with black dots. I did feel a twinge of guilt, but less at the catching than the manner of it. Such a fish deserved to be taken on a fly — which is how Joe caught the biggest of our half-dozen bluefish of the day — 34 inches and more than 10lb.

How he found time to do this I don't know, for he seemed to be everywhere at once: coaching me in the rudiments, advising Jon on the finer points, fetching mineral water, taking the wheel to move us back into 'the zone' when tide and current pulled us away. Sheltered though it may be, New York Harbour is no millpond and it is full of traps for the unwary. Joe, warier than most, none the less gets through six propellers a year.

The harbour was, however, surprisingly free of both noxious smells and noise. We could hear only the slap of water against our boat, the screech of gulls and the sound of metal somewhere being hammered on metal.

Traffic was light. Now and again a rusting barge loaded with containers would slide between us and Manhattan, like some hobos' train that had taken to the water. A top-heavy sport fishing boat, swaggering home, would smack us with its wake. And once, out of the corner of my eye, I glimpsed the orange bulk of the Staten Island ferry making its famous and famously cheap circuit.

Norman Maclean, I remember thinking, would have been appalled at the notion of fishing in such a setting. I loved it.

ALASKA, VIA THE SEA LESS TRAVELLED

MOST PEOPLE SEE THE 49TH STATE FROM THE DECK OF A CRUISE SHIP; **PETER HUGHES** TOOK FERRIES INSTEAD

The idea was simple: to cruise to Alaska without setting foot on a cruise ship. It is one of the classic cruising routes — the Inside Passage from Vancouver in British Columbia to Juneau in Alaska. I would follow it using ferries where possible, a car when necessary, with the freedom to move as I pleased. Not for me the programmed pleasures of big-ship cruising; not for me a cabin and the convenience of one unchanging room for the next sixteen nights.

Instead, I would discover what all those thousands, cooped up in their high-rise, high-seas holiday town-ships are missing on the land they pass so blithely. Well, that was the plan.

Ferries defer to roads. British Columbia has more roads than Alaska, so it has a different system of ferries. They are local, crossing sounds and inlets and plying between Vancouver Island and the mainland. There is no direct route from Vancouver to Prince Rupert, where you pick up the American ferry service — the Alaska Marine Highway. (The Marine Highway service that starts in Bellingham in Washington State does not stop in Canada.) So my progress north in Canada would be partly by car; in Alaska, purely by boat.

Ferries have been running across Howe Sound, north of Vancouver, for 120 years. They leave from Horseshoe Bay, a harbour hemmed in by mountains, today with snow on their tops and diaphanous scarves of cloud chucked over their shoulders. Forty minutes later, the ships dock at Langdale, which for tourists is the start of the Sunshine Coast. For residents, it is the terminal for a string of little seaside commuter villages. At one, Roberts Creek, I arranged a morning's sea kayaking in the Sechelt Inlet.

After paddling for an hour, we landed at a beach, pristine apart from a picnic table and a pole suspended from a tree on ropes like a swing. I was about to say how thoughtful to provide something for the children when my guide said: 'You see the "bear hang"? That's to keep your food out of reach of the black bears.'

The pigeon-grey asphalt of Highway 101 courses between banks of rock and tall forest. Beside it is a succession of villages, dogged little places, all built of timber and each with its store, post office, volunteer fire station and community hall.

Lund is at the end of Highway 101 or, as the locals have it, the beginning. They would also have you believe that Lund is the start of the Pan American Highway. Follow it for 15,000 miles and you'd arrive in Puerto Montt at the southern tip of Chile. Elsewhere, it is generally accepted that the highway's northern end is in Alaska. But then Lund is a take-it-or-leave-it kind of place, run more for the folk who live there than for those who visit.

There are boat trips galore all along this coast, not least for fishing. I went whale-watching from Telegraph Cove, a waterfront hotel prettily converted from the clapboard houses of an old logging camp, redolent with wood-burning stoves and the scent of cedar. The sea had the sheen of stretched clingfilm. In the distance, two cruise ships ambled south. In a few minutes we would be heading back.

Two hundred yards to starboard, a humpback whale surfaced. It performed four laconic breaches and dived. Christie, the on-board naturalist, quivered with excitement: humpbacks hadn't been seen here for three or four years.

We sat, waiting. Christie lulled us with information. Whales, she explained, normally stayed submerged for seven or eight minutes but were capable of holding their breath for 45. Just 30ft away, in a crashing eruption of water, the humpback burst from the deep - 20 streaming tons of it, levitating so close you could look into its tiny, unfathomable eye. It was a *Jaws* moment.

One theme recurring on this journey was the self-conscious, almost expiatory, respect paid to native Americans, whom the Canadians call the First Nation. I had met totem-pole carvers on Quadra Island and now I nipped over to Cormorant Island to see the U'mista Cultural Centre and its Potlatch Collection. Potlatches were – still are – traditional celebrations with singing, feasting and dancing that can go on for days. But in 1884 they were proscribed. Ritual regalia was impounded and sent to museums. By the 1950s the potlatch ban, by then ineffectual, was being quietly forgotten. Gradually, the old artefacts were restored to the communities from which they had been taken, the Kwakwaka'wakw people of Cormorant Island among them. Masks, headdresses and ceremonial gifts, which returned only in 1980, are reverentially displayed at U'mista.

Vancouver apart, little I had seen, and nothing I had done, certainly no one I had met, could have been found on a cruise. Equally, the little towns on British Columbia's coast are completely unaffected by the liners that troop along their summer horizon. That was about to change. The ferries became bigger, the voyages longer and the ports fashioned by the cruising itself. Alaska was a different experience altogether.

More than half the cities on the Alaskan coast are inaccessible by car. Tarmac stops where the wilderness starts, just on the edge of town. That is why the state-owned ferry system — the Marine Highway — was set up as soon as Alaska attained statehood in 1959.

The ocean-going *Kennicott*, which took me to Ketchikan, was nearly twice the size of my largest Canadian ferry. It was built in Mississippi — but then, under an ancient piece of protectionist legislation, any vessel carrying passengers exclusively between American ports has to be built and owned in the US. Cruise ships, which are almost all built in Europe, get round this by stopping in Canada. Vancouver owes much to the US Passenger Services Act of 1886.

Ketchikan is a tourist town and a cruise town. Every day I was there, four huge ships, twenty storeys tall, dwarfed the quayside. The front looks like a frontier town in the same way that Disney's Main Street looks like a high street. The buildings are mostly flat-faced, timber-frame houses painted in browns, greys and greens; some of the sidewalks are authentically planked. But almost every other shop is a jeweller, many owned by cruise lines. Ketchikan has been cruise-ified.

It has a PG-certificate past. It was the first city in Alaska to be reached by adventurers heading north. They quickly converted it into 'Uncle Sam's Wickedest City'. Creek Street was the red-light area, established by city ordinance in 1903, when it was decided to pack all the bawdy houses into one licentious location. It stayed in business for fifty-one years, until prostitution was banned.

Dolly Arthur's house, preserved as a museum, is more homely than salacious. Pink floral paper lines the walls, sheet music ('Gee but I hate to go home alone') lies open on the harmonium and the bed is small and brassy, a bit like a photo of Dolly herself. Her taste in books stretched little further than *Tarzan* and cookery.

Wrangell is close to the mouth of the Stikine River, which, before the railroad was built, was an important pass through the Coastal Mountains — the 'back door' to the Klondike. Prospectors roared into town, among them Wyatt Earp, sixteen years after holstering his Colt at the OK Corral shootout. He was made sheriff on his way through.

A fifth of today's population is native American. I met three elders of the Tlingit tribe on Petroglyph Beach, named because of its primitive rock etchings. Their age is indeterminate: I was told 2,000 years.

One of the Tlingits, Marge Byrd, remembered the bad days, when there were signs in Juneau saying 'No dogs or Indians' and native languages were suppressed. Things have improved. A totem pole, copied from one carved by her grandfather, has been erected in the centre of town. It took years to get permission. 'I cried many times, but the pole had to come back to where it knew it belonged,' Marge said. 'It's very hard for us to live in two worlds. Keeping our native traditions alive is very difficult. But we manage.'

The ferry *Malaspina* sailed overnight. There were cabins, but I had failed to book one. The sleeping possibilities were consequently limited. Here was an experience denied to anyone on a cruise. The top deck was a campsite. Half a dozen tents had been pitched there, their guy ropes stuck to the deck with tape.

The only reclining seats were in the cinema and so uncomfortable that I slept on the deck, immediately beneath a PA speaker. 'Attention passengers! At 06.30 there will be a car-deck break when you may return to your vee-hey-cles. If you're walkin' a critter, it must be leashed. And pick up after...'

For more than 100 years Alaska was occupied by Russia. Sitka – then New Archangel – was the capital of Russian America. Sitka has a cruise business, but about a third of the size of Ketchikan's, mainly because it has so far resisted building a big ship terminal. It was the oddest – and most interesting – of my Alaskan ports.

Russia's abiding legacy is its religion. At the centre of the city is St Michael's Cathedral. Garlic-domed – not quite the full onion – and with a spire the shape of an okra sprout, topped with the three-bar orthodox cross, the green and grey timber building looks exotic in an American Main Street. The congregation is unexpected, too: it is 95 per cent native American. As well as the Tlingit language, services can contain passages of Russian, Greek and two Eskimo tongues.

The original 1848 cathedral burnt down forty years ago, but the nearby Russian bishop's house is original, if restored. A new priest was being inducted in the chapel. It was a ceremony drawn from an extraordinary concoction of cultures. Oil lamps hung from the ceiling; icons shimmered in candlelight. Bishop Nicolae had flown in from Anchorage to officiate. A tall man, elongated by a white Gandalfian beard and bulbous gold mitre, he wore the robes of Imperial Russia, more gold and scarlet.

The liturgy was from the Eastern Church. There was much incense and the rich harmonies of Russian plainsong; a priest tapped a tuning fork on the back of his hand before each chant. But the faces — the women in head-scarves — were Indian, and the hewn-log architecture from the frontier.

My journey ended in Juneau. Most cruises continue across the Gulf of Alaska, but I stopped at the capital. Juneau was one of the earliest Gold Rush towns. The buildings seem to rise from the sea, riding on a mountain-side, and are much as they were a century ago. Cruise ships land about 14,000 visitors a day, so the sightseeing is designed for groups — tours of old gold mines and a thriving brewery; rides on a zip line. Harnessed to a cable-slung pulley, you whizz through a forest 100ft above the ground. It's like bungee jumping without the bounce.

The biggest attraction is the Mendenhall Glacier, accessible by bus. For all the crowds, it is a humbling sight: an enormous river, gushing between high mountains, stopped in its tracks. More humbling still is its rate of retreat — 600ft in 2004, ten times the rate of a decade ago.

In just over two weeks I had caught a dozen ferries and stayed in as many different hotels. Was it worth it? In Canada, definitely yes. The British Columbia coast is serendipity-by-the sea. In Alaska, the ferries go where the cruise ships go. So, unless you want to stay and immerse yourself into that almighty scenery, you miss next to nothing by taking a cruise. After all, that is what so much of it has been made for.

INTO THE WILDERNESS, ON A
RAPID LEARNING CURVE

CANOEING IN NORTH ONTARIO, **MINTY CLINCH**
FOLLOWS THE CREE WAY OF SURVIVAL

On the first day of the trip, Fred's ancestors were not amused. They didn't like the rocks, far too many of them sticking out of the foaming waters of the Missinaibi River. And they didn't like me, a whitewater canoeist who had never even paddled a canoe before.

I had stressed this when I signed on for my heritage adventure in the northern Ontario wilderness and had been told it didn't matter. Fred thought otherwise. How could he share an unstable craft with someone who not only didn't know how to draw and pry, but didn't know what they were? Over the next five days, he would find out. We both hoped it wouldn't be the hard way.

Fred Neegan is a seventy-year-old Cree Indian with more stamina than teeth. He has never married, perhaps because he has never met anyone to equal his mother, an indomitable woman who could shoot a bull moose and carry its parts out of the forest, even after bearing thirteen children. He was born on the Missinaibi, the main stretch of the historic 450-mile fur trappers' route from Lake Superior to James Bay, the southern extension of Hudson Bay. Depending on skills and water levels, a recreational canoeist takes about four weeks to complete the journey.

After the initial 55 miles up the Michipicoten River against the current, a long portage leads to Missinaibi Lake, the headwaters of the river proper. The turbulent upper reaches are for advanced canoeists only, but intermediates can tackle the 45-mile run from Mattice to Bells Bay, taking in the magnificent Thunderhouse Falls, where the river smashes off the hard granite edge of the Canadian Shield on to the Hudson Bay lowlands. No canoeist can negotiate them, though several have died trying, so we faced an 8,200ft portage to circumvent them on the last afternoon before the float plane pick-up.

We ate a last breakfast in Mattice, then set out, a three-canoe flotilla, with

Fred and me in the lead. Our travelling companions were accomplished paddlers — a Canadian businessman and his twelve-year-old son and an American couple who own a sports store on Lake Huron — and we reached the Rock Island campsite, where we would spend our first night under canvas, without incident. We also made our first portage, perhaps 500ft over slippery rocks to a sandy spit. Fortunately the awkward business of carrying upturned canoes is men's work, but women and children are consigned to food, cooking utensils and tents. Factor in personal packs, and everyone has to make two journeys to complete the exercise.

As I lurched and staggered through the water with these unbalancing loads on my back, I thought I'd made a big mistake, an impression that increased throughout an afternoon spent honing canoe skills on the stretch of white water alongside the island. Or, in my case, acquiring them after Fred and I had plunged backwards down the treacherous channels between the rocks. I learnt that drawing or prying (pulling or pushing with the paddle) will move the canoe sideways in the desired direction and that the appropriate stroke should be made instinctively in a split-second reaction to upcoming hazards, but putting theory into practice wasn't easy, especially after Fred admitted that he could be hazy over left and right.

With our tents set up, we began the routine of 'no-trace' camping favoured by Canada's canoe guru, Hap Wilson. 'The degenerate slobs who abuse the rules should be subjected to medieval "trial by ordeal" — public flogging perhaps,' he wrote in our bible, *Journey to the Northern Sky*. And what sort of abuse might earn such a punishment? Not picking up rubbish left by the 'more unrefined adventurer' who preceded you? Or using several-ply coloured loo paper instead of the recommended sphagnum moss?

On the subject of fires, Wilson is torn between spirituality and hygiene. 'The traditional camper requires a campfire to fulfil complete canoe-quest bliss.' Quite so, but a pack stove would be cleaner and safer. For us, it was also compulsory, with fires officially banned after weeks of drought.

Once it was alight, we extricated 'Dinner, Day 1' from the neatly labelled packages inside the bear-proof food barrel. Typically the meals are of the 'add boiling water and stir' variety, easy to prepare in a range of potentially testing weather conditions, but menus are inventive and intelligently put together. Rice, burritos, couscous and pasta, with fillings or sauces to suit, provide the carbohydrate for the next day's paddling, while treats that include chocolate and, memorably, a partially baked blueberry cake, keep expectations high.

'Good morning, Fred.' 'Good morning,' my canoe buddy responded lugubriously, 'although it's really afternoon.' I checked my watch: 6.30 a.m. Fred had already brewed his tea and yearned to be back on his beloved river.

Under the education system imposed on First Native People in the 1930s, he left the Missinaibi when he was five to go to boarding school. The pupils spent half their time studying the history of the British Empire and the other half working in the fields, a form of economic slavery that he resents as much for the loss of his childhood as for its exploitation. Deprived of all contact with his parents, he knew nothing of his heritage until he was released from school twelve years later.

In his early twenties, he was an alcoholic, shutting out reality with cheap wine. At forty-two, he kicked the habit and survived, unlike many of his relations. The Neegans came from a long line of Cree trappers who supplied pelts, primarily beaver, marten and muskrat, to Hudson Bay Company outposts on the Missinaibi.

In winter, they used dog sleds and snowshoes on the frozen river, taking to their canoes in spring once the ice melted. The single piece of birch bark that formed the base was stitched to a cedar frame with roots and water-proofed with resin. The canoes were light but fragile, so the Cree preferred to carry them, rather than risk them on the rocks. Modern canoes, with resilient hulls, are designed to bounce, but Fred's ancestors are always looking over his shoulder, pointing out that hitting rocks is wrong.

With the river lower than he'd ever seen it, there would be no appeasing them over the next few days. Soon after we passed the last of the roads and the end of civilisation as we know it, we entered Fred's natural habitat, the nine-square-mile trap-line in which he is legally entitled to hunt. We had lunch in the wooden cabin where he spends up to three months at a time on his own surrounded by great stretches of virgin forest. As we paddled on, he pointed out neighbouring trap-lines belonging to his cousins and sacred burial sites belonging to his ancestors.

Then we were back in the rapids, the water swirling this way and that, but often so shallow that we had to manhandle the canoes through partially submerged boulders until they could float again. For the next two nights, we camped above Thunderhouse Falls, enjoying a well-earned rest day with time to fish for sturgeon and pike. Throughout the journey, at the height of the summer season, we saw just eight other people – another group of six and a couple. Wilderness indeed.

All too soon we were back on the river, closing in on that menacing final portage. And guess what? It was easy. Back and forth we went, sliding through deep mud, climbing over fallen trees, trotting diligently through the silent forest. OK, we'd lightened the load by eating most of the food, but we were still impressed. So was Fred. 'You made good time,' he said, as we ripped open our celebratory cans of fish at lunchtime. 'Much better than I expected.'

In golden evening sunshine, we were rewarded with a swim in Bells Bay. 'Bronze for effort,' said Fred cheerfully, happy that we'd never overturned. 'You deserve that. And silver for not screaming.' You can't win 'em all.

THESE BEAUTIFUL BEASTS AND THEIR CABBAGE BREATH

THE SEA OF CORTEZ, SAYS **BRIAN JACKMAN**,
IS THE BEST PLACEIN THE WORLD TO
GO WHALE-WATCHING

Since dawn we have been motoring in an oily calm across the Bay of La Paz. To the west lies the coast of Baja California, its cactus-covered slopes glowing in the morning light. There is no wind, and in the ensuing silence when the engines are switched off we can hear the breathing of the great whales all around us. First the hollow rush of expelled air from their great lungs, then the deep intake of air before the next dive.

When they blow, sending columns of moisture 30ft into the sky, the spray drifts over us, smelling faintly of cabbage, and when they surface to peer at us with curious, myopic eyes, it is impossible not to feel one's senses reaching out to them. Here we are – two species from alien worlds – drawn together by mutual curiosity. And who, watching them come so trustingly close, can fail to be moved, knowing how we have persecuted these innocent beasts down the centuries?

Forget the great whales of Newfoundland, the right whales of Hermanus and Patagonia, the humpbacks of Alaska and the orcas of British Columbia. For me the Sea of Cortez is the best place in the world to watch whales – not just for sheer numbers or variety of species but also for silky seas and a blissful desert climate. Yet hardly anyone seems to know about it. So quiet is the Baja, so empty and utterly unexploited, that you cannot believe Los Angeles and its roaring freeways are less than two hours away by air.

Cut off from the Pacific by a thousand miles of mountains, the Sea of Cortez resembles a giant marine oasis in the midst of the Mexican desert. Steinbeck wrote about it. Hemingway should have done. Otherwise it has managed to stay off the map. The Baja itself is longer than Italy, a waterless peninsula hanging off the end of California with its tail in the Tropic of Cancer. Once you leave the main highway from Tijuana to Los Cabos you'll need a four-wheel-drive vehicle to get anywhere. Or a boat.

So, if you want to see whales galore, fly to LA and then down to La Paz, a laid-back ferry-port at the tip of the Baja. There, you sign on for a nine-day cruise with Christopher Swann, a latter-day Ahab who hunts whales not with a harpoon but with love in his heart and a pair of binoculars clapped to his eyes.

The *Jacana*, our live-aboard home for the next nine days, is a 45ft catamaran that Swann has chartered for the season. She has four comfortable cabins and a spacious galley-cum-dining saloon in which Anne, Swann's sister, conjures up delicious feasts of char-grilled fish and enchiladas. Behind us we tow a *panga*, a fast fibreglass launch of the kind used by the local fishermen.

Within an hour of arriving at La Paz we are off into the blue, heading towards the island of Espiritu Santo , where we will anchor for the night. Above us, frigate birds patrol the skies and squadrons of pelicans lumber past. The sun is shining, the sea is calm and Swann is in his element. 'There she blows,' he cries as a pillar of spray erupts ahead. It's a humpback, the first of 175 whales we shall see on this voyage.

Swanny, as he is known to his chums, is a footloose adventurer who should have been born a couple of centuries ago when there were still new trade routes to discover. Instead, he has become the Whale Whisperer of Cortez, seemingly able to summon up whales from the emptiest patch of water.

The last time we met was a decade ago, on his own boat, the *Marguerite Explorer*, a Danish trawler he had converted for wildlife cruises in the Hebrides. Now, at the age of 47, he has swapped his Scottish oilskins for a salt-stained sarong, set up a tour company called Oceanus – based in Brighton, of all places – and spends half the year chasing whales in the Baja sunshine.

Espiritu Santo is a typical Baja anchorage: an emerald cove rimmed with white shell sand, encircled by a Wild West landscape of red rim rocks and cactus forest. Next morning, woken at dawn by the rattle of the anchor chain, I surface for a cup of tea to find we are already under way, with Swanny sitting barefoot at the wheel.

'Today,' he announces, 'we are looking for Moby.' He means the sperm whale, the biggest of the toothed whales, which can grow up to 60ft long. 'They're usually quite shy,' he says, but finds one in half an hour. It's a solitary bull, easily identified by its huge, blunt head and the way it lolls on the surface. When it dives, sliding back into its own weightless world of indigo currents and sonic visions, Swanny switches on the hydrophone and we listen to the barrage of clicks the whale emits as it hunts for squid.

We move on. Swanny is desperate to show us a blue whale, the biggest animal ever to grace our planet. Just how big is biggest? Put it like this: a toddler could crawl through its aorta and you could drop a dog down its blowhole. Fully grown, a blue whale may weigh 190 tons and exceed 100ft in length; even at birth it is 25ft long. And it has the loudest voice in the animal kingdom; its low-frequency calls can be heard across oceans.

In the end, the blue whale finds us. We are floating far out in the bay, enjoying a picnic lunch on deck when we hear the familiar sound of a whale blowing and see the animal heading straight towards us. It is unbelievably huge – like a Polaris submarine. Twice it circles us, no more than a boat's length away, and then it dives, passing directly beneath us. One flip of its tail could have sent us all to kingdom come; but there was no hint of menace in its unhurried movements.

During the 1960s, when whales were being slaughtered at the rate of 60,000 a year, it was feared that the giant blues were doomed. By 1970 no more than 8,000 were left. But by then the tide of international opinion was running in the whales' favour. Even so, it took another fifteen years before commercial whaling was banned. Today, whales are worth more alive than dead. Whale-watching holidays have become big business, worth in excess of $1bn (£588m) worldwide, and the blue whale has survived.

In the days that follow we see nine more blue whales, seventy-nine fin whales, sixty-six humpbacks, thirteen Bryde's whales, two sei whales and another couple of sperm whales. Like Swanny, we have become adept at spotting the distant puffs of drifting spray, the sunlight gleaming on polished obsidian backs and the white shell-bursts of breaching humpbacks.

Yet even these are upstaged by our encounters with dolphins. Elsewhere I have seen maybe thirty at a time, but in the Sea of Cortez they turn up in their thousands. By the time we fly home we will have seen at least 23,000 common and bottlenose dolphins.

Joyfully they race towards us, determined to hitch a ride in our wake, and within minutes we are engulfed by a Mexican wave of leaping bodies. They are chasing fish as they charge along, and they are not alone. All around us, boobies and pelicans are diving into the water. It's a feeding frenzy and we are at the heart of it, with thousands of dolphins strung out for a mile on either side of us.

Peering over the bows I can see them flying beneath us like torpedoes, their dorsal fins cleaving the surface a mere fingertip away. When one of them jumps ahead of us, soaring 10ft into the air and falling back with a crash that soaks us all, I suddenly become aware of this demented voice, hee-hawing like a cowboy, and realise to my horror that it is mine.

Then, as suddenly as they materialised out of the heat haze, they tire of their sport with us and peel away to resume their wild hunt, receding into the distance with a sound like breaking surf.

We, too, continue our voyage, heading north to Isla Coyote, where a score of fishermen, *pangueros*, live in bleached wooden shacks held fast like limpets beneath a simple white chapel. We wade ashore past the horned skull of a steer with a gull perched on it and buy a yellow-fin tuna the men have caught that morning. I talk to one of them. His name is Ishmael and he wears a red T-shirt and a straw sombrero. The fishing is good, he tells me, but life is hard.

Our life, by comparison, has never been sweeter. No longer pale-faced refugees from the British winter, we have kicked off our shoes and become ocean-going nomads. At anchor we snorkel among shoals of tropical fish or go beachcombing for cowries along sugar-white beaches. At breakfast we gorge ourselves on luscious fresh pineapples; and in the evenings, as the islands turn red and gold in the dying light, we drink margaritas and watch the moon come up over the Sierra La Giganta .

No wonder Swanny calls it the Sea of Dreams. Who will ever believe I saw more than 20,000 dolphins? But it is true. The Sea of Cortez pulsates with life. Sometimes, peering down into the Baja's sunlit depths, we spot squadrons of manta rays cruising past like Stealth bombers on a mission. And one memorable morning we go swimming with the friendly sea lions of Isla Partida, whose doe-eyed youngsters are so inquisitive that they peer into our face masks from just inches away.

Birds, too, throng these waters in numbers beyond counting. Flocks of black storm petrels flutter among the wavelets like swallows hawking for insects over an English meadow; and every day we pass huge rafts of grebes and phalaropes, meet lipstick gulls with coral beaks and ospreys perched on cliff-top eyries.

Too soon the voyage is nearly over and I cannot bear the thought of leaving. But the highlight of the trip is still to come. It happens on our last night when we set out after supper to look for whales by moonlight. We jump into the *panga* and race out into the bay, leaving a fiery trail of bioluminescence in our wake.

Our luck is in. The moon is full and the sea is smooth as glass – what Swanny calls 'the Silky'. He kills the engine and in the silence of the moonglow we sit and listen to the deep sighs of spouting whales. There must be at least a score – fin whales, Bryde's and humpbacks – all leisurely circling us on the black-and-silver water.

Away to the south-west I can see the lights of La Paz, a reminder of that other universe from which we have come. But now and for a while yet, we remain in the company of the great leviathans, at peace with them and with ourselves in Mexico's magical Sea of Dreams.

SURELY NO ONE REALLY THOUGHT WE WERE GOING TO WAR...

THE FORMER ITN CORRESPONDENT **MICHAEL NICHOLSON** RECALLS SAILING TO THE FALKLANDS WITH THE TASK FORCE – THE FIRST MASS SEABORNE INVASION BY BRITISH TROOPS SINCE NORMANDY

We pulled away from the Portsmouth quayside in a crazy mixture of commotion and ceremony: the forest of Union flags, the brass bands, young mothers and their babes in tears, amply bosomed girlfriends tearing off their bras and throwing them to their men in a sexy final goodbye. And I, watching it all from the poop deck of HMS *Hermes*, convinced it was all a bit of a sham. I wasn't the only one. A lieutenant-commander standing next to me said: 'We will all be creeping back in a few days.'

Surely no one, on that April morning, really thought we were going to war. It could only be a matter of days before it was settled by diplomacy. It seemed such a nonsense…8,000 sea miles to save a thousand so-called Brits?

It was a fluke that I was even on board. It was all because of a pregnant cow. On the day the Argentines landed at Port Stanley I was on holiday with my family in the Lake District. Our walking routine was to leave the hotel early with a picnic lunch and come back in time for dinner. But that day a cow in calf blocked our path and we detoured back to be met by a breathless porter shouting, 'Your office is after you…you must call London…there's a war on.'

The press were treated from the start with much suspicion. The Royal Navy had at first refused to take us with them. It was only when Mrs Thatcher ordered Admiral Sir John Fieldhouse to do so that the selected few were allowed to sail. Fieldhouse abhorred the media. 'If I had my way,' he said publicly, 'I wouldn't tell anyone there was a war going on until it was all over. Then only tell them who'd won.'

Even as we left England, a coded message was sent from Royal Navy HQ in Northwood to the Task Force captains. It contained a single word: DIET. Decoded it read: 'Starve the Press'. Of all the wars I have covered, and there have been many, the censorship then was the severest of any. I can recall only one instance when the reason behind a cut story was explained.

We had sailed into the Total Exclusion Zone, a 200-mile perimeter of the Falklands that Argentine ships entered at their peril. Three Harriers were on deck, pilots waiting in their open cockpits, ready to fly in combat. But we were enveloped in thick fog; you could not even see the 'ski jump' at the bow. So the operation was cancelled. Later, I said to one of the pilots that it was just as well, as he would have had a job getting back again.

He replied: 'We wouldn't have got back.' He explained that, if they had gone to combat range, on their return they would have had only two minutes' fuel left to find their ship and land.

'But you have radar,' I said.

'Yes…but that only tells you where the Task Force is…it doesn't guide you to your mother ship. In this fog we would have to search for it and two minutes doesn't give you much hope.'

It was some story: a £10 million aircraft that was crucial to winning the war couldn't fly because of the fog. But the censor said no. Then a kindly met officer took me to his ops room and showed me a map of the Falklands.

'There is our patch of fog,' he said, pointing to a blob in the middle of nowhere. 'Now the Argies haven't a clue where we are, but if you broadcast that we are stuck in it [my reports were aired on the BBC World Service] then all they have to do is look at their weather map and send their Exocets to find us. Now do you understand?' I did.

Exocet was the dread word, this French-made missile that could turn the tide of war against us. They had originally been sold to the Argentines to be launched from ships but, despite protestations of neutrality, French engineers were sent secretively to Argentina so they could be modified and fired from the Argentine Etandards and Mirage fighter-bombers.

In my mind there is no doubt that the Argentine light cruiser *General Belgrano* was doomed just as long as she was at sea. On the Sunday afternoon of 2 May, Cmdr Chris Wredford-Brown, captain of the submarine *Conqueror*, without warning and knowing his target was outside the Total Exclusion Zone, fired two torpedoes at her. It was said that the order was given to attack her because 'she was closing in on elements of our Task Force'.

And yet, two days before, the Task Force commander, Sandy Woodward, had told me: 'There's a cruiser sniffing around and I'm going to give it a bloody nose.' The sinking was announced over *Hermes*'s Tannoy. Most listened in silence. Sailors do not celebrate the deaths of fellow seamen. And more than 300 of the Belgrano's crew were killed that day. It was left to the *Sun* to do the indecent thing with its infamous headline 'GOTCHA!'

The Argentines were quick to take revenge. On 4 May, with the Task Force on Red Alert, we saw black smoke rising some three miles away. HMS *Sheffield* had been hit amidships by an Exocet. Survivors were brought aboard, many so badly burnt it was difficult to distinguish charred flesh from charred uniform. As we filmed on deck, one man walked quite calmly past us and nodded at the camera. We learnt later that his nylon shirt and trousers had fused with his skin and he had died in the most horrible way.

We were not told the date or the place of the invasion until the night before, and were flown by helicopter to the smaller, shallow-draught HMS *Fearless* to join 200 men of the Royal Marine Commandos in San Carlos Water.

One memory of that invasion morning is indelible. And of one person, a young marine called Nowak. Visualise the scene: this was the moment we had been preparing for. The first mass seaborne invasion by British troops since Normandy. We could not know what was ahead of us but we all expected the worst. It is 5 a.m. I am below deck surrounded by men with blackened faces, half of England's hedgerows stuck in their helmets, weighed down with weapons and ammunition belts, waiting to disembark. We could hear a lot of artillery and mortar fire. The tension, call it fear, was thick. It was cold, yet men were sweating. Then came a moment of pure Hollywood.

The sergeant-major called out: 'Nowak, stand up!' Up stood Nowak. He could not have been more than 5ft 2in tall and almost as wide. He was carrying a heavy belt of machinegun shells.

Sergeant-major: 'What is that you're wearing, Nowak?'

Nowak: 'It's a bra, sir.'

Sergeant-major: 'And may I ask lad, why you are wearing a bra?'

Nowak: 'Sir, it's my girlfriend's and she told me I had to wear it to remind me what I'm fighting for.'

Sergeant-major: 'Too bloody right, lad, and when this show's over they'll pin a medal on that blooming bra of yours.'

How rapidly the tension evaporated. Soon afterwards, we went ashore in a very different mood. Sadly, Michael Nowak was killed two days before the war ended. No medal was pinned on his bra but his name is among the 258 carved into the granite memorial that overlooks Port Stanley.

We had a week of constant air attacks and, anchored in San Carlos Water, we were sitting targets. The Argentines lost planes but we lost ships. In a telephone report to ITN, I said that it was a gamble on whether they ran out of aircraft before we ran out of ships. I don't know how the censor let that one through. On board *Fearless* we came close to saying farewell when a bomb aimed at us overshot and hit HMS *Antelope*. Had it gone a few hundred yards farther it would have taken out the ammunition ship, full to the brim with high explosive, and most of us in that bay with it.

That same day HMS *Coventry* was sunk at the entrance to the Falkland Sound and the *Atlantic Conveyor*, the container ship bringing desperately needed supplies including more aircraft and helicopters, was sunk by an Exocet. In my war diary, dated 25 May, I wrote: 'This is our lowest ebb. We have now lost five ships, fifty-four seamen have been killed, over 100 wounded, many critically.'

It was the battle for Goose Green that turned things around, a tiny settlement of no strategic value but Mrs Thatcher needed good news and the Paras' overnight victory provided it. Come daylight we filmed the aftermath. The Argentine dead were still out there, half submerged in the mud and water of their trenches. I saw, too, that the Paras had used bayonets as well as bullets.

We witnessed the official surrender of the garrison but the Para major, Chris Keeble, would not let us film it. The prisoners were mostly teenaged conscripts; dazed and shivering, they were herded into sheep pens. One of them threw a hidden grenade into a pile of ammunition. There was an explosion and a fire, many were wounded. A British medical orderly pulled two out of the flames and went back for a third. But his legs had been blown off and he could not be moved. I turned away, then heard a shot. The orderly could not let him burn to death.

The bombing of *Sir Galahad* was the last and worst tragedy of the war. She was anchored in Bluff Cove, and in broad daylight and with no air cover men of the Scots Guards were being off-loaded into landing craft.

We felt the blast and saw black smoke almost enveloping *Sir Galahad*. Her sister ship, *Sir Tristam*, was also burning. I watched as hundreds of men ran along the decks pulling on their life jackets. Those trapped at the stern jumped overboard and the orange rubber life rafts that might have saved them burst as they hit the flaming oil on the water.

The heroes that day were the crew of the Royal Navy's helicopters. They ignored the flames and exploding ammunition and flew into the dense smoke. I watched one pilot steer his machine slowly into the blackness and hover as his crewman winched down to pick men out of the sea.

I saw another helicopter almost touching the water − its rotor blades seemed to be spinning through the flames – to pick up a man clinging to the anchor chain. Then the helpless panic on shore as we saw that the wind was blowing many of the life rafts back into the flames. But the pilots had seen it, too, and they came in low and, using the down draught of the rotor blades, began to push the rubber dinghies back towards safety. I ended my report that night with these words: 'It was a day of tragedy, but I vouch it was a day of extraordinary heroism and selflessness by every man who witnessed it.'

I spent my last days of that short war on top of Two Sisters with the Gurkhas in the direct line of fire of the Argentine 155mm guns in Port Stanley. Just before dusk on the last night we watched the Guards take up positions among the rocks of Mount Harriet, two miles from their enemy's machine gun and mortar positions. In the following nights they would take Tumbledown, Mount William and Wireless Ridge. Harriers dropped their cluster bombs. The casualties were dreadful.

From our positions, we saw the sky lit up with flares and with smoke around them, like the thick mist of a dawn, watched our young soldiers moving forward in line, bayonets fixed. By mid-afternoon of that final day, Monday, 14 June, it was all over. It was snowing and we could see from our summit hundreds of Argentine troops running towards Port Stanley. At 3.55 p.m. (I have a habit of looking at my watch at moments of drama) the Gurkha major came running towards us shouting: 'There's a white flag flying over Stanley. It's all over. Bloody, bloody marvellous!' We weren't filming, so we made him go back and do it again on camera.

For me the day ended in disappointment. Only Max Hastings and I managed to get back to San Carlos to file our story of the surrender, he for London's *Evening Standard* and me for *News at Ten*.

I had the broadcasting scoop of a lifetime…announcing that the war was over and that we had won. But that privilege was being reserved for Mrs Thatcher and the MoD put a blanket stop on all radio traffic out of the Falklands. So Max and I drank whisky together until dawn when the ban was lifted and we shared the story with the rest.

That night, we of the press had something of an end-of-term party in the bar of the Upland Goose. It almost ended in murder. Max had not made himself popular. He has a habit of upsetting folk and that evening he was at his most aloof. He had done better than most and repeatedly told us so.

He had, after all, put on his Territorial Army tunic and walked casually into Port Stanley ahead of the Paras. Some of the reporters had accused him of deliberately sabotaging their copy, although I never did understand how or why. But things got very heated, threatening words were exchanged and even a few parrying blows.

Then an enraged Scot from the *Glasgow Herald* lunged at Max with a bayonet he'd taken off a dead Argentine. With the point almost within touching distance of Max's throat, Derek Hudson of the *Yorkshire Post* hauled him back and immortalised the scene with the words: 'This is not the time or place to kill Max Hastings.' All the while Max had not moved an inch from his whisky glass. Finally someone shouted that Bob McGowan of the *Daily Express* had gone to fetch a gun and the bar cleared within seconds.

It had been ten weeks and one day since we sailed from Portsmouth, and the Task Force, so hastily put together and against all the odds, had done what it had come to do. We had all done our bit. Now it was time to go home.

Chapter 8
ROUND THE WORLD

---

22 APRIL 1995

AHOY, CAPTAIN COURAGEOUS

A HUNDRED YEARS ON FROM THE FIRST
SOLO CIRCUMNAVIGATION OF THE WORLD,
PHILIP DUNN PAYS TRIBUTE TO JOSHUA SLOCUM

You can tell at a glance that Paul Francis is no armchair sailor. He has the look of a man built to withstand a gale on a heaving foredeck...and then there's that pipe, poking from his face like a bowsprit. He doesn't take it from between his teeth very often, but when he does it's usually to let loose a laugh hearty enough to shiver teak planking. He's the sort of chap who prefers doing things to reading about them, but admits that when he's ashore on those long winter evenings he does occasionally put his feet up in front of the fire with a good book – a sailing book, of course.

Paul has been sailing yachts for thirty years and in that time has amassed a library of almost 2,000 books on the sea. There's one he takes down from the shelves more often than the rest, though: *Sailing Alone Around the World*. It was written by his hero, Captain Joshua Slocum.

Before Sir Francis Chichester, Sir Alec Rose, Chay Blyth and the rest; decades before satellite navigation systems and in the days when depth-sounding was done with a lump of lead tied to a piece of string – 100 years ago on Monday, in fact – Captain Slocum set off to become the first man to sail alone around the world. On the morning of 24 April 1895, he weighed anchor and set sail from Boston Harbour. The day was perfect, there was a stiff breeze and his 36ft sailing sloop, *Spray*, dashed through the dancing waves of Massachusetts Bay, 'turning every particle of water thrown in the air into a sparkling gem'. The captain's step was 'light on deck in the crisp air'. His pulse was racing; he knew he was at the beginning of high adventure.

The epic voyage that has made him the patron saint of modern yachtsmen took more than three years. On the way he battled through mountainous seas, fought off pirates, was attacked by 'savages', dined with Robert Louis Stevenson's widow and met the explorer Stanley. The classic lines of *Spray*'s hull are still used as a pattern by the designers of modern yachts – there are about 800 '*Sprays*' afloat throughout the world today, thirty-five of them in Britain – and Slocum's rollicking account of his voyage is now rated alongside the very best of American literature. It is also a bible of seamanship and boat-handling to every yachtsman.

Sixty-year-old Paul, from St Osyth, Essex, is the Commodore of the Slocum Spray Society, and *Hazebra Pride*, the boat he shares with his son, Chris, is a modern steel *Spray*-lookalike. For Paul, Monday will be a very special day. He would like to be in Boston, where the 100th anniversary of the start of Slocum's voyage will be celebrated in style with a giant party and a special postage-stamp issue. A small flotilla of 'replica' *Sprays* will then set sail to follow in the wake of the original, retracing her 4,600-mile route to the Azores, Gibraltar, the Canaries; crossing the South Pacific, the Coral Sea and the Indian Ocean, before rounding the Cape of Good Hope to recross the Atlantic to Newport, Rhode Island.

Paul speaks of Slocum with awe: 'I'll probably come down to the boat that day, sit in the cabin and read a few passages of Joshua's book. Just to pay my respects to the greatest sailor of all time. *Sailing Alone Around the World* is the best book in my collection,' he says. 'It is eloquent; you don't have to be a sailor to appreciate its qualities. I have a framed photo of Joshua in the cabin and I've been known to stand in front of it and salute. He always comes to sea with me when I sail.

'He was the greatest of them all, the forerunner of yachtsmen, the man we all look up to and, when you consider the lack of modern technology at the time he made his circumnavigation, his achievements were absolutely outstanding. The sheer courage and indomitability of the man are almost unbelievable.'

Paul and Chris will take a few weeks off work this summer, when they will sail *Hazebra Pride* to the Azores to meet those '*Sprays*' that will have crossed the Atlantic from Boston. 'It should be quite a party. We'd like to be going all the way round with the others, but three years is rather a long time to take off work. As it is we will have to find some sponsorship,' he says. Then, pulling the pipe from his mouth, he roars with laughter as he tells me how his chance of getting Air Portugal to cough up for a new spinnaker took a dive after he rolled into the marketing manager's plush office and knocked all her bookshelves down. 'It was one hell of an entrance.'

Paul founded the Slocum Spray Society just a year ago and it quickly gained forty-five members from as far afield as America and Australia. Most sail, or are building, their own 'Spray', but the society is open to armchair sailors, too. Some of the members have sailed alone around the world.

'I wouldn't like to do that,' Paul Francis says. 'It takes a special type of person. The solitude would get to me and there is so much that can go wrong. Slocum himself was finally lost at sea. No, I'll content myself with the book.'

A true Yankee sea captain from his cap to his sea-boots, Joshua Slocum was far more than just a brave and intrepid yachtsman. Navigator, master mariner, ship owner, accomplished ship builder, writer – the list is a long one. He went to sea at the age of sixteen and by the time he was forty he owned and was master of the *Northern Light*, the finest American sailing vessel afloat at the time. That was the pinnacle of an extraordinary career.

The advent of steam ships and the death of his first wife, Virginia, who shared his seafaring lifestyle, began a decline in Joshua's fortunes; deprived of the woman he loved, he was like a ship without a rudder. Then he found an old sloop rotting in a meadow beside the Acushnet River at Fairhaven, just up the coast from Boston. He set to work using his skills as a shipwright to rebuild it. For the new keel he 'felled a stout oak' and for the planking he took his axe to several Georgia pines. He worked on the boat for more than a year and conceived the idea of a solo voyage around the globe.

The ship's chronometer, on which Slocum's navigation so much depended, was a $1 alarm clock and had to be regularly boiled in oil 'to keep her at it from noon to noon'. He was attacked several times by natives in the Magellan Straits; one arrow from a Fuegian 'savage' whizzed above his head and stuck in the wooden mast. Ever resourceful, Slocum would spread carpet-tacks on the deck at night to give him warning of the barefoot natives' approach. 'A pretty good Christian will whistle when he steps on the "commercial end" of a carpet-tack; a savage will howl and claw the air,' Slocum wrote. He encountered Moorish pirates off Morocco, tornadoes in the West Indies and, when he returned to Boston, he told his story with a simple gusto that has endured through generations.

CHEERS, SIRENS AND A CUSTOMS CHECK

BY **GUY RAIS** AND **JOHN OWEN**

Escorted by an armada of small boats, which had shadowed him from the Eddystone Lighthouse, and naval vessels, Sir Francis Chichester sailed triumphantly into Plymouth Sound tonight, on the 119th day of his 28,500-mile voyage around the world.

A gun was fired when *Gypsy Moth IV* passed Plymouth Breakwater at 8.56. Sir Francis raised a hand and waved. As he passed the breakwater, a Revenue launch unobtrusively drew alongside and passed a bulky package of official documents requiring a declaration from Sir Francis that he was not carrying dutiable goods and was free from infection.

Sir Francis's arrival came ten hours later than had been predicted and he was hurrying to reach the jetty before darkness. Lady Chichester and their son Giles were aboard as he sailed in. As *Gypsy Moth IV*, her white sails and hull still trim and smart despite her buffeting around the Horn, came into view thousands of sightseers lining the Hoe roared a welcome. For a few minutes nothing could be heard but the ships' whistles and sirens, punctuated by applause and cheering.

Explaining why even the world's most famous sailor was not immune from a check, a Customs official said urbanely that everyone coming in from overseas had to have a clearance. 'In this case we do know who the yachtsman is and where he comes from. There is not much fear of smuggling, but technically we have to issue a health certificate on behalf of the local medical officer before Sir Francis can land. We handed him the papers because at this late hour we did not wish to hold him up. Anyway, we shall issue a certificate. If a man can sail single-handed round the world, he must be pretty fit.'

Sir Francis made a brave effort to reach Plymouth this evening so as not to disappoint the thousands who thronged the Hoe and the surrounding grassy terraces. Some had camped overnight in cars and caravans. Others endured a drenching from frequent showers. But the crowds were good-humoured as they sat picnicking during the fitful bursts of sunshine. On the Hoe a group of girls in mini-skirts carried a banner with the words 'Sir Francis — hurry up. We have had no sleep for two nights.'

HERO'S WELCOME FOR LONE YACHTSMAN

Cannon fire and cheers from hundreds of visitors welcomed home Robin Knox-Johnston, first lone yachtsman to sail non-stop around the world, when he arrived at Falmouth yesterday. His 32ft ketch *Suhaili* (*Fair Wind*) was dwarfed in the harbour by a flotilla of escort vessels and other craft. Television viewers heard Sir Francis Chichester, sailing only a few feet from *Suhaili*, say: 'You can't help admiring him. He's playing it very cool.'

Sir — What a contrast between the still trim and workmanlike figure of Robin Knox-Johnston, after a year at sea, and the dishevelled mob of scruffs infesting the outside of the London School of Economics.

J. O'Connor
Wimborne, Dorset

5 MAY 1969
WOMAN'S VOYAGE

A woman will sail alone and non-stop round the world within the next ten years, Sir Alec Rose predicted last night, speaking at a dinner held by Intercoiffure – an international organisation of women's hairdressers – at Shanklin, Isle of Wight.

YACHT GIRL ENDS WORLD SOLO TRIP

To an impressive welcome, Krystyna Chojnowska-Liskiewicz arrived in Las Palmas yesterday morning to become the first woman to sail solo round the world. She could have sailed into the harbour, which she left on 28 March three years ago, late on Thursday, but the publicity-conscious Poles told her to heave to in her 32ft yacht, *Mazurek*, until first light because of the waiting Press and cameramen.

As the single-masted vessel pitched and tossed a few miles off the harbour, she hoisted the international yellow flag for permission to enter and so end her 31,000-mile voyage. As she arrived she shouted to her husband, one of Poland's marine architects, who designed her yacht, 'I want a long hot bath.' Tugboats gave her an arcade of water jets, the Spanish Navy fired off blank cannon rounds, fireworks exploded and even the Russian and American space-tracking and spy ships took time off to salute her with blaring sirens.

A VOYAGE OF SELF-DISCOVERY

JOHN RIDGWAY AND HIS COMPANION ANDY BRIGGS
TOOK A RECORD 193 DAYS TO CIRCUMNAVIGATE
THE GLOBE NON-STOP IN THEIR KETCH *ENGLISH ROSE*.
DUFF HART-DAVIS JOINED THEM ON THE FINAL LEG

'Another human being!' cried John Ridgway in amazement as he dragged me up out of a rubber dinghy on board his yacht *English Rose VI* at six o'clock on Wednesday morning. I was the first man he had seen — apart from his companion Andy Briggs — since he had left home last September.

In the interval he had smashed the record for a non-stop circumnavigation of the globe by a huge margin, knocking the previous best time down from 286 days to 193. Non-stop meant what it said: for more than six months and 28,000 miles, he had put into no port and taken on no fresh supplies.

A teasing radio message, sent via New Zealand in December, had challenged me to join him for the last two days of his voyage, from the Hebrides to his home at Ardmore, in the wilds of north-west Sutherland. Thus I found myself at a hair-raising dawn rendezvous, in a Force 8 gale, off the south-eastern point of the Isle of Barra.

Considering the ordeal they had been through, both the 57ft ketch and her crew seemed in astonishingly good shape. Apart from barnacles beneath her waterline, the boat was spotlessly clean, and she made a stirring picture in the high seas, her crew like spacemen as they clawed their way about the sky-blue and white deck in crimson oil-skin suits.

For Ridgway — now forty-five — the trip was another leg in his endless voyage of self-discovery, his ceaseless quest to find out what life is about. For Andy Briggs, who is twenty-four, it was a first tremendous experience of ocean sailing. Ridgway thought at first of taking a third person with him, but then decided against it. 'Two people can nearly always get along,' he reckons. 'With three, you're bound to get disagreements.'

His choice of companion proved ideal. A 6ft 3in native of York, lean, wiry and phlegmatic, Briggs built a yacht of his own at the age of twenty-one and sailed it right round Britain, most of the way by himself. His choice of university (Southampton) was governed largely by the yachting facilities available. He now works as the chief sailing instructor at Ridgway's adventure school. During the voyage Ridgway fell into the habit of addressing him as 'Ginger' or 'Ginge,' from the colour of his beard.

Even during my own short time on *English Rose VI* it became clear that, purely as a sailor, Briggs was more enthusiastic than his august skipper. It was he who continually adjusted the sails, he who suggested sail changes, he who handled the boat in tricky situations. After his imperturbable temperament, his greatest asset is skill with his hands. 'He's happiest when something breaks,' said Ridgway, 'because then he can invent a way of mending it.' One minor but vital triumph was his construction of a new razor for the captain, who made a point of shaving every day. Ridgway was distraught when he found that most of the blades he had taken were the wrong sort, but Briggs overcame the crisis by using fibreglass to weld a toothbrush handle onto a piece of alloy cut from a saucepan.

The mariners set out from Ardmore on the morning of 2 September 1983. One of the worst moments of the entire voyage, Ridgway found, was saying goodbye to his wife Marie Christine and his sixteen-year-old daughter Rebecca. 'As the peaks of the mainland went down into the distance, I kept thinking, "What the hell have I done?"'

Both Ridgway and his ketch had been round the world before, in the Whitbread race of 1977–78. Then the boat had carried a crew of thirteen, and the presence of a film team, recording every human foible, made things hellish. This time, with only two people on board, there was – by the standards of ocean racers – a luxurious amount of space. Each man had his own lavatory and washroom, one in the bows and one in the stern. Ridgway slept on a padded bench some 18 inches wide in the main cabin, Briggs in a canvas bunk in a cabin forward. Because they took alternate three-hour watches on duty, they could get away from each other a good deal.

Their routine was soon established. Breakfast, which they had at separate times, was always a hot drink and a bowl of cereal. Lunch consisted of three or four slices of the excellent bread that Briggs continued to bake throughout the trip. The one proper meal of the day was supper, which they took turns to cook. When Ridgway was chef, it was curry, curry and curry again. 'Think of that!' he says with relish. 'A hundred curries, one after the other! But I must say, I can turn out damn good rice by now.' Briggs was more ambitious – and incredibly successful, considering that he had only a single paraffin ring and an oven.

Of the fresh food they took, only onions, garlic, potatoes and cooking apples survived beyond the first thirty days. After that they lived mainly on packets, tins, jerricans of rice and flour, and vitamin pills. Except for one bottle of wine that somebody gave them at the last minute, they had no alcohol. In fact they were so frugal that they arrived home with enough food left to have gone around the world again.

They carried two 180-gallon tanks of fresh water, but with this, too, they were extraordinarily economical, using one gallon a day between them for drinking, cooking and washing. Only during rainstorms in the tropics could they indulge in the luxury of an al fresco shower; in one such storm Ridgeway reckoned there were twenty flashes of lightning every minute for three hours.

Although the ketch has a paraffin heater in the main cabin, they decided before setting out not to use it, to eliminate fumes, condensation and the dangerous temptation that warmth creates — to stay below when you should be on deck. The result was that in cold climates they had to wear a great many clothes, and they were constantly changing in and out of their oilskins.

Their route is easily described: straight down the Atlantic, east round the Cape of Good Hope, across the Southern Ocean to pass south of New Zealand, on to Cape Horn, up past the west side of the Falklands, up the Atlantic, and straight for home. In the whole voyage the only land they saw – apart from a distant glimpse of the Canaries – was Cape Horn itself.

Other yachts have done the circumnavigation faster, but only by stopping to refit on the way. 'If you know you're going to stop,' Ridgway says, 'you can afford to go in a series of sprints and risk smashing the boat up on the way. If you know you can't refit, you have to take it more steadily.'

As it was, they had accidents. The self-steering gear kept breaking. Three times in the Southern Ocean the boat was knocked down flat by freak waves. The first time Ridgway was picked up bodily and flung eight feet across the main cabin, luckily without hurting himself. On the second occasion – a double knock-down – a pole ripped loose, damaging the main mast, and a drum of engine-oil spilt on deck making a filthy mess.

Both men suffered endlessly from seasickness. Ridgway had a recurrence of disc trouble, which made him clumsy about the deck, and in consequence he once fell heavily, spraining both wrists. Briggs was troubled by nothing worse than headaches and toothache.

In the first half of the voyage Ridgway again felt the deep therapy of the ocean. A nervous rash disappeared from his hands; hearing returned to his left ear. When he forgot his telephone and car numbers, he knew that the trip must be doing him good.

Later, anxiety began to rise. As he grows older – he readily admits – he gets more frightened. 'Sitting there at night, under the yellow lamp on the chart-table, listening to the continual bumping and banging, you can't help wondering what would happen if the boat started to break up.'

To let off steam, he gave daily recitations on deck, usually to the sea, but sometimes to astonished audiences of albatrosses and whales. Favourite passages of poetry – 'This precious stone, set in a silver sea,' 'Blow, Bugle, Blow' – would be interspersed with songs delivered fortissimo, always including 'The Lost Chord'. 'I hit my finest form in the Southern Ocean,' he says modestly. 'The surroundings inspired me to great efforts. But seriously, the performances were a very important emotional release. I usually reduced myself to tears, and it did a lot of good.'

Briggs, less emotional and impulsive, wrote marathon letters to his girlfriend, Marie. His hope was that they might meet the odd boat which would deliver the letters for posting. He therefore finished one every two weeks, but, as they never met a ship at all, he came back with all fifteen in a thick bundle.

For Ridgway, the high point of the voyage was his rounding of Cape Horn, in Force 10 snow squalls, the master of his ship, the captain of his soul, which he now knows a little better than before. He loves the Southern Ocean, with its great gales and immense distances, above all others; as he speaks of the albatrosses – to him, the spirits of those seas – the gleam in his eye is that of the Ancient Mariner.

By the last two days of their voyage, as *English Rose VI* came charging up the Minch at eight or nine knots, both crewmen were in fine fettle – 'a little threadbare' after 200 days with never more than three hours' sleep at a time – but delighted to have captured the record, and immensely excited. Ridgway, normally taciturn, was chattering like a monkey.

And so they came home, on a brave and brilliant morning, to a heroes' welcome of siren-blasts, cannon-shots and champagne. They did not know what sort of a winter Scotland had had, or that Andropov was dead; but for Ridgway – himself a marathon runner – all news paled before the fact that Rebecca had won the girls' cross-country at Gordonstoun. 'Now that,' he exclaimed delightedly, 'that really is something.'

REALITY THROWN OVERBOARD

DAVID HOLLOWAY SURRENDERS TO THE NEVER-NEVER EXISTENCE OF THE *QE2*

To join a round-the-world cruise, certainly in a ship as large as the *QE2*, is to enter a different world. There is no real time (where else do you change your clocks in half-hour steps so as not to disturb the habits of your stomach more than is necessary?). There is space, but it can be just your own space. The unreality of the exercise seems to me best expressed by the fact that in your cabin you have a television set with a dozen or more channels, and Channel One is 'The view from the bridge'. There is, you see, no reason to go on deck at all.

From your bed you can see the sea, in that slightly enhanced blue that TV sets prefer, gently slipping by and accompanied by tastefully chosen light classical music. The world outside might not be there at all.

Even the newspaper that arrives every morning (or can be read at any time of day on Channel Four of your cabin TV set) concentrates on such unreal matters as the prices on the New York Futures Market, the sports results or the wit and wisdom of President Reagan. There are no disasters. When you come on board, you surrender to this never-never existence.

And if you have any sense you enjoy every minute of it. It is, after all, beguiling to have two waiters to look after your needs at table and a steward and a stewardess on call to your cabin. And the food: you can (liver permitting) be given nourishment seven times a day, from the early-morning cup of tea with biscuits to the midnight snack of, should you desire it, gargantuan proportions.

Large appetites are catered for: for breakfast if you wish (although I never saw anybody so wishing) you can brush aside the English or American bacon or the English or American sausages (Yankee ones are chipolatas) and tuck into lamb chops, corned-beef hash with an egg or even a soused herring in sour-cream sauce.

But what do you do? Clearly, you can eat and sleep and watch the sea go by. No one would dream of asking you to do more. There is, however, much more. You can, for instance, show off. Where else would you see a man come dressed for dinner in a different jacket for every day of the week, varying from geranium to cloth of gold? In days gone by, so the older hands told me, it was not unlikely that passengers would take one cabin for themselves and one for their clothes. Even in these straitened times I counted, through an open cabin door, thirty-five evening dresses hanging in one cabin. The wardrobe space is awesome.

And then you can play bridge. Each day the card room was full of players until the afternoon, when they moved into larger quarters so that they might take instruction from the travelling professionals. Or they could gamble. Not very seriously: there is a credit limit and serious gamblers, I was told, were not welcome.

For the competitive, a mammoth jigsaw was laid out every day so that anyone with a moment on his or her hands could stop to fit in a few pieces, helped sometimes by the efficient Japanese, who would descend on the table and sort all the pieces by colour. Intellectuals might toy with the daily quiz (results posted in the library at 5 p.m.) or, less demandingly, attend the 'trivia' quiz at tea-time. The energetic can hit golf-balls into a padded target, which gives off a crack like a rifle or, more languidly, play the great courses of the world by computer or putt the nine holes that might have been exciting had there been any sort of sea running.

The swimming pools are there, one flanked by two Jacuzzis, usually occupied by Japanese pumping madly to get more bubbles. When you have swum, you drop your towel: a flunkey will pick it up.

Nothing, as you can see, too energetic, but then our average age was sixty-five, I was told, pulled down by some young companions or granddaughters, jacked up by a couple of game ninety-year-olds and quite a few in their energetic eighties. It was perhaps not surprising that the best-attended lectures were a series on arthritis. The genial American doctor performing looked at us and said, 'I can see 80 per cent of you have got it.' Afterwards he sat on the edge of the stage and gave free consultations; he was much occupied.

Those in search of knowledge could have their handwriting analysed or climb to the signal deck to stargaze under supervision. As evening came and dinner had been reverentially put away, it was time for entertainment. And from whom else but Joe Loss and his sturdy men, each with a pile of sheet music in front of him as thick as two telephone directories so that no request for a golden oldie could go unanswered?

The dance floor was crowded: the social staff seek out the lonely and invite them on to the floor. With great gallantry they picked their way among the solemn Japanese, all performing as if they were in the semi-finals of *Come Dancing*. And there was cabaret of a surreal kind. Where else would you find a Black American comedian telling Jewish jokes?

It was early to bed to be ready to rise in time for gentle exercise sitting down in the Queen's Lounge or more fierce aerobics in the Golden Gate fitness centre. Every two or three days, the *QE2* made a landfall and coaches lined up to take sightseers. But you did not have to go and risk missing a meal: a touch of local culture (the inevitable folk dancers) was brought on board.

Those who did the full 106-day trip (from New York through the Panama Canal across the Pacific and Indian Ocean to Mombasa and back via India, South-east Asia and China) – and nearly 20 per cent of the passengers were doing this – were of course missing winter, suspended somewhere continuously warm if not damned hot.

And they came back to do it again and again. Many were on their twentieth trip, old shipboard acquaintances who kept in touch by postcard during a summer which was presumably spent in amassing a new wardrobe for the next year's cruise.

Some looked sad. Were there many, I wondered, like the people in the next cabin whom I heard telephoning home (at $15 a minute), begging to be allowed to leave the ship at Hong Kong because they were homesick, and evidently being firmly told that they must soldier on? It would be sad to think that this was some sort of open prison for the elderly relatives of the very rich.

I found it wonderfully liberating, but quite, quite crazy. One night we stood on the deck in the darkness as the ship moved serenely and almost silently out of Penang harbour, the spicy smells of the East wafting up, and out of the darkness came the sound of a voice (I never saw the speaker) telling us that the waiters all sneered at her because she wanted plain food and that she was hating it.

It was going to be a long voyage home, poor soul. For me, real life came back too soon.

VOYAGES OF THE IMAGINATION

JASPER REES EXAMINES THE FASCINATION FOR
ARTISTS AND WRITERS IN THE DEATH OF THE
YACHTSMAN DONALD CROWHURST

In 1968, an amateur yachtsman called Donald Crowhurst joined the starting line in Devon for the Golden Globe solo round-the-world yacht race. He had chosen to take part only at short notice, and his lack of preparation began to tell in the South Atlantic. As he fell behind, he took the bizarre decision to radio back fictional co-ordinates to the race judges. In the days before global positioning satellites, these encouraged an excited nation back home to believe that he was actually in the lead.

In fact, he was sailing in a large circle hundreds of miles off the coast of Argentina, all the while keeping a log that charts the slow disintegration of his mental health. His abandoned trimaran, the *Teignmouth Electron*, was found drifting in calm waters, with 16,000 miles on the clock. The logbook revealed the full extent of his deception, and perhaps explained the mystery of his disappearance: presumably he could imagine no future once he was unveiled as a conman. No body was ever found. Aged 36, he left a widow and four children.

It is an extraordinary story that will withstand endless retelling, which is why a succession of writers and artists have found themselves drawn to it like hyenas to carrion. In his bestselling novel, *Outerbridge Reach*, Robert Stone relocated his sailor from England to New York State, but retained the skeletal tale of the yachtsman who keeps two logs, one fake, the other accurate. John Preston's novel *Ink*, set in the world of journalism, hinges partly on one character's obsession with a round-the-world yachtsman who goes missing at sea after radioing home counterfeit accounts of his progress. In the late 1990s, the artist Tacita Dean produced a series of works focusing on the eternal mystery of the sea. Among them were pieces inspired by the Crowhurst conundrum.

She tracked down the wreckage of the *Teignmouth Electron* to the Cayman Islands, and exhibited her photographs of it at the National Maritime

Museum. In the museum's courtyard, she also carved the ghostly, enigmatic final words from Crowhurst's logbook, 'It is the mercy', into a handrail on a platform overlooking the Robin Knox-Johnston yacht that won the race.

Now a company from New York has taken the bare bones of Crowhurst's story and fashioned it into part of an avant-garde, multi-media theatrical experience called *Jet Lag*, based on the audio tapes and film made by Crowhurst in his 243 logged days at sea. On Wednesday, the play comes to London for four performances at the Barbican.

Crowhurst's story, in other words, is the source of inspiration across a variety of art forms. No British wayfarer, possibly not even Captain Scott, has inspired such a breadth of creativity.

His story is seductive not just because of what it tells us about Britishness: 'those qualities,' says Preston, 'which are both admirable and faintly repulsive: that terrible gung-ho keenness and absolute refusal to acknowledge adversity until it is too late.' There is something else at work here; the oddity is that, although his story never changes, everyone who feasts on it takes away a different meaning.

For Dean, the story is 'about human failing, about [Crowhurst] pitching his sanity against the sea, where there is no human presence or support system left on which to hang a tortured psychological state.' Stone's Crowhurst, meanwhile, 'was a bit of a rogue,' he says, 'and his failure has a certain quality that makes it fascinating as an old-fashioned test of character. Yes, he failed, but maybe his failure is more interesting than any victory.'

For Marianne Weems, the director of *Jet Lag*, this is an example of media manipulation. 'His life was enmeshed in and then transformed by technology,' she says. 'Crowhurst fabricated this journey through the airwaves. He existed in this web of radio communication in which he attempted to escape normative ideas of time and space by projecting this enormous journey, projecting this heroic movement. That idea of constructing oneself into the media is of course a very contemporary one, but I think Crowhurst was a prescient example.'

Crowhurst, in other words, has turned into a modern version of a figure from Greek mythology, or a character from Shakespeare. He has transmuted from an individual into an archetype. In most instances his name has been changed and his logbook paraphrased. The memory of the actual Crowhurst, 'a pretty insufferable man who drove a lot of his workmates to distraction', says Preston, has evaporated as completely as did the man himself. The blank that occupies the space is available to limitless reinterpretation, like any unsolved mystery. 'The story has a kind of ancient-mariner dimension to it,' says Preston, 'as well as keying in with all those *Mary Celeste* maritime disappearance stories. It has a yeti-like allure.'

But the abominable yachtsman is also a kind of everyman. 'There's a bit of Crowhurst in all of us,' says Tacita Dean. 'The bit that says we've done more than we have, or talked ourselves into projects we have no hope of achieving. Crowhurst took it to the very extremes of human endurance. He took it to the point of death.'

My own theory is that Donald Crowhurst's story is in the end a parable about the act of creation. He lived a reality but created a beguiling fantasy, a story in which millions of readers wanted to believe. The man in the middle of nowhere who seeks salvation in coining a narrative, in invention, even as the moorings that tie him to his own sanity are loosened, is persuasively analogous. These portraits of a sailor as a young man are also portraits of the artist.

Chapter 9
CROSSINGS

---

4 JUNE 1940

887 BRITISH CRAFT TAKE PART IN EVACUATION

FIGURES TO 'SURPRISE WORLD'
NAVY'S PART AT DUNKIRK

The Germans' use of submarines in their desperate attempt to prevent the withdrawal of the Allied Army from Northern France was disclosed in an Admiralty communiqué issued last night.

The communiqué, which gave a full account of the Royal Navy's great part in the evacuation, announced that losses had been inflicted on enemy submarines and motor torpedo boats. It also stated that, of 222 British naval vessels which took part in the operation, only six destroyers and twenty-four minor craft were lost in spite of incessant bombing attacks. Zeebrugge has been blocked, other ports in enemy hands rendered virtually useless and fuel stocks destroyed.

The text of the communiqué is as follows:

'The most extensive and difficult combined operation in naval history has been carried out during the past week. British, French and Belgian troops have been brought back safely to this country from Belgium and Northern France in numbers which, when the full story can be told, will surprise the world.

'The withdrawal has been carried out in face of intense and almost continuous air attack, and increasing artillery and machine-gun fire. The success of this operation was only made possible by the close co-operation of the Allies and of the Services, and by never-flagging determination and courage of all concerned.

'It was undertaken on the British side by several flotillas of destroyers and a large number of small craft of every description. This force was rapidly increased, and 222 British naval vessels and 665 other British craft and boats took part in the operation. These figures do not include large numbers of French naval and merchant ships which also played their part.

'The rapid assembly of over 600 small craft of all types was carried out by volunteers. These showed magnificent and tireless spirit. Through the operation of the Small Craft Registration Order, the Admiralty already had full details of all available small vessels. The order for the assembly of these vessels met with instantaneous response. Fishermen, yachtsmen, yacht builders, yacht clubs, river boatmen and boat building and hiring firms manned their craft with volunteer crews and rushed them to the assembly point, although they did not know for what purpose they were required. They operated successfully by day and night under the most difficult and dangerous conditions.

'The Admiralty cannot speak too highly of the services of all concerned. They were essential to the success of the operation and the means of saving thousands of lives.

'The withdrawal was carried out from Dunkirk and from beaches in the vicinity. The whole operation was screened by naval forces against any attempt by the enemy at interference at sea.

'In addition to almost incessant bombing and machine-gun attacks on Dunkirk, the beaches, and the vessels operating off them, the port of Dunkirk and the shipping plying to and fro were under frequent shell fire. This was to some extent checked by bombardment of the enemy artillery positions by our naval forces. Naval bombardments also protected the flanks of the withdrawal.

'The enemy was active with submarines and high-speed motor torpedo boats. Losses have been inflicted on both these forces.

'The operation was rendered more difficult by shallow water, narrow channels, and strong tides. The situation was such that one mistake in the handling of a ship might have blocked a vital channel of that part of the port of Dunkirk which could be used.

'Nor was the weather entirely in favour of the operation. On two days, a fresh northwesterly wind raised a surf which made work at the beaches slow and difficult. Only on one forenoon did ground mist curtail enemy air activity.

'A withdrawal of this nature and magnitude, carried out in face of intense and almost continuous air attack, is the most hazardous of all operations. Its success is a triumph of Allied sea and air power in face of the most powerful air forces which the enemy could bring to bear from air bases close at hand.'

THE BARON BLOWS IN ON THE RUSSIANS

A WARSHIP WAS THERE TO GREET ARNAUD DE ROSNAY WHEN HE SAILBOARDED ACROSS THE BERING STRAIT FROM ALASKA TO THE SOVIET MILITARY ZONE IN SIBERIA. **MARK LAW** REPORTS

Russian troops in the eastern extremities of Siberia derive some enjoyment during moments of idleness from tuning to Radio Nome, a US station across the water in Alaska. Apparently they like the music. But on 30 August the most pertinent content of Radio Nome was, for the Russians, a message in their own language from one Baron Arnaud de Rosnay telling them that he was on his way over. A solitary Frenchman was going to cross the Bering Strait by sailboard and was planning to land, uninvited, in one of their most closely guarded military zones.

De Rosnay comes from a family that owns sugar estates in Mauritius. His marriage (since dissolved) to Sir James Goldsmith's daughter, Isabel, was an important event in the young jet-setters' calendar of 1973. For fifteen years de Rosnay has been a photographer. 'But now,' he says, 'I want to make a movie.' He has an idea in mind – 'an inner-vision spectacle' is how he describes it. 'It is basically about nature and sport. It's a new style of movie.'

'Before I began to produce it,' he explains, 'I wanted my name to be associated with nature and sport.' So he planned two expeditions that tested his expertise at sport and knowledge of the natural environment. The first was in March, when he attempted to cross the Sahara from Morocco to Senegal by sailing across the desert on a four-wheeled land yacht. Only part of the journey was accomplished: the Baron was turned back by Moroccan authorities because of the war with the Polisario. On his return he decided he would cross the Bering Strait – the narrow stretch of water (60 miles at one point) that separates the U.S. – the north-west coast of Alaska – from Russia. He would go by sailboard. His original plan was to travel by helicopter from Alaska to Russia with his sailboard and then, taking advantage of the prevailing winds, sail eastwards.

The Baron, who is not without connections in the right places, enlisted the co-operation of the Americans. Then he approached the Russian Embassy in Paris. 'I really had a lot of help at first,' he says. 'I had a long meeting with the Ambassador and he raised such questions as would it be an American helicopter landing on Russian soil, or a Russian helicopter landing in America.' However, the strait is closed by ice from November to June and the Russians later wrote to de Rosnay telling him that they would not be able to make the arrangements in time. 'But never did they say they wouldn't allow me to do it'; and for de Rosnay that was enough, permission by default.

He set off for the U.S. determined to tackle the journey − but in the opposite direction. He arrived to find that American support for the project had suddenly disintegrated in the absence of Russian permission. 'They didn't want to be part of what they considered to be an illegal operation − so they cancelled any help, including coastguard helicopter support. ABC Television, concerned about its position at the Moscow Olympics, withdrew its coverage. No company would hire me a plane to reach the starting point. I had to get one privately. Everybody cancelled. But that made me even more determined to go ahead with it.'

Eventually, at 10.15 one blustery morning, watched by a small group of friends and helpers, he set off. A compass was fixed on the arm of his wetsuit and in a bag on his harness was his emergency equipment − it included small signalling flares, vitamin pills and a knife. In a waterproof bag fixed to the board was a change of clothing, a camera, his passport, a cutting from *Pravda* about his Sahara crossing, the letter from the Russian Embassy, some chocolate and $500 (about £250) in cash. The message he had recorded for Radio Nome was broadcast half an hour after his departure. 'We knew the Russians liked to listen to the station,' he says.

For four months de Rosnay had been studying the waters of the strait. He had learnt that the mountains on either side channelled the wind in such a way that it tended to be stronger at the two sides than in the middle. When he started it was quite light and all went well until he was about halfway across: then the wind dropped almost completely. He spent an awkward two hours trying to maintain his position in the choppy water against the current. In the afternoon the wind changed direction and increased sharply.

De Rosnay had begun to tire and, besides, he was getting extremely cold. During the ten days of training before he set off he had tried to use his gloves as little as possible because their waterproof rigidity made holding the wishbone (the boom of the craft) more of a strain. However, now that his hands were cold, he reached for his gloves − only to discover he had lost them. His fingertips remained numb for weeks afterwards as a result.

After he had been going for six hours the wind was blowing strongly and he began sailing fast — about 20mph. 'It was like waterskiing!' It was then that he first saw the Russian warship. It was about three miles away. It followed him for two hours, until he reached the Russian shore. He landed on a beach under some cliffs. 'The sea was really turbulent here and I fell off several times before I came ashore. The water was two degrees Centigrade — colder than on the American side. It was a big shock. When I landed I was freezing — I did some gymnastic exercises just to keep warm. I ate some chocolate and took some pictures: that was important because it proved I had landed,' he says.

Then de Rosnay saw a launch from the Russian ship coming towards him. 'I didn't know what their reaction was going to be. I decided to go out and meet them.'

The crossing had taken eight hours, and he was now extremely tired. He kept falling off, and when the launch reached him he was in the water, exhausted, clinging on to the sailboard. He was hauled aboard the launch and a Russian officer who spoke excellent English gave him a fur coat, bread and pâté and cigarettes. 'They were very nice to me. They were sailors and they knew what it meant to cross that stretch of water.'

De Rosnay was taken ashore, where other officers were waiting near a helicopter. 'They asked me, "Do you realise that you have entered Russia without authorisation?" and I said, "Well, you know, I'm a bit like a seagull — I came with the wind, I was going back with the wind."' He was later to be proved wrong.

De Rosnay was taken to a town called Uelen and entertained to a meal by several officers. The next day, after being shown around, he was told that in view of his achievement the authorities considered him a guest of honour in transit, and he was to be taken to Moscow and thence to Paris. He tactfully pointed out that he had friends waiting for him across the water in Alaska, but the Russian plan was politely but firmly adhered to.

The origins of this insistence may well have lain in an awkward scene at Kennedy Airport in New York three days earlier when the Americans had held up the departure of Ludmilla Vlasova, wife of the Bolshoi Ballet defector Alexander Godunov.

Although in no mood to deal with the Americans over de Rosnay, the Russians must have been charmed by the endeavours of their uninvited guest, a playboy from the Western world who zigzagged through their defences on a windblown plank as easily as a butterfly might pass through barbed wire.

THE TROUBLE WITH RUNNING AWAY TO SEA

JENNY DISKI INTENDED TO TRAVEL AS SHE USED
TO ON THE CENTRAL LINE IN LONDON, DAYDREAMING
AND SMOKING AND IGNORING THE WORLD.
BUT THE WORLD, FROM THE DAY SHE SAILED
FOR AMERICA, HAD OTHER IDEAS...

Travelling with no purpose is a purposeful business. I had put myself in the way of a long sea journey. The destination was of no concern to me. In fact, when I arranged the trip, the MV *Christiane* was scheduled to travel first to Rio de Janeiro and then up to Georgia. Only two days before I was due to leave, the plans were altered: the ship was leaving several days later and skipping the South American leg.

Freight timetables are notoriously changeable; the profit margins are critical, companies will revise their schedules from one day to the next, sometimes in mid-journey. If you travel by freighter you'd better not have any definite plans or firmly fixed destination.

I was sorry the South American stop had been cancelled, but only because it meant a shorter journey. I was prepared for a trip of six weeks or more before I arrived at Savannah, Georgia, after which I had made no firm plans except to purchase an open plane ticket back to the UK.

A long sea voyage was the only point of the trip. Why? An exercise in sensory deprivation, I suppose. To find out what happened when one day followed another, one mile followed another and each was exactly the same as the last. What was a person left with when there was no landscape except the curve of the horizon, and no anticipation in arriving somewhere you wished to be? How was it when the day-by-day went on, when only the routine demanded by the human needs of eating and sleeping distinguished you from your surroundings, whose single rhythm was the rising and setting of the sun?

To be accurate, it wasn't so much that I wondered about how it was, as that those were the conditions I wanted to be in. But still, in all that silence and lack of interference, wouldn't there be something to listen to? I'm always supposing that if I can get things quiet enough I'll hear something to my advantage. Like the fish on the hooks, I wriggle away from activity, companionship, wanting to launch myself into nothingness where I will find...what?

The fish find themselves gasping on deck, out of their element, suffocating in the poisonous, inimical air. Somehow, I've developed a notion that I am more than a fish. Doubtless that's what the fish think, too. Get out of the water, get away from the circumstantial, and then we'll see.

There is never perfect solitude; a person is a fool to set out in search of it. A fool, at any rate, if disappointed by not finding it.

There were two couples apart from me travelling as passengers. Fogey and Roz were in their seventies, returning home after taking a holiday from a farm in Arizona. She was neat as a button, a large easy-care American matron; Fogey was silent most of the time, though he was known to ask for the peanut butter sometimes when it was out of reach at breakfast.

Neither was talkative, but they weren't unfriendly. They were insular Americans, had taken a peek at Europe, but were uneasy at finding themselves in a strange world, in strange company. At breakfast, lunch and supper, we sat with the officers and after a decent interval of polite conversation – the weather, how they had slept, where we were – they slipped into silence.

The German couple, Stan and Dora, from Lake Constance, were also in their seventies, and they weren't silent. They were travelling with their brand-new, super-equipped, bells-and-whistles mobile home lashed to the top deck. They were planning to spend a year travelling around the States. They talked without stopping, without thinking, it came to seem. They were determined to speak as much English as possible before they disembarked for their New World adventure. What they talked about and how their audience responded appeared irrelevant. They lived in a bubble of their own perceived needs, like children.

They were also a neat pair. Spruce, rather. Stan and Dora were several sizes down from the American couple, with well-nurtured bodies and immaculately cut, short white hair. They were turned out for a cruise: she wore silk scarves with naval emblems on them, he wore studiedly casual slacks, well-ironed polo shirts sporting an anchor or a knot on the breast pocket, and rope-soled deck shoes.

These two had no idea of how to coexist with strangers. They buzzed like flies across all the careful boundaries. They seemed to stalk me, so that no matter which secluded corner I discovered for myself, they found me there sooner or later.

'Ah, you are here.'

Dora babbled. She spoke entirely inconsequentially, staring at me as she talked with intensely blue, intensely vacant eyes. 'I brush my teeth after every meal. We must all brush our teeth after every meal.' 'I love all kinds of potatoes. Boiled, roasted, fried, chipped...' 'You were not at breakfast. Where were you? I said to Stan, "Where is she?"' 'You are reading a book. I like to read books.' 'Ah, you cannot change the past.' 'My mother always said that Hitler would be bad for us.' All of it was spoken in a monotone, with that staring look in her eyes, as if she were trying to recall and practise phrases she had worked up the evening before from her English book.

Perhaps that's exactly what it was, but her eyes were uncanny. Behind her glasses they dragged downwards at the outside corners, as blue and dead as standing pools. Nothing lit them up. She watched Stan, who liked to think he spoke better English than Dora, make his declarations about the world – 'It is good', 'It is not good' – with her unchanging cold fishy eyes, while the rest of her face expressed devoted interest.

Stan talked as much as she, mostly with reminiscences of his travels around Europe thirty years ago. He told the Croatians everything he knew (and they certainly did) about Dubrovnik, and me everything he knew about London, as if he remained familiar with these places he hadn't set foot in for a generation.

At mealtimes he would complain about the state of Europe. Germany in particular. It was being overrun with 'Arabs. Not trust Arabs.' He rubbed his well-manicured fingers against each other. 'Money. Only money. And now they live in our cities with their minarets and their wawawa.'

I left the table at that point, but Roz told me that he had continued unperturbed and gone on to complain of Berlin being overrun by Russians, to which the usually uncommunicative Fogey had quietly murmured, 'Well, that makes a change.'

One morning Dora found me sitting on deck, reading, and after admonishing me for not eating fruit at breakfast ('You must have fruit. Fruit is good for you.') asked me my age.

'Ah, you are one year older than my daughter. I could be your mother,' she announced. While this was chronologically possible, it was, aside from being inane, so historically and geographically inaccurate that I had to fight the gasp that rose in my throat. She then placed a firm hand on my right cheek, and bending down planted a brisk kiss on my other cheek. I froze through the maternal moment. Eventually, I managed a coldly polite and somewhat inappropriate 'Thank you'. But the panic stayed with me.

The next afternoon I was in the wash room, wondering why the hell I was ironing a shirt in the blistering heat of the day. Dora found me again.

'Ah, you iron.' I nodded my agreement, and sweat fell from my chin. She didn't rate my technique.

'No, no, you must open the buttons to iron correctly.'

She approached the ironing board with her hand outstretched ready to correct my sloppy ways. Reality began to slow down for me as she started to open the top button. I had to make a physical effort not to slap her hand out of the way.

'NO.' I actually bellowed at the harmless old woman as you might shout at a child to prevent yourself from lashing out. 'Leave it alone. Don't touch it. Do. Not. Touch. It.'

My face must have matched my warning tone. Dora started and then backed away. She was alarmed and quite baffled by my excessive reaction to her helpfulness. I didn't care to discuss with her how much she couldn't have been my mother.

'Yes. It is your ironing. Yes,' she soothed, leaving the room without turning her back on me. But her surprise was no greater than mine at the rage I'd expressed. My admiration for the crew's capacity to live together increased greatly.

Dora and Stan's blandness and blank insensitivity were monumental. They spoke regardless of who was listening or what anyone else was feeling or thinking. It was a rare, infantile quality that I should have relished having the chance to observe. But the brutality of not observing other people was too stark in these cloistered surroundings, and as it turned out, nothing that happened to other people had any real impact on them.

I appreciated the distant good manners of Roz and Fogey all the more as the days with the German couple passed. Fogey turned out to be a radio ham and had set up an aerial outside his cabin, and without my asking fixed one for me outside my window so I could catch the World Service. He spent most of his time listening in and talking to strangers on his short-wave while Roz sat and did crosswords.

Roz had been widowed, and after two or three years had married her brother-in-law, Fogey. They seemed content together. We were three days away from Tampa when for the first time the two of them arrived late for breakfast, clearly distressed, looking grim and drained, although Roz, who sat next to me, was, as usual, carefully and neatly dressed.

'Didn't you sleep? Was it the heat?' I asked, and then saw that it was more than that.

'We had some bad news last night. Very bad news.'

At ten the previous evening Fogey had got a call on his radio from Arizona. Roz's 48-year-old son, Fogey's nephew and stepson, had died suddenly that morning, probably of a heart attack. Roz told me this in an undertone, her voice just making it to the end of the sentence and her eyes welling but managing to suppress the tears. There was nothing they could do but wait for the ship to get to Tampa and then fly to her son's home in California for the funeral.

The luxury of distance became an agony of time. The vastness of the Atlantic, the immutable sea-ness of the sea, the perpetual horizon that promised more and more of nothing, all of which I was so relishing, transformed in an instant from the mile after mile to the minute after minute that had to be lived through by a woman stuck in the middle of nowhere, cut off from where she urgently needed to be, suffering an unimaginable loss, among strangers. Now the sea was just an intolerable inhuman space to be covered before Roz could get back to her family for the funeral of her eldest son.

Extracted from *Stranger on a Train* by Jenny Diski.

FIRST BRIDES' SHIP LEAVES FOR NEW YORK

FROM OUR SPECIAL CORRESPONDENT
SOUTHAMPTON, SUNDAY

Shortly after the first official contingent of brides left here for New York yesterday, a non-fraternisation order came into force for all ship's officers in the *Argentina*, the 26,000-ton troopship that was specially converted to carry the brides and their babies to their American husbands and fathers.

Some of the officers were indignant when they heard that the United States Merchant Marine War Shipping Administration had placed a ban upon their talking to the brides. One of them said: 'We were told that we must not engage in conversation with any of the brides while at sea, under penalty of immediate dismissal. If we are approached by a passenger and asked a question we can make a formal reply. Otherwise we can talk to them only where necessary in the course of our duty. We have been barred from the promenade deck and the public rooms used by the brides.'

For the brides the ship is a floating paradise, and as soon as she put to sea there was a rush to the store, where sheer silk stockings were on sale at 11s 3d a pair. There was a great demand, too, for all kinds of cosmetics unobtainable in this country.

It was only when the *Argentina* had cast off and begun to move into Southampton Water that many of the brides realised this was goodbye to England. Many of them burst into tears.

The 626 brides and children had been told that the Mayor of Southampton, Ald. Harry Vincent, would come aboard just before the ship sailed, to give a farewell address. But when the Mayor and Mayoress reached the quayside the gangway had already been hauled up. They had to be content with waving goodbye and calling: 'Good luck to all of you.'

The second 'Brides Special' is the *Queen Mary*, due to sail from Southampton next Sunday with another 1,400 women and children.

GIANT LINER'S SLOWEST TRIP

FROM OUR SPECIAL CORRESPONDENT ABOARD
H.M.T. *QUEEN MARY*, WEDNESDAY

The weather is improving, but we were forced to slow down considerably during the night. The sea is still rough, with a moderate south-westerly gale and a heavy swell. The liner's speed is now 25 knots, and by noon we had covered about a third of the way across the Atlantic, 1,060 miles.

This will probably prove to be the slowest Atlantic voyage this ship has ever made, and further alterations in arrangements for the reception and transportation of the United States Servicemen's wives and children we carry will have to be made. The master is easing down solely in the interests of the women and children.

There were more lectures this morning on customs, habits, conditions, clothes, food, and entertainment in the United States. To acclimatise the women to drinking coffee, Chief Steward Charlton is serving it twice daily, but the wives sent a deputation to the Military Commandant, Col. Lane, begging for tea, and that is now being served.

BY CORACLE ACROSS THE CHANNEL

MANDRAKE

The manner of its making must underline it as the strangest record ever set. Without benefit of the Press or television cameras, and watched only by a few incredulous French coastguards, two Welshmen last week in thick fog and darkness stepped gingerly ashore on to the docks of France near Cap Gris-Nez. It had been the first coracle crossing of the Channel in recorded times.

Bernard Thomas, fifty, an electrical contractor of Llechryd, Carmarthenshire, and Denzil Davies, twenty-four, a schoolteacher from nearby Cenarth, had tried last year in the full glare of publicity. After three weeks of waiting for favourable conditions their attempt, made under the sceptical eyes of newsmen, ended in a force-seven gale near the Goodwin Sands. This time they set out to make history by stealth.

The coracle was old before the Romans came to Rye. A frail, flat-bottomed boat, made of tarred canvas stretched across a wicker-work basket, it has no keel, and can rear up and land about the ears of the unwary stepping into it for the first time. It is light enough to be carried on the shoulders.

The crossing on Tuesday night was partly an attempt to solve the riddle of how people of various races crossed from the Continent in the days of prehistory. Their only known craft was the coracle. Yet its frailty had always caused it to be considered a mockery as a seagoing vessel. Old coracle men on the Teify and Towy, the last two rivers of Wales where it is still used, had sneered happily when they heard of last year's attempt, and of its failure.

'Yet we've shown it could have been done,' said Bernard. 'Say 1,000 coracles left France. Perhaps 500 made it.'

The two men crossed in appalling conditions. The great ships in the Channel lurched incuriously by, not checking their speed. The washes to the coracles were of typhoon proportions. They averaged some two miles an hour. Tides and currents increased the 22-odd miles to 30. The crossing lasted more than 14 hours. Shepherded by an escort vessel with professional navigators aboard, they were plotted through the last rocks by French coastguards. For stores they had lemon juice and a few sandwiches.

The feat followed months of rigorous training on the Teify to build up their muscles for the swells and washes of the Channel. No ordinary coracle men could have done it, they claim. They both met the cost of the attempt themselves. The accompanying boat cost them £100, and there were train fares and hotels.

They landed at Cap Gris-Nez at 11 o'clock on Tuesday night. By 2 a.m. they were back aboard the accompanying boat, in Dover, racked with muscular pain. At 10 o'clock in the morning they quietly caught the train home to Carmarthenshire. It had been a famous victory.

It was also a blow in favour of a dying craft. The opposition of fly fishermen has meant a steady encroachment on the rights of coracle fishermen. Thomas's father was the last man to hold a licence to fish the non-tidal waters at Llechryd by coracle; Davies's two uncles are the last non-tidal coracle men of Cenarth. Both feel strongly about this.

Blistered horribly, but buoyant with achievement, the men were speculating yesterday about new seas to sidle across. The grey waters of the Irish Sea are just 10 miles away, all 54 miles of them. 'Now that,' said Thomas. 'We've been thinking about that...'

IRISH SEA CROSSING BY SIX IN A CORACLE

FROM **L. MARSLAND GANDER**
DAILY TELEGRAPH RADIO CORRESPONDENT
WEXFORD, EIRE, THURSDAY

Six 'Stone Age men' set out in a curragh (coracle) from here today bound for Fishguard on a BBC expedition across the Irish Sea. The object is to provide filmed material for a 'Buried Treasure' archaeological programme proving the remote common ancestry of the peoples on both sides.

Four Kerry fishermen provided the professional oar power, supplemented by Paul Johnstone, the BBC producer, and Lt.-Cdr. A. de M. Leathes, of HMS *Dryad*, the Royal Navy Navigational School. All six wore cowhide outfits simulating the dress of our Neolithic ancestors.

The resemblance to Robin Hood and his Merry Men was purely coincidental. In the curragh they carried the cranium of a human skull for baling, not symbolical, purposes, and for food had a store of nuts, apples and wheatcakes. Just in case anything went wrong there were also cold mutton chops and the curragh was being followed by an Irish fishing trawler, the *Dewy Rose*.

The curragh was a replica of the earliest Neolithic boats except that canvas was stretched over the framework instead of skin and that it was painted in the colours of the Irish Republic. The average age of the tough crew was well over fifty. Maurice O'Connor, the senior member, was sixty-six and the others were Thomas Grommell, Sean O'Criothan and Patrick Fearney. They are being paid £2 10s a day during the rehearsal period and will receive prize money of probably £20 each when they arrive.

Originally it had been intended to use a raven for navigational purposes, the idea being to launch the bird when in doubt with the certainty that it would head straight for land. But the only raven available, 45 miles from here, turned out to be a cripple and most reluctant. In any case, the owner demanded £5 for the loan. A crow offered as a substitute was deemed to be unsatisfactory for temperamental reasons and the curragh went off birdless.

Mr Johnstone explained to me the object of the exercise during a preliminary experiment which demonstrated that the curragh could carry protesting hog-tied sheep. He said that archaeological authorities believed that in the period 2,500 BC England and Ireland were invaded from the Continent by Neolithic peoples who introduced cattle and agricultural practice.

The chief danger to the expedition is that it crosses regular shipping courses and the curragh will carry only a small safety lantern. But under their skins the Kerry men will wear Mae Wests. The row, over a distance of about 60 nautical miles, is expected to take about 24 hours.

At dusk, after six hours' rowing, it was reported by radio from Tuskar Rock lighthouse that the curragh was going 'strong and steady' and had covered about 18 miles. The sea was calm.

CORACLE MEN BEATEN BY THE WEATHER

FROM **L. MARSLAND GANDER**
FISHGUARD, FRIDAY

High winds and choppy seas caused the BBC to abandon its 'Stone Age' curragh crossing of the Irish Sea, 20 miles from here, early this morning.

The four Kerry fishermen had rowed their 25ft canvas craft 45 miles in 15 hours, stopping only for a few minutes' rest. They had one narrow escape in the small hours. The curragh's safety lantern had been extinguished by the waves, and so the craft had to keep close to the escorting drifter, *Dewy Rose*. It was pitch-dark, raining and beginning to blow.

Out of the blackness a French trawler cut right across the curragh's bows. Mr Paul Johnstone, a BBC producer, who was in the curragh, said to me: 'We had to stop rowing abruptly to avoid being cut in two.'

When the weather worsened soon after dawn the curragh was making only one knot. Hoisting it on board the *Dewy Rose* was a tricky operation.

My own crossing was more civilised in the mail steamer *St Andrew*. It provided a strange contrast in methods ancient and modern. I spotted the *Dewy Rose* on the ship's radar screen, spoke to her on the radio-telephone. I even heard Paul Johnstone's voice, picked up by the radio, when he used a loud hailer. When I met the *Dewy Rose* in a launch and boarded her, the four Kerry fishermen, unshaven and dressed in sheepskin and cowhide, looked more like pirates than Neolithic men.

Chattering happily in Gaelic among themselves, they were all smiles and showed no sign of fatigue. Mr Johnstone said they had had no sleep and only one cup of tea each since starting on the previous afternoon. They willingly launched the curragh again and got into it to row into the harbour here, where Mr Richard Williams, chairman of the urban council, welcomed them.

The final blow came at Fishguard, where Customs officials detained in bond a BBC film camera and thirty reels of exposed film. Mr Johnstone and his team had to leave for London without the pictorial record of the voyage, but there are hopes of early release.

BRITISH SUBMARINE CROSSES
ATLANTIC UNDER WATER

A British 'A' class submarine, the *Andrew*, 1,385 tons, yesterday made naval history by completing a 2,840-miles (2,500 sea miles) Atlantic crossing from Bermuda entirely under water. Just before dawn she surfaced off the south-west approaches of the English Channel.

There is no record of a previous underwater crossing of the Atlantic. Throughout the trip the *Andrew* used the modified Snort breathing tube fitted to the hull and serving as a snorkel, it allowed a submarine to spend longer under water, having previously made extensive tests with the apparatus. The original type was banned after the *Affray* disaster; the unexplained loss of a submarine with 75 crew in April 1951.

An Admiralty spokesman said the voyage was 'just an ordinary training trip. The crew have not been in special training for it. They just decided to do it.' Soon after surfacing the submarine was ordered to proceed to Portland.

The *Andrew* is commanded by Lt.-Cmdr W.D.S. Scott, R.N., who joined the submarine service in 1941. A-class submarines have a surface displacement of 1,385 tons, and 1,620 tons when submerged. They have a complement of about sixty.

During most of the passage the *Andrew*'s crew kept in touch with the outside world through daily news bulletins. They heard about the Coronation, the conquest of Everest and the Test Match.

An Admiralty statement said that since January the *Andrew* had been operating with the Royal Canadian Navy. At the end of May she was working off Bermuda. 'It was decided that to gain experience she should make the return passage to England using her Snort, and this morning she completed the 2,500-miles journey.' The duration of the voyage is being kept secret.

There was disappointment among the crew when, on surfacing, they received a signal to proceed to Portland. 'We had hoped to steam between the lines at Spithead this morning,' one crew member said on arrival.

On board the *Andrew* at Portland last night Lt.-Cmdr Scott said: 'I was astonished at the depth-keeping qualities of the boat under heavy seas, and the performance of the machinery, which was first-class. On a trip of this kind everyone needs to be on his toes the whole time. It is the biggest strain of all, but luckily I have the best crew I have ever sailed with. Everyone behaved magnificently.

'Our biggest danger, of course, was of being run down. The main periscope went out of action the second day out from Bermuda, but we managed. One day in dirty weather when we were rolling badly and we had to move some heavy machinery, we went down to 80 feet for eight hours. On two other occasions we went down to 80 feet to avoid passing ships and idle curiosity.

'We had two lots of really bad weather. On the third day out we encountered a gale which lasted for twenty hours. We had only two days of flat calm during the whole trip.

'On the way we heard bits of the Coronation service on the radio and we were receiving the cricket scores. We also heard about Everest, and I can only confess that at the time we felt we would rather have a foot on Everest than be where we were.'

Lieut. M.H. Friend, R.N.V.R., thiry-three, of Coulsdon, Duty Officer, said last night: 'We "spliced the main-brace" on June 3 to mark the Coronation. The toast was "The Queen, God bless her". At that time we were at periscope depth. There was terrific excitement when we heard Coronation descriptions over the radio.'

Petty Offr. Court, of Betteshanger, Kent, said: 'My biggest thrill was being awakened one morning by a fanfare of trumpets. I couldn't make out what it was at first. Then I realised we were hearing the Coronation broadcast from the Abbey.'

16 MARCH 1996

THE INDOLENT LURE OF THE CARGO SHIP

VOYAGING ACROSS THE SOUTH PACIFIC IN A
'BAG LADY OF THE SEAS' REQUIRES AN
INDIFFERENCE TO TIME – EVEN BEFORE YOU BOARD,
SAYS **PETER HUGHES**

She arrived in the night. Yesterday the wharf had been empty, this morning she was there, berthed beyond the fishing fleet and French warships at Mota Uta, the commercial port of Tahiti. Dented, rusting, streaked and stained, the *Moraybank* was a bag lady of the seas, the antithesis of suave cruise liners that swan around the world.

Tufts of ochre derricks sprouted round her masts; the black paint on her hull was pocked and pitted; containers were stacked on her decks. She was everything I had imagined and more than I had hoped for in a cargo ship that would take me through the South Pacific.

I had been waiting four days: unpunctuality is the prerogative of kings and cargo ships. It had been an expensive stay. Tahiti may look like a grass-skirt society, but the labels are Courrèges; in Papeete, the capital, South Seas simplicity comes at Parisian prices.

But this morning you could see the *Moraybank*'s custard-yellow funnel across the harbour from the scarlet tables of the Retro Cafe, where expats linger to read back numbers of *Le Monde*.

She was bigger than I had expected, 530ft long and 12,000 tons, built at Wallsend in 1972 to carry general cargoes to the South Pacific. For more than twenty years she and three sister ships, operated by the Bank Line, have made round-the-world voyages out of Hull. This was to be the *Moraybank*'s last, through the South Seas at any rate; a replacement fleet of newer and bigger ships had been bought from Russia.

The port agent showed me to my cabin along an air-conditioned corridor panelled in pale plastic laminate. Cabin C had two beds and a suite of cabinets in beech veneer. For a ship it was quite spacious. Two windows, fastened with big brass catches, looked out to starboard. Above the basin in the shower a sign read: 'Not drinkin [sic] water.'

The Bank Line ships had not long been converted for passengers. Cabin C had been a recreation room and its loss did nothing to allay the reservations among the ship's company. According to the young Yorkshire captain, Eric Pallister, their initial reaction to passengers was 'absolute disgust'. But that attitude soon changed. 'People like to have fresh faces aboard.'

Amin, my cabin steward, a Bangladeshi like the rest of the crew, delivered my luggage, as he would deliver my morning tea, with grave dignity. Certain accessories set the cabin apart from a bedroom ashore: a canister of insecticide and a carton of detergent; a short-wave radio with an aerial of green flex; books – Thomas Hardy, Mario Vargas Llosa, two Trollopes and a Robert Ludlum. The ship had a video library but unfortunately my television was 'in maintenance'.

Andy Pring, the purser, had already stocked my fridge. Beside it was a list of drinks obtainable from the 'slop chest' and their prices – £5.58 for a litre of gin, £8.25 for malt whisky, £3.28 for a bottle of wine, £7.55 for twenty-four cans of beer.

According to Andy, the qualifications for a round-the-world passenger include an indifference to time and an occupation. 'There are only so many books you can read.' Some painted, others took an interest in navigation. On one voyage one man spent almost the entire time in his cabin devising a new language. It is also important to get on with people: Andy told of the couple who boarded in Antwerp only for the husband to disembark in Le Havre two days later.

At lunch I met my fellow passengers. Of the eight on board, six – all Americans and cargo-ship veterans – were making the whole 110-day circumnavigation. They had been on board for a month and had not made landfall since leaving Le Havre. Now there would be a port every few days all the way to Singapore. In the next month they would be calling at Western Samoa, Fiji, New Caledonia, the Solomon Islands, Vanuatu and Papua New Guinea. My intention was to stay ten days, as far as New Caledonia.

In the dining-room shared with the officers – half of them British, half Polish – we were distributed among three tables, overlooked by a black-and-white photograph of a young Queen Elizabeth. I had little trouble deciding who was who: the passenger list gave everyone's date and place of birth, officers and crew included.

On one table were Rod and Mary, both in their seventies, he a retired United Airlines pilot, she a former nurse, gentle and demure. With them were two sisters, Yeta and Bessie. Yeta scurried about like one of those tough little up-and-at-'em cartoon rodents, while Bessie, in her eighty-first year, was rather stately.

At the far end of the room was a Swiss couple who had joined with me in Tahiti and would be getting off in Singapore. Hans-Peter and his wife, Rosalind, had brought a wardrobe more suitable for a yacht than a cargo boat: white chinos, Docksider shoes and a lot of smart silk.

At my table was Gary, who had been a stockbroker in Miami and now lived in Spain. For him the voyage was the fulfilment of a life-long dream. He spent hours on the bridge, tracking our progress against the course he had plotted before leaving home. And then there was Roy.

Roy was always first in the dining-room, usually filling a polythene bag with a snack that would see him through to the next meal. A big man, he was dressed this day in a pink cotton jump suit.

He had two disconcerting habits: he repeated the last words of every statement he made and possessed a laugh like an unsilenced single-cylinder diesel engine running on half throttle – eh eh eh eh eh. It was not just distinctive, it obeyed no law of humour or breath control. There was no predicting what would set it off or, once started, when it might stop. Roy took it upon himself to show me the dining-room ropes. 'The food is real good. One day they had hot dogs, eh eh eh eh. But I didn't eat them. I get enough of them at home. Enough of them at home; eh eh eh eh.'

Amin had already advised me of meal times – breakfast at 7.30, lunch at noon and dinner at 5.30. There would be nights when I would return to the cabin, read for a while, and then find it was still only 7.30.

Cargo-ship cruisers will tell you there is a romance to this kind of travel unavailable in any other kind, certainly where there is any element of organisation. Cruising by cargo ship is travel for the sake of travelling, ships for the sake of ships, not hotels afloat. It is an adventure where nothing is predictable beyond breakfast, a defiance of time when your days belong to no one but you.

The *Moraybank* shuffled along with a lulling roll, the sort of ship the sight of which helps convince cruise passengers they really are at sea. In Apia she discharged flour from France and loaded copra for Antwerp, the staples of her trade.

At sea again Rod approached me after breakfast: 'It's a delicate matter. It's Roy's laugh. It drives Bessie crazy, she has to leave the dining-room.' I said I was not sure there was much I could do about it. 'But it's you who makes him laugh.' From then on I ate in trepidation, fearful that anything I might say or do would trip the mysterious switch that detonated Roy's humour and send Bessie to her bunk.

The day before we were due to arrive in Fiji, three of us were having morning coffee in the passenger lounge. Andy Pring came in, looking dishevelled when normally he was immaculate. 'There's been a tragic accident,' he said.

Two Bangladeshis, who had entered an empty tank used to carry vegetable oil, had been asphyxiated, apparently by a residue of gas. The British second officer went to their aid; he too died. Sorrow fell upon the ship like drizzle. Andy said things would go on as normal for the passengers but in such a small community grief cannot be compartmentalised.

At Suva next morning the bodies were carried down the gangplank on stretchers by Fijian police and laid in the back of a truck. The Swiss videoed the procedure from the boat deck.

Three months later I received a phone call from Gatwick. It was Rod. The *Moraybank* had just returned to Europe and he and Mary were on their way home. He sounded fit and cheerful but the line was breaking up. 'If ever you get round to writing that article of yours,' he said, 'tell them we had a terrific time.' Then we were cut off.

CRACKNELL AND FOGLE CONQUER THE ATLANTIC

CASSANDRA JARDINE SEES THE OLYMPIC CHAMPION AND THE TV PRESENTER REACH LAND

A tiny light on the horizon was the first sign for the loved ones of James Cracknell and Ben Fogle that the men were alive. It was midnight and the sea was pitch-black as they motored towards the light. So big were the waves that, even from their 53ft rented boat, the view was obscured much of the time. They could only hope that Cracknell and Fogle could see them.

The rowers' VHF radio had survived their capsize nine days beforehand but was not working properly. As the glimmering light came closer they made contact. 'It's Ben!' screamed Marina Hunt, Fogle's girlfriend.

A cheer filled the boat of supporters who had come out to watch them approach the end of their seven-week ordeal. Only Inca, Ben's dog, was absent from the party, which included James's wife, Beverley Turner, his two-year-old son Croyde, both sets of parents, sisters and friends.

Amid 12ft waves it was only possible to get near enough to see that Cracknell was rowing – 'as long as his sore bum will hold out', said Fogle. Shortly before reaching the finishing line he handed over the oars to the slower rower, a gentlemanly gesture in acknowledgement that this dangerous challenge had been Fogle's idea. It was late last year that the presenter of television wildlife programmes bounced up to the Olympic gold medallist oarsman at a party and asked him to accompany him on the Atlantic Rowing Race to raise money for BBC Children in Need.

They made an odd couple. Cracknell had trained all his adult life for three Olympic Games, in an event for which he had to row with all his might for six minutes. He had lived, his wife says, 'in a pressure cooker of competition' with only one aim, to come first. She wondered if this race would be 'kill or cure' for his hyper-competitive spirit.

Fogle was, by his own admission, 'useless' at rowing, but with a passion for tough challenges. As a teenager he climbed the volcano Cotopaxi; in 2000 he accepted the challenge of being marooned for a year on a remote

Scottish island for the television show *Castaway*; and in 2004 he ran the 155-mile Marathon des Sables. But Fogle is not competitive. 'Ben just wants to do things, he doesn't want to win,' Miss Hunt says.

As rowers, they both knew that they would have their differences. That much was evident before the start of the race at La Gomera in the Canaries. And yet they made it, emerging from their boat forty-nine days later looking skinny, wearing their last two pairs of tattered shorts (having rowed naked much of the time out of necessity as much as to prevent chafing), burnt brown by the sun and with heavy beards.

As they stepped out of the boat their legs were scarcely able to support them after so many weeks when they were unable to stand. On land, they embraced one another. 'Thanks, mate,' said Cracknell. Fogle, hugging him back, said: 'You saved my life.'

It was an extraordinary feat for them to have made it to the end of the 2,937-mile race. To have arrived ahead of all the other pairs was little short of a miracle to all those who watched them before they set off on 30 November.

The other competitors in the 26-boat, 58-competitor race had spent two years or more preparing themselves physically and psychologically. They had assembled their flat-packed boats and mastered their equipment well in advance and had deliberately put on extra weight to burn during the voyage.

Cracknell and Fogle did none of that. They ordered their boat two months before they set out and only then started to look for sponsors and to source equipment. Too busy to practise, they had no idea whether they would get on.

'I wondered how James would cope with taking part in a race in which he wouldn't know how he was doing, couldn't see the other competitors and had little control over his ability to win,' said Turner, a television presenter, who feared that Fogle's inexperience as a rower would infuriate her husband.

Miss Hunt, a children's party planner, was worried as to how her laid-back boyfriend would cope with Cracknell's insatiable will to win. 'At La Gomera,' she said, 'James was shaving millimetres off their oars to give them the competitive edge and Ben was beginning to regret asking him to row with him. Ben is non-confrontational and James can be a bully. I kept begging Ben to stand up to him.'

The race was three days late in starting because of bad weather. This was a boon for Cracknell and Fogle: their boat had acquired a hole in transit and they discovered at the eleventh hour that their oars were in the wrong position for ocean rowing and that their pins were breaking. But even with this extra time, they were in such a rush that Fogle did not have his rowing shoes, and they were completely unprepared for the stress they would suffer when fighting water that felt as heavy as treacle as they rowed in adverse currents.

For the first ten days they were so miserable that they could not bear to speak to their families at home. It was only after they began to make some progress that they dared to share their gloom, which, at times, was intense. 'I was worried that Ben was over-straining himself, rowing faster than he would have done on his own or with someone else in order to keep up with James,' said Miss Hunt.

Meanwhile, Turner was anxious about the mental stress her husband was suffering. Used to Olympic training in which everything was done for him and all he had to do was row, he was unprepared for the psychological stress of ocean rowing. 'I never heard him say one positive thing about the race when he called home. At times, he was sobbing down the phone,' said Turner. 'I thought he might throw himself overboard.'

This was the worst of all years to take part in this race, which is timed to start after the end of the hurricane season. Usually, the seas are calm and the winds favourable, but the rowers were hit by three low-pressure systems, two tropical storms and Hurricane Zeta. For days on end they were confined to their airless cabin, the size of a car boot, trying to distract themselves with card games and anecdotes while Cracknell fretted about the time they were losing and other boats pulling ahead.

Christmas marked the nadir of their spirits. They were bobbing about on their sea anchor or rowing in such constantly veering winds that they feared they were going backwards. Added to that, thick cloud cover prevented their desalinator from working, so they were getting dangerously dehydrated.

Miss Hunt said: 'On Christmas Eve James rang me in secret asking me to call Ben as he was too miserable to ring me. I begged him to break into the fresh-water ballast even though it would mean a time penalty.'

To her great relief, Fogle rang back some time later to say that that was what they had done, although Cracknell now feared that they would lose the race. Sense only prevailed once they realised that, if they had to give up because pride prevented them from drinking the fresh water, it would take them even longer to reach Antigua and their waiting families.

They swallowed painkillers to mask the agony of the inflamed tendons on Fogle's hands and the infected sores on Cracknell's bottom. They cut back on their rations of 10,000 calories a day because they feared that the race would take them more than the fifty days they had anticipated.

Apart from the occasional pilot whale and dolphin, and the letters from home containing tiny presents and quiz questions, they were alone with their frustrations and their spirits swung. They were rowing two hours on, two hours off, sleep deprivation making their task still harder. 'I kept telling James to think about all those others in the race who were far behind, some of them rowing solo, no thought of winning,' said Turner, 'but he would say, "Whatever" and ask about his position again.'

As the final storm left them, with another boat taking the lead, Cracknell told his wife that he was going to put on a three-day spurt. From then on, they started to race ahead of the other pairs, learning to surf waves that sometimes reached 50ft and threatened to overwhelm them. When one finally did so, turning them over and depriving them of much of their equipment, they thought of raising the alarm. It was James's competitive spirit that kept them going. 'For days afterwards, I was too scared of it happening again to sleep in the cabin,' said Cracknell, 'and Ben was too frightened of another wave tipping us over to row. But I was not going to give up, especially since just before it happened we had our best ever morning.'

Nine days later they came into land looking like Robinson Crusoe and Man Friday but, despite the disagreements that had arisen from time to time, they were firm friends. 'We helped each other when the other was down,' said Cracknell. 'I have learnt that I am not always right from Ben's more subtle perspective on life.'

'And I am grateful to James's competitive spirit that kept us going. I hope some of it has rubbed off on me,' said Fogle.

As they stepped ashore, the bond between them was evident. While Cracknell hugged Turner, Fogle, with his arm around Miss Hunt, announced: 'James and I are thinking of having another adventure. It will have nothing to do with boats or rowing.'

Now safely in Antigua, they can spare a thought for those still rowing. They include a French pair of amputees (the support boat is carrying spare legs for them). A British photographer has missed the birth of his twins because he could not let down the cancer charity for which he was raising more than £1 million. Towards the back is Roz Savage, a former City high-flyer who capsized and is on her own.

Of the twenty-six boats to start, three have given up, one of them because the boat sprang a leak following an attack by a 12ft shark. Two others who capsized were not as lucky as Cracknell and Fogle in that they could not right their boats.

A pair of American women spent sixteen hours sitting on the upturned hull waiting for rescuers after their life raft went adrift. Another woman had to be winched off her foursome boat because she had consumed all its supplies of painkillers and feared that she would permanently damage her back.

Cracknell now has two months in which to decide whether to take part in the Beijing Olympics. Fogle has television programmes to make. For the moment, all they want to do is sleep and eat, and feel proud that they are now among the select band – fewer than 160 – to have rowed the Atlantic.

Chapter 10
COMMANDERS, PASSENGERS AND CREW

---

9 JULY 1995

TIME YET FOR THE ANCIENT MARINER

WITH HIS PERILOUS RAFT VOYAGES BEHIND HIM,
THOR HEYERDAHL WAS STILL SEEKING TO PROVE
HIS THEORIES ABOUT EARLY SEAFARERS.
HELENA DE BERTODANO REPORTS

Even as a child, there was something different about Thor Heyerdahl. While his classmates frolicked in the water and learnt how to swim, the young Norwegian boy stood alone at the edge, petrified. He had nearly drowned in a millpond at the age of five, and nothing would induce him to return to the water.

Yet a few years later, in 1947, while his classmates pursued their careers as bankers and teachers, Heyerdahl embarked on what seemed an absurdly perilous voyage: binding together some balsa logs, he crossed 4,300 miles of ocean in 101 days, risking his life to prove that Peruvian Indians could have settled in Polynesia.

Now eighty and with several more voyages on glorified hay-bales to his name, Heyerdahl is in London for two days between visiting pyramids in Tenerife and Peru, where he is finding exciting evidence to support his seafaring theories about early civilisations.

We meet at the Royal Geographical Society where his name is emblazoned in gold letters at the entrance; he has been awarded the Society's gold medal for his geographical explorations in the South Pacific Ocean. In the council room where we talk, he becomes enthused by a nineteenth-century globe, using it to give me a crash course in ocean currents and feasible routes around the world.

He has shoulder-length white hair and is wearing a blue blazer with gold buttons imprinted with tiny ships. Jacqueline Beer, his partner of the past four years, is at his side. They are coy about the exact nature of their relationship; Heyerdahl refers to her as his wife, but then adds that there are many ways in which one can be married. 'I consider her my wife; that is the important thing.'

A former actress and once Miss France, Jacqueline, now in her sixties, accompanies him everywhere, picking fluff off his jacket during the interview and nodding enthusiastically at me when he is telling remarkable stories – as if to corroborate his words.

Over lunch later, they order exactly the same. Heyerdahl confuses the waiter by initially asking for roast guinea pig. 'Guinea fowl,' says Jacqueline, laughing. 'You've spent too long in Peru...' He talks so much that he hardly touches his food. 'You must eat,' Jacqueline keeps reminding him. But he is in full flow describing a pyramid he is about to visit in Ecuador and, in his excitement, the food is irrelevant.

There is more than a hint of Coleridge's Ancient Mariner about Heyerdahl these days. Not only does he describe sights that most people cannot even imagine – such as a white-spotted sea monster with a five-foot mouth and 3,000 teeth – but he also has an extraordinary narrative gift, even in English, his second language.

He recounts the first time he saw the pyramids of Túcume in northern Peru: 'The sun was setting and spreading gold over the sloping sides of the twenty-six pyramids, which resembled the jagged spine of a dragon against the night sky.'

His blue eyes are alight with such excitement that you become as curious as he is to know what is inside the pyramids. The most significant find to date is a huge mud frieze depicting reed boats – further proof of his theory that there were experienced voyagers among early Peruvians. It is the subject of his latest book, *Pyramids of Túcume*, published last week.

He uses that same visual intensity to describe his childhood fear of water. 'I used to watch the tremendous surf smashing against the rocks off the coast of Norway. I had heard of people who had been washed over the cliffs and my nightmare was that such a wave would sweep me away.'

Then one day, aged twenty-two, he fell into the water in Polynesia and managed to swim. 'I realised that the ocean buoyed me up instead of sucking me down.' At the time he was living on the primitive island of

Fatu-Hiva with his first wife, Liv, seeing if it was possible for man to abandon civilisation. But their bodies could not cope with tropical diseases, and if they had not sought urgent medical help they would have died. 'I discovered that today neither man nor nature is what it was.'

Once back in civilisation, Thor and Liv had two sons but they grew apart. 'He was hardly ever at home,' says his son, Thor Heyerdahl Junior, a marine biologist. 'Although he was a warm and caring father when he did appear, it was so rare that he was more like a strange uncle to me.' Heyerdahl married another Norwegian, Yvonne, and had three daughters, the eldest of whom recently died of cancer. This marriage foundered in 1979.

Heyerdahl is the only child of two elderly parents who were very protective of him. 'I'm afraid I was terribly spoilt,' he says, grinning. His father was president of a brewery in Larvik and his mother was chairman of the local museum. 'I reacted against them by going on treks with a Greenland dog, braving storms and sleeping in the snow just to prove that I could do things alone.'

Fatu-Hiva marked not only a total break from his parents and the modern world, but also the beginning of his fascination with the movement of ancient peoples. On the Polynesian island a native told him about the god Tiki who had led his ancestors there from the East. According to Peruvian mythology, the Inca name for their departed god-king was Con-Tici. Heyerdahl made the link and called his first voyage the *Kon-Tiki Expedition*.

Although the public sees him, as he puts it, 'as a super Viking sailor jumping from one raft to the next', he has spent more time organising archaeological digs, most memorably in Easter Island. His projects are all related, he says, 'like pearls on a string'.

Subsequent genetic tests have challenged some of Heyerdahl's migration theories, suggesting for example that the original Easter Island settlers did not arrive from South America, as he insisted, but from the opposite direction. When I put this to him, he shrugs and says there were probably two migrations.

We may never know for sure. But even if every one of Heyerdahl's theories were to be punctured by science, his life would not have been in vain: he has sparked our imaginations and stimulated valuable debate.

Heyerdahl happily admits that he owes a lot to his critics. He only undertook the *Kon-Tiki* expedition because everyone said it was impossible. Yet he is the first to concede that just because he reached the islands on a balsa raft does not necessarily mean it happened before. 'I can only disprove a dogma which is false.'

It is a mistake to assume that he undertakes his voyages in a daredevil spirit. Ninety-nine per cent of each expedition lies in the planning, he says; the journey itself is a holiday in comparison. 'I am a very careful person and anyone who accompanies me knows how much I love life. Even when I cross a street, I do it with great caution. I have always known that unless I had extreme bad luck we would make the crossings alive.'

Only once has an expedition failed. *Ra 1*, aimed at proving that a papyrus reed boat could cross the Atlantic, collapsed after a storm sliced the vessel almost in half. Heyerdahl's insistence on abandoning ship, against his crew's wishes, illustrates his sense of responsibility. The following year, in a more carefully crafted boat, *Ra 2*, he completed the voyage.

The Tigris expedition in a Sumerian-type reed boat also ended prematurely – but not through any fault of the vessel. It foundered when North Yemen refused Heyerdahl permission to enter its waters. With war raging on three sides, the crew set fire to the vessel as a protest against the supply of weapons to the Third World.

It was a gesture typical of Heyerdahl. He abhors warfare and is astounded at the temporal chauvinism of our society, which believes it is better because it is more technologically advanced. 'To think that nuclear is superior to bows and arrows is insane.' He has just signed a protest against Jacques Chirac's decision to resume nuclear bomb tests in the Pacific. 'It is one of the greatest disappointments of my life,' he says. 'If the president of an elite nation can do such a thing, who knows what the leader of Iraq will stop at?'

He believes that societies that are less encumbered with modern wizardry are more contented. 'I define civilisation as a way of complicating simplicity. I am not only sure that primitive people are happier, I am 100 per cent convinced of it. In Túcume you rarely hear a child crying.'

Christopher Ralling, a TV producer who has travelled extensively with Heyerdahl and become a friend, describes him as a curious mixture of stubbornness and humility. 'He will fight for every frame in a programme but he has no sense of superiority. I remember a Hamburg taxi driver who could not believe Heyerdahl was in his car. Yet when he conveyed his delight, Thor showed equal enthusiasm and five minutes later both men had spread photographs over the bonnet and were showing each other their families.'

It is this ability to empathise and integrate that has opened doors – and tombs – for Heyerdahl around the world. In Peru, the Túcumanos were initially suspicious of the strange foreigner building himself an adobe hut in their village. Yet soon he was carrying statues in their religious processions and was overwhelmed with invitations to become godfather to their children.

Thor Junior says that his father has never lost his boundless capacity for wonder. 'Standing with him on the rim of Vesuvius is like being with a child on New Year's Eve. He is a highly emotional man with an imagination that is closer to an artist's than a scientist's.'

Sometimes he completely loses me. When I ask him whether ferreting among ancient tombs gives him a heightened sense of his own mortality, he says that it does not, because he has no sense of time. 'Age only exists within our awareness. For me it is logically impossible to accept that the three of us are here exactly now, when we know that everything before us is dead and everything afterwards is yet to come. The percentage of probability is so infinite.'

Surely it is not so bizarre, I say. If I had lived 5,000 years ago and was tucked away in one of his tombs, then someone else would be sitting in my place and he would be none the wiser. But he still insists that it is remarkable that I am here today. 'I can't explain it, but I'm sure there is something out there beyond our conscious selves. Call it God or what you will, but the one thing I am absolutely certain of is that we are not confronting reality.'

When he lists his itinerary for the next few weeks, it does indeed seem astonishing that we have coincided at all: he is planning to cover Peru, Ecuador, El Salvador, China and Tenerife, chasing after pyramids and mummies.

'He is like a mackerel,' says his son. 'If it loses its swim bladder it sinks to the bottom. When my father is no longer able to explore, he will die. But there is no danger of that yet. He still exhausts everyone, and if anything, he's getting worse...'

'I WANTED TO COME BACK KNOWING I COULDN'T HAVE DONE MORE'

AT TWENTY-FOUR, **ELLEN MACARTHUR** BECAME THE YOUNGEST AND FASTEST WOMAN TO SAIL ROUND THE WORLD SINGLE-HANDED. ON BOARD KINGFISHER, SHE TOLD **ELIZABETH GRICE** ABOUT HER FEARS, HER TIMES OF TRIUMPH AND HER 'AMAZING FRIEND'

If you have stood in a forest of giant pines and craned so far up to see the treetops that you almost fell backwards, you have some idea of what it is like to stand on the deck of Ellen MacArthur's boat and try to see the tip of the mast.

This is the giddy point to which she climbed, in seven utterly desperate crises, to effect the running repairs that kept her in the Vendée Globe. It is so high it quivers and vanishes. You feel sick just looking at it.

It goes without saying that this boat was nearly the death of her. You do not finish an unforgiving race such as the Vendée without being close to annihilation. One unsure step, and she would have been in the freezing, boiling ocean; or spreadeagled on the deck 90ft below.

'When you are up there,' she says, eyes shining, 'it's like trying to hang on to a telegraph pole in an earthquake.' Yet she revisited the scene of so much torment yesterday as if she were a child on a treat.

Two days' enforced separation from her boat had put Ellen in a state of high excitement. These two have been round the world together in an incredible ninety-four days. They are a symbiotic union, working as one. The hardest thing, she says, was approaching the finishing line, knowing it would soon be over. 'I had been so happy out there.'

I thought perhaps I knew what she was talking about until we actually boarded *Kingfisher* yesterday. The boat, after all, is a beautiful piece of technology, built for speed, dangerous even in repose. You can imagine it making a sailor happy 'out there'. But descending into the cramped, unventilated quarters that have been Ellen's home for the past three months, you realise that this is a serious challenge to any conventional notion of happiness.

The blue and yellow livery is cheery enough. The low ceiling of the cabin is decorated with stars and suns and moons. You edge forward, head bowed to investigate further, and meet a bank of winking screens and instruments. That is all there is to it. 'Just a little world that has been turning and turning', as Ellen memorably put it on her dazed landfall a few days ago. Surely not this little? But, yes, the hub of her working life at sea is a mere nutshell.

A bunk is slung invitingly to our left, but Ellen never once used it; to sleep even at arm's length from her instruments would have been too far. Instead, she simply propped herself up on the long seat in front of the screens. For three months, she never had more than five hours' sleep in twenty-four, usually taken in twenty-minute catnaps. If she nodded off from exhaustion, a strident alarm would automatically sound if conditions changed.

We have entered a zone where the concept of leisure, of relaxation, does not exist; where surveillance is never-ending and the body-clock wildly reprogrammed. There is day, night, storm, calm, crisis and the occasional magical encounter with sea creatures. But there is no let-up. Ellen seems surprised that anyone should think otherwise.

'When you are exhausted from dealing with some big problem, you still have to fight, even when all you want to do is collapse. It's that relentless. You are pushing yourself the whole time – for you, for the team, for everyone who's following the race. You push yourself because you want to come back knowing you couldn't have done more.'

A kettle rocks on its ring above a tiny gas stove. This is the galley: hot water and a collection of foil-wrapped freeze-dried food – far more of it than she ever needed, not because she has a small appetite, but because she came home so fast. The boxes of food containing provisions for days 95-110 were never even started.

In her matter-of-fact way, Ellen demonstrates the delights of apple and raisin crumble-in-the-bag. Nothing in this tiny space was a pain to her, neither the unappetising food nor the confinement. While the photographer and I lumber about like visitors to Lilliput, she darts around in her element, checking the instruments, putting things back where they belong, already back in maintenance and housekeeping mode.

'People think the Vendée Globe's about sailing,' she says, 'but it's about a partnership with a boat. She is an amazing friend. We have had the most amazing adventure together and it was our adventure, out there, going through all that.'

She speaks about *Kingfisher* with the fondness of a lover, dwelling on its injuries – the broken daggerboard, the shredded sails – far more than on her own wounds and bruises. Could she ever feel this way about another boat? 'Can you fall in love five times in your life? She is the dream I've had since I was a kid.'

Once you have toured this incredible machine, you cannot think of Ellen MacArthur ever again as a mere sailor – albeit one of the most proficient, daring and determined of our times. She is also an engineer, a technician, a plumber, an electrician, a computer expert, a meterologist, a sailmaker and a rope-splicer.

Her hands are still shiny and calloused from hours of physical work. They are small hands like a child's, with short fingers. It is impossible to imagine them, cracked with salt sores, wrestling down a sail three times her own weight. But then so much about Ellen MacArthur is impossible to comprehend, not least her diminutive size in relation to her achievement. She doesn't mind in the least that people draw attention to the fact that she is female, 5ft 2in and weighs about eight stone. To her, all this is an irrelevance as great as it is a fascination to her admirers.

'It's all about mental approach,' says Matthew Sheahan, an experienced sailor who has briefly handled the *Kingfisher*. 'This is a race run with brain, not brawn.'

In her uncomplicated, pragmatic way, Ellen says she was never lonely, only that she 'missed people a bit'. Despite the radio satellite contact, the e-mails, she says that when times were most desperate 'the hardest part was the lack of physical contact. There was no one to hug.'

Far from being fearless, she admits to often having felt pure terror. When she woke to find icebergs outside her window. Up the mast. When she hit a half-submerged container, and the grinding wrenching noise made it sound as if her boat were holed.

In the iniquitous Southern Ocean, a place where no human being would choose to be alone, icebergs stole up on her out of nowhere. 'I was so close, I could feel the wall of cold. They were half a mile long, as high as a cliff. Very blue. There was an aura about them, like presences. They are fascinating and frightening at the same time.

'I will never be able to recall my most frightening time because, usually, the last thing that happened to you is the worst. You forget, or rather your body preservation system makes you forget just how bad things were – otherwise, you would be in too much shock. And it's that which allows you to go back out there and do it again.'

She admits that when a mast baton broke in shelving water near the Galen Islands she was close to despair. 'Going up the rig took absolutely everything out of me. I was hanging off the rig with one hand, with no energy left. I was in a mess. It was very windy and rough and freezing cold. Not only did I have to get up the rig, get the baton down and get back down again, but I also had to take the mainsail down, repair the baton and get the sails up and carry on. When I got down, I was so shaken I couldn't see properly. My eyes had stars. I could hardly feel my skull.'

Strangely, once such crises were resolved, they were usually followed by depression – her only concession to weakness. 'There were times when you'd start spiralling downwards without really understanding why. You're tired, and a lot of little things pull into that spiral, and before you know it, you're at rock bottom and there's no one to pull you out. It never happens at the big moments, but after them. The hardest thing about being out there, alone and exhausted, is decision-making. After a big problem, you don't usually have nice stable conditions where you can recover. You have changes to cope with, decisions to make – when all you want to do is sleep.'

Two nights running, her anemometer (a vital directional aid) broke when she was near the Equator, and she came down from the mast 'black and blue'. Her leg had been mangled after becoming trapped between the sail and the mast. The scabs from her wounds are only now beginning to fall off.

Did she ever doubt her ability to get out of these and other catastrophes?

'No, because you cross the start line with the object of crossing the finishing line. The moment you doubt yourself, it's too late.'

It is not fanciful to imagine that Ellen MacArthur may put a lower price on her life than most of us would. She disagrees. 'You put a higher price on everyone else's, because you don't want to hurt them by not coming home.'

She says she realises that the voyage may have been more difficult for her parents than for her. 'It is hard for them, sometimes harder for people on land because, whereas you have some control over what's going on, they have none. I just hope that my being in a dangerous situation is outweighed for them by the amount of good I can do with it: to show people that if you really have a dream and you want to achieve it, you can.'

Nevertheless, Ellen is as superstitious as any other sailor. Crossing the Equator, she offered a libation to Neptune in the form of a small bottle of champagne poured into the sea. The second time, she made the supreme sacrifice of throwing overboard her second-to-last packet of Ginger Nuts – again to placate the sea-god.

She is still wearing the green jade Maori 'hook' pendant she acquired in New Zealand, where *Kingfisher* was built. Her mother gave her a silver St Christopher medallion, which also accompanied her on the 25,000-mile voyage.

Did she pray? Well, not exactly. 'I did look at the sky, and I talked to it a few times. Sometimes, I said just thank you, and sometimes: "Please help us. We are in desperate times and it's hard to cope" '.

Practical and down to earth as she is, Ellen is not the unsentimental professional adventurer she has sometimes sounded. Tucked into a corner of her chart is a dog-eared collection of photos from home, a few battered soft toys and a piece of wood from her grandmother's oak tree. She also took a poetry anthology and *Wuthering Heights* – although neither became well-thumbed.

In her few peaceful moments, she was more concerned with natural wonders. Whales, lit up by phosphorescence, visited her at night; dolphins 'glowing, like underwater shooting stars', followed her for miles. Detached from any island, albatrosses would hang around the boat for days. 'When the wind died and the sea was glassy, they would sit down and chat. It made me feel there were friends out there.'

Flying fish would land on the boat, smashing into things, and usually she would slip them back into the water. The day she cooked a flying fish in butter in her all-purpose metal bowl – as a variation from freeze-dried food – was not a success. 'I don't like to take from the sea.'

Ellen does not know when she began wanting to race. To begin with, her competitive instincts were channelled into a quest for marine knowledge. From the age of eight, when she spent holidays on her Aunt Thea's old boat at Burnham-on-Crouch in Essex, she says she discovered the extraordinary peace of being on water. By eleven, she was going without school dinner to save money to buy her first boat, a dinghy.

Regarded by her fellow pupils as a bit of a geek, she would spend lunchtimes on the floor of the school library, poring over books by her heroes – Sir Francis Chichester, Robin Knox-Johnston and Chay Blyth. 'They are probably still in the library, with my name ten times on the sticker in the front, and no one else's since.

'At sixteen, I suddenly realised that all the books I had were about single-handed sailing. I didn't realise till then how obsessed I was by it. Then when I bought my little corribee, *Iduna*, I stripped her down inside and removed a bunk. So there was only one left. I did that without ever consciously think-ing I would sail on my own.'

Sharing her boat with a crew when she next races is going to be difficult. To see her yesterday, after *Kingfisher* had been sailed briefly by three friends while she was reconnecting with her land life, was to realise how dedicated she has become to solitude and control. They had spent all morning metic-ulously tidying up, but she found things in the wrong place and rubbish in the food department, tut-tutting like a houseproud biddy.

'I'm used to things being in a certain place,' she says, laughing. 'Sailing with a crew will be hard at first. Not that I mind sharing things, but I'm so used to doing everything myself, and doing it a certain way, that I'll find it difficult to watch.'

In a way, a tiny space on a wide, unpredictable sea is the ideal habitat for someone like Ellen MacArthur. She never seems to have acquired any possessions. The material bits and pieces from her twenty-four years – and that is all they are – are scattered around the country, with friends.

She has slept on people's floors, on her small yacht while it was being refitted, in boatyards. The only thing she has been interested in acquiring seems to have been the sponsorship money needed for her immense labour.

It is somehow surprising that she has collected a boyfriend along the way – though, naturally, Ian Mackay is a sea-going man, and part of the young, close-knit *Kingfisher* team that has sustained its star for three months, to the detriment of families and social lives.

How was it for him, knowing she was really in love with a boat? 'He was just thrilled I was out there. He is a very unselfish person.'

As one of the yachtsmen on board *Kingfisher* yesterday pointed out, Ellen has achieved in four years what others aim for all their lives. You wonder where she will go next. But, of course, as a sailor who lives no further than the next race, she is no help. Seafaring is an end in itself.

We have talked of terrible storms and even more terrible calms, of icebergs and submarine dangers, but I still do not know what her worst enemy has been.

'Me,' she says. 'In wanting to give everything, maybe sometimes I gave too much. I should have known when to throttle back rather than keep pushing. But I was learning.

'That's the great thing about sailing. You can never know it all.'

NURSE KNEW BEST WHEN THE SHIP WENT DOWN

ON THE 74TH ANNIVERSARY OF THE INQUIRY INTO THE SINKING OF THE *LUSITANIA*, **HUGH MONTGOMERY-MASSINGBERD** MEETS THE NANNY WHO DREW ON 'GOOD OLD-FASHIONED DISCIPLINE' TO DELIVER HER CHARGES TO SAFETY

Always keep a-hold of Nurse, as Belloc cautioned, for fear of finding something worse. Never was this precept more admirably exemplified than one May afternoon in an ocean liner off the Irish coast, when seventeen-year-old Nurse Alice Lines – then feeding her infant charge Audrey Pearl with the four-year-old Stuart Pearl in attendance – heard 'a terrible bang'.

The liner was the *Lusitania* and the bang was caused by the first of the two German torpedoes that sank the great Cunarder in a mere twenty minutes, with the loss of some 1,200 lives.

Only a few hundred survived this act of piracy and today, 74 years on, it seems likely that Nurse Lines (now Mrs John Drury, 91) and her 'baby' (now Mrs Hugh Lawson-Johnston, sister-in-law of Lord Luke) are the only two left.

The redoubtable Mrs Drury, the most vigorous and alert nonagenarian it has ever been my privilege to meet, recalls the events of 7 May 1915 with precision. In the best nannying tradition, she attributes the saving of herself and the two children to 'good old-fashioned obedience and discipline'.

After the first torpedo hit the ship, on which the children's parents were also travelling, Nurse Lines tied Audrey, the baby, in a shawl round her neck and held Stuart tightly by her hand. 'No matter what happens,' she told him, 'hang on to me. If I fall down, hang on to me. Don't let go.' As the trio made their ascent from the cabin to the boat deck the second German torpedo rocked the ship and water was soon swirling round the nurse's waist.

On her way up the stairs Nurse Lines met her Danish under-nurse, Greta Lorenson, with Stuart's sister, Susan Pearl; another sister, Amy, had been taken by a stewardess to a lifeboat. In the event, Susan, Amy and Miss

Lorenson (whose brother had gone down in the *Titanic* three years earlier) all perished.

Once on deck, Mrs Drury recalls: 'A sailor snatched Stuart from me and threw him into a lifeboat, but as it was so full they wouldn't let me get in with the baby. Then I am afraid I became slightly hysterical. I screamed "He's my boy! I must be with him!" and fought with the sailor.'

She wrestled free of the seaman and then, without a lifejacket, jumped over the rail into the sea as the lifeboat was being lowered.

'It was my long hair that saved me,' she recalls. Now flowing freely in the water, her locks provided a lifeline for one of the men in the lifeboat to haul the nurse and baby on board.

Mrs Drury remembers the frantic efforts to prevent the lifeboat from being sucked under by the sinking ship. 'All I could see was bodies everywhere. And the thing that I'll never forget was the sight of the submarine that had torpedoed us. There it was sitting on the surface – with the German sailors just looking at us.'

Nurse Lines passed out in the lifeboat before they were picked up by a British ship. She did not lose her sense of humour. 'I remember finding it amusing that a Frenchman in the lifeboat, on seeing me with the baby, said: "If you've lost your husband, don't worry – you can come and live with me!"'

Back on shore at Queenstown (now Cobh) near Cork, Nurse Lines was asked if she wanted to contact anybody. Instinctively she telegraphed the Pearl children's grandmother in New York. 'I forgot all about my parents,' she says, 'and did not remember for a fortnight to let them know I was alive.'

Nurse Lines – like all the best nannies – had become part of the family. When she had confessed to Mrs Pearl that to get the job she had pretended to be older than she really was, 'Mrs Pearl put her arm around me and told me not to worry. "You're family," she said. "From now on you're one of us."'

A stout-hearted Suffolk lass, Alice Lines was born in December 1897, the daughter of a Saxmundham cabinet-maker, and trained at the Norland School of Nursing in London.

She soon showed her qualities when, in the early part of the 1914–18 War, her employers, Surgeon-Major Frank Warren Pearl and his wife, Amy, were briefly held by the Germans on suspicion of espionage, leaving the young nurse to cope alone with the children in Denmark.

'We were staying in a seaside hotel at Skager when war broke out,' she recalls. 'One minute I was flirting with these two German officers; the next, they had suddenly become the enemy.'

After the *Lusitania* sinking, Nurse Lines was staying at Queenstown with Stuart and Audrey when their father, who had also survived, turned up for an emotional reunion. But Mrs Pearl was still missing and Nurse Lines accompanied the Major on grim tours of the morgues. Eventually Mrs Pearl was washed up – alive – floating on a deckchair. Nothing was ever heard of Greta Lorenson or the two girls.

Following the ordeal of the inquiry in June, Alice Lines recuperated in Suffolk with her own family. She married Francis ('Bunny') Page from Yorkshire; and then, after his death, John Drury, a retired hairdresser from Manchester who recalls trimming Charlie Chapman's moustache and George Robey's eyebrows. The Drurys now live in Bexhill-on-Sea. 'My Audrey' keeps in close touch and earlier this year the Lawson-Johnstons presided over a celebration dinner to mark the Drurys' silver wedding.

Both survivors love the sea and treasure their *Lusitania* 'medals' – those notorious German commemorations of the ghastly tragedy. On one side the figure of Death is depicted issuing tickets at the booking office; on the other the *Lusitania* is going down.

The Germans should have known better than to underestimate the English nanny.

UNSTEADY AS SHE GOES

ADAM NICOLSON SET OUT TO SAIL THE ATLANTIC
COAST OF BRITAIN IN HIS BOAT, THE *AUK*, WITH HIS
OLD FRIEND GEORGE FAIRHURST. IN THIS EXTRACT
FROM HIS BOOK, *SEAMANSHIP*, HE DESCRIBES HOW
TENSION ERUPTED BETWEEN THEM

As the summer wore on, and as we made our way north up the Irish coast
and then crossed over to the southern Hebrides, something seemed to go
wrong between George and me.

A day on Skellig – eight miles off the coast of Kerry – had been followed
by a bad night in the Blaskets. George had been unable to leave the *Auk* at
the Skelligs. All day he had put up with the difficult combination of anxiety
and tedium, sitting alone on the boat, wondering if its anchor was going to
hold, knowing that the rest of us were on the island, drinking in its every
element, while he could only watch from the side.

Demand without stimulus, accommodating the necessary and ever-
present watchfulness, needing to check at every turn that the boat was
continuing to cling to its tiny underwater shelf with its toothpick of an
anchor, 10 or 12 fathoms below. He was, as a result, exhausted, even before
we arrived late, at one in the morning, at the frankly unsatisfactory shelter
we had chosen. The anchorage in the lee of Inishvickillaun had scarcely
been sheltered from the westerlies and the swell had poured through the
gap to the north of the island.

The *Auk* had been unsettled all night. None of us had tightened the
mizzen sheet, and so its jaws were twisting and grinding against the mast all
night. In the broken water that came round the top end of the island,
halyards and their blocks were slapping against the mainmast. The anchor
chain was continually grinding against its fairlead in the bow, a low
rumbling.

All night long, George was up and down, more aware than the rest of us
of the possibility that the anchor might not hold. He was clearly angry. On
one occasion as he went past my bunk to the companionway steps, the boat

tipped so severely that the kettle fell off the cooker and veered all over the floor. I lay where I was and said, 'Can I do anything to help?'

'That's what's called a BSR,' he said.

'A BSR?'

'A Bum Slightly Raised. And none of you need bother with the f****** kettle.'

Then, sharply, and at other times more subtly, my hopelessness and lack of responsibility were twinned with his anger. It became something of an underlying theme. George, of course, knew a great deal more about the psychology of the sea than I did. He had watched it at work on people, including himself, for too long not to be familiar with the dynamics of crews and with the way that adequacies and inadequacies overlapped at sea. He had often talked about the way the sea draws people who do not feel entirely whole on land. Even my presence here, this year, was a symptom of the belief that a boat could solve your problems. George had known glamorous yacht skippers in the Caribbean. As he saw it, there was always something hollow about their potency because everyone at sea, in one way or another, had run away to sea. The cool of a cool yacht skipper belonged more to the yacht than the skipper. Divorced from his craft, in all its senses, the sailor becomes a diminished man, his prop not there for his elbow to lean on.

George knew all these things but was at times subject to them too. There can be few people in the world as capable as him: a natural athlete, a charming and funny man, an incomparable mimic, a gifted musician, a man who sticks to tasks and knows how to dig deep, who will go 10 miles before you have asked him to go one.

But alongside all that, his need to exert control over the boat and its inhabitants, particularly when tired, could be powerful. He would ask me, say, to lash a dinghy to the deck, come back when I had done it and kick it to show I had done it wrongly or badly. He would ask me to attach a line to a mooring buoy or a quayside without showing me how, and allow me to struggle before showing me the right way.

Rarely would he accept that anything I had done was done right. Some of my children had left their beach buckets and spades on the boat: they became somehow symbolic of my messiness and unsuitability to boat life, or my 'guilt', as he said one day, about leaving the children behind. In part, I felt, what mattered to him most was the boat, as a destination in itself, when what mattered to me was what the boat might do and where it might go. An air of frustration hung between us.

I don't wonder, because what I had asked him to do for me was not easy. Not only was I George's employer, but also his crew. I would tell him what I would like to do and he would then tell me to do it. The poor man had to look both ways, listening to and instructing the same person. No wonder he felt taut.

This difficulty was made worse by my own lackadaisical, freedom-searching and non-mechanical frame of mind. The qualities I love in my son Ben – a kind of disengaged ease about things – George found wildly frustrating in me. He dreamed, he often told me, of the two of us becoming such a good crew together that there would be no need to talk. The boat would simply happen. It would go on its way as sleekly and neatly as an Atlantic panther.

In his eyes anyway, that never occurred. Although he did once say that maybe it was because he was refusing to let me grow out from under his shadow, George never felt that I could skipper the boat myself. I did! I learnt, well enough, how to read the weather, how to set the sails, how to navigate, how to anchor and weigh anchor, how to make our way along a difficult shore, how to stick with it, how to take the *Auk* out into a wind-strewn sea, how to bring her home, how to choose shelter for her.

I could look up and read from the rigging what every stay and halyard was doing. But George never thought I could. What a sadness that is: the dream we both had at the beginning of the year, of a deepening friendship, of a trunk full of intimacies, of us becoming bound together, that never really developed.

Of course, he was right. If a halyard block broke in a storm, or a bilge pump blew; if the fuel supply to the engine became clogged, or if we were being blown, with no power, on to a lee shore, embayed and unable to escape, with a frightened crew, then I would have been at a loss. I simply did not have the hours, the days and the months for sea habits and sea knowledge to have been creased into my mind as they had been over the years into his.

Nor was I progressing fast enough. Too much time was spent away from the boat, filming various adventures underwater and down cliffs, for my sea knowledge to be deepened and enriched in the way it should have been.

I was both a neglectful employer and a skiving pupil, arriving back at the boat from time to time, saying, 'Right. Everything OK? Let's go. Now. Aren't we ready? I know how to do it. Jump to. Tell me how. Why isn't this working? Haven't you mended that yet? What a mess it is down here. Help me. Listen to me. Don't talk to me like that. Let's try and have a good time, can we?'

Inch by inch, yard by yard, over the weeks, George was improving and honing the *Auk*, and I can only imagine that in all of this, half there, half not there, half critical, half engaged, I was a nightmare.

'YOU CAN DO THE ORDINARY THINGS IF YOU WANT...'

PAUL WEAVER HEARS WHY ROBIN KNOX-JOHNSTON PUTS HIMSELF TO THE TEST

Stroking his beard, Robin Knox-Johnston looks a little like Hemingway. The old man of the sea is off again, attempting to sail around the world in seventy-seven days, win the Jules Verne Trophy, and prove that he remains one of the world's outstanding long-distance yachtsmen.

He looks so ordinary in many ways. He is very British, fifty-four, conservative – with both a small and a large 'C' – and lives in modest comfort in a couple of cottages knocked together near Totnes in Devon. However, there is a calmness that marks him out, a remarkable self-containment that would unnerve you if you had the misfortune to be his adversary.

'I do lead a normal businessman's life for much of the time, and this is partly deliberate,' he explains. 'But there is a difference. You can do the ordinary things if you want to lead an ordinary life. But if there's something in you, some deep curiosity to find out what life can be like...then I think you will always be looking for that thing which is just a bit different, where you can find stimulation.

'That's why I went parachuting and why I went climbing with Chris Bonington in Greenland. I wanted to find out what it was like. I have no need to test myself. I'm just a very curious person.

'When I sailed around the world non-stop and single-handed, it wasn't to test myself. It was to prove wrong the people who said it couldn't be done, people who had a low standard of expectation. I have a very high standard of expectation.'

For Knox-Johnston and Peter Blake there is a feeling of unfinished business. Last year's attempt to win the Jules Verne ended in failure when their catamaran, *ENZA*, struck a piece of flotsam which split one of the hulls and allowed the French team, led by Bruno Peyron, to claim the trophy.

'We don't mind getting to the end of 1994 and looking back on another failed attempt. But we would hate to look back on a year in which we hadn't even made an attempt to put the record straight.

'I find the whole thing so challenging. This is the fastest ocean sailing boat in history. It's so exciting to sail. And the concept of the race is so simple. Round the world in less than eighty days.

'It will be a head-to-head against the French boat and also a race against the clock and the record of seventy-nine days and six hours. I regard cruising and pottering about as my hobbies these days, but this is something I just couldn't resist.

'OK, it may not be quite as epoch-making as sailing round the world single-handed, but I feel this race could really capture the imagination.

'The only rule is no outside assistance. Apart from that anything goes. First boat home wins.'

It was boating, rather than sailing specifically, that galvanised the young Knox-Johnston. Forty years ago he built a canoe. He went on to join the Merchant Navy and in 1967 built a boat in India and sailed it home. 'Francis Chichester had just sailed around the world and I thought to myself, "I can do that". So I did. I also enjoy solitude occasionally. It allows your mind to drift to depths it would otherwise not find.

'Single-handed sailing also teaches you to pace yourself. It makes you calmer in business decisions. I am now less easily frightened because I have faced so many potential disasters in sailing and come through them.

'There was a nasty moment coming back across the Atlantic forty years ago when things got a little bit out of control. We went down four times and eventually lost our mast.

'And I remember, in the Southern Ocean, seeing a huge wave coming and wondering whether I would still be alive in five minutes' time.

'Now, forty years on, I still get the same enthusiasm. If someone said to me, "Robin, take this boat and go to a race", I would be off like a shot.'

He is, you sense, a rather difficult man to live with. 'Unpredictable' is how he prefers to describe himself. He is not ideally suited to quiet family holidays. 'My wife and I did try a package holiday to Tenerife a while ago. I stuck it for two days, then I found a local sardine fisherman to take me out. He didn't speak any English and I didn't speak any Spanish. But I had a great time and I learned all about sardine fishing.'

ENZA has been substantially refitted for the attempt to win the Jules Verne Trophy, which will get under way as soon as the weather is right. They have added five feet to the stern and two feet to the bows to give more buoyancy. They have also changed the underwater shape to give extra speed and will be looking to travel regularly at more than 20 knots.

'There will be times when we will have to cover 400 miles in a day,' he said. 'But we have a great crew.'

The boat has changed substantially but Knox-Johnston, you sense, is the same. 'I still feel in my forties,' he said. But eyes change very little, and in his you can still see the youthful passion of that fourteen-year-old Ulster boy who built his first canoe.

BLASHERS' BASH-ON WORLD

TIM HEALD IS GIVEN A LESSON IN LEADERSHIP BY COL. JOHN BLASHFORD-SNELL

JBS was in town the other day to touch base with CHQ. Phase two of the operation has been completed, so he was able to fly out from Central America, take a quick shufti round London and then rejoin TACHQ in Chile.

Now I will translate. JBS is the celebrated, if improbable, explorer, Col. John Blashford-Snell, known to Fleet Street as 'Blashers'. I have never believed that anyone in real life calls the colonel 'Blashers' and was pleased to have this confirmed. 'People call me a lot of things, not all of them complimentary,' he says, 'but never "Blashers".' My personal observation suggests that most colleagues call him 'John' or 'JBS'.

CHQ is 'Central Headquarters'. This is rather like something from an early episode of *The Avengers*. You go to a drab electricity generating station in Chelsea, enter through very unpromising anonymous doors, pass up flights of empty echoing stairs and emerge into a set of offices full of rather military-looking men in shirtsleeves, crisply pretty girls and a great many computer screens.

'The Operation' is 'Operation Raleigh', successor to 'Operation Drake', another of JBS's grand designs. The idea is wonderfully barmy. You get a couple of ships – one a converted ocean-going trawler, the other a picturesque brigantine. You spend four years sailing them round the world, stopping here and there for some exploring, adventuring, helping out the natives, doing whatever seems appropriate. Each stop is called a 'phase' and there are sixteen of them. You have a hardcore of senior chaps to lead and organise; appropriate boffins – archaeologists, botanists, zoologists, etc. – as and when required; and on each phase you have about 250 'venturers' aged between seventeen and twenty-four and from all over the world.

'TACHQ' stands for 'Tactical Headquarters' and is the mother ship, the 1,900-ton *Sir Walter Raleigh*, a gift from the people of Hull.

The popular image is of a man who should really exist only in a series of

'Blashers' books written by Captain W.E. Johns ('Blashers and the Blue Nile,' 'Blashers of the Congo' etc.). If I were casting 'The Blashford-Snell Story' I would have used a middle-aged Terry Thomas for the colonel, who has the same sort of hair and the same sort of moustache. Not nearly as languid, though. 'He's in his office,' said one girl at CHQ; 'I can hear him shouting.' This is slightly unfair, but he is a loud talker and seldom, I should guess, silent. He also has – despite a breezy and usually genial manner – a way of looking very straight ahead with his head lowered that suggests an animal about to charge. A bull on the lookout for a red rag.

It would be unwise, however, to treat JBS simply as some sort of joke because the story of Operation Raleigh really is rather astonishing and its success so far is largely due to his energy, enthusiasm, his powers of persuasion and, above all, the quality he admires almost more than anything else – leadership.

He talks long and eloquently about leadership. 'In Panama,' he says, 'we were a bit apprehensive because they'd voted against us over the Falklands.' After the Raleigh team's visit to that country he was told: 'We were suspicious about British military people, but now we say: "The Malvinas conflict is dead." The one thing you British can do is to teach "leadership."'

JBS said that he had heard exactly the same thing from the Prime Minister of New Guinea back in '69. A few weeks ago, he adds, he was rocking at anchor in exactly the same spot as Drake and Raleigh all those years ago – off the coast of North Carolina, composing a radio message to be broadcast at a special St George's Day bash at the London Hilton – 'and I suddenly thought: the answer is we're still mucking around with this business of leadership. We may be a funny little nation but one of the things we can still do is to lead.'

Being extremely resistant to the idea of 'leadership', I was rather relieved when he changed the subject and told me that the expedition had completed 1,775 man hours under water without a single accident. And how they searched for buried treasure and found fourteen 'major wrecks'. And how one of the diving instructors pulled a barracuda's tail. And about 'dear old Pat from Fort Bragg' who taught them how to photograph jaguars and make napalm from soap and candles. And how Princess Alexandra's daughter got a native village to install dustbins.

And how the boat capsized in a hurricane but everyone was rescued. And being mistaken for a spy ship by the Nicaraguans – or was it the Salvadoreans? And Union Jack Hayward. And alligators in swamps. And the most poisonous snake in the world in someone's airline bag. And great leather-back turtles laying eggs. And how they saved the sight of about 300 Indians. And found all the gear de Lesseps left behind after building the Panama canal. And gold mines.

I could go on for ever. So could he. The whole dotty enterprise sounds tremendous fun and is chalking up all sorts of improbable achievements. It is largely voluntary; heavily sponsored by business — 1,000 benefactors; and it's British. Nobody else would have pulled it off. Perhaps more to the point, nobody else would have thought of it in the first place.

ONE STEP FURTHER UP THE NILE

INSPIRED BY THE VICTORIAN ADVENTURERS,
CHRISTOPHER ONDAATJE ABANDONED HIGH FINANCE
TO GO EXPLORING. **BRIAN JACKMAN** REPORTS

In the Fifties, when Christopher Ondaatje was twenty-two, he arrived in Canada with $13 in his pocket. It was barely enough to rent a basement room in Toronto, where he survived on a dime-a-day diet of toast and coffee. But he worked hard and soon managed to put by $3,000. Thirty years later — during which time he was a member of Canada's 1964 Olympic bobsled team — he was presiding over a corporate finance empire worth $500 million. But by then he had become disillusioned with the greed of the business world. 'In 1988 I decided I could take it no longer,' he says. 'So I sold everything and got out, and devoted myself to the life I had always craved — a life of adventure and writing.'

His latest book, *Journey to the Source of the Nile*, describes his most recent exploit, a gruelling three-month trip through Africa retracing the routes of the Victorian explorers, Burton, Speke, Grant, Baker and Stanley, in their search for geography's greatest prize — the beginnings of the world's longest river.

Like Burton and his contemporaries before him, he travelled by dhow from Zanzibar to Bagamoyo on the Tanzanian mainland, the old slave port whose Swahili name means 'lay down the burden of your heart'. From there he headed inland to Lake Tanganyika, turned north and travelled around Lake Victoria and then on to Lake Albert and the Ruwenzori Mountains in Uganda, before returning across the Serengeti plains. By the time the expedition was over, he had covered 6,270 miles — one-and-a-half times the length of the Nile.

The clue to this extraordinary U-turn in Ondaatje's life is a Victorian portrait that hangs in his home. It shows his hero, Richard Francis Burton, the nineteenth-century soldier, orientalist, writer and adventurer, in the Afghan disguise he wore to enter Mecca in 1853. 'This was painted after Burton's trip to Mecca and before his expedition to the Nile in 1856,' says

Ondaatje. 'It was referred to in Isobel Burton's will, but was lost for ages. Then somehow it surfaced in Australia, where I managed to obtain it.'

His obsession with Burton dates from the early Seventies. 'I read an incredible book, *The Devil Drives*, by Fawn Brody, on the life of Burton. It made me realise that here I was in the modern world but there was another world and that was where I really belonged,' he says. 'His was the life I most wanted to live.'

The result was two expeditions in Burton's footsteps, first to India and Pakistan and now his epic journey through East Africa. 'My greatest fear was that I should die with the word financier carved on my gravestone,' he says. 'Now I have taken the journeys of the Victorian explorers one step further. That's a much greater achievement than making a couple of million bucks.'

We are in the oak-panelled library of his north Devon home, a haunted Gothic manor on the Exmoor coast. By the window, framed by a view of the sea 200ft below, stands the desk where his younger brother, Michael, wrote part of *The English Patient*.

Does he feel overshadowed by his novelist brother? 'Heavens no,' he says. 'Michael is a romantic. He writes fiction. I write fact. He's ten years younger than me and I am hugely proud of him. I pulled him out to Canada and put him through college. I was a financier. I had already sold my soul to the devil, but Michael never compromised. He has a great dramatic ability and love of words, and has lived always in the world of literature.'

The house – Ondaatje bought it in 1984 – lies at the bottom of a three-mile track. 'It was built in 1825 by Walter S. Halliday, a Victorian recluse, and is so remote that every stone had to be shipped in by sea,' he says. 'I remember it as a boy. It had this long drive and we used to say that if you ever went down there you would never come back.'

Ondaatje was born in Ceylon in 1933. His family were tea planters, descended from Dutch burghers who had settled there in 1636. 'I grew up on a tea estate,' he says. 'Then, at the age of twelve, I was uprooted and sent to England for an education. So there was this wild unruly colonial boy from the jungles of Ceylon suddenly flung into Blundell's School in Tiverton and taught to be an Englishman.'

The structured society of Devon came as a shock. Luckily, he had an English uncle, the Rev. David Cockle, vicar of Timberscome on Exmoor. 'So I had a place in the English scheme of things. I was the vicar's nephew.'

When his education was complete he went to Canada and had to learn a new set of rules. 'When you're young and hungry you learn fast. You learn to think for yourself,' he says. 'If you want to do well you must be single-minded. You have to have guts, to take risks, to know everything you possibly can about yourself and the world at large.'

That philosophy stood him in good stead when he set out to relive Burton's 1856 journey to the Nile. 'Mind you, there were a few differences,' he says. 'Burton's caravan consisted of almost 200 men and dozens of pack and riding animals. Mine had five men and two Land Rovers. And the locals are better armed these days.'

At Kigoma, on the shores of Lake Tanganyika, Ondaatje met the horrific sight of boatloads of refugees from Zaire fleeing the conflict between ex-President Mobutu and Laurent Kabila's rebel army. The refugees had arrived in their thousands, but were prevented from landing by soldiers with machine-guns. 'As we cruised north, we encountered similar scenes,' he says. 'It was a scary business, and we sometimes found ourselves travelling between the refugee boats and the soldiers.'

Fear, Ondaatje says, is a curious thing. 'At first you're scared; then you go one step further and feel you're invincible. It's like photographing a charging elephant. Hidden behind a lens you feel separated from reality. Apart from the first ten days, I felt very little fear, but there is no doubt that Africa is going through a very dangerous time. It is only fifty years since Africa was being opened up by missionaries, explorers and colonisers. Now much of it is in the hands of dictators and tyrants, giving rise to the terrible bloodbath we are seeing in places like Rwanda. We are living through a terrible post-colonial hangover in which white men's boundaries are being blurred, where Islam is moving in, where tribalism is returning and natural frontiers, like the Nile, are replacing artificial lines drawn on the map.'

One of Ondaatje's main objectives was to measure the discoveries of the last century in the light of modern scientific knowledge. In 1874, on a journey partly sponsored by the *Daily Telegraph*, Stanley set out from Zanzibar, circumnavigated Lake Victoria the following year and confirmed Ripon Falls as its only northern exit. Even now, children are still taught that Lake Victoria is the source of the Nile.

The truth is more complex. 'Lake Victoria is not the source of the Nile, and neither is Lake Albert,' he says. 'They are merely its reservoirs. The Kagera River, feeding Lake Victoria, and the Semliki, pouring down from the Ruwenzori Mountains into Lake Albert – these are the Nile's two main sources.'

Towards the end of his book he makes a huge leap of the mind by suggesting that the geological spasms that shaped the present course of the Nile may also have sparked our own evolution. 'To the west of the Rift Valley, where the gorillas and chimps still live, Africa remains wooded, wet and steamy,' he says. 'But to the east arose the open savannahs where the first humans learned to stand upright and scan the plains for animal kills as they scavenged like hyenas.'

It is time for lunch. He is sorry that Valda, his wife, is away but the butler has laid on a little something for us in the dining-room: a delicious home-made game soup, smoked salmon, pâté, fruit and cheese.

'I love England and the life here,' he says. 'I'll never get it out of my system. But I also love Africa. Like Burton, you go there and experience it for as long as you can. Yet, in the end, you must always come back, because England is one of those centres of culture and civilisation where you must write and strive for acceptance by one's peers.'

Today he is a governor of Blundell's, a director of WWF Canada and a philanthropist with a passion for cricket (he funded Somerset County Cricket Club's school of excellence in Taunton). Yet he remains an enigma, a restless, complex Renaissance man like those Victorian giants whose exploits he so admires, torn between his home in England and the desire to see that other, older world before it vanishes for ever.

'When I set off on my Nile trip,' he says, 'I thought I could write some-thing fantastic about Africa, its past and present, and even, with guts, to speculate about its future, but ultimately I had to admit defeat. Africa will always have its problems, which it will solve in its own way. At the end of it, I realised Africa will always be a mystery.'

ALL IN THE SAME BOAT

THE RIDGWAYS ARE PLANNING TO SAIL TO
THE ENDS OF THE EARTH AND BACK. AS THEY
ARRIVE IN THE CANARIES ON THE FIRST LEG OF
THEIR ADVENTURE, **TREVOR FISHLOCK** EXPLAINS
WHAT DRIVES A FAMILY TO SEA

It was a sweat carrying my bags up the steep grassy hill to Ridgway's place. He was pleased to see the sheen on my brow. He thinks life isn't worth living if there is no physical struggle. 'Hello, old top,' he said, extending his Cape Horner's paw. 'Bit hot?'

The handshake was what you would expect from a man who has kept a ferocious grip on life in desperate hours. His broken-nosed face seems carved from the granite on which he has wrested his living. The blue eyes are merry and candid, the smile warm and mischievous, though one tooth was recently bested by a baguette in France.

He led the way up the ladder into his private tower on the roof of the solid white house that commands his croft. In this library-eyrie he writes his books and broods and prowls, not least in the hours before dawn, for he is a restless and questing man, impatient of slumber.

Ridgway's kingdom is at Ardmore, 12 miles south of Cape Wrath, where Scotland's north-west edge juts into the Atlantic. The croft, beside a sea loch of crystal water, the haunt of seals and otters, is enfolded by stern mountains. It is a dramatic and enchanting place and the Ridgways gave their hearts to it long ago.

At the foot of the sheep-studded hill stand the timber buildings of the adventure school they have run for twenty-five years: bunkhouses, dining hall, kitchen, workshops, boathouses and stores. For the first seventeen years they had no electricity. One of the sheds houses the 20ft boat in which Ridgway and Chay Blyth rowed across the Atlantic in ninety-two days in 1966. Ridgway fashioned the idea for his school during that trip. He reckoned he could earn his living helping others to meet physical challenges. Ten thousand people have been to the school, to climb, sail, canoe, dive, walk, fish, to confront the elements and also themselves.

In the kitchen, Marie Christine Ridgway cooked dinner for forty-two, as she does seven days a week during the seven-month Ardmore season. She is slim and fair, quick and vivacious. Serene, too. She met Ridgway at a roulette table and married him at twenty.

That was twenty-nine years ago. He was a penniless paratroop officer with a strong spring of adventure, a compulsion to strain nerve and sinew, to feel more alive by confronting danger.

He is demanding, sometimes difficult to live with and, as Marie Christine has related in her book about life at Ardmore, she has at times resented living in the shadow of an extraordinary, driven man who is determined to force a gallon of life into his pint pot. Asserting her own individuality is one challenge of her existence.

From his tower, Ridgway indicated two kayaks flitting across the water. Twenty-two months ago he and his daughter Rebecca, twenty-six, paddled them around Cape Horn. He watched a boat ferrying stores to a white yacht, his 57ft ketch *English Rose VI*. He has raced it around the world twice. On the latter occasion, he walked out of the croft, down the hill, climbed aboard the yacht with a friend, turned left and did not sight land again until Cape Horn; and he did not see land after that until he sighted Scotland.

Now the ketch is at sea again, shouldering through the Atlantic at the start of an amazing voyage. Ridgway had been simmering the idea for months before he launched it in May upon his family: Marie Christine, Rebecca and Elizabeth, the Ridgways' fourteen-year-old adopted daughter.

They would sail across the Atlantic and the Pacific, round Cape Horn and brave the ice of Antarctica. He gave more detail: they would close the adventure school for a season and be away for eighteen months. They would leave Ardmore, push out into the North Atlantic and head for the Canary Islands, pick up the trade winds for Barbados and Antigua, transit the Panama Canal, visit the Galapagos and cruise the South Pacific, the Marquesas islands, the Cook islands, Tahiti and Pitcairn, before dropping south to the roaring forties and the shrieking fifties to pick up the westerlies that would blow them to Chile.

Here the yacht will rest for two months while the Ridgways make a remarkable expedition to the highlands of Peru. They have promised Elizabeth they will do their best to fulfil her dream of meeting her mother.

Elizabeth is the daughter of a Quechua Indian mother and a Norwegian-Quechua father, Elvin Berg. In 1970, the ever-adventuring Ridgway met

Berg during an Amazon expedition. Berg saved his life and they became friends. In 1985 Ridgway trekked with his wife and daughter into the Peruvian mountains to meet Berg, but found he had been murdered by Shining Path terrorists.

By chance, they discovered that he had a daughter. She was in a remote jungle village, a malnourished six-year-old cared for by her grandmother because her mother, simple and stone deaf, could not do so. Grandmother asked the Ridgways to take the girl home with them, to give her a future.

It seemed to the Ridgways the stroke of fate. Ridgway was himself an orphan, adopted at three months. 'I was very fortunate, given a loving upbringing, given my chance. With Elizabeth I felt I was being shown the way to help someone, in my turn.' He also felt strongly that he could repay the debt to the girl's father, who had saved his life. One glance told him that Marie Christine and Rebecca felt the same way. The following year, after negotiations with the Peruvian government, the Ridgways adopted Elizabeth and she came to live in Ardmore.

'I want to see Elizabeth right,' Ridgway said, 'and show her many things. She is curious about her origins and knows she looks different. I want to show this vivid and volatile person from Peru that there is more to the world than a bleak corner of Scotland. I want her to see herself in context. It will be a geography lesson on a grand scale, a boost to her self-confidence. I don't know how she will react. It would be traumatic at any age. But she is a Quechua: tough and stoical.'

After Peru the Ridgways will rejoin the yacht and sail through the Patagonian islands of Chile to Cape Horn. The plan is to sail 600 miles south of the Horn to Palmer Station, Antarctica, for Christmas next year.

Ridgway showed me the orange patch he has had made in case the yacht is holed by an iceberg. From Antarctica the family will head north up the Atlantic to South Georgia and Tristan da Cunha, returning to Ardmore and their warm, woodlined home in March 1995 in time to reopen the school of adventure and reclaim their platoon of cats.

'A little test,' is Ridgway's laconic description of the voyage. But the ocean and the storms, seasickness and fear, will make it at times a big test. Ridgway worried about it all summer. 'I know the dangers and I'm responsible. We are setting off tired after a long summer, into the North Atlantic, a major risk. No wonder I wake up at two in the morning.'

He may sometimes sound a hearty action man – 'Stir the stumps, old top' – but he is often tormented, wrestling with self-doubt, and he is cautious, not arrogant. He concedes that some think him crazy to seek danger, but he would not be true to himself if he did not construct a challenge and submit to it.

At fifty-five he has mellowed a bit, the old granite may be a little smoother, but he is not slowing down. He is a great inhaler of cold air. *Carpe Diem* — Seize the Day — is the motto carved in large gold letters on a beam in his house, and he lives by it.

He feels the march of the years, but this gives an edge to his battling. There's something of Ridgway in the lines in Tennyson's 'Ulysses': 'I cannot rest from travel: I will drink / Life to the lees… / To strive, to seek, to find, and not to yield.'

In his tower he reached for some books to take on the voyage. 'Must take Chichester,' he said. 'Always my inspiration, never gave up.' He added surprisingly: 'I've never particularly liked sailing. I don't like the sickness and the boredom and I'm frightened of the dark and other things. But down at the foot of the croft is a magic carpet and the means to travel it: the yacht, which will take us anywhere the wind blows.

'I want to see whales and dolphins and albatross again, trade wind clouds, islands emerging from the sea, green and restful. I want the adventure that is proof of being alive and vibrant. You can't postpone such things, you cannot be a waiting-to-die figure.' He recited a favourite phrase: 'The opportunity of a lifetime must be taken in the lifetime of the opportunity.'

Marie Christine sat on a rock high above the croft, looking out to the mountains of Foinaven and Arkle. 'I sailed with John in the 1977 round-the-world race. There were some terrific moments, but most of the nine months was an ordeal. I hated the sickness and squalor, the tensions and lack of privacy. When I returned I said, "Never again."

'So sailing isn't really my bag. Yet here I am again, squeezing into a 57ft plastic tube with all the attendant discomfort and seasickness. It is a wrench leaving Ardmore, but in the end I didn't want to miss out on the trip of a lifetime. And this time it will be different. We are going as a family, which means so much to us, and it isn't a race. We have two young men in the crew, Will Burchnall and Andy Adamson, and friends will join us from time to time. I shall continue Elizabeth's education on board. I've stowed a big box of books for her and there will be daily lessons.

'It won't always be easy with John. Living with him can be like living with a lion. On the other hand, he's a grand chap with immense humour, and he really is inspiring. Of course, we are all single-minded people, and that is why the rows start, when we object to his self-appointed leadership. Any couple would find it extremely difficult to be with the partner morning, noon and night as we are. Lively is the word for our family life. John feels henpecked, but...' – she smiled – 'we Ridgway women have him sussed.

'He has a granite core and he can be severe and uncompromising, but never brutal. He is a frontiersman who has to carve an existence for himself and, if you do not let him do it, he is diminished. He needs a platform, to be an inspirer, a general running a campaign. If he doesn't have a great project the frustration makes him sick. He comes to life in situations of physical danger and he is a man of such vitality that it is hard for him to come to terms with the fact that it all ends. The recent death of a friend of his own age shook him terribly. But at the same time he puts himself into life-threatening situations, half-taunting death.'

Rebecca was brought to Ardmore in a fish basket when she was three weeks old. She is as much in love with the croft as her parents. She lives in the cottage next door to them and works in the adventure school. She has her mother's gentle manner; and her toughness, too.

'There are often arguments. We are all competitive and Dad can be annoying. He expects an awful lot of people. But we know each other well and don't fight over important things. Dad has qualities I don't match up to. He pays close attention to detail and planning, leaves nothing to chance. He is meticulous and hates untidiness. He is demanding, but he believes you don't grow unless you are stretched. As for Mum, she is tougher than any of us.'

Ridgway paused in his planning for the voyage. 'The family is the main reason for the trip, the most valuable part of my life. It is about time I did something in a more leisurely fashion. I've been in a rush during my first fifty-five years. I'm still young and life is unfolding for me. At sea you become a different person, you get away from the corrosive pressure to conform, from increasing bureaucracy. I've seen too many people eaten by the worms of discontent.

'As for family life, we get on well, but it won't be easy all the time. There may be threats of flying home to mother. Jugs have been thrown in my direction and I've survived only by being alert, cowering back. Wanting my own way, that's the trouble. Not being a milksop saying: "I'll just take the dog for a walk, dear." But Marie Christine and I have worked together for nearly thirty years. She is the sunlight in the whole thing. I believe we will have a tremendous time.'

Tennyson speaks for men like Ridgway: 'How dull it is to pause, to make an end, / To rust unburnished, not to shine in use'. Or, as Ridgway himself says: 'All you have is time. As long as head and body hold together, keep wriggling about, mate, keep wriggling about.'

WHEN THE BOAT CAME IN

EIGHTEEN MONTHS AGO JOHN RIDGWAY AND
HIS FAMILY SET OFF TO SAIL THE ATLANTIC AND
THE PACIFIC AND RETURN VIA ANTARCTICA.
TREVOR FISHLOCK JOINED THEM ON THE LAST LEG
AND SAW A HOMECOMING THAT REVEALED THE
IRON MAN'S SOFT CENTRE

'Breakfast, a hero's breakfast,' John Ridgway said. 'Black pudding and kidneys.' He braced at the wheel, steering the yacht down a whaleback wave. 'Bacon,' he added, 'and scrambled eggs.' Tiki from Tahiti, the ship's ginger cat, squeaked and skedaddled as a sea broke into the cockpit. 'Tomatoes and mushrooms,' Ridgway commanded.

A faraway look lay in his blue eyes. His gaze monitored the grumbling ocean, the rainy sky and the sails as full as aldermen's waistcoats; but his imagination projected him 1,000 miles to the north, to a croft by the loch and a kitchen table set with a white cloth. 'Lots of sausages,' he insisted. The sound I heard was the smack of his lips, or the crack of a sail.

The family Ridgway had been wandering the oceans for a year and a half when I joined them for the final 1,500-mile leg from the Azores to their home at Ardmore in Scotland. I found all four in a fever's grip. Channel fever, the old-time sailors called it: the ache for home after months at sea.

Ridgway had fantasised about his end-of-voyage breakfast since he set course for home from Antarctica after long journeys in the Pacific and South America. His wife, Marie Christine, yearned for a kitchen that stayed still, a chance to wear her black velvet dress. His daughter Rebecca longed for reunion with her boyfriend and, like her sister Elizabeth, for her own bedroom.

Ridgway had hungered for this adventure. He needed to know danger again. He had rowed the Atlantic, sailed twice around the world, trekked the Amazon and had made his living from his belief that life is colourless without physical struggle: for twenty-five years his adventure school at Ardmore had provided the means for others to confront the elements.

In Marie Christine the iron man had met his steel magnolia. They celebrated their thirty-first wedding anniversary during their odyssey. Later, they went ashore in Chile to see the film *The Piano*. She loved the film, he loathed it. Rowing back to the yacht, they argued fiercely and she pushed him out of the dinghy. When he tried to scramble back, she whacked him on the head with a paddle. 'He was much better after that,' she said.

The trip had started badly. 'We were tired after the school season and soon sailed into storms,' Ridgway said. 'We felt rotten. Only two of us could steer: the rest were too seasick or inexperienced.' Marie Christine's bunk was swamped and she wrapped herself in dustbin liners to keep dry. Rebecca quarrelled furiously with her father. Gear was smashed by waves. Mutiny loomed. A queasy Ridgway, no great lover of the sea, had to remind himself how much he wanted an adventure that was proof of being alive.

Rebecca, twenty-seven, and her boyfriend, Will Burchnall, endured the frustration of conducting their romance in a confined and lurching space. 'Life on a yacht is public,' Marie Christine told me as she sat in her tiny cabin, stitching one of the tapestries that she and her daughters worked on through the journey.

'Before we set off I wondered whether we would fight all the time. John's a very strong character and sometimes I longed to leave the boat to get a breathing space. But, overall, we got on harmoniously. We have spent a lot of time in each other's company, have had time for each other, time in which to show compassion. It was a test for the relationship, but we have been united by the fun and the fights, the forced sharing of hardship. And you couldn't run away in mid-ocean.'

Ridgway admitted he had 'the glooms' in the Caribbean. 'All I saw was the conveyor-belt of tourism, jaded New Yorkers offloaded from cruise ships.' The others didn't share his grumpy view. They loved the islands.

Thereafter, though, Ridgway found the satisfaction he sought. For months the ketch sailed the Pacific and Polynesia. 'We were united and in great shape,' he said. 'Everything seemed worthwhile.' In Tahiti a stray cat joined the yacht and was soon devouring the flying fish that flipped into the scuppers.

The next stage formed one of the reasons for the whole trip. The Ridgways left the yacht in Chile and travelled for two months in the mountains of Peru. The aim was to show Elizabeth her roots. They trekked for three weeks to Elizabeth's native village and found her family, fulfilling her grandmother's wish to see her granddaughter before she died. Elizabeth's mother was astonished to meet her daughter, a healthy schoolgirl of fifteen. 'Marie Christine had feared that Elizabeth might want to stay in Peru,'

Ridgway said. 'But Elizabeth worked it out: she understood who she was and she wanted to be with us.'

Rebecca's boyfriend left to continue his farming studies in England, Rebecca reflecting that at sea they had seen each other in the worst circumstances – and the relationship had survived.

'There were still great mountains to climb,' Ridgway said. 'Patagonia lay ahead and fearsome Antarctica. If something goes wrong there, it goes badly wrong. You can't be happy without paradox and contrast – and that is what made this trip so fulfilling.'

From Cape Horn the yacht sailed south for 650 miles, through the icebergs. Ridgway revelled in the adventure and everyone was thrilled by the Antarctic spectacle. When it reached the British Antarctic station at Faraday, *English Rose* was the southernmost yacht in the world.

At last, the Ridgways turned north, sailing to South Georgia and on to Tristan da Cunha. From there they sailed three weeks to Brazil and then three more on to the Azores.

Ridgway met me at the airport. Everyone was in cheery humour. I shared the Ridgways' watches: 6 a.m.–8 a.m., noon–2 p.m., 6–8 p.m., midnight–2 a.m. Hungry for news, they devoured every word of the newspapers I had brought. Off watch, when it wasn't too rough, Ridgway pounded the deck doing circuit training, the iron man's anti-rust routine. At night, under the stars, with dolphins for escort, he summarised. 'We'll look back on all this and see a symmetry in it. It was our last chance for a voyage like this as a family. We have done it and we are stronger.'

Ten days from the Azores, the island of Barra loomed out of the mist. Gannets and fulmars circled in salute. We sailed around Skye, into Ardmore and moored below the croft, the home the Ridgways had endlessly discussed, down to the last beloved cracked tile. In the yacht's saloon one of the family pinned up the word 'HAPPY' cut from a happy birthday streamer. Ridgway, the granite rock himself, was moved: 'It says something when you've been with your family 554 days and they stick that up.'

Friends were there to greet them. Ridgway hugged Marie Christine. Rebecca reflected on the wonder of it all: 'Well, Dad was right. He's always right.' Tiki stayed aboard, to be collected by a quarantine official.

In the house the Ridgways took off their red ocean suits and sat down with a mingled sense of disbelief and triumph. Ridgway poured whisky and everyone toasted the ship and survival. 'We've had appalling times and wonderful times,' Marie Christine said. 'We've dealt with the monster.' She meant the ocean.

She went on to the mountainside and dug up the small brooch she had buried there in 1993. That evening, indefatigable, she cooked for fourteen friends and crew. Someone told Ridgway that the VAT inspectors were coming next week. 'Welcome to Britain,' he said with a wry smile. Towards the end of dinner, Rebecca's Will arrived and she looked radiant.

Ridgway surveyed the jolly table. He looked very happy to be home. But I wondered how long it would be before he would submit himself once again to pain and danger just to prove that he's alive.

Chapter 11
IN THE WAKE

SLOW DAYS, LONG NIGHTS ON THE CONGO

TO TRY TO RESTORE CONFIDENCE IN RIVER TRAVEL,
THE UN HAS TEN BARGES SHUTTLING ALONG THE
WATERWAY. **TIM BUTCHER** JOINED ONE OF THEM

My time on *Pusher Number Ten* [a boat attached to, and propelling, a barge] passed at its own strange pace. My diary tells me we sailed for seven days, but it felt as if I travelled years back in time. After leaving Kisangani, we did not stop at any other town until Mbandaka, 1,000 kilometres downstream, and in between I felt as though I saw an Africa unchanged from that which Stanley saw.

Without any major towns all I saw was the endless forest, an unbroken screen of green that was reeled slowly past me. It would grow fat when we neared the water's edge and thin when our course took us far into the mainstream, but for 1,000 kilometres it never quite broke. At first light the rising sun would colour in the forest with a rich spectrum of greens from emerald to lime, pea to peridot, before they steadily faded as the sun tracked upwards. By midday, the overhead sun would wash out all but the most vivid tints, before they were slowly restored as the sun dipped towards the western horizon.

And there was the river. Conrad's uncoiling serpent grew fatter and fatter each day that we descended. There are places where the river swells to a width exceeding five kilometres. We were constantly slaloming through eyots and islands, some of which were enormous, running to twenty kilometres or more in length. Every day we passed villages that had the same design Stanley had described. There would be a clutch of thatched huts built on raised stilts to avoid the seasonal high water and, through the smoke from cooking fires, I would see people moving around wearing rags, while down on the river's edge a clutch of pirogues hung in the current.

For the first few days our progress was slow and cautious, as the Congolese skipper sat up in the wheelhouse barking at the helmsman to cut the revs, nudging the boat forward, while one of his crew stood right at the bow of the barge, more than forty metres away from the skipper, using an old branch to probe for a safe course through the sand banks. There was no sonar or depth sounder, just a branch broken off a riverside tree to save us from being marooned. The bowman had no radio or intercom, so our progress depended on wild gesticulations and the occasional scream. And after some days, as the chocolate-coloured waters deepened and the safe channel widened, the engine settled into the high-end rattle of full power and the bowman put down his stick and sat on a home-made chair that hummed with the vibration coursing through the boat's superstructure.

I entered a zone of mental torpor. Normally I am the sort of person who needs to be doing something constantly. I am not a napper. But on that river passage there was nothing I could do to influence our progress. We would reach our destination when we reached our destination, and not a moment sooner, so I took off my wrist watch and let my days flow with the rhythm of the river.

At night the boat would stop. Night navigation was too dangerous, the navigable channel too tricky to follow in the dark. So just before sunset the skipper would look for a suitable section of river bank, steep enough to ensure we did not become beached. He would then gently kiss the bow of the barge up against it. By the time the bowman had jumped on to the bank and wrapped the large rustling anchor cable around a tree, the rest of the boat would have swung around in the current and now be hanging down-stream. When the first Belgian-era steamboats started regular journeys on the Congo River, they used to pull over on the river bank just like this. Woodcutters would then be sent off into the forest to cut fuel overnight for the following day's steaming, while the white crew would struggle for sleep in the still heat under bombardment from mosquitoes.

It was exactly the same for me. When the boat tied up on the river bank each evening, the now motionless air would clot with heat and moisture. Insects would swarm to any flicker of torchlight, so I clung to darkness, teaching myself how to feel my way around the boat, to the stern-plate to have a pee, to the store of jerry-cans for a drink of clean water. Ali let me sleep on the carpeted floor of his cabin and I would huddle there in the dark, cocooned in my gossamer tent of mosquito netting, nervously fidgeting so that my skin never came into contact with its sides. Congo River mosquitoes are notorious. Conrad himself took six months to recover from the fever he caught during his single passage up and down the river, and I knew the little bleeders were more than capable of biting through netting if I was foolish enough to let it come into contact with bare skin.

Ali had been brought up in rural, tropical Malaysia and was clearly tougher than I was in dealing with disease-carrying insects. His passion for fishing meant he would slip out of the cabin at night wrapped in a hooded cagoule from which only his face protruded, and take up position on the side of the pusher, crouched over his fishing rod, constantly puffing on cigarettes to keep the insects from his face. In our time together he did not catch a single fish, but this did not deter him. Around midnight, as I thrashed in shallow sleep, he would tiptoe back into the room, shed his coat and, invariably, twang the web of strings I had set up to support my mosquito net.

Nights were grim and I would lie awake waiting for the first throaty cough of the diesel engines that marked dawn. The skipper liked to get away at first light, and by the time the eastern sky was beginning to lighten he would be back up in the wheelhouse ready for a day's passage. Once I had extricated myself from my straitjacket of sweat-sodden bedclothes and netting, the whole cabin would be vibrating as the engines powered the boat upstream to take the tension off the anchor line so that it could be retrieved by the bowman. Then the boat would pirouette and, once again, we would be reeling in kilometre after kilometre of the green scene.

This was one of my favourite times of day. I had brought plenty of clean water for the trip and I would spend the first few hours up on the top deck drinking mug after mug of black tea, enjoying the sensation of motion and the muggy waft of air moving across my face. My normal mindset would have found our progress infuriatingly slow. The boat rarely reached its top speed and even then it only managed 18kph. But I had entered a Zen state and every metre we moved was a metre closer to the end of my ordeal.

I loved watching our wake. The mocha whirls of white water whipped up by the propeller would rush out from under the stern-plate, dancing and churning before growing steadily calmer and calmer. Slowly the creamy lather would lose its fizz and darken, merging into just another featureless reach of flat, brown water. But the thing I loved most about the wake was that it meant we were moving. A wake meant slightly closer to our destination. I loved watching our wake.

Out of boredom I found another way to monitor our progress. Up in the wheelhouse the skipper had a solitary navigational aid, a thirty-year-old map book. Each page was mouldy to the touch after years of exposure to the humid river air and the edges were as tattered as week-old leaves in a rabbit hutch. Grubby pencil messages, written and over-written, had been scrawled on each page, as well as a dotted line that marked the navigable channel. I could see it had been rubbed out and redrawn numerous times. The entire route from Kisangani to Kinshasa, the descent of 1,734 kilometres, was covered by this old map book, so every time one of its sixty-four pages turned, I knew I was thirty kilometres or so nearer my destination.

By ten o'clock the morning heat was too much for me to stay out on deck. After crossing the equator a short distance upstream from Kisangani, the Congo River prescribes a slow but momentous westward arc, eventually dipping back across the equator for a second time at Mbandaka before its final run to Kinshasa, and thence the coast. The climate gets crueller and crueller with the descent. As altitude is lost, with it goes any hope of a cooling breeze. I found by late morning, even on a hazy day, the steel panels on the decks would be throbbing with heat. They were studded with rice-grain-sized bulges for grip, and through the soles of my sandals I could feel each one radiating warmth.

I would surrender to the heat by late morning, seeking shelter in the darkness of Ali's blacked-out cabin. Tired from the uncomfortable night's sleep, I would nap in between attempts to read some of the trashy novels Ali kept.

I entered the same odd mental zone that I reach on overnight flights, the state of consciousness when I am awake enough to watch a film, but not awake enough to actually take anything in. Plane movies have a special quality. Within a few hours of watching them I never seem capable of remembering the smallest detail about the film – the name, the plotline, the actors. I felt exactly the same during my boat journey on the Congo. I would turn the pages of the book and my eyes would work through the paragraphs, but to this day I have no recall of what I read.

To pass the time I would drag out my daily ablutions, taking perverse pleasure in the slow process of boiling water for a meticulous, slow shave, before taking one of the world's most dangerous showers. The water for the shower came straight from the river. Against the creamy ceramic of an old shower cubicle, it ran brown like tea. It reminded me of Scottish hill water tainted with peat, only it was much warmer and the chemicals that leached brown into the Congo River were more terrifying than those found in Highland soil. Somewhere to our north ran the Ebola, a tributary of a tributary of the Congo River, but a name that is associated with a horrific medical condition. It was near this river that a virus was first discovered that caused its victims to die in a spectacularly horrible way, bleeding to death from every orifice. Several of the world's other spectacularly horrible haemorrhagic fevers were first discovered in the Congo. I kept my mouth tight shut whenever I showered.

Ali was a gracious host. He had kitted himself out with a Congo survival kit from the duty-free shop at Dubai airport while flying from Malaysia to Africa. He had bought himself a microwave, a kettle and a rice boiler. The diesel generators on the *Nganing* offered ample power, so he would provide me with meals of noodles and litres of water, boiled clean.

By late afternoon, when the temperature had begun to dip, I would venture outside once more. Most days I would go all the way to the bow of the barge, picking my way over the straining hawsers and cables that connected the barge with the pusher, to join the Congolese bowman. His name was Pascal Manday Mbueta and he was entered on the crew list with the lowest possible grade of deckhand. Pascal lived inside the barge. He had no cabin and there was no furniture. He simply slept on the rusting metal, squashed up against a bulkhead. I peered through the hatch and down a ladder into his living space one day and winced at the smell. With the motion of the boat I could see a broken beer bottle floating down there in a malodorous swill of bilge water and God knows what else.

Pascal had the rheumy eyes of a confirmed drunk. He had brought a large stash of Primus beer from Kisangani but, if I got to him when he was sober, he was good company. Mostly we would sit in silence, listening to the hiss of the water working its way down the side of the barge. Occasionally he would blurt out something about how the river used to be.

'See there,' he would say, pointing at the river bank. 'There used to be a marker showing the safe channel. The authorities kept the channel clear and kept the markers in the right place, but all of that has gone. Now, you have to work by memory alone – 1,734 kilometres from memory alone. It's crazy.'

Our constant companion out on the river was water hyacinth. For each of the thousand kilometres of my river descent, floating alongside me in clumps that could be as small as a single tendril or as large as a tennis court-sized raft, I was accompanied by the plant.

The story of the water hyacinth in the Congo is a wonderful allegory for the white man in this country. The plant's intended role was innocent enough. It was brought here as a garden ornament decades ago. According to one story, a Belgian colonialist who had seen it in its native South American environment imported the first seedlings to prettify a waterway near his remote colonial outpost. Another account blames an American Baptist missionary who was attracted by its delicate pastel flowers.

There was nothing innocent about the alien's behaviour once it took root in the Congo. It grew and grew and grew, spreading a deadly mat across much of the Congo River basin, suffocating the life out of ponds, lakes and slow-moving rivers and upsetting entire eco-systems. It is now categorised as a dangerous weed that should be eradicated before it clots even the main arteries of the river system. And I saw with my own eyes the extent of its grip on the Congo River. Downstream from Kisangani I saw barely a single stretch of river free from floating knots of water hyacinth.

As the sun neared the horizon, picking out the lilac blooms of the water hyacinth on their mattresses of matted tuber and leaf, the day's cycle would repeat itself. The skipper would look for a suitably steep river bank, Pascal would grab hold of the anchor line and I would return to the cabin and brace myself for another night of battle with mosquitoes.

Extracted from *Blood River: A Journey to Africa's Broken Heart* by Tim Butcher (Vintage).

BEATING THE BOUNDS OF BLIGHTY

PYTHEAS THE GREEK WENT ROUND BRITAIN BY
BOAT 2,300 YEARS AGO. **NICHOLAS CRANE** FOLLOWS
HIS EXAMPLE – ON A SHIP WITH SAUNAS AND FIVE BARS

Three hundred years before Caesar landed in Kent, an audacious mariner from the Greek colony of Marseilles left the balmy, civilised Mediterranean on a mission to explore the freezing, barbarian north. Pytheas 'the Greek' returned home having completed the first recorded circumnavigation of Britain. In his book, *On the Ocean*, he noted that the British lived modestly and peacefully without 'shrewdness or vice' on an 'extremely cold' but 'thickly populated' island.

Some 2,300 years after Pytheas challenged the North Atlantic in a timber sailing-boat, travellers can follow much of his course aboard MV *Discovery*, a 20,000-ton cruise ship equipped with saunas, an internet centre, two restaurants and five bars. Twice each year, *Discovery* departs from Harwich, Essex, and loops around Britain in an eight-day, anti-clockwise circumnavigation. It is one of the world's great, unpredictable voyages, and for Britons it offers the chance to gaze upon the homeland from afar, with foreign, Pythean eyes.

Sea-voyages began with 'coasting', and I was as curious as the other 500 passengers to orbit Blighty. This would also be *Discovery*'s maiden voyage following a multi-million-pound refit and a change of name; at a quayside ceremony the day before we sailed, bagpipes had skirled, a prayer by Sir Francis Drake had been intoned, and a bottle of Champagne had been sacrificed against the freshly-painted hull. New to cruise ships and their mysterious rituals, I was quickly adopted by a passenger who had stepped straight from the pages of Mark Twain's burlesque cruise classic, *The Innocents Abroad*. After a muddle over my dinner table on the first night, it was 'The Oracle' who informed me that I had failed to queue for a numbered table ticket. 'If you see a queue,' he advised, 'join it. It might be a line for the lifeboats.'

I spent much of that first evening lingering at the rail as we cruised the low coasts of Suffolk and Norfolk. Through binoculars I searched in vain for places that had been absorbed into the unsteady pencil line that divided the grey tones of sea and sky. Where were the mouths of the Deben and the Alde? And residual Dunwich, the town that fell into the waves? To the writer W.G. Sebald, the east was the coast of lost causes and of encroaching tides; the point of departure for westward migrations. It is where I grew up and, as the light failed, I stared harder at the long string of embers that had flickered into lifelike camp-fires in the black veldt of the night. Each glowing coal was a place I knew as a child, each name (Caister, Scratby, Waxham) recalling Romans, Scandinavians and Saxons who had prised wealth from these shores.

When I woke next morning, we were off the edge of the Dogger Bank. For part of the night, *Discovery* had been threading her way through the rigs of the Leman and Indefatigable gas fields. The Oracle, who had managed to stay awake until the early hours, reported over breakfast that the rigs had seemed almost incandescent with electric light and bursts of flame. The Captain, Erik Bjurstedt, likened the experience to 'driving through a forest'.

At noon on our first full day at sea, Captain Erik announced on the Tannoy that we were 12 nautical miles from Northumberland. Off the port bow was a long blue ripple of land, which soon became an intricate pattern of islets, cliffs and silver strands backed by billowing fields, woods and distant mountains. A fishing boat bucked through the swell towards Alnmouth and we passed so close to the Farne Islands that the guano-streaked rocks appeared to be a short swim from the ship's crowded rails. From the seaward side, St Cuthbert's chapel looked as if it could be snatched by a passing wave.

Behind the islands, Bamburgh Castle resembled one of Rommel's concrete blockhouses on the Atlantic Wall, while its near neighbour, Holy Island, rose from the sands like a chiselled volcano. Twenty miles behind Holy Island, the grey, elephantine shoulders of the Cheviot Hills domi-nated the entire horizon. Compared with the barely discernible coastal topography of East Anglia, this was the most emphatic of shores; a land-sea frontier characterised by big geology and man-made bastions.

Shortly after we passed Holy Island, the massive Elizabethan ramparts of Berwick-upon-Tweed crept into view. A few years earlier I had spent a week in Berwick at the start of my own Pythean journey, a walk from one end of England to the other along the line of longitude marked on maps as two degrees west. For most of those miles on foot, I was as far from the coast as it is possible to be, and the England I found often felt vast, landlocked and introspective. Viewed from a hardwood deck moving at 13 knots, England had become small and coy. And the next three days increased the gap in comprehension.

The Scotland I had holidayed in since teenage years revealed itself as wildly unapproachable, the soft hills of the Lammermuirs appearing as oppressive black cliffs, while St Abb's – which I had always known as a grassy viewpoint – came across as a violent cape thrashed by breakers. But it was the northern scatterings of Orkney and Shetland that provided the most startling cruising, and two of the most remarkable archaeological relics I have seen anywhere in the world.

On Orkney, I joined a coach tour to Skara Brae, where the walls and stone furniture of a Neolithic village cling to the lip of a low cliff. Stonehenge and the pyramids of Egypt didn't exist when the village was engulfed intact by drifting sand at least 2,000 years before Pytheas threaded the Pentland Firth. Now the houses have reappeared, with their box beds, hearths and stone dressers, which would have displayed family treasures: bone necklaces, pendants and armlets. Running beneath the settlement is a drainage system. It is impossible not to succumb to a profound awe at the ordered life of Britain's first settlers. Along the road is the Ring of Brodgar, the largest stone circle in Scotland. Twenty-seven of the original sixty stones remain, encircled by a rock-cut ditch that took 10,000 man-days to excavate.

The other revelatory site was on the little island of Mousa near the southern tip of Shetland. Rising from the greensward above the shore was a tall stone tower, like a windmill shorn of its sails. But this tower – or 'broch' – was at least a couple of thousand years old and would have been clearly visible to Pytheas had he sailed along this shore. Most of Scotland's brochs have been dismantled for building stone, and Mousa's is the best preserved. There are no windows, but a tiny ground-level door leads into a central chamber from which a spiral staircase curls up between the tower's double-skinned walls. The exact purpose of a broch is still not known, but to the Orcadian writer George Mackay Brown the spiral-staired tower was 'the guardian of the tribe', a sanctuary into which a community could withdraw in times of threat, re-emerging to resume the 'wide fecund circle of their existence'.

Back on *Discovery*, the cruise was about to take a series of unexpected turns. From Shetland we were due to land at St Kilda, Oban, Holyhead and Milford Haven. But wind and tide forced the abandonment of a landing at St Kilda, and the following morning we woke in Dublin instead of Oban, the swell again to blame. There are worse places to be blown ashore, and I ran out of time before getting further than the Book of Kells, the National Gallery and a musically intoxicating pub by the Liffey. After crossing the Irish Sea by night, we cruised the precipitous flanks of Snowdonia beneath a Mediterranean sun. Dolphins were spotted, and — emboldened by an on-board bird-watching lecture — I directed The Oracle's enormous binoculars towards a floating guillemot. 'Plastic carrier bag,' he corrected, 'Safeway.'

In an attempt to repair my ornithological credibility, I joined the bird-watchers' shore excursion to Skomer — a two-mile-long block of rock anchored off the end of Pembrokeshire. Our guide was Anna Sutcliffe, a marine biologist who had lived as a warden on the island for seven years.

On cliff paths, puffins pottered about our ankles, building nests and looking unamused by the tearing wind and rain. 'In good weather,' explained Anna, 'you won't see them. They'll all be off having a good time fishing.' At The Wick, a sea-sluiced chasm on the west coast, we watched thousands of sea birds adhering to the cliff, guillemots on a long luxury ledge at the bottom, kittiwakes clinging to toe-holds farther up, razorbills in cushioned nooks where the cliff angle relented, and at the top, fulmars gazing down imperiously from sheltered grassy belevederes. The evolved sense of order on Skomer's cliffs would not have surprised Pytheas, for it had been the orderly flights of migratory birds that had helped to guide him around the coast of Britain.

That night we turned Land's End, then looped past Guernsey and Sark for breakfast. By evening, *Discovery* was humming along the English Channel's contra-flow shipping lane towards Harwich and home. Across the moonlit sea, the lights of Hythe, Folkestone and Dover blazed like grass fires along the rim of an unseen hinterland. Behind that glowing shore were darkened paths to be trodden anew.

Looking at Britain from the outside had turned a place I had known and tramped since childhood into somewhere fresh and unexplored. A circumnavigation is a wilful act of separation, a breaking of bonds as much as a beating of bounds. The places that most surprised me had been the islands: the ornithological Farnes, Neolithic Orkney and treeless Shetland, lonely Rona. spiky, seagirt St Kilda, the Hebridean arc, black-cliffed Anglesey and rowdy Skomer. The Britain I knew as an island had become an archipelago.

A CELTIC KON-TIKI

DAVID HOLLOWAY REVIEWS
THE BRENDAN VOYAGE BY TIM SEVERIN

It does not matter tuppence whether St Brendan did in fact sail in a leather boat from Ireland to America in the sixth century AD with a crew of fellow monks. What does matter is that Tim Severin, with three, sometimes four, companions, did just this in 1976 and 1977.

Mr Severin's description of his journey is the most exciting sea story that I have read for a long time. He is first and foremost a writer and so what one is given in *The Brendan Voyage* is not just a bald or, still worse, an overwritten account but the reactions of a sensitive man with a feeling for words to the sort of adventure that is beyond most people's wildest dreams.

To travel with him through the tide race in the Faroe Islands where his tiny craft survived when it should by rights have been dashed to pieces, or to battle with the giant waves and the ice floes between Labrador and Newfoundland is to share in adventure of the highest kind because Mr Severin knows exactly how to put action into words.

Indeed the astonishing thing about his account is that the preparations for the voyage become in his narrative quite as thrilling as the actual journey.

In brief, Mr Severin set out to do a 'Kon Tiki' on behalf of St Brendan. Medieval accounts said that the Irish Saint had gone to the 'Promised Land'. An amount of circumstantial detail is supplied that could have been either the usual flummery of moral fables (dragons, giants and the like) or exact descriptions of natural phenomena observed while island-hopping across the North Atlantic. The giant smiths who threw hot rocks at Brendan, for instance, might have been an Icelandic volcano in eruption.

The only way to test the 'Navigatio', the narrative of Brendan's voyage, was to put to sea in the sort of leather boat the Saint might have used. So financed by a couple of publishers, Mr Severin set to work. The right leather came from a tanner in Cornwall who still used the oak-bark method; the wood for the shell came from, indeed was donated by, the one timber firm that still processed ash.

An Irish boatyard built the wooden structure and then Mr Severin picked out all the nails and substituted the leather thongs that Brendan would have used. A retired saddler led the team that stitched the leather, sometimes a quarter of an inch thick. The trick was to push through an awl to make a hole for the needle and then move the needle through before the hole closed.

The boat set sail with a crew of five. Two, for different reasons, soon dropped out and, on the way to Iceland where the first year's travel ended, were replaced by a jokey old Etonian from the Hebrides and an artist picked up in the Faroe Islands. The second of these, who returned to complete the journey, became, certainly in Mr Severin's account, the most striking personality of the expedition.

This is perhaps unfair, for George, the ex-Army officer sailing master, and Arthur, the Irish fisherman, were less spectacular in their contribution than Trondur, the giant Faroese, who kept them alive by fishing for cod with long line and 5lb weight that only a giant could handle and by snaring sea birds. In addition Trondur Patursson has left his mark on the book with a selection of delightful, wholly individual, drawings, which supplement the good but more conventional photographs.

This is a very 'British' book with a lot left unsaid, but a sensitive reader can glean a great deal from between some of the lines. It was for much of the time a hell of a journey, but one which seemed to bring out the best in almost everyone involved – from the radio operators at many shore stations to the Icelandic coastguard, even to the puzzled trawler skippers who spotted the leather anachronism tossing in the North Atlantic swell.

In the way that only really modest accounts of deeds of great daring can be, this one is deeply moving. The descriptions of the night the big waves crashed in and the later day when an ice floe finally succeeded in doing what so many others had threatened to do and pierced the hide hull should rank with the best prose produced by the sea.

SIR RANULPH, WE PRESUME

WHO BETTER TO REPLICATE LIVINGSTONE'S DISCOVERY OF VICTORIA FALLS, 150 YEARS ON, THAN OUR GREATEST LIVING EXPLORER? **RICHARD GRANT** REPORTS ON AN EXERCISE IN RIGOROUS AUTHENTICITY – UP TO A POINT

The Livingstone commemorative expedition spent its first evening in a campground bathroom facility on the banks of the Zambezi, taking shelter from a thunderstorm. Here we were at last, after nearly two years of planning and preparation, with our dug-out canoes tethered in the water, 120 miles of river ahead of us, drinking beer in an African toilet.

Our guest of honour and expedition figurehead, Sir Ranulph Twisleton-Wykeham-Fiennes, 3rd Baronet, OBE, the world's greatest living explorer according to *The Guinness Book of Records* and the nearest modern equivalent we could find to David Livingstone, looked tense and ill at ease. His leg twitched restlessly. He slapped viciously at a mosquito alighting on his cheek and swung his stump-fingered left hand at a larger, leggier insect flying towards his ear.

The ex-SAS man and veteran polar adventurer, who got those fingers frostbitten at the North Pole and sawed off the dead fingertips when he got back to his garden shed in Exmoor (going down to the village midway through the process for a fretsaw blade that snagged less on the bone), confessed that 'creepy-crawlies' unnerved him and he disliked them intensely.

His wife, Louise, patted him reassuringly on the leg. 'I'm the absolute opposite,' she said. 'Snakes, spiders, I love them all. I want to pick them up and get a good look at them.' Louise was the only woman in our party, which didn't seem to bother her in the least. A tough, capable, no-nonsense Cheshire countrywoman, devoted to Range Rovers and rescuing stray animals, she trained horses for a living and her hobby was endurance horse-racing – 100 miles a day if the horse was up to it.

She married Ran in the spring of 2005. She was thirty-eight, divorced with a ten-year-old son. He was sixty-one and recently widowed. She couldn't believe how cutting and cruel the British press were about their marriage and Ran's achievements in general. 'Female journalists in particular,' she was sorry to say. 'Quite frankly, I think a lot of them have gone off their trolley.'

She spent her honeymoon at base camp on Everest − 'a nasty, filthy, spooky place' − and returned to England while Ran tried and failed to reach the summit. Then they went climbing in the Alps and to a film festival in the frozen Canadian Rockies. 'This is the first hot place I've got him to take me since we got married, and it's raining like bloody Exmoor,' she said.

'We met in the Garden of Eden,' said Ran in his precisely enunciated Old Etonian English, 'which is Louise's terminology for Cheshire.' 'It is paradise compared to Exmoor,' she retorted. Ran smiled. Their hands entwined. Rain dripped through the grass-thatched roof.

Simon Wilde, our chief organiser, a white African who owns a luxury guest lodge further down the Zambezi, apologised for the weather. We were here to replicate Livingstone's historic 1855 journey down the river and celebrate the 150th anniversary of his 'discovery' of Victoria Falls − or Mosi-oa-Tunya, Smoke that Thunders, as the locals had always called it. It was perhaps unfortunate, offered Simon, that Livingstone had been here in mid-November, when the hot dry season reaches its scorching crescendo and the first big storms of the rainy season arrive.

He called on Russell Gammon, a burly, red-bearded Zimbabwean safari guide and African history expert, to give us a safety briefing. 'Do you all know what a Jeep Cherokee looks like?' said Russell. 'A hippo is longer, taller and weighs twice as much. They might look cute or even comical but, as most of you probably know, hippos kill more people than any other animal in Africa. We will be keeping our eyes peeled and giving them a wide berth because a hippo could easily bite one of these canoes in half. In fact, a hippo can bite a one-ton crocodile in half, which brings us to our other major danger. You do not want to be in the water. Do not trail any limbs in the water. Approach the water after dark with great caution. Crocs are nocturnal predators that hunt from an ambush at the water's edge.'

What should we do, I asked, if a hippo upended our canoe or bit it in half and put us in the water? We would be croc bait. 'You worry about the hippo,' said Russell. 'You want to drift away or swim away with as little commotion as possible. If a croc comes for you, which is unlikely, you'll hear stories about jamming an arm down its throat to make it let go, but if it's a big croc in deep water, you're basically buggered.'

Down by the river, waiting out the storm in a tent, talking softly in the Lozi tongue, were the three men most responsible for our safety and our basic locomotion on the river. The African dugout canoe, or *mokoro*, is not a very stable craft and, like Livingstone, we would be travelling with experts who had been paddling these hollowed-out logs up and down the Zambezi since boyhood. It seemed odd to me that Lemmy Nyambe, Saad Mweemba and Victor Sikushaba ate their dinner separately from the rest of us and called us boss and bwana. But it was my first time in Africa.

We slept in puddled tents and crawled out of them at 5 a.m. The rain had stopped and our mighty expedition kettle was on the fire for tea and coffee. The first grey light revealed a huge sky filled with high storm clouds, and shortly afterwards our small flotilla cast out into the wide Zambezi.

Replicating a historic journey is always a tricky business. You want to be authentic but you don't want an 1855 medicine kit or weevils in your porridge; and would it really spoil the experience to bring along some folding camp chairs? Our canoes were rigorously authentic. We would be trying to camp in the same places on the same days of the year as Livingstone, and if all went to plan, we would arrive at Victoria Falls for the 150th anniversary of Livingstone discovering them. On the other hand, we had mobile telephones, GPS navigating systems, coolers full of ice, beer and Cokes, and a support motorboat carrying our food and camping supplies.

The boatmen stood on the back of the *mokoros* with long wooden paddles that doubled as punt-poles. We sat on low chairs – one at the front, one in the middle – and used short modern paddles. I was in the narrowest, wobbliest *mokoro* with Guy Hammond, the expedition artist, and Saad paddling silently at the back. It was alarmingly easy to lose your balance in those chairs. The *mokoro* was always tipping one way or the other, often in quick succession, and if you failed to counterbalance it, you would start to topple over. Soon after we started I had one horrible, heart-pounding lurch to the right which nearly put all three of us in the river. An hour later, despite vigilant concentration, it happened again. 'Third time lucky, eh, sport?' said Guy with his usual blunt sarcasm.

When I first heard there was an artist coming along, I envisaged a sensitive, refined type, but Guy was an ex-army Zimbabwean tobacco farmer with a hyena grin and a way of calling a spade a shovel. He was fiercely right-wing, bitterly funny about losing his farm to Mugabe's comrades and glad that it had turned him into a professional painter. He specialised in African wildlife scenes and was planning to make a series of paintings from our trip. 'To commemorate the commemoration?' I asked. 'To make some f***ing money,' he replied.

The river was entering a flat treeless floodplain now, and the sky grew even bigger and more epic with shafts of light piercing the storm clouds. Silhouetted against the sky on the riverbank, two oxen pulled a cart made from the back end of an old Datsun pick-up truck. We passed fishermen in *mokoros* and cattle-herders on the banks who called out, 'Hello, how are you?' and then, 'How is your family?' The river was low after a long drought, and on the exposed islands and sandbanks there was a dizzying multitude of birds – skimmers, waders, herons, storks, kingfishers, cormorants, ibis, fish eagles soaring overhead and gyres of vultures wheeling over the plains.

Ran Fiennes seemed largely oblivious to his surroundings. Head down, a look of determination on his face, he paddled away like a machine all day. Louise sat behind him and did no paddling. She leant back in her chair, smiling and relaxed, pointing at birds and waterlilies and saying things like, 'Ooh, look at that lilac one. Isn't that lovely?'

Late in the morning Saad uttered his first word from the back of our *mokoro*. The word was 'hippo', pronounced with a silent 'h'. Two dark heads were visible a hundred yards downriver. Then two more heads surfaced and swivelled their little round ears to get the water out. They looked at us suspiciously and then submerged. We hugged the bank, paddling fast and smooth, wondering where they would surface and hoping it wouldn't be under our *mokoro*, but we never saw them again.

We pulled up on a sandbar and ate sandwiches made of some dubious Zambian pressed-meat product. Simon called out to one of the paddlers: 'Hey, Victor, is it going to rain?' 'Ah, no boss. No rain today.' Ninety seconds later the heavens opened and Ran coined the nickname Victor Fish – a reference to Michael Fish, the BBC weatherman, that took some explaining to the paddlers. For the rest of the trip, Victor's weather forecasting was absolutely dependable. If he predicted rain, it would stay dry. If he suggested more wind, it would calm.

We paddled 28 miles that first day and most of it into a headwind. When finally we found a sandbar to camp on we were tired and hungry, and Victor said his arms were ready to fall off. We put up the tents in a whipping wind by tying Coke bottles to the guy ropes and burying them in the sand as anchors. Then the wind died away suddenly, the storm clouds lifted slightly on the western horizon and a narrow strip of purple sunset appeared. A hippo rose and grunted, and Russell handed me his binoculars. 'The biggest mistake people make on safari is to buy a brand-new expensive camera,' he said. The hippo opened his enormous jaws in a territorial display, then sank down backwards into the purple river. 'They get so focused on trying to get that photograph that they miss half of what's going on. I always tell people to buy expensive binoculars instead.'

We ate pre-cooked curry and rice around the campfire and then the talk turned to Livingstone. What drove this pious Scot to spend his life tramping around Africa? He called himself a missionary and yet in thirty years of trying he converted only one African to Christianity, and the convert later backslid. 'Livingstone never grew disheartened by this because he loved being in Africa and the company of Africans, especially when it involved a long, arduous journey to some remote place where no white man had been before,' said Russell. 'More than anything I think he liked the sheer animal pleasure of moving through wild, unexplored country.'

It was a short step to questioning Ran Fiennes about his motivations. What compelled him to drag a 485lb sled across 1,350 miles of Antarctica, for example? He gave his usual answer: 'It's my job. I was thrown out of the SAS for trying to blow up the film set for *Doctor Dolittle*, which was an environmental eyesore, and I started doing expeditions because I could get paid to do them and it was the only sort of thing I was trained to do. I enjoyed solving the problems, I suppose, and beating the competition, which was usually the Norwegians.'

Was it true that the Norwegians spread a rumour that he and Charlie Burton had hauled prostitutes on their sleds to the North Pole in 1979? 'Absolutely true and absolutely ridiculous,' Ran replied crisply. 'At 48 below zero what possible use could you have for a prostitute and why on earth would you want to pull the extra weight? We didn't give them a hard time about it because one of the Norwegians had to have his foot amputated that year.'

The next day trees started to appear on the riverbank, isolated acacias and fat-trunked baobabs at first, and then a lush green forest studded with palms. The sun came out for the first time and tried to sear holes in my skin. I've spent most of my life in hot places but nowhere had my white skin ever felt so worthless, so fundamentally impractical, as under that African sun.

We turned up a side channel lined with papyrus reeds, and a man poled his *mokoro* towards us, wearing a shirt with David Beckham's face badly reproduced on the front. The temperature was now 40C, yet like so many African men along the river he was wearing a thick woollen ski cap. 'It is the fashion,' explained Saad.

We heard rapids ahead and then saw the white water rushing and tumbling through a maze of jagged black rocks. The boatmen told us to put away our paddles; they could steer more accurately by themselves. We gripped the sides with white knuckles, got splashed and jolted and thrilled, and all made it through safely. Villagers cheered from the riverbank. A topless woman washed a blue plastic chair. Soon afterwards we pulled into shore, put up our tents at the Mambova Safari Camp and spent the rest of the day compromising our authenticity.

There was an outhouse with showers, an open-walled thatched bar and a small round shaded swimming-pool well populated with biting water beetles. Ran and Louise waged a campaign against them – she pointed, he squashed and scooped – and then stayed in there for much of the afternoon. Ran in his swimming-trunks was taut and lean with well-defined stomach muscles, in superb shape for a man of sixty-two. He runs for two-and-a-half hours every other day and lifts weights on his off-days. He has trained like this all his life ('not much choice in my profession') and even more rigorously when preparing for expeditions.

The puzzling thing is the long white vertical scar down his chest. In June 2003, at the age of fifty-nine, he suffered a major heart attack while boarding a plane, lost consciousness for three days and had double-bypass surgery. He has often been described as the fittest man on the planet, so how was it possible for him to have heart disease?

'Chocolate,' answered Louise bluntly. 'Ran used to eat a family-size bar of Cadbury's Whole Nut every day and sometimes more than one.'

'I had 2,600 of them left over from an expedition and I do have a terrible sweet tooth,' said Ran. 'I used to smoke a pipe and roll-up cigarettes, too, and I don't suppose that helped.'

At the time of his heart attack, Ran and Mike Stroud, his partner from the 1993 crossing of Antarctica, were getting ready to run seven marathons in seven consecutive days on seven different continents. Ran wasn't the sort of chap to let a double-bypass disrupt their plans. Five months after his surgery, he completed the seven marathons with Stroud running alongside him with a defibrillator. A year later he finished second in the North Pole marathon, running in snowshoes at -25C, and decided he had finally had enough of the poles. What next?

He had always been afraid of heights, so he decided to climb Everest. Training on Kilimanjaro, he felt a worrisome tightening in his chest and turned back down. He had bad luck with weather on Everest but he was also concerned about the way his heart felt high on the mountain. I wondered if he was planning to scale back his exertions now and take more pleasure trips like this one. 'That's certainly the right term for it,' he said. 'I don't know if this qualifies as an expedition. It's far too pleasant and relaxing.'

Louise later explained this remark: 'Ran's never done anything like this before. He's either doing an endurance event or an expedition in some godforsaken frozen wasteland or he's on the lecture circuit getting inter-viewed left and right. This is not easy for him. He finds it very hard to relax.'

Like Livingstone we left our dug-outs at the beginning of the Katambora rapids and went on a two-day walk around them. Unlike Livingstone we had a support truck which carried our supplies and many plastic bottles of water. The truck drove ahead and stopped every few kilometres. We would lean against it, guzzling water and Coke, panting, sweating and pink-faced. The heat was now up to 42C. Then the truck would drive off and we would start walking again. To the villagers watching this, it must have been puzzling, to say the least. Why would people walk through the hottest part of the afternoon when they had a perfectly good truck?

At first glance – conical thatched huts, bare packed reddish earth, chick-ens and goats, no electricity or running water, a man binding together a stone-age axe with a strip of rawhide – the riverbank villages looked much as Livingstone would have seen them. Then a man would ride past on a bicycle wearing a football shirt or you'd catch an earful of fuzzed-out African pop music coming from the blown speakers of a boombox. The villages were poor but people didn't look hungry, grim or troubled. They asked after the health of our families. They shook our hands and wished us a good journey. They invited us to sit down in the shade and talk, but for some mysterious reason we had to keep marching after our truck.

'The locals threw stones at us during the Reading canoe race,' said Ran. 'They've got better manners here, haven't they?' said Louise. The decline of morals, manners and character in modern Britain is a favourite topic for both of them, and Louise thinks the first step should be to bring back corpo-ral punishment in the schools. Ran is often called eccentric in the British media and this is partly because his belief system – patriotism, decency, self-reliance, pluck and perseverance, a stiff upper lip, disdain for the nanny state and pampering in general – has fallen by the wayside of modern British culture.

He wouldn't have been called eccentric in Victorian England. The Empire would have made good use of a man like Fiennes, plucked him from the regiment, dispatched him to its remotest frontiers and made a hero out of him at home. Livingstone was admired for his fortitude in sewing up his own wounds after being attacked by a lion. When Fiennes sawed off his frostbitten fingertips, modern Britain wondered what was wrong with him. Surely the man must be mad.

On the second day of our trek we left the roads and villages behind and struck out through the bush. We were joined by Isaac Sitali, one of Simon's employees, who used to be a poacher and knew the land and its wildlife very well. He took Ran, Louise, Guy and Ian (the expedition photographer) ahead. Simon, Russell and I were about fifteen minutes behind, following their tracks in the sandy ochre soil. It was the hottest day yet – 'hotter than a snake's arse in a wagon's rut,' in Russell's phrase. 'A merry heat doeth like a good medicine,' I said, quoting Livingstone. Maybe it was all the steak I had eaten the night before, but I was coursing with energy, senses peeled and alert, feeling chock-full of life.

We lost their tracks, fanned out looking for them and found them overlaid on big round footprints the size of dustbin lids. They were tracking elephants, and both sets of tracks looked very fresh. When we caught up with them they were gawping at an enormous bull elephant tearing branches off a tree and stuffing them into his mouth. He was looking right back at us, about 50 yards away, and we could hear what sounded like many more elephants behind him.

It turned out to be two herds of about fifty, moving parallel to each other so the males wouldn't have a confrontation. They seemed to walk in slow motion, with each raised foot taking a long time to descend, although the babies sometimes had to hurry. Then the sound of an engine on a nearby road set off an alarm of trumpeting and both herds thundered off at speed.

The elephants were here because this was the last piece of untouched, unpoached forest on this stretch of the river. Part of it was owned, unfenced, by a burly white Zimbabwean former park ranger called Doug Evans. He showed us to some tents by the river and told us to be extremely careful. Not only were there 'ellies' around but hippos came up here to graze and there were a lot of big crocodiles, plus the usual array of venomous snakes and scorpions.

I found it hard to sleep that night, not because I was nervous. I felt too excited and exhilarated. I went down to the river in the moonlight, treading very slowly and carefully, stopping short of the water because of crocodiles, and listened to the hippos grunt and the distant whooping of a hyena. Coming back to camp I stopped in my tracks. There was a large animal of some kind making a long, drawn-out grunting noise. Was it a hippo? An elephant? A warthog? No, it was Russell snoring.

For the rest of the trip we were back in the *mokoros*, paddling and camping in protected National Park land with a super-abundance of wildlife – hippos and crocs by the dozen, elephant herds on the banks, warthogs, kudus, waterbucks. We were treated to one particularly rare sighting: Sir Ranulph Fiennes in the act of relaxation and enjoyment, sitting back with his paddle across his knees and a smile on his face, pointing at elephants and saying how marvellous it all was. 'Nearly all my travels have been in places with no living things except polar bears that wanted to eat you,' he said later, pouring himself a rum and Coke at our last campsite on Kilai Island.

Huck Finn was right. There's something mighty free and easy about floating down a river, even if the river is full of hippos and crocodiles. We had one tense moment with a lone male hippo when we encountered him in a narrow channel, but otherwise it was straightforward to paddle around them. A closer call, perhaps, was the hippo that waddled through our last camp while we slept, well sedated by rum and beer, and revealed itself by its footprints in the morning.

The annoying whine of a sightseeing plane flying upriver from Victoria Falls reminded us of our upcoming appointment with civilisation. We wanted to see the falls but none of us wanted the trip to end, except maybe to get out of the heat. It was 48C, or 119F, when we paddled through the last rapids and around the last hippos and came into view of Livingstone Island with the smoky spray of the falls behind.

We had been sleeping in tents for six nights. We were grubby and greasy, dizzy from the heat, and we smelt of sweat, wood smoke and mosquito repellent. Waiting for us on the shore were guitarists and crooners in traditional African costumes, a man holding a silver salver with glasses of fruit punch, journalists, photographers, dignitaries and the British High Commissioner, Alistair Harrison, standing under a golf umbrella and wearing a suit, tie and panama hat.

We shook a lot of hands and were led up a trail to a furnace-like marquee laid out with white tablecloths, silverware and finger foods. We could hear the falls but we weren't allowed to see them yet. There were pleasantries to be exchanged, photographs, introductions, interviews and costume changes. The British High Commissioner changed into red swimming-trunks but kept on his white shirt and hat because of the sun. Then swimming guides and native towel-bearers appeared and led us over the rocks towards the Smoke that Thunders, 'the most wonderful sight' Livingstone ever saw in Africa. 'Very impressive,' said Ran. 'That's a lovely rainbow in the spray,' said Louise.

The falls were astounding, but in my heat-dizzied state I kept getting distracted by photographers and the surreal formality that surrounded us. Our towel-bearers waited patiently on the banks while the swimming guides took our hands and led us into the river and through some rocks to Devil's Pool, a deep roiling pocket of water on the very lip of the falls that filled Ran with boyish delight. 'This is absolutely brilliant,' he shouted over the roar of the water. 'I can't imagine a better place in the world to go swimming. Louise, over here!'

Then there were speeches, and a plaque of Livingstone to unveil. Ran said how proud we were to commemorate such a great explorer. Russell pointed out the sad irony that Livingstone, who devoted so much of his career to trying to end slavery, died of dysentery in a remote African village, eighteen years after seeing and naming Victoria Falls, and never learnt that the slave markets had been closed down.

We all stood there dutifully in the scalding, blinding sun. The British High Commissioner had put on a tie, black socks and lace-up shoes but was still wearing his red swimming-trunks. Guy, whose ancestors came to Africa from Scotland, had donned a kilt and sporran. He played 'Amazing Grace' on the bagpipes, and then we all scurried off like stricken moles to find some shade.

Chapter 12
FIRSTS AND LASTS

---

23 JULY 1988

ALIVE ON THE OCEAN WAVES

HAMMOND INNES, BESTSELLING NOVELIST AND
COMPULSIVE SAILOR, REFLECTS ON HOW HE FELL
UNDER THE SPELL OF THE SEA

'There is nothing – absolutely nothing…' That was written when messing about in boats was a bucket-an'-spade occupation for adults at the seaside. A far cry from the trapeze artistry of high-speed dinghy racing or the flippety-gibbetry of windsurfers finding air as they flip their boards through the overfalls of a tidal race; even further still from the America's Cup, or maxi-driving round the world, or doubling the Horn single-handed under sail.

These are the extremes of a sport that has so gripped people during the latter part of this century that boats now present almost as big a parking problem as cars.

What is it that has so captured people's imagination? I wrote a book about Captain Cook's third and tragic voyage of discovery, writing it as Cook might have written it had he kept a private journal, trying to think myself into the mind of that great navigator. You would expect it to be well-received in places like Australia and Canada, even Japan since he was searching for a way through from the Pacific to the Atlantic. But Bulgaria! Why would people in Bulgaria want to read about Cook?

Why should the America's Cup have become a billion-dollar industry? Why do we lean into the wind, plastering our faces with salt delivered wet at gale force? Why do we buy dreams we cannot really afford? Why the hell do we take pleasure in pushing ourselves to the limit in a rough, hostile, lonely environment?

There is no simple answer to these questions, for there are more facets to sailing than to any other sport.

On a night in Greek waters, my *Mary Deare* treading the dappled surface of the Aegean under a full moon, the splash of a dolphin close alongside and Dorothy dreaming of Odysseus on the foredeck under the pale curve of the genoa — idyllic moments like that stay in the memory when all the rough stuff is forgotten.

Another night and the sight of the American Sixth Fleet coming up over the horizon, the fireball blaze of the carrier's masthead warning light, the slab side of the great warship striding past like a breakwater, two destroyers heading us off. And near the entrance to the Dardanelles the rumble of engines as we sat drinking wine in the cockpit and a whole fleet of ships bearing down on us, trawlers in line astern, a supply ship and a factory ship — our first sight of a Russian pelagic expedition bound for the Antarctic via Suez.

A thousand sea-going vignettes, but the most vivid are not always of far places and great moments. The first time you actually hoist sail, that breathtaking moment when you watch it belly out, feel the sudden power of it as the boat heels to the breeze. The first night watch, alone at the helm. The first time you go foreign in command of your own vessel. Above all, perhaps, the moment you first push off from the shore, your very first sail. Either it grabs you or it leaves you cold, and if the former it never lets go, no matter whether your baptism is a dinghy, an ocean racer or a sail training square-rigger.

For myself it was a dinghy. Not one of those clinker-built clung-bungs, but, of all things, that thoroughbred of a racing machine, an International Twelve. The owner, poor fellow, was appalled when he realised I had never sailed in anything before, let alone a racing dinghy. I was a journalist and with a dozen or so others I had been offered a weekend break from London to sample the delights of Exmouth. 'We have every form of leisure activity,' the resort's publicity manager assured us. 'It's all yours — golf, tennis, bowls, sailing...'

I was the only one who opted for sailing, and on the Sunday morning, with a cool breeze blowing across the sandbanks of the Exe estuary, I found myself helping to heft that varnished beauty down to the water. The sails up, a lot of slatting and banging, and then we were off, the owner hauling on the mainsheet, his feet braced to hold the helm, myself precariously seated with the jib in my hand. 'Haul it hard in and make fast.'

Suddenly the little vessel was heeling over, my bottom wet with the water rushing along the side, and there was peace – no slatting, no banging, just the bubbling, creaming sound of water as we powered away into the sun, the estuary ahead blinding us with a myriad reflective surfaces.

Power! That was the overriding impression I had in that first instant of sailing. A complex little coracle of a boat, and suddenly it had come alive with a fearful, thrusting sense of power.

I remember, too, a feeling of intense, nervous exhilaration. The sheer joy of that moment is something I shall never be able to recapture. God gives us only one bite at life's cherries, which is why, as a traveller, I never go back on my tracks.

But sailing is a kaleidoscope of intensely experienced happenings. There is always something more to reach out to, some new challenge, and the ownership of your first boat is a sort of milestone. I bought mine at an auction beside a level crossing, at one of the few places in Britain where you can virtually step off the train straight on to your boat. The fact that *Sonia* should never have been rigged with mast and sail and was a menace in anything over Force 4 didn't seem important. It was ownership that counted. My boat, my first boat.

Having discovered the hard way that it was unsafe to take her outside the estuary, I was soon searching the ads of the yachting papers, scouring East and South Coast ports for something with a bunk that I could actually take to sea. Like everybody else, I was looking for the boat of my dreams, which is akin to house-hunting, except that it isn't a houseboat you're searching for, it's a sea-going machine, with smaller versions of the gear to be found on cruise ships and supertankers, navigational instruments that will take you across the sea to foreign countries and into places no car can ever go.

There are no filling stations at sea. But so long as you have the wind to power you and your home on your back, all lands are open to you, if you have the nerve.

Armchair dreamers, of course, fantasise in safety the making of splendid voyages; but there are others, like the lone sailor Donald Crowhurst, lost mysteriously on a round-the-world voyage in 1969, who fantasise for real and lose their lives in the process. Now that I am reasonably experienced, most of my sea-going friends seem to have walked on the water since childhood. What do they know of the tensions of the tyro, new to the game and scavenging crew from the likes of himself, the blind leading the blind?

The great majority of the sailing fraternity – and it is still very much a fraternity despite the vast increase in numbers – come to the sport, like myself, through an inborn, urgent desire. That's all right for dinghy sailors in the confines of estuary or lake, but for those intending to go to sea, who shop around the various boat shows or pick up something secondhand from an ad in a yachting glossy, it is different. They are the ones at risk. It is they who take the chances, and sometimes find themselves featured as a rescue in the RNLI's *Lifeboat* magazine.

Triune of Troy came to me through an ad, a dream of a boat – so white, so slender, so graceful. And so tender! Our first voyage together was when I brought her down the East Coast from Blyth to the estuary nearest my home in Suffolk – a scratch crew of three, the boat an unknown quantity and short on safety equipment, and myself with only a learn-it-yourself rudimentary knowledge of navigation. An almost certain recipe for disaster!

But what the hell? Taking risks is half the fun of life, and anyway I had beginner's luck, the sea glass-calm off the Humber estuary and nothing over Force 3 all the way. The things one does at that age! I, a sailing novice, had bought an ocean racer.

Is this the attraction of sailing? Always a little further, pushing oneself to the limit? Chichester, Tilman, Lewis, all the great names – for them it is satisfaction rather than pleasure, the fulfilment of something deep inside them.

And that's something very different again from the motivation of the mini-sailor who can be seen, wet-suited and bent-kneed, skimming across almost any patch of open water. Board sailing is another world with its own language, its own peculiar excitement, and the wind-surfers, those who drive their boards into rough water to find air, to flip and somersault, turning cartwheels of multi-coloured sail in the spray, these are a breed apart.

Different again is the other end of the sailing spectrum, the tall ships that move with such stately beauty. How does it feel to be a youngster going to sea for the first time in a square-rigger? I have watched them come aboard *Royalist* and within an hour the motley crowd of kids is processed, kitted out and into watches, clambering up the ratlines and over the tops.

Some are scared, like the black girl from Birmingham – she had only joined the Sea Cadets because it was a good introduction to the boys. Yet two days later she was spidering her way over the futtock shrouds as though she had been doing it all her life. The sea is a catalyst, teaching self-reliance, the impersonal hostility of it enabling the young to find a new dimension within themselves.

For obvious reasons my own enjoyment of sailing has always been travel-orientated, my sights set on the islands, coves and inaccessible little bolt-holes that bring to life the history of ancient peoples: the great stones once worshipped on the islands and headlands of Brittany; the Viking feel of Ny-Hellesund at the south-western tip of Norway as we lay one night with a full gale roaring over us; thoughts of Magellan as we rolled our guts out at the bottom of the Bay; above all perhaps, Santorini in a golden dawn, the cratered remains of Atlantis opening up before our eyes.

To see the origins of our civilisation from a vessel no bigger than that which took Odysseus on his wanderings, to see Scylla reach down and explode the sea from the safety of Ventotene's Roman port, to lie the night in the little horseshoe cove of Fourni on Delos, having come down the Sacred Way from Mount Cynthus after watching the sun set over the Cyclades...

So much of Europe's coastline, from Scandinavia round to Turkey, is now imprinted on my mind; a hand reaching up out of the sea to place the remains of a Greek amphora on our deck as vivid a memory as the brush with a Cretan earthquake that nearly lost me the boat.

But sailing, thank God, is all things to all people, the motives urging us to hoist sail as varied as our choice of craft. Because the elements of wind and water are ever-changing, the uncertainty of life afloat, whether inshore or trans-ocean, is always a challenge. That, to my mind, is the real joy of sailing.

YACHT THIEF TOOK LEFT TURN FOR AMERICA

A jobless man with no experience of sailing stole an ocean-going yacht so that he could voyage to America in search of work, the Cardiff stipendiary magistrate was told yesterday.

Alan Mattock, nineteen, told police he thought the Atlantic was about 500 miles across and his passage would take three days. His food supplies consisted of three packets of biscuits and a tin of baked beans. But when he took the 33ft, £20,000 boat *Stowaway* out of Cardiff docks he turned left instead of right and headed up the Bristol Channel towards the Severn Bridge, said Mr Brian Jones, prosecuting. After 20 miles he ran aground, and a rescue operation involving a helicopter, lifeboat and coastguards was mounted to save him.

Placing Mattock on probation after finding him guilty of the theft of the yacht, Sir Lincoln Hallinan, the magistrate, urged him to seek a reconciliation with his parents, who live in Nottingham. The magistrate said: 'This is the only real way you will get back on an even keel.'

Mattock had told docks police: 'I tried to get a job in this country but there was no work. I decided to give life a try in America. I tried to go right but the wind was too strong and the boat went left. When I got out in the Channel I realised I couldn't make it to America and decided to try for Ireland.'

Asked if he would try again, Mattock replied: 'No, it's too bloody dangerous by boat. Next time I'll try to steal a plane.'

CASTING OFF RESTRAINT

TREVOR GROVE DISCOVERS WHAT CRUISING REALLY
MEANS FOR THE BRITISH

Somewhere in the middle of the Bay of Biscay, after thirteen days at sea and just one day from home, the SS *Oriana*, 42,000 tons, eight bars, three swimming pools, four dance floors and the length of some dozen cricket pitches, ceased to be a floating holiday camp and became a ship.

The rollers rolled, foam was flung, brown paper bags appeared at discreet points on the stairways, and we were fewer for breakfast. The sea-legged weaved up and down the promenade deck, exchanging beams of mutual admiration. For the first time since our fortnight's voyage to the Aegean had begun it was possible to find an empty deck-chair on the Stadium Deck after 10.30 a.m.

If P&O had its way, one imagines, the Bay of Biscay would be erased from the cruiser's atlas. For the audacious and highly successful stratagem that lies behind the popularity of ships such as the *Oriana* and *Canberra* consists of a kind of geographical sleight of hand: what cruising offers is a means of journeying vast distances, crossing mighty oceans and seeing the world... while never really leaving home.

The essence of the cruising adventure, it seems, is not so much in being at sea or visiting exotic ports of call (where many passengers do not even bother to leave the ship), as in the opportunity to pursue all the traditional British pastimes with all the traditional restraints uninhibitedly cast aside.

Twelve midday (eight bells to us). Over the Tannoy the navigating officer tells us where we are and describes the sea, which seems to have done for at least a third of the passengers, as 'choppy'. At about the same time there is a violent ringing of bells. This is not the 'abandon ship' alarm, but the signal that someone has won the jackpot on one of our two dozen fruit machines. As fruit machines go, *Oriana*'s are prodigal. Jackpots are frequent and the noise of cascading 10p pieces must now be considered, I fear, the contemporary version of the call of the sea.

One p.m. Pre-lunch drinks in the Ocean Bar — the most imaginatively decorated of all the public rooms, with jolly rope-work umbrellas and lime-green woodwork. Why do the designers of passenger ships feel that any hint of a nautical atmosphere must be so rigidly eschewed? *Oriana*'s décor might be described as hotel-anonymous. It would be wide of the mark, though, to liken *Oriana* to a floating hotel in other respects. Few hotels, for example, could boast a one-to-two staff/customer ratio. Few could match the extraordinary efficiency and good humour with which the operation is run.

Even ashore, P&O takes good care of us, conveying us to dry land in the ship's own lifeboats, where the amiable deputy captain, looking like an immensely dapper pirate in white shorts and a villainous black beard, supervises operations on the quayside. The young sailors who man the launches look even more piratical, with Botticelli locks, earrings, dirty jeans and curiously out-of-place bovver boots.

One-thirty p.m. The chimes go for the second-sitting lunch in the Elizabethan Restaurant – slightly posher than the Drake, since this was the old first-class dining room in the days when *Oriana* was a class-conscious passenger ship on the long haul between Britain and Australia. Now, of course, democracy reigns, and everyone is on first-name terms.

Four-thirty p.m. Time for the last After-Tea Dance of the voyage in the Carnival Room. These cruises are just made for the ballroom brigade. There are lots of bands and lovely, shiny floors and quicksteps and cha-chas and foxtrots and waltzes to be hummed while executing a showy little reverse.

These lumpy, elderly people in their floral print dresses and their Aertex shirts really know what they are about. Curiously, as they steer each other expertly around the floor, they bring a touch of dignity and style to *Oriana* that recalls the grand old days of the Blue Riband liners – whereas the white tuxedos and the lilac dress shirts sported by the flashier male dressers in the evenings seem a mockery of them.

The fact is that posh, in the old port-out-starboard-home and drinks-in-the-captain's-cabin sense, cruising is not (though that is still the image the cruise lines like to convey). Posh, in the Castella-after-dinner-and-a-crème-de-menthe-for-the-wife sense, it is. And the cruisers love it.

Ten-fifteen p.m. Our final Cabaret Showtime. The 'Star Comedian', Bobby Dennis, says goodbye and that we've been a wonderful audience. He's been jolly good, too, and we clap him like mad. The 'Sensational Personality', Stuart Gillies, goes round pecking wrinkled cheeks and singing 'Love Thy Neighbour' for what must be the umpteenth time.

1 October, 7 a.m. We dock at Southampton and muster for the last of Chef T. Friday's excellent breakfasts. Have I enjoyed my first cruise? I have a lovely tan. I cherish the memory of Bill Lowndes, our port lecturer, who looks a bit like Harold Wilson and sounds a lot like Arthur Lowe, downing an ouzo and rendering 'I Am the Very Model of a Modern Major General' on the quayside of a little fishing port in Mani. The museum in Thessaloniki is exquisite.

I relish the cultural impudence with which P&O celebrated our arrival in Greek waters by staging a Hawaiian Night. And I am content that as the only male member of the Ladies' Keep Fit Class, where we did an exercise called The Pussy, I have put on slightly less weight than I might have otherwise.

As we get ready to go ashore, we realise that the BBC's splendid World Service is no longer crackling through on our cabin radio. What we are getting instead – what I assume P&O's planners have decided comes closest to the cruise passenger's habitual tastes – is Radio Two. We are home. Did we ever go away?

SPELL OF THE SWELL

NICHOLAS CRANE, A FIRST-TIME SEAFARER, BOARDS NORWAY'S COASTAL EXPRESS AND BRAVES A FORCE 7 GALE IN A SAUNA

As the *Harald Jarl* drew away from the quayside at Rörvik, my travelling companion leapt across the widening void, then clung for a second to the outside of the hull before slipping inexorably towards the black water.

He had been warned, of course; the ships of the Hurtigruten – Norway's Coastal Express – have schedules to keep. They are not cruise ships that wait upon ill-disciplined passengers but working cargo boats calling at thirty-four ports on a 1,250-mile, eleven-day round trip to Kirkenes, a snowball's throw from the Russian border beyond the top of Norway.

Hallam – who had once served in the merchant navy – had advised me to bring long johns, condoms (for carrying fresh water in the event of ship-wreck) and a supply of brandy and ginger ale for seasickness. We boarded *Harald Jarl* at Bergen, which next year celebrates its 100th anniversary as the southern terminus of the Coastal Express. Of the eleven ships in the fleet, *Harald Jarl* is the oldest and smallest, a tiddler of 2,600 tons, built in 1960 with ninety cabins for passengers, a cargo capacity of 25,500 cubic feet and space on the foredeck to carry four cars.

Lying against Bergen's Puddefjorden dock in the wet twilight, she looked diminutive and dented, as if a boxer had given her a good pummelling. 'That's the effect of Atlantic storms,' said Hallam as we carried our bags up the gangplank. 'This could be a rough voyage.'

As we slipped out of Bergen, a quick recce of our new home revealed a couple of saloons overlooking the cargo hatches on the foredeck, a dining-room with fresh flowers on every crisp tablecloth, a small library with Charlotte Brontë in Norwegian, a bar and a shop selling snacks and rubber trolls.

My cabin was small, but it had a large window on to the sea, and a loo and shower. It was spotlessly clean, the heater worked and the desk was big enough for a laptop computer, with a 220-volt socket for the juice. To a first-time seafarer, it seemed luxurious. The rhythmic heartbeat of *Harald Jarl's* engine lulled me to sleep.

While I slumbered in Cabin D we called at the port of Florö for fifteen minutes, and at 6.45 a.m. we stopped at Malöy, where the yellow derrick on the foredeck unloaded drums of Mobil oil and cases of salmon.

Breakfast was called early, so that we could eat in the sheltered waters between the island of Vagsöy and the mainland. I had just finished my porridge, pickled herring and fried eggs when the ship's Tannoy warned us to prepare for rough seas.

In the wheelhouse, Captain Nilssen explained that *Harald Jarl* had no stabilisers and just one propeller. 'This is a real ship,' he grinned as *Harald Jarl* buried her nose in a wave then rose through the spray.

Ottar Nilssen started as a fourteen-year-old deck boy. He has served on cargo ships, sailing the world's trade routes, for the past twenty-six years as a captain. His has been a life ruled by avoidance: of rocks; of other ships; of bad weather; of mechanical failure.

He had once been on a ship whose engine room had caught fire. It was night, and stacked on the deck were bottles of gas and crates of dynamite. 'We covered the air-intakes,' he said matter-of-factly, 'and the fire went out.'

We passed a little orange freighter, the *Jungmann* from Bergen, lurching gamely northward with timber on deck. Off the starboard rail, shark fins of reef cut through the surf. Nilssen sat rock-like in his big chair, one eye on the sweeping radar screen and the other on the chaotic ocean beyond the dribbling windows.

On a recent trip, one of his passengers jumped overboard at midnight when the *Harald Jarl* was steaming through a narrow channel. Nilssen managed to turn the ship, spot the victim with searchlights, manoeuvre the *Harald Jarl* alongside, then haul him to safety.

'The odd thing was,' said Nilssen, 'that he jumped over the rail carrying his suitcase.'

Among the other twenty-five 'round-trip' passengers on *Harald Jarl* was Aubrey, a retired manager of a Japanese art gallery in Brighton; Bruce from Maine who had flown Liberator bombers in the Pacific War; John and Kerry, computer boffins, who had read about the Coastal Express in the *Seattle Times*; and Barbara, a 28-year-old economics student from Frankfurt who was hoping for heavy weather.

'Some people like cars or planes,' she said. 'I like ships.' It was, she explained, the 'up and down, you know the...swell. I especially like the storms'. Barbara had made thirty sea voyages over the past ten years and she was the only passenger on *Harald Jarl* who knew by heart the length of every hull in the fleet. Europe's last great coastal cargo voyage has an addictive pull.

I, too, fell under the spell. *Harald Jarl* worked waters so thin that there were times when 18 inches separated our keel from the bedrock. Skerries and cliffs would bar our way and then part at the last moment to let us slip through chicanes of lichen-covered granite. The weather was alternately benign and wild; one moment we were sliding frictionless on polished glass and the next we were colliding with walls of grey water.

There were up to five shore trips a day. Some lasted only ten minutes, others were long enough for sightseeing. At Alesund (a three-hour stop) Hallam and I dashed up Aksla Mountain to gape at the town's spiky archipelago. At Trondheim (six hours) we wandered in warm sunshine up to the Gothic cathedral and then to the art museum.

Bodö (three hours) had the Norwegian Aviation Centre, where we clung to the seat of a Sopwith Camel simulator during a dogfight with the Red Baron, then staggered queasily back to the ship in time to hear of an impending Force 7 gale.

At Rörvik (45 minutes), Hallam forgot to look at his watch and *Harald Jarl* left without him. His plummet after his leap to the ship was arrested by the rail of the lowest deck, on to which he flipped with the alacrity of a gymnast.

On our third morning out from Bergen, we sailed across the Arctic Circle into the shadow of the Lofoten Wall, the 62-mile chain of islands that rises sheer from the sea to heights of 3,300ft. By night, *Harald Jarl* squeezed through one of the tight gaps between the islands, with cliffs seeming to brush our elbows.

Hallam and I disembarked in the Lofotens and waited a couple of days for one of the flagships of the Coastal Express fleet to come by. The *Nordlys* was a slab-sided monster five times the size of *Harald Jarl*, launched three years ago and carrying 700 passengers. It was so vast that I kept losing my cabin – a spacious affair with bunk, sofa bed and shower room. Shipboard life revolved around meals, window-gazing and reading.

'It's a floating hotel, isn't it?' said Stan from Brisbane, Australia, a veteran of twelve cruises in miscellaneous oceans. Where *Harald Jarl* had been tasteful (good art in the saloons, curvy lines with brass and varnished wood), *Nordlys* was like a city hotel, with glittery ceilings and a TV monitor in 'Reception' instructing passengers how long the ship would stop in harbour. On *Harald Jarl*, the crew used to hang a blackboard over the side.

'You're being sentimental,' said Hallam. Agreed, *Nordlys* did have stabilisers, which apparently cut out 75 per cent of the rolling. She also had a sauna, where we sat out a Force 7 with scarcely a wobble. Indeed, the technology was amazing. Where *Harald Jarl's* single engine was a glorious contraption crowned by pumping rods, *Nordlys'* four propulsion units were snugly boxed in an engine room cleaner than most kitchens. Instead of levers and dials, the engineers roamed with a mouse across a computer screen. The bridge was a lofty conservatory stuffed with boxes like electronic games machines.

'We have 15,000 horsepower,' Captain Noralf Robertsen told us. 'That's big, wild horses.' He could steer the ship with a joystick the length of a pencil.

The big ships may mark the beginning of the end for the traditional Coastal Express. In 2001 the government subsidy will be lifted from the operating companies and they will be looking for ways to cut costs. Some of the ports may be dropped to reduce the number of days taken for the round trip, or 'super-fjords' such as Geiranger may be added to the itinerary as a lure for the cruise-ship market. The two surviving 'old ships', *Harald Jarl* and *Lofoten*, may get the chop.

The farther north we sailed, the bleaker became the shore. The woods and farms that had decorated the rugged coast south of the Arctic Circle were replaced by a barren tundra darkened by stands of silver birch or fishing hamlets.

Shore trips became surreal snapshots: a morose, stuffed musk ox in Tromsö's Polar Museum (which also had the framed letter written by Amundsen to Scott at the South Pole); a gang of solemn Danes in Hammerfest — the world's most northerly town — being inducted into the Royal and Ancient Polar Bear Society by a woman brandishing the bone of a walrus penis. At Honningsvåg our trip overland to the North Cape was cancelled by a freak snowstorm and I found myself warming up over hot chocolate in a fishermen's bar decorated with Leeds United and Chelsea scarves.

The day before we docked at Kirkenes, the ship's Tannoy announced that we were passing a Coastal Express ship. Seesawing through the Atlantic swell and dwarfed by a backdrop of cliffs came *Harald Jarl*, battered but indefatigable.

How many more trips this little Argo will manage before the accountants close the Clashing Rocks around her hull is anybody's guess, but when she is gone, the Coastal Express will not be the same.

'A VOYAGE IS A PIECE OF AUTOBIOGRAPHY AT BEST'

IT WAS NOT IN HIS NOVELS BUT IN HIS FIRST TRAVEL BOOK THAT ROBERT LOUIS STEVENSON CREATED THE CONFIDENTIAL LITERARY PERSONA OF 'RLS'. **RICHARD HOLMES** EXPLAINS

I was eighteen years old and lying on Mont Lozère, high up in the remote Cevennes, when I first read Robert Louis Stevenson's heady paean to travel and travel writing. I was burning with sun and wind and loneliness, but had just found a spring, bubbling up out of the stony turf. I drank the ice-cold water, and read Stevenson's words, in deep, alternating gulps. Both made me wonderfully giddy. They sharpened rather than slaked my thirst.

> For my part I travel not to go anywhere, but to go; I travel for travel's sake. And to write about it afterwards, if only the public will be so condescending as to read. The great affair is to move; to feel the needs and hitches of life a little more nearly, to get down off this feather bed of civilisation, and to find the globe granite underfoot and strewn with cutting flints.
>
> [*Cevennes Journal*]

This is obviously a young man's declaration (Stevenson was twenty-seven), and written for other young men, too. But, less obviously, it is also the angry declaration of an invalid against his fate. The tone and quality of this defiance make Stevenson's travel writing unique and enduring. And also magically uplifting to read.

Born in Victorian Edinburgh in 1850, Stevenson undertook his earliest journeys from a feather bed, though it was a lonely and often frightening one – an only child's sickbed. As a fragile, coughing, often feverish little boy, marooned beneath the bedclothes and besieged by nightmares, he escaped as often as he could into 'the pleasant Land of Counterpane'.

Here he founded vast empires, navigated down mighty rivers, and crossed fantastic oceans. In the poem 'Travel', written years later from another, adult sickbed in Hyères, France, he recalled these childish longings with perfect fidelity:

> I should like to rise and go
> Where the golden apples grow;
> Where below another sky
> Parrot islands anchored lie,
> And, watched by cockatoos and goats,
> Lonely Crusoes building boats…

> [*A Child's Garden of Verses*]

Unlike most of us, Stevenson remained wonderfully faithful to his childhood dreams. Fidelity, like stoic courage, was intrinsic to his character. All his life he fought chronic illness with chronic adventure. The incurable invalid (whose tubercular lungs haemorrhaged with terrifying regularity) became one of the most intrepid and inveterate travellers of his generation.

Teenage rambles over the Pentland Hills and sailing trips round the wild shores of the Scottish Highlands led southwards in his twenties to Belgium, France, Italy and Switzerland. His first published essay, written when he was twenty-three, was entitled 'Roads'. He wrote: 'Sehnsucht – the passion for what is ever beyond – is livingly expressed in that white riband of possible travel…' The harsher counterpoint between illness and escape is hauntingly explored in another early essay, 'Ordered South'. Here he wrote movingly of the 'imprisoned life' of the conventional Victorian invalid that sometimes threatened to overwhelm him.

> The world is disenchanted for him. He seems to himself to touch things with muffled hands, and to see them through a veil…Many a white town that sits far out on the promontory, many a comely fold of wood on the mountain-side, beckons and allures his imagination day after day, and is yet as inaccessible to his feet as the clefts and gorges of the clouds.

Later his search for love, for family happiness, and always for health, led him to increasingly remote and exotic locations: to pioneering California (to find his future wife, Fanny Osbourne), to the wild Adirondack Mountains, to Australia, and – finally – to those 'parrot islands' of the South Pacific. When he died at the painfully early age of forty-four (from a brain haemorrhage rather than a tubercular one), the Land of Counterpane had been transformed into Stevenson's estate of Vailima, on Samoa. Nor was he lying in bed. He was standing on his own balcony, after a full day's writing, watching the beautiful Pacific dusk come down, and opening a bottle of his favourite old burgundy.

The extraordinary story of these lifelong wanderings is reflected in a remarkable three-volume set of Stevenson's miscellaneous travel writings, published later this month by the Folio Society. Covering some twenty years of work, they are hugely varied in length, tone and location. They include individual books, separate short essays, and a number of longer, serialised articles written for English and American magazines. Among the rarer pieces is Stevenson's long-forgotten but highly diverting first book, *An Inland Voyage* (1878). It was this work that launched the literary persona of 'RLS', the dandyish adventurer and whimsical stylist. The elegant initials gave Stevenson a brand name, much prized by his literary advisers Sidney Colvin and Edmund Gosse. It also served to launch a new kind of fantastical traveller upon the Victorian reading public.

Stevenson's whole biography could be set down in the form of a dotted line across the map, and eventually round much of the globe. He often spoke of the 'little pictorial maps' he held in his head of each of his journeys, and how many of his books began as imaginary expeditions through a landscape. In an essay on Walt Whitman he once remarked that 'there is a sense, of course, in which all true books are books of travel'. And his account of the conception of *Treasure Island* famously begins with the drawing of a map for his stepson, Lloyd. His wife Fanny later remembered:

> To the end of his life he found the keenest pleasure in the study of a map, especially one of roads. Like Branwell Brontë, of whom he could never speak without emotion, he would sit poring over maps, making imaginary journeys...he knew the hours when railway trains of London and Paris started, and when outgoing passenger ships left English and French ports.

Unlike many Victorian travel writers, Stevenson does much more than give a record of things seen and the strangeness of 'local colour'. Nothing could be further from a Bradshaw, a Baedeker or a Murray guide. Nor does he have much in common with the epic travel writers of the British Empire: Charles Doughty, Alexander Kinglake, Isabella Bird or Mary Kingsley. His writing is always extraordinarily intimate. It is picturesque, but intensely personal. It is a conscious exercise in style, but also a continuous self-portrait. He once wrote, 'a voyage is a piece of autobiography at best'.

It was in his travel writing, not his novels, that Stevenson created the confidential persona of 'RLS'. His fiction, for all its pace and colour, is a curiously impersonal machine, with its strong 'carpentering', its well-oiled suspense mechanisms, and its dependence on a powerful historical tradition of adventure writing: Daniel Defoe, Walter Scott, Alexandre Dumas, and later maybe Émile Zola.

But his non-fiction influences are different ones, and perhaps less expected. He admired, imitated and learned from Samuel Pepys, James Boswell, Charles Lamb and William Hazlitt. He practised their styles – 'playing the sedulous ape' – and wrote critical appreciations of their work. He praised Pepys's 'unflinching sincerity' (remarking that we all would like to write 'such a diary in airy characters upon our brain'), and intended to write a biography of Hazlitt – 'the great master' of intimate Romantic prose. Hazlitt's 'On Going a Journey' is the basis for his own essay, 'Walking Tours'. Each of these admired writers is master of a recognisable, intimate, autobiographical voice. They are the deliberate 'personalities' of our literature: vivid, eccentric, confidential. Stevenson set out to create his own travel voice and persona: stoic and sincere, but also teasing, enchanting, flippant and seductive. The traveller becomes a storyteller who is always tempting us over the hills and far away: RLS as the Pied Piper.

An Inland Voyage, published in 1878, was RLS's first book and the first time he deliberately set out to turn a private travel diary into popular literature. It was based on a canoe trip made with his aristocratic friend Walter Simpson in September 1876. Canoeing had become a fashionable sport, and RLS had canoed regularly on the Firth of Forth with his 'mad' cousin Bob Stevenson and Simpson. *An Inland Voyage* was partly inspired by this vogue, and also by J.L. Molloy's successful account of a similar cruise down the Seine and into the Loire, *Our Autumn Holiday on French Rivers*.

Stevenson's original, modest idea was to navigate from Belgium all the way to the Mediterranean. What he actually achieved, mostly in driving rain, was a desultory trip from Antwerp to Pontoise, just north of Paris – a distance of some 200 miles covered in some three weeks.

They sailed or paddled south-westwards through a network of canals and locks, and then into France down the river Oise. They took two wooden 10ft canoes with sails, the *Cigarette* (made of English oak) and the *Arethusa* (made of French cedar).

The basic humorous device of the book is that the two travellers are given the names, and characters, of their boats. So Simpson is Cigarette, a solid, philosophic, totally reliable and very English presence, largely uncomplaining but often rather silent. While RLS is Arethusa, voluble, flighty, inventive, generally unsafe on the water, rather pro-French and foolish, but a good deal of fun. There is a wonderful sense in which nothing at all happens throughout the entire book: 'It was nothing but clay banks and willows, and rain.' They paddle along, get wet and cold each day, and then warm and dry and mildly drunk each night. Admittedly RLS nearly drowns at one point, knocked out of his boat by a fallen tree; and Simpson nearly loses his temper at another, when insulted by a French landlady. Yet the book is brought alive by its style. Out of tiny haphazard incidents, RLS spins a brilliant series of improvised essays on such things as church bells, balloons, wine, pedlars, patriotic songs, French logic, canal barges and cathedrals. They are sententious, but also highly observant. In a melancholy riverside inn he notices an empty birdcage with a slight bend in the bars where a lump of sugar used to be pushed, an emblem of lost care and love.

These mini-essays are presented as pure, dexterous improvisations, casually thrown off and allowed to spin and glitter in the light. Like a street juggler, Stevenson shows off his literary wares: his elaborations, digressions, inversions, exclamations, apothegms, asides. All is written in the fast, precocious, highly decorative, "tuppenny-coloured" style of the early RLS.

Naturally, RLS develops a philosophy of canoeing. The beauty of his watery surroundings, the rhythmic simplicity of paddling, the detachment from the world of business and cities, is both physically and mentally healing. Travel becomes therapy, and even spiritual revelation.

> I was about as near Nirvana as would be convenient in practical life; and if this be so, I make the Buddhists my sincere compliments... A pity to go to the expense of laudanum, where here is a better paradise for nothing!
>   This frame of mind was the great exploit of our voyage... It was the farthest piece of travel accomplished.

RLS's dandyism includes a continuous, flirtatious interest in women. Typical are the three girls he archly christens the Graces in the episode in Origny Sainte-Benoite. The girls admire the canoes, suggestively stroking their wooden sides, and amorously comparing them to violins. Arethusa gallantly remarks that they are more usually compared to coffins. Later these maidens modestly turn their backs on the travellers, in the village street at dusk. But the next day they make a memorable farewell, chasing after the canoes along the river bank...

the foremost of the three leaped upon a tree-stump and kissed her hand to the canoeists.

Not Diana herself, although this was much of a Venus after all, could have done a graceful thing more gracefully. 'Come back again!' she cried; and all the others echoed her; and the hills about Origny repeated the words, 'Come back.'

Self-mockery is also part of the RLS persona. Their glorious reception by a democratic Belgian boating club, ironically named the Royal Sport Nautique, is painfully compared with that of the humiliating rejection by the landlady of the snobby inn at "La Fère of Cursed Memory", who bundles them out into the street.

This mockery deepens to a more subtle and pervasive sense that the travellers are suspect and *déclassé*. They are frequently mistaken for pedlars, carrying their faintly sinister 'india-rubber bags' into each village at dusk. They are stared at suspiciously in villages, turned away from inns, followed by crowds of small children who sometimes spit at them from the bridges. (Here RLS remarks genially that these small boys have acted 'with a true conservative feeling'.)

Yet the subversive idea that the traveller sees the true underside of society and the real conditions of poverty and rejection was soon to become a major theme of Stevenson's writing. 'As long as you keep in the upper regions, with all the world bowing to you as you go, social arrangements have a very handsome air; but once get under the wheels, and you wish society were at the devil.'

The Epilogue adds an incident where RLS is arrested as a vagabond or a spy. He is only released when Simpson - identified as the son of a Scottish baronet on his passport - comes to vouch for him. Here the whimsy has gained a distinct, satirical edge.

It also touches unexpectedly on a larger, grimmer moment of history. Their whole journey is shadowed by the memories of the recent Franco-Prussian War (1870-1) and the national shame of France's defeat. The French towns often hold military garrisons, and there are troop manoeuvres, reveille trumpets, and the firing of distant guns. They encounter drunken, prickly militia in the inns. The nervousness they excite in the small riverside villages, and the noisy chauvinism in the larger towns, is set uneasily against their own holiday nonchalance.

For the modern reader this also holds a tragic prophecy. The bucolic route of the canoeists traverses the flat frontier countryside where many of the most murderous battles of the Great War were fought a generation later. In 1918 the English poet Wilfred Owen was killed on exactly this section of the Sambre-Oise canal. Nevertheless, at the time the little book may be said to have launched a whole flotilla of innocent, Arcadian, riverside adventures. Not least of these were Jerome K. Jerome's *Three Men in a Boat* (1889) and Kenneth Grahame's *Wind in the Willows* (1908).

One of the revelations of these Folio volumes is how fast – and yet how profoundly – the RLS brand altered and matured. Within a dozen years, the deliberate charmer, the *fumiste* and phrase-maker of *An Inland Voyage* had been transformed into the impassioned advocate, realist and unflinching reporter of *In the South Seas*, published in 1890.

The man who flirted with the fluttering Graces of Origny Sainte-Benoite in 1876 seems totally different from the one who solemnly played croquet with the schoolgirl lepers of Kona in 1889:

> I am fresh just now from the leper settlement of Molokai, playing croquet with seven leper girls, sitting and yarning with old, blind leper beachcombers in the hospital, sickened with the spectacle of abhorrent suffering and deformation among the patients, touched to the heart by the sight of lovely and effective virtues in their helpers: no stranger time have I ever had, nor any so moving.

Yet more than ever, I realise this is still the same brave, true, inspiring Stevenson I met early one morning on Mont Lozère.

This is an edited extract from Richard Holmes's introduction to a three-volume edition of *Travels with Robert Louis Stevenson*, published by The Folio Society.

ON THE QE2'S LAP OF HONOUR

WITH THE LINER ABOUT TO BE RETIRED,
GAVIN BELL JOINED ONE OF HER LAST VOYAGES
AROUND BRITAIN

When I was a young reporter on a Scottish newspaper, the sun vanished. It happened as I was approaching a Clydeside shipyard where shop stewards had called a 24-hour strike. One minute the sun was blazing from blue skies, the next it was obliterated by the hull of a gigantic ship rising from John Brown's yard like a Biblical revelation – a twentieth-century Noah's Ark of riveted iron and steel.

It was a vision of colossal grandeur and, as I stood gaping at the scale and beauty of it, a worker said: 'We're oot the day, laddie, but we'll be back, and she'll be the best one yet.' You could hear the pride in his voice, and he was right.

When the *Queen Elizabeth 2* was launched in September 1967, she was destined to become a ship of superlatives. Four decades later she is still the fastest non-military ship afloat (she can go faster backwards than most cruise ships can move forwards) and has travelled farther than any other ship. At the last count she had logged more than 5.6 million miles, the equivalent of twelve journeys to the moon and back.

In the process, she has become a symbol of a lost age, when Britain made the finest ships in the world. The last in an illustrious heritage of transatlantic liners, she has barely six months left as the grande dame of the Cunard fleet before retiring to Dubai as a floating hotel and entertainment venue. A measure of the esteem and affection in which she is held is that her final voyage from Southampton in November sold out in 36 minutes.

A fortieth-anniversary cruise last September – billed as 'a lap of honour' around Britain – was also fully booked months in advance and, from a rousing send-off at Southampton by the band of the Royal Marines to a celebration concert at Liverpool's Anglican cathedral, it was a voyage of pride, nostalgia and sadness.

The military band in red tunics and white pith helmets set the tone with a repertoire of patriotic spine-tinglers as the *QE2* slipped her lines to a chorus of popping champagne corks on the sundeck and a fireboat spraying plumes of water high into the air off our stern.

Her pedigree was apparent as we cruised past the Isle of Wight, followed by a modern cruise ship. We were barely a mile, yet a world, apart: the long, sleek profile of a thoroughbred ocean liner slicing through the waves in sharp contrast with the multi-decked floating holiday resort wallowing in her wake.

This is a ship whose regular passengers fall somewhere between a faithful fan club and an extended family. 'You feel an emotion on this ship you don't get on any other,' confided Carole Williams, a retired education consultant from Norwich. 'She's a British legend, and this is our last chance to sail on her. We feel fortunate to be part of history.'

Her husband, David, agreed: 'They don't build ships like this any more.'

Viscount Christopher Wright, sporting a tie emblazoned with Union flags and a red rose in his buttonhole, summed up the general mood as we powered serenely through a near-gale in the Dover Straits: 'She makes you proud to be British.'

Distinguished guests included Ronald Warwick, a former *QE2* master, who had an interesting encounter with a hurricane on a transatlantic crossing in 1995. Having avoided the worst of it, he was appalled to see the approach of a 'rogue' wave almost 100 feet high. Later he wrote in his log: 'It looked as though the ship was heading straight for the white cliffs of Dover.' All that happened when the wave broke with phenomenal power over the bow was that the ship shuddered and carried on, with many of the passengers unaware of the incident. 'She shrugged it off. She was built to handle rough weather,' he concluded.

Happily, hurricanes and rogue waves are fairly rare off Yorkshire and the only event of note as we cruised north was the arrival of Sir Jimmy Savile in a fishing boat from Scarborough. His unorthodox approach was announced by Captain Ian McNaught, who intimated that, weather permitting, he would do his best to 'fix it for Jimmy'. In the event, he had to bring us to a halt to allow Sir Jimmy to scramble on to a rope ladder, to a ragged cheer from passengers. He could have boarded the ship at Southampton, but that's showbusiness.

Newcastle had waited forty years to welcome the *QE2* to the Tyne and it waited patiently for a few hours more after strong winds delayed our arrival. When eventually we passed the breakwater it was the signal for a fusillade of fireworks, a cacophony of hooting from a flotilla of yachts, ferries, dinghies and the local lifeboat, and cheering and flag-waving from tens of thousands of spectators crowding quays, bridges, streets and rooftops. The *QE2* responded with deep, resonant blasts of her distinctive whistle and a blizzard of fluttering Union flags handed out to passengers for the occasion.

It was an exuberant celebration of national pride on a river that had built great Cunarders such as *Carpathia* — the saviour of *Titanic* survivors — but that, like the Clyde, had seen the shipbuilding life ebb out of it. Next day the local newspaper, the *Journal*, captured the sense of occasion with a headline: 'The day the boat came in.'

Shore excursions were hardly the main attraction of this voyage, but our next port of call, at South Queensferry, on the Firth of Forth, offered an opportunity to visit the Royal Yacht *Britannia*, moored at Leith. Designed more as a floating country house than a palace, it still has in its drawing-room the baby grand piano at which Noël Coward entertained guests ranged on floral print sofas and armchairs. It was the one place, the Queen observed, where she could enjoy privacy and truly relax.

The service on *Britannia* was no doubt impeccable, but it could not have been appreciably superior to that on *QE2*. From the start she has been a class act, and maître d's in her silver-service restaurants are determined to keep it that way until the end. Dress codes apply throughout the ship from 6 p.m. and are strictly enforced. The most relaxed code requires gentlemen to wear shirts and jackets, the only concession being that ties are not obligatory.

It is said that, over the years, the *QE2* has had more facelifts than Liz Taylor, who once famously drove aboard her in a white Rolls-Royce. From a rather brash child of the Sixties, the ship has matured into a stately lady, staging Ascot Balls in the Queen's Room and nostalgic 'Swinging Sixties' concerts in the Grand Lounge that end with the audience on their feet singing 'You'll Never Walk Alone'.

James Murray, who supervises waiting staff in the Mauretania Restaurant and has been with the *QE2* since her maiden voyage, rising from commis waiter to the lofty heights of maître d', has seen the likes of James Cagney, Dame Vera Lynn and the Sultan of Selanghor being fêted at glittering banquets. He recalls the wife of the US Army General Lewis Hershey coming to dinner wearing $7 million worth of jewels, because she felt it was the only place left in the world she could wear them.

After *Queen Mary* was retired to Long Beach, California, James went to visit her and was saddened by what he saw. 'The *Queen Mary* had a soul, but it was gone. Only the shell was left. There was no warmth in her. I hope the same doesn't happen to *QE2*.'

It is a common sentiment among passengers who regard the *QE2* as a second home. So far, Leonard Carson of London has completed ten world cruises and sixteen transatlantic crossings, and he has secured a prized stateroom for her final voyage. 'It's the staff that make her special,' he says. 'They always welcome you as if you're coming home. We'll all miss her very much, the regulars.'

The point was taken up by Carol Thatcher, daughter of the former prime minister, who was on board to sign copies of a souvenir *QE2* book and was warmly applauded when she told a packed auditorium: 'I think she could have gone on sailing for a while yet. The British have a knack of getting rid of icons too early, like Concorde.'

Happily, a surviving British icon, the RAF Red Arrows, turned out to welcome the *QE2* home on the Firth of Clyde on her fortieth birthday, roaring out of clouds over the Cowal hills to thrill spectators with their high-speed aerobatics.

Among local dignitaries invited to an anniversary lunch at Greenock was an elderly man with indelible memories. As a machine shop foreman, Ross McLelland supervised the fitting of the *QE2*'s propeller shafts in John Brown's yard; this was the first time he had set foot on her since they began turning.

His father had helped to build the *Queen Mary*, and he had worked on *Caronia* and *Britannia*, but the *QE2* was always special. 'It was the size and beauty of her. Even men who worked on her day in, day out were impressed when they saw what they were building.

'It annoys me she's not staying in Britain. *Queen Mary* is a hotel in California, *Queen Elizabeth* is lying at the bottom of Hong Kong harbour and we have not been left with any remembrance of these great ships. I feel closer to the *QE2* than any other ship...' At this, Mr McLelland's voice broke, his eyes became moist and he apologised for 'feeling a wee bit sentimental'.

Another emotional farewell awaited in Liverpool, the erstwhile HQ of Cunard, where the Royal Liverpool Philharmonic Orchestra and Choir joined the Band of the Scots Guards in stirring renditions of 'Rule Britannia' and 'Land of Hope and Glory' that soared to the rafters of the Anglican Cathedral amid a flurry of Union flags.

Heaven knows what the final voyage will be like. One imagines Lord Patten of Barnes carrying off the *QE2*'s masthead flag at Dubai to a crescendo of skirling bagpipes.

Cunard, now owned by the Miami-based Carnival Corporation, says the investment arm of the Dubai government made an offer it could not refuse: $100 million and assurances that the *QE2* would continue to be treated like royalty as Queen of the Desert.

But a ship comes alive only at sea and, no matter how much attention is lavished on her, Britain's last great transatlantic liner will be no more than a hotel and tourist attraction far from home.

When the Scots Guards concluded the Liverpool concert with the traditional air 'Will ye no' come back again?', it had special pathos.

BEYOND THE WORLD'S END

AT THE TIP OF SOUTH AMERICA, **SOPHIE CAMPBELL** MAKES A FINAL EFFORT TO ENJOY CRUISING

The world is changing for Tierra del Fuego, the final vertebra in the coccyx of South America and an island that has always styled itself 'The Uttermost Part of the Earth'. The frontiers of tourism have slid beyond its peat bogs and snaggle-toothed mountains, and crossed 600 miles of the Southern Ocean to Antarctica, leaving the once remote island as much a handy jumping-off point for visitors clutching guidebooks to the White Continent as a destination in itself.

What endures, though, is its sense of being on the edge. The port of Ushuaia, on the Argentine half of the island (the other half belongs to Chile), has the air of a settlement rather than a town. Its surviving wooden houses, tin-lined and decorated by convicts, still have a pioneering feel — even if they do include a video shop. And the duty-free status that fills its shops with electronics and trainers gives it a rakish, trading mien. Fueginos call the museum beside the bay El Museo del Fin del Mundo, and the town can still claim to be one of the world's southernmost communities.

As I stood on the main drag, my hands aching from the cold, this end-of-the-world ambience suited my mood. I had tried cruising twice before and cordially disliked it. This was my final attempt and I felt that if I was going to enjoy it anywhere it would be here. In the harbour, I could see our ship, the *Terra Australis* — flying the Chilean flag — which would take us west along the Beagle Channel (part of Fitzroy's 1830s route), expose us briefly to the ill-tempered oceans and then turn north into the Strait of Magellan and up to the Chilean port of Punta Arenas — four days in all.

There were three small decks of surprisingly cosy cabins, a dining-room, one comfortable lounge/bar in the bows and another scruffier one in the stern. Two black Zodiac rafts were clamped to the back like limpets. There was not a shred of glitz, not a chandelier, none of the things I hate about cruising. In fact, it looked more like an icebreaker than a cruise ship. The only thing that could spoil it was the passengers.

Two hours later, the *Terra Australis* shuddered gently. Winding, coiling, gesticulating sailors could be seen through the long, raked windows of the Magellan Lounge as we assembled for our official welcome. The ship's officers acknowledged that there had been 70mph winds on the way over and pointed out that the forecast was good, 'although down here, any weather is normal at any time of year'. As the navigation officer outlined our route, passengers of sixteen nationalities savoured the names of innumerable islands and channels – Bulnes, Dawson, Fitzroy – bestowed by earlier, braver visitors than us.

The passengers were fine. They were mostly middle-aged and clearly definable by their dress: the Spanish diminutive in expensive, warm casuals; the Italians chic, but definitely glittery; the Americans towering above everyone in brilliant white trainers and leisure-wear more comfortable than flattering. They might have looked soft, but most of them leapt from their beds at 4 a.m. to admire 'Glacier Alley', their hands warmed by cups of brandy-laced hot chocolate. We – the photographer and I – mistakenly leapt from our beds at 3 a.m., stared puzzled into the empty darkness, helped ourselves to the hot chocolate and went back to sleep, thereby missing a spectacular row of glaciers and having nothing to show off about at breakfast.

So, what do you do on a cruise ship with only three meals a day, no step classes and minimal shopping opportunities? You watch, that's what you do. You watch as the ship ploughs a furrow through the glacial waters, between the same grey, woolly islands that Darwin saw. You watch the odd, slovenly glacier slipping into the sea. You watch as a burly sailor sits down in the Magellan Lounge to teach knot-making, patiently unravelling the efforts of his adult pupils. You watch the officers on the bridge – which is open to passengers twenty-four hours a day, a real pleasure – as they wield their weapons of high and low technology: radar, sonar, global positioning system, fax, brass clock, barometer, charts, set square and dividers. And you do excursions.

The first of three was to Garibaldi Fjord, where a great glacier was spitting ice into the water and a walk was organised on the opposite shore. There was a tough walk ('many people think they can do this, but it's hard'), a medium walk (same route, slower pace), or no walk at all – there would be a talk on nature instead.

As the ship nosed its way into the fjord, there were soft, resonating thumps as tiny icebergs hit the bow and rolled over like rubber ducks, showing undersides of startling blue. Below deck, people pulled on yellow-and-orange storm suits and juggled with binoculars, specs and cameras. Several opted for the tough walk. The crew smiled glassily, obviously calculating how many of them would need rescuing midway.

The beach smelt of seaweed and was strewn with icebergs. The bigger the iceberg, the bluer it was. The small ones were clear, shot through with needles of stress. Between them strolled orange-and-yellow passengers, a strange vision against the blues and greens of the landscape. I stayed by the water's edge, enjoying the peace and the mountain tops – the last gasp of the southern Andes – dusted with an unseasonal fall of snow. By the time I went to collect my hot chocolate and brandy, the first casualty was down, bleeding from a small cut on his head.

I had forgotten how beautiful it was down here. The humid Magellan jungle – the climate may be cool, but it dumps about 9ft of rain annually – with its hairball parasites and fallen logs jacketed in moss. The clear rock pools and red spots of calafate berries, the streaked slabs of rock with threads of waterfall coming down from above.

That night we would feel the other side of it, the open ocean as we rounded Peninsula Brecknock. 'Will we notice?' someone asked. 'You can't not notice,' came the bald reply. The word went out among the passengers that the *Terra Australis* was no icebreaker; she had been built flat-bottomed for the inland waters of Chesapeake Bay. There were murmurings of discontent, but when a Spaniard voiced them we all looked blandly into our cups of coffee and thought him ill-mannered. The ship thumped and rolled, plucky in the face of adversity.

Seasickness has never been a problem for me. The problem for me, I now realise, is the sea per se. I don't really like it. This struck home on Excursion Two, a visit to the first southern Chilean colony at Fuerte Bulnes, founded by one John Williams, who arrived from Santiago on the *Ancud* in 1843. As we climbed off the Zodiacs on to the stony beach, with its tufts of grass and flowers trembling in the wind, I could have wept for joy. Beautiful daisies! Lovely curls of cow dung! Land! We had been on board for two-and-a-half days.

As we strolled through the southern beeches with their huge tumours known as *pan de Indio* (Indian bread), it was explained that Bernardo O'Higgins, the founding father of Chile, had died saying 'Magellanes! Magellanes! Magellanes!', which was taken to mean, 'Go forth and colonise'. The Chileans claimed Tierra del Fuego and Patagonia in 1843 and ended up sharing both with Argentina. They still engage in regular territorial spats over outlying islands.

We, meanwhile, got back on the boat to see more territorial spats at the penguin colony at Isla Magdalena, where thousands of grey and white Magellanic penguins waddled about and sat in their shallow burrows, watching in frank amazement as alien creatures in strident orange and yellow plumage waddled about uttering cries of 'So cute'.

Somebody nearly stood on an egg that had been laid in the middle of the path. A floating colony of seabirds, shocked by the invasion, exploded into the air and tumbled down again like tickertape as we straggled back to the Zodiacs.

Back on board, there was a purposeful air. Everyone on the bridge was in full uniform. As the ship turned into Punta Arenas harbour in parchment light, two vast storm petrels gave us a flying escort. Hundreds of gulls and cormorants, perched on pier piles, gazed as two tugs bustled out and eased us towards the dock. The captain stood on deck for the final manoeuvres. Boiler-suited sailors wound, coiled and gesticulated. There was a gentle thud and we had arrived. My cruising career had come to a graceful end, in the Penultimate Part of the Earth.

NOTES ON CONTRIBUTORS

———————

JONNY BEARDSALL loves water and foxhunting. A regular freelance contributor to the *Telegraph Magazine*, *House & Garden* and other publications, he wrote a country diary in the 'Weekend' section of the *Daily Telegraph* for three years. When not on a horse he can be found paddling his canoe or at the oar of his rowing boat, usually wearing one of the distinctive fox fur hats that he makes and sells.

JAMES BEDDING's experiences of exploring waterways include wading through a pungent canal in Venice to retrieve a suitcase he had dropped off a motorboat taxi; receiving a verbal thrashing from a French lock-keeper after jamming a cruise boat in a lock in the Canal du Nivernais; and falling into the slimy Grand Union Canal in the Chilterns while attempting to skipper a narrowboat. He recommends leaving anything that looks like work to the professionals, and simply sitting back to watch the scenery glide by – as he did in Kerala on a converted rice boat.

GAVIN BELL is a former foreign correspondent of the *Times*, who has found that travel writing makes an agreeable change from reporting on wars and coups d'état. He won the Thomas Cook/*Daily Telegraph* Travel Book of the Year Award with *In Search of Tusitala: Travels in the Pacific after Robert Louis Stevenson*, and his latest book is *Somewhere Over the Rainbow: Travels in South Africa*. He is still travelling hopefully.

HELENA DE BERTODANO is an interviewer and travel writer/feature writer. She has worked for the *Telegraph* group in Madrid and Washington, D.C., and for eight years wrote the weekly celebrity interview in the *Sunday Telegraph*.

DAVID BLAIR spent ten years as a foreign correspondent for the *Daily Telegraph*, based in Africa, Asia and the Middle East. After being forced to leave Zimbabwe by Robert Mugabe's regime in 2001, he wrote a book about the country, *Degrees in Violence*, which probably did not help the local tourist industry. The farthest he has travelled by water is across the Channel by ferry.

TIM BUTCHER was on the staff of the *Daily Telegraph* from 1990 to 2009, serving as chief war correspondent, Africa bureau chief and Middle East correspondent. His first book, *Blood River*, an account of his crossing of the Congo, was a number one bestseller and a Richard and Judy Book Club selection and was shortlisted for the Samuel Johnson Prize. His latest book, *Chasing the Devil*, recounts his adventures in two more failed states: Sierra Leone and Liberia.

SOPHIE CAMPBELL has been a freelance journalist for twenty years, working for national newspapers and magazines, and writes a monthly heritage column for the *Daily Telegraph*. She is about to qualify as a London tour guide and now juggles writing, guiding and lecturing for a living.

MINTY CLINCH, a long-time contributor to the travel pages of the *Daily Telegraph* and the *Sunday Telegraph*, has written biographies of Robert Redford, James Cagney, Burt Lancaster and Harrison Ford, and a novel, *Clean Break*.

GRAHAM COSTER is the author of two travel books, *Corsairville: The Lost Domain of the Flying Boat*, and *A Thousand Miles from Nowhere*, about riding with long-distance truck drivers. His fiction has appeared in the *New Yorker*, *Granta* and the *London Review of Books*. He is now publisher at Aurum Press.

NICHOLAS CRANE is a writer and broadcaster. *Clear Waters Rising*, his account of a mountain walk from Finisterre to Istanbul, won the Thomas Cook Travel Book Award in 1997. He has written a biography of the map-maker Mercator and presented two television series for BBC2: *Coast* and *Great British Journeys*. His latest book, *Coast: Our Island Story*, is due to be published by BBC Books in October 2010.

TERRY DARLINGTON was brought up during the Second World War between an oil terminal and a flying-boat base. He survived and went to Oxford University, where he passed unnoticed. In Stone, Staffordshire, he founded Research Associates, the international research firm, and Stone

Master Marathoners, the running club. He likes boating but knows nothing about it. *Narrow Dog to Carcassonne* and *Narrow Dog to Indian River* have both been bestsellers. *Narrow Dog to Wigan Pier* will be published in the spring of 2012. For the latest on his adventures, see www.narrowdog.com.

MAX DAVIDSON is an author and journalist who has travelled extensively, often by boat. Whether he is cruising down the Nile or chugging along a canal in Wales, he never tires of the romance of the waterways and the colourful eccentrics who use them. Highlights of his aquatic meanderings include a cruise along the west coast of Norway, against a backdrop of spectacular mountain scenery, and a gourmet-themed trip from Hong Kong to Bangkok in the company of Raymond Blanc. His latest book is *It's Not the Winning that Counts: The most inspiring moments of sporting chivalry*.

JENNY DISKI was born in 1947 in London, where she has lived most of her life. She is the author of eight novels, two collections of essays, a volume of short stories and two books of travel/memoir: *Skating to Antarctica* and *Stranger on A Train*. The latter (from which the extract in this anthology is taken) won both the Thomas Cook/*Daily Telegraph* Travel Book Award and the J.R. Ackerley Prize for Autobiography. Her latest book is *The Sixties*, a personal exploration of the decade.

PHILIP DUNN is a professional photographer — and sometimes writer — who has had countless publications in the *Daily Telegraph* and other newspapers and magazines. He has had a lifelong passion for sailing and the sea and in 2001 went round Britain in a 27ft yacht. He now runs photography holidays in Menorca. His most recently published book is *Kirkcudbright — Your Town*, available online: www.photoactive.co.uk.

TREVOR FISHLOCK is a writer and broadcaster. He was staff correspondent of the *Times* in India and New York, and Moscow bureau chief for the *Daily Telegraph*. He has worked on assignment in more than sixty countries and has written books about Wales, India, America and Russia, and a study of nineteenth-century exploration and discovery. He wrote and presented the popular *Wild Tracks* series for ITV and *Fishlock's Sea Stories* for BBC Wales. With John Ridgway he sailed twice across the North Atlantic, and through the Roaring Forties from Cape Town to Melbourne. His forthcoming books are descriptions of Pembrokeshire and the controversial Welsh Assembly building in Cardiff.

MARTHA GELLHORN (1908–1998) was one of the most distinguished journalists of the twentieth century. In the 1930s she travelled across the United States, summing up the effects of the Depression in a collection of four linked novellas entitled *The Trouble I've Seen*. With world war looming, she chronicled the rise of fascism in Europe for *Collier's* magazine: her reports on the Spanish Civil War are among the best dispatches of the time. Her reportage on war – from the Battle of the Bulge to the invasion of Panama in 1990 – can be read in *The Face of War*. A collection of her other journalism, *The View from the Ground*, was published in 1988.

RICHARD GRANT is a freelance journalist and author based in Tucson, Arizona. His first book, *Ghost Riders*, was a history and memoir of wanderlust in North America, and won the Thomas Cook Travel Book Award. His second, *Bandit Roads*, was about drugs and lawlessness in the Sierra Madre mountains of Mexico, and nearly got him killed. The next will be about East Africa.

ELIZABETH GRICE has been a staff feature writer on the *Daily Telegraph* since 1992. She is the author of *Rogues and Vagabonds*, the story of nineteenth-century travelling players on the Fisher Circuit of theatres in East Anglia. Her hobby, yet to be committed to print, is tracking down and documenting medieval dovecotes.

TREVOR GROVE has been deputy editor of the *Daily Telegraph* and editor of the *Sunday Telegraph* and is now a freelance writer. He wrote *The Juryman's Tale* after a long trial at the Old Bailey and *The Magistrate's Tale* (both published by Bloomsbury) after becoming a JP. He is also the author of *One Dog and His Man* (Atlantic), about walking a Dalmatian on Hampstead Heath. He owns a veteran wooden motor cruiser on the Thames called *Deglet Nour* (like the dates), which means 'fingers of light' in Algerian.

DUFF HART-DAVIS was associated with the *Sunday Telegraph* from its launch in February 1961, joining as a junior in the literary department and rising to assistant editor of the paper. His books include novels, a biography of Peter Fleming, histories of deer-stalking and of the *Telegraph* (*The House the Berrys Built*) and *Hitler's Games*, a study of the 1936 Olympics. His latest is *Philip de László: His Life and Art*, a biography of the Hungarian portraitist.

TIM HEALD is an author and journalist. His collection of Richard Cobb's letters is due to be published by Frances Lincoln in 2011 and he has been commissioned by John Murray to write a book marking the sixtieth anniversary of the Queen's accession (1952–2012). He is also writing a history of his old school, Sherborne.

DAVID HOLLOWAY (1924–95) was a journalist all his working life and literary editor of the *Daily Telegraph* for twenty years from 1968. His books included *Lewis and Clark and the Crossing of America* (1971), *Derby Day* (1975) and, as editor, six anthologies of *Telegraph* writings (1977–93). His grandfather, the actor-manager W.J. ('Bill') Holloway, founded one of the most celebrated theatrical touring companies which, after his retirement, was taken on by his son, W.E. ('John'). Their exploits and travels from Trinidad to Shanghai and from Swiss Cottage to Wagga-Wagga were recounted by David Holloway in *Playing the Empire* (1979).

RICHARD HOLMES is an award-winning author best known for his biographical studies of major figures of British and French Romanticism, among them *Coleridge: Darker Reflections* and *Shelley: The Pursuit*. He is a Fellow of the Royal Society of Literature and a Fellow of the British Academy.

PETER HUGHES was founding editor of ITV's *Wish You Were Here...?* Since turning from television to full-time travel writing, he has received three Travel Writer of the Year awards, although his first foray into travel journalism was nearly his last. In 1968 he attempted to drive a family car from London to Timbuktu and back in a fortnight. The journey took a month and the car was abandoned in the Sahara.

RALPH HAMMOND INNES (1913–98), having been a journalist at the *Financial Times* from 1934 until 1940, served with the Royal Artillery in the Second World War, during which he began publishing the thrillers that would make his name. Four of his early novels were turned into films and *Golden Soak* (1973) was adapted into a television series. Many of his books reflected his love for and experience of the sea. In his will, he left the copyright to much of his work to the Association of Sail Training Organisations.

BRIAN JACKMAN is a freelance writer who spent two years as a national service able seaman on board a Royal Navy minesweeper, and later became part-owner of an ancient Hillyard sloop. He is best known for his abiding interests in wildlife and wild places – especially Africa where he has undertaken almost 100 safaris. His books include *The Marsh Lions* and *The Big Cat Diary* (with Jonathan Scott), and *The Countryside in Winter*. He now lives three miles from the sea in Dorset with his wife, two cats, seven chickens and a donkey.

CASSANDRA JARDINE is no sailor, but all her most enjoyable holidays in recent years have been spent on water: pottering around canals, lagoons, rivers and, in occasional moments of bravery, the open seas. Rowing the Atlantic, however, is one holiday that she is happy to leave to James Cracknell and Ben Fogle. Her five children, for whom she wrote *How to Be a Better Parent* and *Positive not Pushy* (Vermilion), agree.

JOANNA KAVENNA is the author of *The Ice Museum*, *Inglorious* and, most recently, *The Birth of Love*. She is currently writer-in-residence at St Peter's College, Oxford.

STEPHEN LACEY is principally a gardening writer – he is currently revising a new edition of his book *Gardens of the National Trust* for publication in spring 2011 – but he is also a keen naturalist, ornithologist and tropical traveller. He has been to rainforests in Africa, Asia, Central America and Australasia, and is returning to the Amazon at the end of 2010.

MARK LAW is the author of *The Pyjama Game: A Journey into Judo* (Aurum Press), for which he was named Best New Writer in the 2008 British Sports Book Awards. Having been a publicist for theatre and film business clients and the new city of Milton Keynes, he went to Fleet Street to work on the *Mail on Sunday*, the *Times* and the *Daily Telegraph* as a features editor and writer. He was comment editor of the *Sunday Telegraph* until September 2004 and then founding editor of the *First Post*, the online news magazine.

SAM LLEWELLYN is a novelist for adults and children, a columnist and an environmental campaigner. His sea thrillers have won him an enthusiastic readership in at least fifteen languages, and he contributes to maritime and horticultural journals worldwide. He is a historian of the Isles of Scilly, on the most beautiful of which he had the good luck to be born. His latest book is *Black Fish* and the first volume of his next venture, *The Marine Quarterly: A Journal of the Sea*, is due to appear in February 2011.

MALCOLM MACALISTER HALL nearly drowned, aged four, after toppling out of *Petrel*, his father's old wooden sailing dinghy, in North Berwick harbour in Scotland in the mid-1950s. He has loved boats and the sea ever since. He has written investigative and travel features for the *Daily Telegraph*, the *Observer*, the *Mail on Sunday* and the *Independent*, and won the Magazine Writer of the Year award in 1988.

JAN MOIR is a columnist and writer on the *Daily Mail*. She previously worked for the *Daily Telegraph* as an interviewer, columnist and restaurant critic. You can find her restaurant reviews on her website, areyoureadytoorder.co.uk.

HUGH MONTGOMERY-MASSINGBERD (1946–2007) contributed to the *Daily Telegraph* from 1986 until shortly before his death. He wrote feature articles about the nobility and country houses (leading *Private Eye* to christen him 'Massivesnob'), reviews of books, restaurants and television, and celebrity interviews (in one of which he confessed a desire to kiss Hugh Laurie). He also found time to write or edit more than twenty books. But he is best known for his tenure as editor of the obituaries page, when he reinvented the form, substituting for the grave and ceremonious tribute the sparkling celebration of life. The paper's celebration of his own can be read at http://tiny.cc/0ltgr.

TIM MOORE was named Travel Writer of the Year in the 2005 UK Press Awards. His books include *French Revolutions* (about his attempt at the Tour de France), *Do Not Pass Go* (which follows the Monopoly board around London) and *I Believe in Yesterday*, an account of his adventures in living history. As these notes were being compiled he was working on a book about a tour of 'the worst places in Britain'.

CHRIS MOSS was born in Lancashire, educated in London, Liverpool and Leeds, and lived for ten years in Buenos Aires, where he worked for the *Herald*. He contributes travel features to the *Daily Telegraph* and *Condé Nast Traveller*, is editor of *Time Out Beijing* and *Time Out Flight Free-Europe* and co-editor of the *Time Out* guides to Buenos Aires and Patagonia. He also reviews and compiles world music CDs. His book *Patagonia: A Cultural History* is published by Signal Books/OUP. He is currently working on a bestselling novel about maps, steak, sex, tango and *mujeres*.

MICHAEL NICHOLSON is one of the world's most travelled, most decorated and longest-serving television foreign correspondents. He joined ITN in 1964, retired in 2009 and over forty years reported from eighteen war zones, from Biafra to the Gulf. His books include *Across the Limpopo* and *Natasha's Story*, which was filmed as *Welcome to Sarajevo*.

ADAM NICOLSON writes books on history and the landscape, has worked widely as a journalist and for many years wrote weekly columns in the *Daily Telegraph* and the *Sunday Telegraph*. He is a Fellow of the Royal Society of Literature and of the Society of Antiquaries in Scotland. His latest book, *Sissinghurst: An Unfinished History*, won the 2009 Royal Society of Literature Ondaatje Prize.

ANTHONY PEREGRINE is as far from being a sea-dog as is consonant with having been schooled in Fleetwood, Lancashire. But now he lives near the Mediterranean, likes the look of the thing and, occasionally, can't avoid being taken out on it.

JASPER REES is the author of *I Found My Horn: One Man's Struggle with the Orchestra's Most Difficult Instrument* (Orion). He learnt to row a coracle for *Bred of Heaven*, his book about Wales and Welshness, which is to be published by Profile in 2011.

NIGEL RICHARDSON was on the staff of the *Daily Telegraph* for thirteen years. He has written five books, including a bestselling travelogue, *Breakfast in Brighton*, and a critically acclaimed novel for teenagers, *The Wrong Hands*, as well as radio drama. He continues to contribute to the *Daily Telegraph* and to other leading publications.

CHRISTOPHER SOMERVILLE has had some thirty-five books published, and several thousand articles, mostly about his explorations on foot, often within the United Kingdom, with an emphasis on obscure, remote and disregarded places. As author of BBC2's *Coast* series of books, he has travelled the coasts of Britain from Shetland to the Scilly Isles, but retains a fondness for the muddy mysteries of the Thames Estuary and its moody, out-of-the-way corners.

NICK SQUIRES spent eight years in Sydney as the stringer first for the *Sunday Telegraph* and then the *Daily Telegraph*, covering not just Australia but the islands of the South Pacific. He had a kayak outside his apartment, which he regularly paddled round Sydney Harbour and, on one occasion, round a couple of southern right whales. Since September 2008 he has been the *Daily Telegraph*'s man in Rome.

HENRY MORTON STANLEY (1841–1904) was the most famous journalist of his day. Indeed, his scoop in finding David Livingstone has overshadowed his later and much greater achievement: filling in the last blank in the centre of the map of Africa. Towards the end of the twentieth century, historians accused him of crimes against humanity and biographers painted him as the most brutal of all the Victorian explorers. More recently, his reputation has been reappraised in Tim Jeal's *Stanley: the Impossible Life of Africa's Greatest Explorer*.

STANLEY STEWART has won numerous awards for his articles, including most recently that for PPA Magazine Writer of the Year. He is the author of three books – *Old Serpent Nile*, *Frontiers of Heaven* and *In the Empire of Genghis Khan*. The latter two both won the Thomas Cook Travel Book of the Year Award, and have been translated into a dozen languages. He is currently writing a book about Rome, and divides his time between London, Dorset and Rome.

CATHERINE STOTT began her career on *Vogue*, then worked as a feature writer on the *Daily Express*, the *Daily Mail* and the *Guardian* before spending ten years as women's editor of the *Sunday Telegraph*. She later wrote travel features for the *Daily Telegraph*, specialising in cruising.

ROB STUART worked for many years in the media, mainly in television, before going freelance. His travels took him to Sweden, Singapore and the United States (to do the rafting trip he recounts on page 166). Unfortunately, illness has recently put an end to his nomadic life.

GRAHAM TURNER was BBC economics correspondent from 1964 to 1970 before escaping back to newspapers. He initially resisted the idea of going on cruises but succumbed to their charms. His books include *Elizabeth*, a biography of the Queen. A new book about Mahatma Gandhi – *Catching up with Gandhi* – is due to be published by Penguin in India in October 2010.

MAURICE WEAVER was born in Coventry and, as a boy, expected to follow the rest of his family into the motor industry. Instead he joined his local newspaper and aimed for Fleet Street, working on the *Daily Telegraph* for thirty-four years at numerous locations, including London, Manchester, Birmingham and Washington, D.C., and in a wide variety of roles. These included news reporter, feature writer, foreign correspondent, royal specialist and (harking back to his roots) industrial reporter.

PAUL WEAVER was cricket correspondent for the *News of the World* and the *Daily Mirror* before joining *Today* as senior sports writer and then becoming a regular contributor to the *Sunday Telegraph*. Now a sports feature writer for the *Guardian*, he is co-author of two books on Sussex cricket, *The Longest Journey* and *The Flight of the Martlets*.

ACKNOWLEDGEMENTS

The contents may have been chosen by one man, but in common with the newspapers on which it draws, this book is a team effort. I should like to thank my staff colleagues and the many more freelance contributors who said I could use their work again here.

My thanks too to Graham Coster, who is not only publisher but also contributor; to Caroline Buckland, his counterpart at the *Telegraph*; to Nick Trend and Joanna Symons, who saved me from nautical infelicities; to the staff of the *Telegraph* library, especially Gavin Fuller and Nick Alexander; to John Coldstream, who helped with a note on a *Telegraph* veteran I am too young to have worked with; and, as ever, to my wife, Teri.